Advance Praise for

𝔇angerous Coagulations?

"Citations abound from Foucault in education: everyone wants a piece of power-knowledge, it appears. But much use is greatly oversimplified. In this excellent collection of papers brought together by Baker and Heyning, the complexity and variety of Foucault's own nectar (his methods and topics) is well represented and well applied to education. In my view, this is altogether a sparkling work and the contributors and editors are to be congratulated."

Lynda Stone, Professor, School of Education,
The University of North Carolina at Chapel Hill

"An outstandingly crafted introduction that is insightful and revealing about Foucault and his work, and the work of others regarding Foucault, which alone makes the book a must read. Following the introduction are brilliantly researched chapters divided into two sections: the first of which invites historical re-readings of Foucault, along with presenting discussion of timely topics (e.g., school uniforms and dress codes; student bodies and biopower; cosmopolitanism; and professionalism); and the second section, which offers a rethinking of Foucault in a more sociological context (e.g., Foucault in the classroom; in interviews of teachers and students; in educational policy-making), all of which have been written by an excellent group of scholars. This volume is a compelling invitation to both novice readers and Foucault-familiar audiences—a stellar contribution to the field!"

Carl Grant, Hoefs-Bascom Professor and Chair,
Department of Curriculum and Instruction, University of Wisconsin-Madison

"In *Dangerous Coagulations?*, Baker and Heyning point the way forward for a Foucauldian research agenda for educational studies. Their collection of conceptually rich and provocative essays offers us a picture as few other volumes have of the diverse ways in which contemporary researchers use Foucault's ideas as a lens for interrogating a range of important educational issues. This is a marvelous collection of essays for both scholars who work within the Foucauldian tradition as well as for those who wish to learn more about the interplay between Foucault's ideas and educational research."

Barry M. Franklin, Professor and Head, Department of Secondary Education, College of Education, Utah State University, Logan, Utah

"No one reading this volume will doubt the vitality of Foucault's approach to the governance of social and personal life. Here a rich array of studies investigate schooling not as an ideological mechanism but in terms of the whole variety of ways in which it forms and informs, nurtures and disciplines the children of the liberal state."

Ian Hunter, Australian Professorial Fellow, Centre for the History of European Discourses, The University of Queensland, Australia

DANGEROUS COAGULATIONS?

ERUPTIONS
New Thinking across the Disciplines

Erica McWilliam
General Editor

Vol. 19

PETER LANG
New York • Washington, D.C./Baltimore • Bern
Frankfurt am Main • Berlin • Brussels • Vienna • Oxford

DANGEROUS COAGULATIONS?

The Uses of Foucault in the Study of Education

EDITED BY
Bernadette M. Baker
& Katharina E. Heyning

PETER LANG
New York • Washington, D.C./Baltimore • Bern
Frankfurt am Main • Berlin • Brussels • Vienna • Oxford

Library of Congress Cataloging-in-Publication Data

Dangerous coagulations?: the uses of Foucault in the study of education /
edited by Bernadette M. Baker, Katharina E. Heyning.
p. cm. — (Eruptions; v. 19)
Includes bibliographical references.
1. Foucault, Michel—Contributions in education.
2. Education—Philosophy. 3. Postmodernism and education. I. Baker,
Bernadette M. II. Heyning, Katharina E. (Katharina Elisabeth). III. Series.
LB880.F682D36   370'.1—dc21   2002156044
ISBN 0-8204-5814-7
ISSN 1091-8590

Bibliographic information published by **Die Deutsche Bibliothek**.
Die Deutsche Bibliothek lists this publication in the "Deutsche
Nationalbibliografie"; detailed bibliographic data is available
on the Internet at http://dnb.ddb.de/.

Cover design by Lisa Barfield

The paper in this book meets the guidelines for permanence and durability
of the Committee on Production Guidelines for Book Longevity
of the Council of Library Resources.

In

Loving Memory

of

Anna Marion Heyning

and

Jesse Nicholas Baker

—we miss you—

Table of Contents

SECTION TWO: DANGERS

PART ONE: In Tutelage

PART TWO: Inter-views

Acknowledgments

What is an author indeed! This book would not have been possible without the help of many. Our first and most special thanks go to those closest in our lives who supported us in innumerable ways through the long journey of production. Katy wishes to thank Judi for picking her up when she fell and reminding her of the truly important things in life, as well as for her patience, care, and willingness to listen to all things Foucault. And from Bernadette, for burdens halved, sorrows shared, and joys multiplied, the most sincere thanks to Pat, for everything, and then more.

We also cannot help but admire the efforts of our contributors. Their patience with our editorial styles and the dialogues back and forth have been part of the pleasure of working on this book. In those conversations to and fro is where the Academy lives. They have crystallized in the volume, making it an interesting and innovative one that takes seriously the responsibility to think deeply and beyond the immediate or easy analysis.

Several colleagues gave us timely feedback and suggestions for the Introduction. To Ruth Gustafson, Erica McWilliam, Thomas Popkewitz, and Lynda Stone—thank you. Also a deep thanks to the staff at the Foucault Archives in Paris for their assistance with accessing the collections.

None of the book would look the way it does without the work of our project assistant, Christopher Gaalaas, and the support of Carl Grant, chair of the Department of Curriculum and Instruction at the University of Wisconsin-Madison. Chris went above and beyond the call of duty, working in so many positive ways with the manuscript. His industriousness and enthusiasm came at the exact time that we needed it most. Such words cannot really capture the extent of our gratitude for Chris' conscientiousness.

For formatting and extra copyediting assistance, we thank Laura Alvarez and Katherine Gilbert. Both took care with the detail that got everything looking "right" for the publisher. The volume also benefited from the skills and expertise of Chris Kruger of the Department of Curriculum and Instruction at the University of Wisconsin-Madison. Her organization and willingness to handle various tasks throughout the book's production was such a relief as the chapters passed from hand to hand across multiple formats, computers, and countries.

Without the initial encouragement and support of the series editor, Erica McWilliam, this volume would not have come to fruition. We wish to thank Erica for the opportunity to honor our conference participants' requests for copies of papers, for opening her series to an international volume on Foucault, and for her constant good humor. We also extend a special thank you to Sylvia Wynter for reading and giving encouragement to this project. We wish her well and our thoughts are with her.

Penultimately, there are several sources of funding that made this collection possible. We appreciate immensely the University of Wisconsin-Whitewater's College of Education for support of the first International Foucault and Education Conference at New Orleans in April 2000, which set things in motion. This seed money brought the initial group of scholars together to discuss the uses of Foucault in the study of education. Katy would also like to specifically thank the Teaching Scholar's Program at the University of Wisconsin-Whitewater for its summer 2002 support that gave her time to work on the book without interruption. And Bernadette similarly appreciates the Graduate School at the University of Wisconsin-Madison's support, made possible through WARF, for summer funding.

And finally, we end our acknowledgments on a very sad note. Our dear friend, colleague, and contributor to this volume, Kenneth Hultqvist, Professor at the Stockholm Institute of Education, passed away during the printing of these pages. Kenneth's work in the educational field bespeaks his intellectual savvy, his insightfulness, the breadth of his scholarship, and of course, his playfulness! His elegant analyses hold a unique place in the discipline. His chapter is indicative of the perceptiveness he has demonstrated across his career; a pulling-together that is laced by his deep commitment to intellectual challenges, fertile debate, and a genuine curiosity and receptivity to new ideas. We have dedicated Part Two of Section One of the volume to Kenneth. The eloquence is his.

bb and kh

INTRODUCTION

Dangerous Coagulations? Research, Education, and a Traveling Foucault

Bernadette Baker and Katharina E. Heyning

I absolutely will not play the part of one who prescribes solution....My role is to address problems effectively, really: to pose them with the greatest possible rigor, with the maximum complexity and difficulty so that a solution does not arise all at once because of the thought of some reformer or even the brain of a political party....It takes years, decades of work carried out at the grassroots level with the people directly involved....Then perhaps a state of things may be renewed. (Foucault, 1978/1991, pp. 157–159)

I've never clearly understood what was meant in France by the word 'modernity'....I feel troubled here because I do not grasp clearly what that [modernity] might mean, though the word itself is unimportant; we can always use any arbitrary label. But neither do I grasp the kind of problems intended by this term—or how they would be common to people thought of as being 'post-modern.' While I see clearly that behind what was known as structuralism, there was a certain problem—broadly speaking, that of the subject and the recasting of the subject—I do not understand what kind of problem is common to the people we call post-modern or post-structuralist. (Foucault, 1989, p. 205)

The above quotes from Michel Foucault, which also appear in different chapters in this volume, highlight limit points in mainstream educational depictions of his work in anglophone settings.[1] On the one hand, refusing to play the part of one who prescribes solutions has seen Foucault's work jettisoned to an imagined camp called postmodern theory. This positioning is not always a positive one in the field of education. The salvationist, redemptive, and reform rhetoric that has historically accompanied the professionalization of the field has also generally required the scholar to be a confident expert on how to change others or "the system" in mass form. To be positioned as stepping aside from the role of expert who disseminates prescriptive and transcendental principles for change can be taken to mean that the writer is unethical, uncaring, amoral, weak, lacking, or in desperate need of a cop-out. On the other hand, a refusal to be located in a postmodern camp—a "there" that Foucault cannot find—troubles the simplicity of such a reflex. A reconciliation usually follows diagnoses of apparent dis-ease around Foucault; in anglophone assessments his work has been rendered as postmodern or poststructural *precisely because* he refused to be labeled these or to prescribe universal solutions. The net result is a circularity that militates against a broader conversation over the grounds for debate: the questioning of the label *post* and the questioning of the label *modernity* seem to thrust Foucault's work further under a nomenclature that he contested. In short, the desire to not prescribe solutions, to write as one who has no face and who will not say who he is or remain the same, is taken as the index *par excellence* of "postmodern" or "poststructural" reasonings.[2]

Whatever such reasonings are assumed to be, they have at times been objects for anxiety, mockery, or charges of irrelevance in noticeable parts of education's discursive domains, with Foucault's name proffered as exemplar of what is wrong. It is around Foucault's name that a noticeable target has been drawn in mainstream or critical theoretical work for instance (see Schrag, 1999). This is by no means a unilateral positioning, however. In other locales in education, the name Foucault and the prefix *post* are brought deliberately and unabashedly together as positive signifiers (e.g., Lather, 1996; McWilliam, 1999; St.Pierre, 2000). In still other anglophone educational work, Foucault's name does not automatically lead into the postmodern versus not postmodern debate at all. It is considered to already hold a secure and positive place as marked by a series of publications, doctoral theses, and conference papers that make use of him without apologizing. As such, scholars have taken this opportunity to reflect on the conditions of discourse that might have enabled a "Foucault turn" in educational research (e.g., McLeod, 2001).

It is noticeable, then, that multiple and contradictory positions have coagulated around the name Foucault in studies of education. It is also noticeable that the heritage of positivistic research, of discourses of rescue, and of a general criticality that privileges terms such as agency and empowerment, without necessarily questioning their cultural specificity, tensions, or foreclosures, has obscured the historicity of criteria for judgment around Foucault's name. There is a potential for debate over the "validity" of educational research to thus limit determinations of good or contributory work to only those studies that offer "quantifiable" outcomes, checklist prescriptions, or bullet-point solutions for what to do on Monday morning. As a result, how, when, and where criteria for determining "useful," "contributory," or "good" work came to be is not given deep consideration. How criteria differ—how irreconcilable the grounds for truth are across forms of study—and how this ushers in unique styles of research and narration that cannot be reduced to each other remain unscrutinized.[3] The conversation, or lack thereof, can tend to minimize the complex tapestry that has emerged in education as a field and miss the variety of ethical positions that underwrite many different approaches to scholarship.

In this Introduction, we engage in a deliberate conversation with the uses of Foucault that acknowledges the diversity of Foucault (both to himself and across others, if such distinctions can hold at all). We position this volume as a coagulation point that makes conversations over approaches to educational research around Foucault's name explicit. We do not, however, conflate this explicitness with a desire for definitional statements or a list of criteria for "truly Foucaultian research." The chapters contained herein are more a sharing of "what work his works have been made to do," with editors and contributors writing under multiple scholarly labels—as longtime teachers, readers, researchers, and university workers—coming together in such a site.

The volume presents a series of chapters in two major sections. Section One of the volume, "Coagulations," focuses on historico-philosophical problematizations in/of education, and Section Two of the volume, "Dangers," focuses on more sociological uses of Foucault. Such disciplinary boundaries are contestable and have difficulty holding, especially around the name Foucault. Our hope is that by the end of this Introduction and the volume as a whole the stickiness that dangerous coagulations forge in rethinking educational work will be both apparent and food for further thought.

We perceive the need to express at the outset certain commitments that mark this volume's contribution to the wider "Foucaultian literature" and educational research more specifically. As editors we feel no reason to distance ourselves from the uses of Foucault (by himself and across others) as though such work constitutes an evil new or trendy empire. Nor is the goal of such a volume a race to the presumed opposite position, to acquire disciples. Instead, we want to problematize such binaries of Foucault = Saint and Foucault = Villain by addressing several themes with an important under-standing—that there are no "complete" or even "essential works" of Foucault to report and summarize, although there are, as it seems, plenty of "differences" with which to play.

To give form to the direction that such an "although" has taken us, we delineate our editorial commitments with an apparent clarity that ends up in a deliberate stickiness and haziness—in a kind of dangerous coagulation that the confluence of multiple fluids can render. Readers looking for a summary of what Foucault really said or really meant will be disappointed here. We do not engage with the act of "proving" the extent to which we have studied Foucault by quoting prolifically from his texts in order to assert an authentic understanding or shore up a summary account of his works.[4] Rather, we express our editorial orientation to an "epistemological Foucault" or "traveling Foucault" through an equally traveling or epistemological analysis of the ways in which his work have been commentated on and deployed.

In stating that what we offer below is a reading of the different ways in which commentators have been drawn to and have redrawn Foucault, we expect that this will, in turn, be read and critiqued differently. Enunciating such a traveling or open orientation to styles of commentary renders the problems of language visible.[5] In invoking an epistemological orientation to Foucault's name in this Introduction, we mean it is an *under-standing*, an under-stance that is neither originary nor linear nor foundational in what "under" means, nor assertive of what Foucault "really" meant. It trusts that in paying attention to the multiple uses of Foucault there are qualitative differences to be felt and that the expression of those differences presently runs up against the limits of the languages in which they can be constituted and expressed and, predictably, against the limits of the same/different binary.

Thus, while we draw the title of this volume from Foucault's writing, we under-stand the work from which it was drawn as a springboard, as "our" (nonpossessive) interpretation of the analysis of the art of distribution in *Discipline and Punish: The Birth of the Prison* (1975/1995), a citation that stimulated and catapulted further thoughts around the study of education:

> But the principle of "enclosure" is neither constant, nor indispensable, nor sufficient in disciplinary machinery. This machinery works space in a much more flexible and detailed way. It does this first of all on the principle of elementary location or *partitioning*. Each individual has his own place; and each place its individual....Disciplinary space tends to be divided into as many sections as there are bodies of elements to be distributed. One must eliminate the effects of imprecise distributions, the uncontrolled disappearance of individuals, their diffuse circulation, their unusable and *dangerous coagulation*....Discipline organizes an analytical space. (Foucault, 1975/1995, p. 143; emphasis added)

The discussion below organizes analytical spaces. It moves through four layers that elucidate how Foucault has been partitioned by others and ourselves, how disciplinary practices (in both senses) of contouring locations, bodies, impressions, or behaviors and disciplines-as-fields make analytical spaces around the name Foucault. The academic battles, sometimes waged as war by another name, become apparent in the commentaries discussed, but that transparency does little to prevent new coagulations that exceed efforts to enclose Foucault in this or that interpretation, or to make him unusable. Thus, in Part One of the Introduction below, from the vast array of commentaries now available pertaining to Foucault's work, we portray differing styles of commentary, foreshadowed above, that have coagulated around his name outside of education. Here, we document the proliferation and swarming that have occurred, as well as investigate instances of how he has been divided, received, and positioned in various anglophone commentaries. In Part Two we overtly map lines of inquiry that have become possible/noticeable in educational uses of Foucault since publications have been more widely available in English. We offer a delineation of major ways in which Foucault has been used in educational literature, especially since the late 1970s. In Part Three we explicate the implications of such debates and deployments for editing a volume on the uses of Foucault within education. Here we tie our rationale to three issues that, from our review of the literature, and importantly, from much unpublished conversation in educational sites, seem pertinent to discussions of Foucault and education: translation, composition, and the limits of the toolbox metaphor. And, last but most significantly, in Part Four we examine both the continuities and ruptures with such lines of inquiry that the chapters in this volume present, thereby offering a framing and interpretation of contributors' insights that are shared through the volume's chapters.

PART ONE
Dividing Foucault: Epistemological and Traveling Orientations

In 1990, Bernauer described a significant pattern in many commentaries on Foucault: Bernauer argued that while there is a commonly asserted awareness of the multiplicity of positions that have formed around Foucault's name, there has been less cognizance of how nearly every account of his work embodies some of the same analytical moves that appear across his texts. In the early 2000s, we see what Bernauer identified as a lapse or an absence as, now, an active presence.

For example, in more recent commentaries around the name Foucault there is a very cautious, self-conscious, and even contorted effort to acknowledge how one is mired in the limits of discourse being mobilized and critiqued while also playing in a space that Foucault's work, among that of many others, helped to carve (e.g., Dumm, 1996; Falzon, 1998; O'Farrell, 1997). That is to say, a special kind of reflexivity in extended readings or commentaries on Foucault has become apparent. Commentators acknowledge that they may be using some of the very strategies, vocabulary, or techniques that are being attributed to Foucault, either positively or negatively or in-between, or that they are departing from what he cautioned *on purpose*. The "feel" is that commentators want the reader to know that often they notice two things: first, that writing about and around and in relation to the name Foucault carries with it question marks as a project, or more dramatically, this writing is part of a "crisis" of re-presentation and author-ity; and second, that there is a stable/accepted understanding of Foucault that a studious and familiar audience shares. This then dictates which statements appear "un-Foucaultian" and need justifying as departures and which ones are okay to run with because they are clearly are in line with what Foucault said.[6]

There has been an enormous proliferation and swarming around the name Foucault across multiple sites of production that challenge any such determination of what is shared or given and what constitutes a departure, however. While it may not have been the case twenty years ago, it is currently physically impossible to locate, compile, and review every piece ever published about or around Foucault's name in anglophone scholarship. It is equally impossible to substantiate *unilaterally* within or across disciplines how Foucault is "different." This does not suggest that what has been done with his name has not spawned work that is perceived as unique from the partial perspectives of sub-disciplinary or interdisciplinary locations. Rather, it speaks to how impossible it now is to make any kind of transcendental claim as to what that difference might be as marked by uses of his name. This is no doubt a "dangerous" position to articulate in a volume with his name in the title, and it is an articulation that presumably would not be well received in the "Foucault industry" or "inner circles." It is, however, an acknowledgment of the extent to which different readings of Foucault now militate against neat summaries of "him" and it also gestures toward an openness that faces the partitioning that occurs when his name is invoked.[7] This acknowledgment forces a decoding of the criteria or axes along which something is identified as singular, new, or a departure, and an investigation of whatever is appointed as the foil, the designated or preexisting location, state, or understanding.

We used several research strategies to substantiate the claim to proliferation, swarming—and contestation—around his name. These included humanities, social science, and alternative press index and database searches, surveys of Internet searches and sites, and "physical" visits to archives in Paris in which are housed materials that are not always widely available to anglophone readers or researchers. We have found such extensive surveys extremely helpful in thinking about conditions of discourse in specific fields and sites where Foucault's name has been presenced.[8]

Proliferation and Swarming

The name Foucault has appeared in more traditional academic sites (such as within disciplinary locations), and in claims to interdisciplinary or antidisciplinary work. The variety of fields is demonstrable, as are the number of references within, around, and between such fields (see notes for citations in the fields listed here). For instance, Foucault's work has been engaged within African studies, African American studies, anthropology, architecture, art, Biblical literary criticism, Caribbean studies, disability studies, environmental and planning studies, family therapy, feminist studies, gay and lesbian studies, geography, Latin American studies, law, history and its subfields (e.g., art history, histories of the child, histories of the discipline of history, histories of medicine and science, histories of statistics and mathematics, and the new disability history), library and information sciences, nursing, (non-Biblical) literary criticism, media studies, philosophy, political science, postcolonial studies, psychology, psychiatry, psychoanalysis, social work, sociology, theology, and, of course, in education (discussed below). The proliferation is difficult to deny.[9] The citations we provide in the notes do not in or of themselves really begin to capture the range of literature that our surveys have compiled. As we take up below, they also do not speak to *how* Foucault's name is being presenced or the manner of engagement.

We argue, however, that because such proliferation has occurred, it tells us something rather than nothing.[10] It is more than just documentation.[11] We suggest that this proliferation of references to Foucault's name has been accompanied by a swarming in anglophone scholarship, most noticeably across the decade of the 1990s. We note, for instance, several patterns that have emerged via our survey of cataloging devices. Using Academic Search, ProQuest, the Alternative Press Index, the Social Sciences Citation Index, the Arts and Humanities Citation Index, the Philosopher's Index, and Sociological Abstracts, as well as ERIC and Education Full Text search engines (discussed in Part Two), we found a late 1990s burgeoning of citations to Foucault, appearing in abstracts, titles, or as keywords, even allowing for when search engines appear, how far they go back respectively, and when they add new journals/sources to their databases (see Table 1).[12] In the largest databases, for instance, similar trajectories appear. In Academic Search, it is between 1996 and 2002 that a proliferation relative to previous years occurs, with 430 records appearing in that period. A similar trajectory occurs in ProQuest, with a sharp upturn between 1996 and 2002, where 411 records appeared. This is further paralleled in the Alternative Press Index, where relatively few citations appear until between 1996 and 2002, when 200 records appear.

These patterns cannot be reduced to the availability of translations alone. Most of Foucault's histories were translated into English during the 1970s, fewer in the early 1980s. After his death in 1984, before finishing *The History of Sexuality* volumes, his final letter, taken as his will, requested no posthumous publications. Since then *Dits et Écrits* has been published in French in the 1990s by Éditions Gallimard (and selected from in English).[13] It compiles published works that fall outside of his books. The swarming seen in the 1990s, then, does not parallel the appearance of his works for the first time in English. The intensification of anglophone references to his name occurs considerably later. While this might provide entertaining fruit for the theory that English-language scholarship is where old French theories go to die, it does little to explain either the initial lag or the more recent upsurge in referencing such work.

In addition to more traditional academic sites, a virtual cottage industry has grown up around Foucault's name on the Internet, a disparate industry with no center, manager, or assembly line but with many homes where he is made to live. The search engine Google (preferred in library and information studies because it was not initially designed to list shopping sites first) indicated 103,000 hits for the name "Michel Foucault" in mid-2002.[14] This does not mean that every site listed in the search results is centered around Foucault but that his name (or at least all people with exactly the same full name) appears on that many. Of those that do take Foucault as a central subject, the range of

Table 1

	Academic Search (1984–)	Alternative Press Index (1969–)	Arts and Humanities Citation Index (1975–)	Education Full Text (1929–)	ERIC (1966–)	Philosopher's Index (1940–)	ProQuest (1988–)	Social Sciences Citation Index (1956–)	Sociological Abstracts (1952–)
1954–1955	0	0	0	0	0	0	0	0	0
1956–1960	0	0	0	0	0	0	0	0	0
1961–1965	0	0	0	0	0	0	0	0	0
1966–1970	0	0	0	0	0	2	0	0	0
1971–1975	0	0	2	0	0	14	0	4	3
1976–1980	0	10	40	0	1	26	0	23	43
1981–1985	5	38	171	4	1	71	0	83	118
1986–1990	54	95	236	6	24	204	109	138	240
1991–1995	252	69	320	18	54	292	310	278	452
1996–2000	342	136	251	35	83	242	320	430	674
2001–present	88	68	76	13	13	37	91	131	88

what he is made into is notable. In addition to discussion groups that exist around his works, such as the Spoon Collective, he appears as a subject of extended commentary in sites dedicated to philosophy and social theory, pop culture and music, love, rhetoric, religion, management and organization, and other disciplines. He is also the object of pictorial and audio sites, such as photo galleries and lecture series, and he is a focal point of extended commentary on Internet discourse itself. The sample list of web addresses and titles in the appendix gives some sense and flavor of the diversity of positionings and presencings of Foucault on the Internet, from the "serious" philosophical sites to the "playful" (e.g., a site that offers Michel Foucault trading cards).

Finally, there are both public and privately funded places that can be "physically" visited such as centers and archives dedicated to the works of Foucault in France. The Centre Michel Foucault, located in Paris, is administered (using some public funds) by an office in association with a scientific committee[15] and has organized several symposia and conferences on Foucault's work. A collection of Foucault's work and secondary material relating to his work that used to be held at the Bibliothèque Saulchoir (associated with the Centre Michel Foucault) is now held at the private Institut Mémoires de l'Edition Contemporaine (Institute of Contemporary Works [IMEC]). The IMEC is devoted to collections from twentieth-century France: selections from publishers, writers, intellectuals, artists, graphic artists, bookshop owners, printers, journalists, critics, translators, and literary directors appear here. The material in these archives has been deposited by individuals, enterprises, and institutions, and the institute describes itself as constituting the principal private collection of archives in France.[16] It holds tape recordings of Foucault's lectures, many photographs, and a smaller collection of his unpublished writings. All of his publications are available here, many of them in translation in a variety of languages, and collections of newspaper clippings and other material are also available. The archive purchases and is sent *gratis* commentaries and analyses pertaining to Foucault. The shelves of commentaries and analyses are in multiple languages as well, with many editions not commonly found in other places, such as those that have been published by smaller or less-advertised publishers from around the world.

The lists could go on, both in terms of disciplinary cites and other sites. There is an impossible-to-summarize series of "literary," "virtual," and "physical" locales that could be referred to, compounded by the epistemological problem of naming or classifying works as belonging strictly to this or that disciplinary locale (e.g., some locales are named, such as Caribbean studies, while others remain unmarked). Furthermore, with 103,000 hits to examine on the Internet and two different sites to visit in Paris, one could quite easily become all Foucault-ed out.

Such survey and review tasks around the name Foucault may indicate that something different or special has been perceived in relation to his work, but they do not actively describe what or how such differences are asserted within the literature. This is further compounded by the blending and coagulation that defies neat parceling, not only in regard to traditional notions of disciplines, but also in regard to shifting commitments by particular scholars, and moreover by the different ways in which Foucault's name has appeared in and been used within and across works.[17] To have been given appearance is not necessarily to have been approved of and to have approved of something is not necessarily to have engaged with it. That is, to demonstrate the proliferation and swarming, or to list where the name Foucault has appeared, tells us that this phenomenon has become noticeable, that this volume is part of the same effect. It tells little, though, of the manner of engagement or the burden under which existing discourses receive and make his name anew.

Inside Out: Coagulations in Anglophone Scholarship

To consider not just where or when Foucault's name has been made to live but what has been done around it substantively, we examined a variety of commentaries on Foucault, considered the nature of the partitioning, and analyzed the kinds of coagulations that have occurred. Commentaries appeared across fields such as philosophy, history, sociology, literary criticism, and so forth. While we found commentaries were partitioned along different analytical axes in "home" disciplines, we also noted some common tendencies, patterns of discussion and critique, repetitions both within education and beyond. One particular tendency in anglophone scholarship outside and inside education has been to read Foucault through different versions of identity politics. These versions range from wanting to "give" Foucault a unique "identity" to marshaling his work toward more familiar versions of identity politics struggles.

For example, outside of education, positionings around Foucault as a "problem child" have occurred. In mainstream historical commentaries in England, elaborated below, the reception of his work generally has been a hostile one, but not one that has remained uncontested. The grounds for dismissing Foucault have played off of identity politics familiar within Europe, and on grounds that are expressed in terms of an evidentiary warrant in anglophone "history debates." Foucault has been described, for instance, as being unable to write accurate empirical histories. This judgment is tied to notions of historical documents as objective and as evidentiary snapshots of reality. A version of ethnocentrism circulates through the critique: Foucault's identity is cast as a poor historian because he does not focus enough on anglophone documents and England's uniqueness relative to France (see Midelfort, 1980; Scull, 1992; Stone, 1982, 1983).

Similar positionings occur in anglophone debates within education. Although some scholars believe that "the uses of Foucault" now hold a secure place within educational studies, this does not mean we are unable to notice a prior tendency toward dismissal which still circulates through the identity politics debate. For instance, Foucault's not saying who he is has been taken as evasion, as signs of whiteness and/or of maleness refusing to mark themselves or admit their privileges (e.g., Flecha, 1999; Stoler, 1995).

The tendency to read Foucault in relation to identity politics as broadly conceived here is notable but is not the only frame of analysis for invoking his name. Such readings of Foucault have not been left unchallenged and can be unpacked in ways that demonstrate how such critiques can end up turning on themselves. For instance, because the lines of reasoning described above typically make appeal to an identity politics that is exponential and almost infinite, other forms of Otherness are inevitably left out of the preferred list in the critiques. Foucault is reduced and read through one set of variables like "nationality," "race," or "gender" while others like "ability" or "hemispheric location" remain below the threshold of interrogation. It becomes possible, then, to notice further absences in critiques of the absences in Foucault. For example, why has Foucault rarely been criticized for not looking at documents written south of the equator, or, why is the equator not perceived as an important a dividing line as are race, gender, ability, class, or religious affiliation in the North? If Foucault never gazed past the navel of the northern hemisphere as though only that disastrous, overanalyzed, overpopulated, and overexposed zone of the earth mattered, then why should anyone south of the equator ever read him?—and so it could go on. The upshot is that what is expected or demanded of Foucault's work around more high-profile forms of "-ism" or "-ness" cannot be reflexively demonstrated by the critic who is charging Foucault with a lack of reflexivity or confession. Critiques that position Foucault as being in trouble for not having studied everything intensify according to their own logic, running up against the limits of present affiliations and checklist thought. The tiger gotten by the tail turns back to bite its holder and the circle keeps spinning.

Such reactions and counterreactions to Foucault's work thus foreshadow some of the complexities and paradoxes of approaching anglophone scholarship outside and within education. The reactions and counterreactions are underpinned by a further identity crisis—there is palpable confusion/conflation between "reading Foucault" as though independent and separating out charges directed at "users of Foucault," at "interlocutors" or "disciples" as distinct from Foucault "himself." As indicated above, what is less obvious and not an outcome that we anticipated from our survey of literature was how much the reaction to Foucault's work, whether interpreted as an "itself" or as "applied by others," has been commented on via various versions of identity politics. There is constant reference to seeming crises of identity over "who" Foucault was and whether "he" or his work was coherent. Furthermore, disrupting perceptions of a priori subjects, or reinforcing them, or pointing to their historicity and paradoxical complexities seems a persistent focus in humanities and social-science fields where Foucault has been made to live in anglophone scholarship. Thus, while the name Foucault has been positioned positively, as being of a problematizing kind that troubles taken-for-granted practices or rethinks universalizing tendencies in old-style identity politics, his work has also been viewed negatively, as being *in trouble* for where he looks and doesn't look, whom he cites and doesn't cite, and what he studies and doesn't study. This has set in motion critique and countercritique, attack and defense, a pointing to the limits that circulate within charges of being *limited*. The question that is rarely posed out of the critique and countercritique is why identity politics, in all manner of manifestation, have become almost the only terms of debate for reading, using, not reading, or not using a text?

Some possible responses perhaps lie within the very ruptures that Foucault's histories discuss. One might argue that in *Madness and Civilization: A History of Insanity in the Age of Reason* (1961/1965), Foucault historicizes what he calls a key dimension of the West's originality, the mad-reason nexus where Europe's range is confronted by its own derangement. In *The Birth of the Clinic* (1963/1975), *The Order of Things* (1966/1970), and *The Archaeology of Knowledge* (1969/1972), one could say that Foucault demonstrates how knowledge is made for cutting—how the formation of the human sciences placed humans at the center of knowing, where knowing Man eventually equals recognizing ourselves as scientific objects that can be dissected. If extended into understanding the above kinds of debates over where Foucault has and has not looked, the dissected object of Man might now be understood in terms of "variables of identity" in much educational discourse. The emergence of such variables, or of historical ontologies that are not innocuous or superficial in their effects on, to, and between humans (and where human itself is understood as a variable of identity) indicates how possible it has become to split Man into pieces around which identity politics can form and criticism and reception of texts proceed. In *Discipline and Punish: The Birth of the Prison* (1975/1995), and *The History of Sexuality: Vol. 1* (1976/1978), it could be claimed that there are additional narratives to mine for how the very act of criticism, or of reading, writing, and using, has been tied to both the constitutive experience of institutional confinements and their dividing practices (where confinement and division do not necessarily equal "bad") and the formation of different kinds of desiring subjects as new forms of confinement. Under this line of argument, then—to critique Foucault in terms of presumed identities, entities, and essences that he mentions or doesn't mention, or for where he looks or doesn't look, for whom he cites or doesn't cite, or to label or not label his work, to place him at center or margin, to locate or not locate his "true identity," or to celebrate or denigrate, to use or abuse his work—is to play in some sense on the grounds for debate that he took the effort to historicize.

As such, our analysis of a traveling Foucault below takes seriously the coagulations, the difficulties, the tensions, and the limits suggested in criticisms of and responses to the various uses of Foucault in anglophone work. The binaries that swirl around the name Michel Foucault (e.g., Saint or Villain) speak with a productive and wonderful irony to the conditions of possibility for persuasion, truth telling, narration, and assertion in educational discourse and beyond.[18] These binaries prove themselves useful and suggest to us a fluidity rather than a fixity, with this book reveling in the stickiness of such passionate coagulations. What we consider, therefore, are a range of commentaries that do and do not overtly frame Foucault around identity politics and that have engaged extensively with his name

We offer in this next section of Part One, specific examples of the range of positionings with which Foucault's name has been associated in scholarly discussions across disciplines. It is not and could never be a comprehensive survey. What we aim to demonstrate is how Foucault's name has been and still is divided, and in some cases unified after the division. As indicated above, we suggest that attention to such multiplicity renders a different qualitative feel and entrée into Foucault debates. This attention to multiplicity cannot be explained away by simplistic critiques that see the heeding of such "difference" as just another furtive homogenization operating within a passion for sameness. In offering an epistemological orientation to the uses of Foucault we do not position the scaffolding provided here as the last word, nor as something that is amenable to a naïve reading which might posit that our claim to an "epistemological or traveling Foucault" is really a singular stand anyway that eradicates the moves it makes toward multiplicity before it even begins (see also note 5). Significantly, we propose that the partitioning practices around Foucault constitute neither unilaterally good or bad strategies for interpretation, which is not to say that our position is neutral. Rather, what our analysis is attuned toward demonstrating is how wider (i.e., outside of education) "interpretations" of Foucault constitute interpretations that are already in motion, already edited, already nonneutral in their effects, and already have the potential to (and do) dialogue with education-specific approaches to his name.

Styles of Commentary:
On Concepts, Periods, Single Works, and the Corpus

Commentaries on Foucault generally take four forms: 1) analyses around one work or concept by a given scholar (e.g., journal articles or book chapters); 2) extended investigations around one work or concept by multiple scholars (e.g., edited volumes on Foucault's sense of ethics); 3) extended investigations around select works or concepts (e.g., edited volumes on several chosen topics like the subject, aesthetics, and power-knowledge); or 4) an extended introduction to or reading of the breadth of his work by individual scholars (e.g., general introductions to Foucault).

I. In anglophone publications where a particular concept has been selected for treatment by an *individual scholar*, Foucault's work in relation to that concept is brought to bear usually in a discussion of the implications, merits, or otherwise of such work. Young's (1995) "Foucault on Race and Colonialism," Elden's (2002) "The War of Races and the Constitution of the State: Foucault's '*Il faut défendre la société*' and the Politics of Calculation," and Elliott's chapter in *Concepts of the Self* (2001), "Technologies of the Self: Foucault, New Technologies, New Selves" are such examples.

II. In scholarship around a given work or concept by *multiple scholars*, it is edited volumes in the main that have materialized (sometimes appearing out of earlier journal-article exchanges). Such volumes can cohere around the exploration and explication of specific terms, such as "governmentality" or "power" (e.g., Barry, Osborne, & Rose, 1996; Langsdorf, Watson, & Smith, 1998). They can also appear around publication dates, e.g., volumes on his later works which describe their focus as being on government and ethics (e.g., Moss, 1998), while others have taken a group of concepts and theories as their foci (e.g., Miguel-Alfonso & Caporale-Bizzini, 1994). Still others form around what are called "critical readings of Foucault" (e.g., Burke, 1992; Racevskis, 1999; Smart, 1994) or more directly around refuting Foucault "representing careful counterarguments to Foucault's own theses, or assessments of his thought by other contemporary thinkers with their own visions" (Hoy, 1986/1996, p. 2). In edited collections generally, then, each chapter makes use of Foucault's works to either argue over what he meant by particular terms or concepts, or to apply key concepts to other situations, or to challenge the usefulness and accuracy of his works altogether.

III. Commentaries on a specific history as opposed to a discrete term or group of concepts have also emerged. These can be single-authored commentaries such as Stoler's (1995) *Race and the Education of Desire: Foucault's* History of Sexuality *and the Colonial Order of Things* or Goldhill's (1995) *Foucault's Virginity: Ancient Erotic Fiction and the History of Sexuality*, as well as edited volumes on a particular history such as Larmour, Miller, & Platter's (1998) *Rethinking Sexuality: Foucault and Classical Antiquity*.

As an example of the commentaries in this third group, that is, of the proliferation, swarming, and contestation that has played out around a particular text, we refer to debates over *Madness and Civilization: A History of Insanity in the Age of Reason* (1961/1965), the first of Foucault's books to be translated (partly) into English. The chapters in Still and Velody's (1992) *Rewriting the History of Madness: Studies in Foucault's* Histoire de la folie are illustrative of the partitioning practices around Foucault. They speak not only to different francophone and anglophone depictions that are rarely a central focus within education-specific accounts, but also, without traveling across the variety of his works, they still manage to convey the disparate grounds for reception of an individual one.[19] We go into some depth in regard to these commentaries for several reasons—because such quarrels bring into relief what has and has not appeared in educational debates over Foucault; because in a field obsessed with determinations of dis/ability, *Madness and Civilization* is rarely the focus of educational researchers, including those who draw on Foucault; and because the debates around *Madness and Civilization* in mainstream history highlight a disciplinary specificity that speaks beyond the avenues through which Foucault is taken up or made to enter educational circles.

The Range of Derangement?
Madness and Civilization as Object of Critique

In *Rewriting the History of Madness* (Still & Velody, 1992) Foucault's *Histoire de la folie à l'âge classique*[20] is evaluated by scholars writing primarily from institutional locations in England, France, and the United States.[21] While many of the contributors agree that one of Foucault's main points in *Madness and Civilization* was that the meaning of madness had changed, being defined only relatively recently as a form of "mental illness," this is where the compatibility ends. Of the many different positions taken around the text, two stand out for us in terms of indicating the range of ways in which Foucault's work has been treated. The first is in the difference between francophone and anglophone receptions within the discipline of history and the second is in the diametrically opposed positions expressed in the anglophone receptions. In regard to the latter, for example, Gordon (1992a) argues that a full translation of *Madness and Civilization* would have accounted for many of the misreadings and criticisms of the book by professional historians[22] while Scull (1992) argues that a full translation would simply reinforce the already accurate negative assessments of the abridged translated version.

In generally supporting Gordon's position over the problem of different versions of the book in French and English, Castel extends the debate to consider how the book was received in France. He suggests that an historical gap existed between the intellectual context of the early 1960s when the book first appeared and the end of the 1960s and early 1970s when it began to reach another audience and to assume what he calls a political/practical meaning rather than a theoretical one.

While the book was received very positively, described as a "very great book" and "a magnificent book" in terms of an academic text at the point of its publication in France, after May 1968 *Histoire de la folie* was read as "political/practical" in the sense of having themes in praise of folly and in criticism of constrictive systems, being made use of as a model for challenging exclusions, segregation, the setting of limits to desire, and honoring a subjectivity (madness) freed from constraints of social adaptation or concession to established order. Thus, in noting how the book was reinterpreted through currents of thought "far removed from the system of preoccupations at the origin of the work," Castel states that to him it is important to underline that Foucault did not see this dual reading as representing an opposition between truth and error in interpretation of it or between good and evil uses. He never disowned the militant reuse of his work. "He even collaborated in it, to the extent that he committed himself to a number of ventures inspired by such a trend by participating in the 'antipsychiatry' movement, in the broad sense of the term" (Castel, 1992, p. 67).

Gordon (1992a) identifies four reasons for how the book was received, mostly negatively, in anglophone scholarship: First, British and American historians were not as comfortable as their French counterparts with interdisciplinary work; second, its uptake by a nonspecialist antipsychiatry movement was apparently an indicator of its lack of serious scholarship and its appeal to a broader general readership not trained in the routine constraints of scholarly work; third, Foucault later reflected on the book relative to his newer works in a brief series of self-critical remarks; and fourth, the degree of animosity his book provoked among psychiatric practitioners via his treatment of the historical beginnings of the discipline, which have been misread as a polemic against medical rationalism, hindered its reception.

Gordon also summarizes Midelfort's (1980) critique of the book: that Foucault was wrong about the date of the first psychiatric hospitals in Europe, that Foucault completely overlooked the extensive development in the eighteenth century of numerous purely private madhouses, especially in England, that Foucault repeatedly and erroneously implies that prior to the nineteenth century madness was not a medical problem, and in taking Pinel's liberation of the mad as central to his narrative, Foucault had not considered the "careful research" that had cast doubt on Pinel's famous gesture as ever having occurred.

Scull (1992) agrees with such criticisms and suggests that anglo-american problems, difficulties, and negative assessments of *Madness and Civilization* would be reinforced by its fuller translation, not undermined. He states that Gordon finds it hard to believe that someone such as Scull could read the book in its full French version and still find it a poor history. He does not see the pointing out of historiographical difficulties as Gordon charges as deriving from the "xenophobia of a bluff Anglo-Saxon historian, resistant to 'foreign' ideology and unwilling to grant 'French facts' but rather as due to Foucault's weak, inaccurate, and untested historical scholarship" (Scull, 1992, p. 159). Specific problems for Scull include the limited documentation for comparison across European settings, the taking of the "symbolism" of the Ship o' Fools as a "factual" or "real" ship, and the ignoring of the advent of private English madhouses in the eighteenth century. On this latter point Scull argues that what Foucault attributes to the French occurred earlier and differently in England. He describes Gordon's defense of Foucault's text as invoking "smear tactics" against critics who are not "disciples" and refers on multiple occasions to Foucault sarcastically as "the master." He argues further that Foucault deliberately sought to influence the fate of his ideas "through a strategic deployment and concealment of texts" in life and death (Scull, 1992).[23]

None of this explains though why it would even matter. *Who cares* how *Madness and Civilization* was received by "the historians?" Moreover, why would it even be an issue in regard to *educational* uses of Foucault? Gordon responds to questions such as "Why worry about Foucault's reception by 'the historians' if he was not writing especially for them, and, if he was not one, why read him as one?" (Gordon, 1992b). He explains that how historians have positioned Foucault matters partly because of why nonhistorians (or nonmainstream historians) take it to matter; and because it conditions views of what other kind of thinker or writer Foucault may actually have been:

> I have not tried to show that Foucault is just like any conventional professional historian, but only that such historians can profitably read him, and even read him with some care. This is not a matter, as [Allan] Megill suggests, of drafting Foucault into an inappropriate discipline. It is rather a matter of what needs to happen for the disciplines, including history, to live and breathe: or of what Foucault himself calls "work in common by people who seek to 'de-disciplinarize' themselves." (Gordon, 1992b, p. 170)

Thus, the above debates indicate how Foucault's work has been made into a placemarker for discipline-specific debates within history and in scholarship over "standards," interpretation, and truth. It further indicates how such debate can take the form of an identity politics familiar within Europe, expressed in terms of evidentiary warrants for who or what constitutes Europe's "center." Moreover, it demonstrates how criteria for judgment can remain obscured not just in educational debates over Foucault but elsewhere. For example, the common point of appeal in both sides in "the historians' circle" around *Madness and Civilization* is an uncontested belief in the terms "empirical," "facts," "evidence," and the allied notion of "comparative history" that hangs on them. Each side claims points for or against Foucault on these criteria rather than interrogates, as Paul Rabinow suggests, such grounds for debate to begin with. The very different structures of narrative and warrants for persuasion that Munslow (1997) has unpacked, albeit subsequent to 1992, in regard to reconstructionist, constructionist, and deconstructionist styles of historiography would have perhaps summarized and/or preempted such debate.

IV. Extended commentaries that are dedicated to the breadth of Foucault's work as opposed to a single work are the fourth kind and have a different feel. They may contain some of the same points as are embodied in the exchanges above but the activity of critique coagulates around different analytical axes than those of mainstream European or Euro-American historiography. What is notable, however, is how such commentary coagulates in many instances around still other versions of identity politics. For Example, they are undergirded by either a desire to give Foucault an identity or to make sure that he speaks to that of presumed others. Foucault's "identity" has been divided implicitly, in some instances, according to institutional classifications such as research, teaching, and service. That is, he has been divided according to what is seen as his research trajectory, or lack thereof, according to his teaching posts (Lille, Uppsala, Warsaw, Hamburg, Clermont-Ferrand, Tunisia, Vincennes, Paris), and according to assessments of his political activism (e.g., PCF [French Communist Party] affiliations in the 1950s, antiracism and anticolonialization demonstrations of the 1960s, antipsychiatry movement of late 1960s and with Daniel Defert, in 1971, participation in le Groupe Information sur les Prisons (GIP: Prisons Information Group), etc.[24] Second, in biographies, he has been divided implicitly in stage-of-life narratives around childhood, adolescence, studenthood, and adulthood (Eribon, 1991; Macey, 1993; Miller, 1993). Given the developmental logic lacing biographies, it is not surprising that sexuality becomes a bone of contention, with biographers apparently either trying to "queer" Foucault or "straighten" Foucault.[25] Third, in discussions of "how to read Foucault," he has been implicitly divided in terms of his style of writing and comprehensibility. In regard to the latter, he is in some places considered difficult to read, puzzling in his thought, esoteric, jargonish, ambiguous, and abstract. His work has been called these things by those who are in support of his projects (Bernauer, 1990; Goldstein, 1992; Privitera, 1995) and those who appear not to be (Midelfort, 1980; Merquoir, 1986; Stone, 1982). In other places, his work is considered clearly written, a nonspecialist style developed for a popular rather than disciplinary-based audience to engage with. Again, these comments are not simplistically aligned. Those who dismiss Foucault and those who do not have seen his writing as clear, nonspecialist, and as more suitable for a broad audience (Dean, 1994; Scull, 1992). He is given "identity" in regard to writing style, then, as either of and for "the people" or the underdog, conversely as elitist and abstract, or both.[26]

A fourth, more common strategy for reading Foucault, though, is to overtly or explicitly position him in relation to existing frameworks for reception within a field—how theoretical frameworks are grouped, already labeled, and constitutive of the conditions for receptivity—the kind of strategy used to open this Introduction. Several examples of this fourth *explicit partitioning* approach can be found, and it is here that Foucault's name gets most obviously deployed in regard to more familiar versions of identity-politics-as-categories-of-Being. Some extended commentaries thus overtly position his work as constituting major insights in regard to political struggles founded on categorical identity politics, while other extended commentaries do not center their analysis around this. In the former, the axis used to narrate Foucault does not so much put Foucault back together in order to master, clarify, or provide handles on perceived ambiguity in his works or to stamp a unique "identity" onto him via analysis of writing style, biography, or university employment as in the above examples. Rather, it is one that makes Foucault visible in regard to existing institutional dilemmas or field-based struggles that have emerged out of and through overt connections to the production of populational or identity categories. These commentaries take categorical identity politics struggles as the site through which Foucault is narrated and gelled.

The positioning of Foucault in regard to identity politics is complicated, however, and not just because identity politics has more than one form or meaning.[27] Foucault gets positioned in some accounts as a problem and as part of the problem regarding local identity politics and in others as a pleasure and a necessary political device for changing the terms of debate. For instance, Stoler's (1995) criticism of Foucault for not focusing on race and racism enough is homologous to Sawicki's (1991) *Disciplining Foucault: Feminism, Power, and the Body* critiquing him for not focusing on women and sexism enough, which is homologous to Moi's (1985) view in "Power, Sex, and Subjectivity: Feminist Reflections on Foucault" that the seductiveness of his discourse will depoliticize the interrogation of sexuality and homophobia. Alternatively, West's (1982/2002) "A Genealogy of Modern Racism," Stiker's (1999) *A History of Disability*, Bell's (1993) *Interrogating Incest: Feminism, Foucault, and the Law*, and Halperin's (1995) *Saint=Foucault: Towards a Gay Hagiography* have found Foucault useful for identity politics projects.

In *Bodies and Pleasures: Foucault and the Politics of Sexual Normalization*, McWhorter (1999) discusses in detail such a series of conflicting assessments around the usefulness of Foucault in regard to local identity politics. While obviously hers is not the only work to undertake such discussion, and while sexual normalization is not the only or even the most commented on of sites around the uses of Foucault in regard to identity politics, working through parts of her narrative lays out some similarities in Foucault's positionings within education and the nature of responses that have arisen, including chapters in this volume.

Overt Categorical Identity Politics and Extended Commentary on Foucault

In the chapter titled "Why I Shouldn't Like Foucault…So They Say," McWhorter identifies the oft-heard critiques that she went from in order to reexamine the works' effects. They resonate so strongly with the types of discussion and critiques mounted from within educational research that they are worth considering at length. McWhorter explains that she "gave rein" to the "maliciously meticulous-scholar me" who proceeded to isolate three lines of criticism typically aimed at Foucault (p. 65). These were:

1. Foucault leaves us with no criteria for preferring one set of values or courses of action over another; thus we cannot justify our political agenda any more credibly than proponents of the status quo can justify theirs. The main reason why Foucault's work leaves us in this undesirable position is that it undermines humanism and puts nothing comparable in its place.

2. Foucault's work destabilizes agency. It brings into question the very possibility of individual freedom, because it suggests that one can never get free of power relations, and it gives no account of how to develop agency within networks of power. Foucault's universe appears to be fully deterministic. Thus, further, it offers no affirmation of the potential agency (freedom, self-determination) of oppressed people. Further still, since it denies agency even in our opponents, it eliminates our justification for holding oppressors responsible for their actions.

3. Foucault's work destroys the basis for community, which is the basis for political action. This worry typically comes to the fore when critics examine Foucault's suggestion that identities—both individual and collective—are the products of power and that subjectivity is subjection. On Foucault's view, they say, identity is something we ought to resist, not something we ought to affirm and reinforce by building communities.

McWhorter argues that if any of these criticisms held, then her fascination with Foucault's work was a dangerous thing indeed. She felt they were so widespread as criticisms that she had to address them. In the process, she examines proponents of each view and argues against each position. For the first she suggests that it is because humanists cannot imagine questioning the category "the human" that they cannot understand politicizing the subject as Foucault does and thus remain in a circular logic that they attribute to Foucault, largely because they assume that: a) political action is always the work of a logically prior subjectivity; and b) good actions are always premeditated, reasoned actions based on universalizable normative criteria:

> What appears politically questionable, then, are the assumptions and requirements embedded in humanist critiques themselves. Indeed, I cannot reason my way out of humanism, since humanism precludes my particular existence from the outset. I cannot start with humanism, then, even as a departure point; it is imperative that I start somewhere else. The fact that Foucault starts elsewhere means new possibilities are opened and questions themselves—not simply answers—are transformed. (McWhorter, 1999, pp. 73–74)

In response to the second critique regarding a loss of agency, McWhorter contrasts her undergoing of Foucault's texts with other commentators such as Linda Alcoff who argue that Foucault's analytics of the subject and power deny subjectivity and agency. Alcoff, she argues, sees power still as an entity, as an external cause of effects, and subjectivity simply as a form of being subject to control or dependence by someone else (McWhorter, 1999, p. 78). McWhorter reads Foucault's analytics of power in terms of events rather than causes and effects, where power does not hold or grip us as though from the outside but where we emerge historically within repeating circuits of events: "Power is—occurs as—the events that are sets of relations" (p. 77). She reads his notion of subjectivity as having no difference between what subjects and what is subjected—they are not external to each other, hence subjugation refers to how the subject is tied to identity by a conscience or self-knowledge (p. 78). To say "subjugation" or "subjection of the subject" is to describe this process that is not necessarily a "bad" one. She concludes that "I can exercise agency despite (and even because of) the fact that my very existence as a subject is a form of subjection" (p. 79).

Third, McWhorter challenges the view that "Foucault will make you lose your identity and alienate you from your community" (McWhorter, 1999, p. 79). She states that Foucault's work historicizes subjectivities but that it does not thereby expose subjectivities as illusions or advocate their destruction, and she states that the same can be said for identity. For example, she sees Foucault as arguing that sexual identities are historically produced but never suggesting that they are unreal. She argues that there are three questions to ask about the assumptions embedded in claims regarding loss of identity, community, and political action: first, whether Foucault actually does undermine or destabilize identity as critics claim; second, whether community actually does require the existence of shared identity in order to ground and maintain itself; and third, whether political action to end oppression really requires the existence of a community of those who are oppressed (Is political action really dependent in turn upon each of the other two—identity and community?) (p. 79). After treating the complexities around each "if" via the essentialist/constructionist debate, McWhorter concludes

> I have come to respect my lifelong resistance to the label homosexual and to the status of those who bear that label. I have come to understand that my earliest responses to the label and to the oppression that accompanied and depended upon it were good, appropriate, and healthy and that my earliest flickerings of knowledge about how that oppression worked were real and valuable insights....That is not, of course, what most analysts, even gay-friendly ones, would say. Most people would view my youthful refusals,

concealments, silences as the very opposite of self-affirming, positive, political response to heterosexism. Practically every day I hear both gay and straight people speak disparagingly of non-heterosexual individuals who refuse to name themselves homosexual or gay, as if refusal of the label is synonymous with self-hatred and cowardice. Practically every "gay-positive" account of homosexual identity development I've ever seen insists I rid myself of my loathing for the label homosexual or gay and embrace my homosexual identity as if I had chosen it myself. (p. 98)

Foucault's analyses are then placed by McWhorter as the springboard toward a different understanding of what a political action is or entails:

Foucault's analysis, by contrast, allows me to remember my early resistance. No, I didn't stand opposed to my tormentors' *appraisal of homosexuality*. I stood opposed to the very idea that sexuality is a domain of facts before it is a domain of values and powers. The issue was never simply overcoming the stigma attached to homosexual identity. I was never interested simply in convincing those around me that gay people are just as good as straights. I was suspicious of the whole damned sexual and gender identification project. I believed it served dangerous interests and was perpetuated precisely because of its power to limit freedom of all people—not queers only but straight people as well. Foucault's analysis lets me affirm these suspicions and explore them....Other analyses cut me off from the knowledge and strength that first made my resistance possible. Foucault's analysis puts me in touch with that knowledge and that strength. It helps me to remember where the sources of my deepest and hardest and strongest resistance to my oppression actually lie. (pp. 98–99)

McWhorter's undergoing of Foucault's texts toward identity-politics projects and her response to the three criticisms of relativism, loss of agency, and lack of identity, community, and political action thus arrive at a "reconciliation" that is homologous with many of the strategies in educational uses of Foucault discussed below.

Extended Commentaries and Other Kinds of Identity Politics: Developmentalizing Foucault

Other styles in this fourth group, i.e., of extended commentary where Foucault is partitioned in regard to disciplinary or institutional debates, do not pay homage to identity politics of the above kind. Instead, after dividing him in different ways, some commentaries tend to put Foucault back together through other discipline-specific concerns that make him appear as a coagulated mass. They argue that there is coherence or evolutionary-style development or stages in his thought between his first published book in 1954 and his last publications in 1984.[28]

In philosophy, Bernauer's (1990) *Michel Foucault's Force of Flight: Toward an Ethics for Thought* is an example of a commentary that self-consciously makes these moves simultaneously, i.e., division, connection, and developmentalization. It offers a view on the available positionings of Foucault by other scholars up to 1990, labeling the analytical axes along which Foucault's work had been received and positioned to that time. Bernauer's commentary is one of the more elaborated anglophone commentaries of the late twentieth century that is so explicit over the dividing and unifying practices it uses and that are used by others.[29] It displays a tendency to "developmentalize Foucault" that sits in paradox with how educational scholars who draw on Foucault use him. That is, in education Foucault has been deployed to question the dominant idea of evolutionary, linked, or coherent stages and to trouble a priori notions of child or scholar development (see Baker, 2001; Cannella, 1997; Lesko, 2001; Walkerdine, 1984).

Bernauer (1990, pp. 17–20) suggests, for instance, that there are four domains or elements to Foucault's ethics for thought that unite across his career and that over time formed into four arts of questioning:

1. Substance: "What was it necessary to think today in contrast to the traditional domain of the thought-worthy? What should the substance of thought be?"

2. Subjection: "What sort of understanding should be sought? What mode of subjection should the thinker take up?" This refers to "Foucault's effort to denature or historicize Immanuel Kant's great questions on knowledge, obligation and hope. Not 'What can I know?' but rather, 'How have my questions been produced?'"

3. Asceticism: "How should the search for understanding find its way? What asceticism must it practice on itself in order to be enabled to think differently?" This refers to a shift from Kant's central question of Man to three other types of intellectual responsibility that Bernauer identifies, "a practice that entails the work we do to ourselves along the axes of discourse, power, and self."

4. Aspiration: "What goal is pursued through this definition of substance, mode of subjection, and practice of asceticism?" Bernauer

argues in regard to this element, for instance, that Foucault "realized there was never to be a definitive escape from configurations of knowledge-power-self relations and yet he was unyielding in his conviction that no specific configuration was necessary and unchangeable."

The action in Foucault's work across these questions/elements is further parsed along three distinct axes Bernauer identifies in Foucault's work: the knowledge axis (what knowledge does, and not reads), the power axis (how power is constructive and not repressive), and the subject axis (how the self is invented and not discovered). Bernauer uses this grid to argue that commentators have tuned into and out of different lines of analysis in Foucault's work, foregrounding some axes and domains while downplaying others.[30] He suggests that "While there are numberless disagreements among Foucault's commentators on both significant and minor points in his work, this disagreement has often obscured the very dissimilar levels on which they are reading him. This incongruity of levels has largely prevented the emergence of a meaningful dialogue, or even conflict, among interpretations" (Bernauer, 1990, p. 21).

In sum, the above has offered a reading of commentaries on Foucault's work, commentaries that flow around individual concepts or terms, single works or periods, or the wider ensemble of his publications. The analysis of such commentaries indicates at least three things: 1) the different criteria/axes along which Foucault is being read implicitly and explicitly (e.g., research, teaching, service activities; biographically; via writing style and comprehensibility; via field-specific versions of identity politics struggles; via developmental and periodized notions of his work's coherence and the coherence of 'his' identity as a scholar); 2) the irreconcilability of positionings of Foucault; and 3) how an "epistemological" approach to his name brings those things to view. In short, it has documented "the very dissimilar levels" on which commentators have read him and how the incongruity of those levels might be marshaled toward "the emergence of a meaningful dialogue, or even conflict, among interpretations" (Bernauer, 1990, p. 21).

PART TWO
Foucault and/in the Study of Education, 1954–2002

The above illustrates in some ways how Foucault has been crisscrossed and gridded into "clear visions" that simultaneously acknowledge the importance of "ambiguity" or interdisciplinary movements in his work. In this section we overtly perform the same, our point of departure being that mapping the uses of Foucault in the study of education from his first publication in 1954 to 2002 does not arrive at a complete and pure point of clear vision but rather leads back to a stickiness experienced in the very undertaking and effects of such a mapping project at all.

In keeping with the above, our commitment was not to defend the uses of Foucault among scholars who already use him nor to eradicate different uses of Foucault by writing an Introduction that resolved and demarcated once and for all his "real" contribution. Rather, here we analyze *already existing contributions* that have been made in educational scholarship around Foucault and try to discern if there are any patterns at all, dubious though that question might be, in his uptake in anglophone educational literature. Although Foucault's name has been kept in flux and presenced differently as per the wider literature surveyed above, we have been able to identify some consistent uses of Foucault in the educational field.

Because of the amount of literature we have surveyed and unearthed we, again, do not claim to provide comprehensiveness in the citations offered or even selectivity toward some kind of Foucault and education canon. Two other edited volumes that we know of which are specifically focused on Foucault and education have appeared: Ball's (1990) *Foucault and Education: Disciplines and Knowledge* and Popkewitz & Brennan's (1998a) *Foucault's Challenge: Discourse, Knowledge, and Power in Education*. The introductions and chapters in these volumes provide overviews of Foucault's earlier entry into education and are records of already existing contributions to scholarship that we do not summarize here. These volumes cut a wide swath in which others have the luxury of now wandering. They were first in their respective locales of publication (England and the United States) to draw diverse scholarship under the name of Foucault in book-length form, and we recommend them to readers who wish to gain insight into earlier deployments of his work and the analytical pathways through which he entered. We offer citations, then, from more recent years that traverse the kinds of emphases that have become available within educational scholarship[31] and acknowledge the problem of both demarcating and classifying previous uses of Foucault. The lines of reasoning/uses we have noted can appear, for example, within the one piece of scholarship and not simply across pieces.

The uses of Foucault that we have grouped are not linked unilaterally to particular time periods in any evolutionary sense, e.g., "from 1980 to 1985 Foucault was used in one way and now we have progressed to better ways." Rather, the uses of Foucault have winnowed and swayed within and across educational literature, with an intensification in references across the 1990s as indicated in both ERIC and Education Full Text databases.

The first pattern in educational scholarship is absence. We do not find Foucault's name objectified as a keyword, title, framework, or focal point of study in published educational literature until 1977. In 1977 an article by Maxcy appeared in *Paedagogica Historica* entitled "A Structural View of American Educational History" which compared Levi-Strauss, Foucault, and Kuhn's work around structuralism, without seeing Foucault's name as titular or a keyword but engaging in particular with his *The Order of Things* (1966/1970). From 1977 onwards,[32] we identified three predominant uses of Foucault in anglophone educational scholarship to which we have given arbitrary labels. The three predominant uses that we have identified over approximately the last twenty-five years are:

1. historicization and philosophizing projects with relativization emphases
2. denaturalization projects without overt historical emphases and with diversity emphases and
3. critical reconstruction projects with solution emphases

Historicization projects have drawn on the terms archaeology, genealogy, and history of the present and/or modifications or departures from what these are argued to be to offer insights into the "conditions of possibility" for certain discourses to take hold, for questions to be posed as they are currently posed, and for ascertaining when/how things were formulated into being an "educational problem" relative to other timespaces. These can include histories that focus on specific subjects like the urban teacher, the child, the basic writer, the educated person, the lesbian teacher, or the feebleminded (Baker, 2001; Cavanagh, 2002; Davis, 1995; Fendler, 1998; Franklin, 1994; Gray-Rosendale, 1999;

Hunter, 1994; Kirk, 1998; Middleton, 1998; Popkewitz, 1998; Willis, 2002). Educational scholarship in the historicizing vein can also be research that treats Foucault's work as something that must be historicized and introduced (Davies, 1995; Drummond, 2000; Gore, 1994; Jones & Ball, 1995; Marshall, 1996; Popkewitz, 1998; Stone, 2002; Tamboukou, 1999).

Such histories generally take as their starting point a particular subject position, a presumed identity, existing ways of reasoning, or a state of affairs and map the conditions of possibility for their emergence. Here there is often both a break with and reinvocation of identity politics in a very different sense. In moving to "decenter the subject" and historicize meanings or constructs, especially through genealogical approaches, the "givens" of the present are contested and re-presented in new light through the import of the historical analysis. Historicizing approaches in educational work have questioned the normativities of historical narrations—for example, what an appeal to linear time, three-dimensional space, evolution, or origins might mean. They are not necessarily found most commonly within history of education journals, however, perhaps because they challenge what Munslow (1997) calls a conservative reconstructionist approach to history. As Popkewitz, Franklin, & Pereyra's (2001) citational analysis has indicated, in anglophone history of education journals, there has been a more general pattern of censorship or absencing around Foucault's name.[33] As our literature review has also indicated, historicizing analyses have appeared mainly in edited volumes on Foucault (e.g., Ball, 1990; Popkewitz & Brennan, 1998b), in curriculum-based or philosophy of education journals, or as conference papers.

Philosophizing projects do not necessarily draw on what are attributed to Foucault as his historical senses but draw Foucault's work into comparison with other philosophies/ers to unpack the orientations to a particular concept relied on in education, such as "self" or "reason" (Biesta, 1998; Butler, 1999; Erevelles, 2002; Kerr, 2001; Marshall, 2001; Mourad, 2001; Papastephanou, 2001; Peters, 2000; Seals, 1998). In this work there is frequently a reconsideration of the problematic of knowledge, a refiguration of the everyday meanings attributed to time and space, and discussions of Foucault that lead back to translations from continental European interpretations as opposed to anglophone debates within education. Furthermore, in the historicizing and philosophizing veins, the scholarship that has emerged has not necessarily paid homage to or drawn on debate within "the mainstream historians' circle" as described in Part One above, nor taken as its primary citational circle other educational accounts. Rather, Foucault enters this strand of educational work in regard to debates found within wider and varied literatures, such as political philosophy, sociology, cultural geography, or art history which mobilize his name toward what Castel calls a *problematizing approach.*[34]

The relativization aspect of this strand of work emerges from insights into how difficult it is to adjudicate the one best moral position for the topic or periods under study. While in some critical literature this raises the ire of those who don't quite believe that judgments are not made anyway (e.g., Bridges, 1998), the thrust of such historicization and philosophizing projects is not necessarily to play arbiter of the one true or best moment or position but to describe, contextualize, or understand differences that are now noticeable between positions.

Denaturalization projects without overt historical emphases and with diversity emphases draw more "sociologically" on Foucault. They have focused specifically on classroom-based or pedagogical-moment approaches as well as looking at beyond-school settings for the site of education (Gore, 1998; Walkerdine, 1984). They have highlighted how practices/systems of reasoning/ways of saying and doing can have different meanings contemporaneously across places, how classification and categorization within specific institutions might homogenize and normalize that which is marshaled beneath the label for better or for worse, and how current discourses produce their objects. The latter is especially apparent through uptake in the analyses of concepts such as power-knowledge, discipline, surveillance, and governmentality. These four concepts repeatedly emerged as key foci of such projects, indicating a heavier reliance on much of Foucault's later work. Analyses within subfields include and extend beyond areas such as art education, educational administration, literacy, science education, athletics, and higher education studies (e.g., Atkinson, 1998; Blades, 1997; Broadhead & Howard, 1998; Brookfield, 2001; Cladis, 1999; Comber, 1998; Danforth, 2000; Duncan, 1999; Hennon, 1999; Heyning, 2000, 2001; Holligan, 1999; Kivinen & Rinne, 1998; Lechner, 2001; Mayo, 2000; McWilliam, 1999; Middleton, 2001; Olssen, 1999; Opfer, 2001; Pignatelli, 2002; Qi, 1998; Sackney, Walker, & Mitchell, 1999; Spencer, 2001; Thomas & Glenny, 2000; Vinson, 1999).

The research here also demonstrates vacillation around the notion of identity politics, with some studies coagulating around challenges to a priori subjects and questioning liberal notions of agency and empowerment, while others take Foucault's name as a further instance of how subjects can be better empowered and "made" more agentive than "critical theory" has currently allowed. Interesting to us in this strand of research was how many studies drew on the latter approach and also how little crossreferencing there was between subdisciplines of education. While Foucault is engaged centrally within specific pieces of scholarship in such areas as physical education, nurse education, math education, science education, educational administration, school counseling, and so forth, there is little citational cross-fertilization between such areas. Furthermore, there is little between such areas and more generalist research in curriculum studies, histories or philosophies of education, teacher education work, and so on that has utilized Foucault. The slough of individual publications that drew on Foucault's work within such a strand was thus noticeable, but researchers seemed, citationally at least, unaware of each other and of the diversity of subdisciplines in which his name has been made to live. Many pieces of scholarship drawing on Foucault in this strand, do not, for instance, show up in more "official" and recent circles like the Foucault and Education Special Interest Group of the American Educational Research Association or the annual Foucault Circle conferences in the United States.

Critical reconstruction projects offer analyses that can share features of the first two lines of inquiry above but marshal that inquiry toward delineating and reconstructing a stated new vision or practice.[35] Within education, Skrtic's (1995) work is an example that deploys Foucault to critique traditional practices of the special education profession and in order to overtly and explicitly reconstruct the field in specific ways. In a different kind of reconstructionist approach, Flecha (1999) argues that antiracist pedagogies based on Foucault or Derrida promote postmodern racism in Europe, thereby making use of Foucault as a foil toward a reconstruction overtly indebted to Freirean and Habermasian views. In a wide range of subdisciplinary areas from adult literacy to early childhood to mathematics education to teacher education "next steps" or "what to do specifically on Monday morning with the outcomes of this analysis" are provided (Butin, 2001; Faust, 1998; Gore, 1998; Karagiannis, 2000; Ryan, 1998; Veri, 1999; Walshaw, 1999).

The implications of ascertaining such patterns are at least threefold. First, they speak to conditions of receptivity that make certain discourses more likely to appear, be taken up, or coagulate, in a field. Specifically, we have found most uses of Foucault to have taken place around denaturalization projects. The research here brings to visibility certain of

Foucault's texts and not others, suggesting perhaps the limits of education's receptivity. It is not, for example, *I, Pierre Rivière, Having Slaughtered My Mother, My Sister, and My Brother: A Case of Parricide in the Nineteenth Century* (1973/1982) or *This Is Not a Pipe* (1968/1983) that educators have most turned toward in this line or any of the other lines of scholarship. These texts appear noticeably in discussions in law and criminology and in art and art history, respectively, but not in education. The "preferred works" in education seem obvious: those thought more related to specific institutional analysis or forms of institutional regulation as well as the texts that are seen as containing overt "methodological" statements such as "Nietzsche, Genealogy, History."[36]

Second, the discussion/deployment of Foucault in much of the research embodies many self-conscious acknowledgments of, acceptances of, or rejections of the tensions that McWhorter outlined and responded to, which we discussed above. These seemed to be profound and consistent returning points. Questions considered included such things as: Is Foucault's name to be associated with identity-politics projects of any kind? Should Foucault's name be "drawn into" a critical theoretical framework that robs him, as Gilbert-Rolfe (1999) puts it, of its Nietzschean volition? Should Foucault's name be associated with reconstructionist, salvationist, or empowering projects with a priori subjects, religious vestiges and prescribed courses of future action? Should Foucault be used only to denaturalize rather than reconfigure new groupings? Should Foucault's name ever be used outside of an effort at historicization?

Third, the three main kinds of uses we have arbitrarily identified seem both to inform and be defied by the chapters in this volume, problematizing our very act of comporting, labeling, and pegging them— hence the aforementioned stickiness that we arrive at through such a dividing practice. This is a deliberate contradiction that leads such a project into collapsing in on itself, the purpose of which is to ascertain from the process rather than the product insights about the study of education and its discursive limits. Thus, in providing the above categories/maps we hope to have constituted both a handle with which to grip educational literature and a metal bar that can no longer be clung to by sweaty hands; we have slipped off our "own" structures, falling with outstretched legs onto a springboard that has sent us flying somewhere else and with no landing pad in sight until the next deadline.

PART THREE
The Next Deadline: Translation, Composition, and
the Limits of the Toolbox Metaphor in Editing Foucault

Editing Foucault cannot really be thought of as a unique task, for Foucault is always already edited. The contributors to this volume are cognizant of the debate that has formed around positioning Foucault. It would be hard not to be given the knee-jerk rejection directed at users of Foucault's name in education in some places and the delight with which "close" but divergent readings of Foucault are received in others. As such, three reemergent and interrelated conversations have contoured our editorial approach: concerns over translation, concerns over composition, and concerns over the limits of the toolbox metaphor and the term "uses of Foucault."

Translating Foucault

There is a noticeable but misguided snobbery around discussions of Foucault that has emerged in crossovers between francophone and anglophone readings in particular. The argument often occupies the beginning confessional statements of translator's explanations or appears in reviewers' or audience members' comments, especially where the reviewer or audience member actively disagrees with the analysis just presented. The argument goes like this: Unless you have read Foucault in the French, you are not qualified to comment on him or use his name at all. A "better" or "truer," more believable, closer, accurate, considered, reasoned, sensitive, or persuasive reading of Foucault requires reading him in French. The only bottom line to overcome the crisis of author-ity that exists around interpretation in general but Foucault in particular is, therefore, to take the argument back to the base language in which it first appeared. Failure to engage Foucault's texts in the language in which they were first written is the first sign of a poor or weak reading of Foucault.

   This line of argument is not, however, a discussion that arises only in regard to Foucault or European languages. The same line of reasoning is heard when "Western" scholars undertake interpretations of "Eastern" texts without reading the parchment on which they were written, or when "Southern" writers draw concepts presumed exclusive to "Northern" languages to theorize a situation that, in the South Pacific, for instance, was not previously expressed in such terms.

These issues arise under certain presumptions that have to do with, most immediately and obviously, how to weigh the issue of language, especially in regard to a scholar who took it so seriously, but secondly and less immediately, with colonization of what constitutes the political and a site of origin in scholarship, especially scholarship overtly focused on difference in a positive sense. We see Foucault's work in the French and English as launching pads that can be made to do work. Some of our contributors have read him in the French and English and some have not and to this we give no weight other than a belief that different kinds of launching pads allow for different imaginings. We see documents in general, then, as springboards, with languages providing different kinds of springboards and offering other possibilities for the kinds of work that can be done or arguments that can be built.[37]

The reading of Foucault in one language or another does not, then, hierarchicize the worth of an analysis. We would go further; not only is there not one form of French or English, but the act of translation changes the kinds of documentary springboards available in "both" or multiple directions. As might be surmised from Bertrand and Houssaye's discussion (1999, p. 16), the issue of translation when waged in regard to authorization is part of the game of references. This is a game in which Foucault, they suggest, participated quite differently by respecting the texts he worked with so much that he integrated them with very few quotation marks and without comment "because his proposal is theirs."[38]

The chapters throughout this book therefore indicate multiple analytical tactics around the word Foucault. The number and different manner of appearances that Foucault's name makes actually beg a different kind of question, not "What do all users of Foucault have in common?" or "What did Foucault *really* say in French?" but "What work is the name *Foucault* doing at specific sites?" In the book's chapters there are isolated and strategic deployments of the word Foucault, extended engagements with the concept of Foucaultian, swift sidestepping around implied baggage called Foucaultian, and deliberate centering of particular texts by Foucault. Our contributors may use pom-poms and tsk-tsks, cheersquads and big yawns in relation to what are seen as key Foucaultian ideas. Foucault is treated as though unto himself and also in camaraderie with others who are thought of as "along the same lines," such as Judith Butler, Jacques Derrida, or Gilles Deleuze. These varying uses of Foucault do not occur just between chapters but within them as well. The diversity of orientations and deployments, the different starting points, conclusions (to prescribe or not to prescribe?), labels (postmodern or not?) and analytical objects in-between illustrate for themselves what St.Pierre states outright: "Simply put, there is no 'original' Foucault to find." As indicated throughout, however, and as the volume's chapters demonstrate, there are plenty of differences and distinctions with which to play.

Composition around Foucault

The thing that may quiver uncertainly in light of such claims is that there is a chosen name. This book's subtitle is not, to put it satirically, *The Uses of Elephants in the Study of Education* or *The Use of Just Anything in the Study of Education*. Patterns appear prevalent and seem to arise across chapters—for example, the noticeable repetition of the quote "Everything is dangerous" in the "Dangers" part of the volume. What is done with such citations, what they are taken to illustrate, demonstrate, or discombobulate is not repetitive, however, and it is here that such incoherence is understood as productive in the sense of inciting further debate and more openings for ways of saying and seeing.

For example, the compositions around Foucault in this volume do not reduce readings of his work to one line of analysis even where similar texts are referenced. The contributors drawing on *The History of Sexuality*, for instance, do not necessarily ask Foucault about where he grew up, nor do they read him in relation to "confessions" about "influences" in order to proffer singular and causal explanations for why particular foci are taken in a given text. Collectively, the chapters place the burden on the reader to consider the historicity of processes of attribution in the first place,[39] to locate them as historical artifacts, and to work with and through how a conversation with Foucault, as with anyone, recomposes him and you. Still, something niggles: that contributors are indeed citing the name Foucault surely says something about similarities between "authors" and "his" uniqueness, does it not?

The similarity does not pertain to the content, argument, absences, or foci in chapters but to the site of production, mentioned above. All the contributors to this volume spoke at the International Foucault and education conferences, held in 2000 and 2001 in New Orleans, Louisiana, and Seattle, Washington, USA, respectively. Out of multiple requests for proceedings, papers by the international panel of keynote speakers at both conferences were compiled. In addition, we were frequently approached to disseminate copies of further papers presented at the sessions and those requests, too, have been honored in this volume.

These consecutive conferences enabled extended discussion and revisiting of issues around using Foucault's work—issues that not surprisingly arise if Foucault is positioned functionally by terms such as "uses."

Limits of the Toolbox Metaphor and the Use of "Uses"

The beauty of extended conversations lies precisely in the effects of languages in which they are conducted. If the term "uses" is simply taken to imply a distinction between the real Foucault and the "pretenders" who make use of him in some kind of imitation or application, then the kind of politics that opens around the toolbox metaphor shouldn't surprise anyone—levels of approximation are created under such an interpretation of "uses," and work is thereby judged as "accurate" or "inaccurate."

For example, the issue of the Foucault police came up at both conferences—whether there was a body of scholars who presumed themselves to know more, most, or better about Foucault and to censor or weed out "inappropriate" uses of him that might muddy some presumed purity and unique contribution. Was there a guard who tried to prevent the bringing of Foucault "back into" critical theory, salvationist rhetoric of solutions and prescriptions, or to censor his use in utopian structural analyses that contained a priori conscious actors, modernist historical narratives whose focus was social control as a negative phenomena, or neo-Marxist resistance theories where conceptions of power were still understood as sovereign, static, and binary?

Whether the terminology of "the uses of Foucault" implies a binary distinction between the real and the applied, the primary and the secondary, is an open issue for the contributors in this volume. Some contributors actively distance themselves from the view that Foucault can be applied by stating that is not what they are doing. Others have no qualms about positioning Foucault's work as a template for understanding things that have arisen in education, acknowledging the context is different, and running with what can be noticed through the idea of application. Which of these is "better," whether one is "truer" to Foucault or not, and so on, is not part of our editorial style to arbitrate within a given chapter. As editors, we have gained a view from across chapters. We do not see an original or real Foucault whose purity is then "used," but there *are* different uses of Foucault. To play on Bertrand & Houssaye (1999) cited above, "his proposals are ours," and the use of quotation marks doesn't necessarily help clarify the him, me, or us. Writers and readers are, then, left to their desires regarding what "uses" means and whether this is purely functionalist or something beyond and whether this falls within the domain of a toolbox metaphor or not. Such desires include the desire not to compare uses of "uses" at all but to just get on with it, especially where there are no stable grounds for "controlling contaminating variables," on which most notions of comparison and functionalism implicitly and dangerously hinge.

In regard to these commitments, then, we have engaged a particular and deliberate editorial strategy; whether our contributors were aware of our stylistic perversions or not is another matter. To arbitrate definitively is to miss the point; to argue is the process. As editors, we have argued with our contributors and to our delight they have argued back (but maybe not to their pleasure given the viscerality of time pressures!). The temporary, shifting, and irresolved debates over the uses of Foucault in education are what are gathered here in and as the chapters of this volume. The chapters are diaries of those arguments, but they also go beyond. They represent thoughtful orientations to a body of literature that has been drawn on to rethink boundaries and taboos, to challenge previous forms of question-posing and problematization in educational discourse, to raise to the threshold of investigation that which has not previously been seen as an object of study. We outline below, then, how each chapter provides such rethinking.

PART FOUR
Continuities and Rupture

Our refusal throughout the above to ask the transcendentally real or original Foucault to step forward does not belie a lack of attraction. It is Foucault's name in this book's title and not another one. And it is clearly around the name Foucault that contributors have coagulated. This might suggest that there are facets to his works that we perceive drawing us; we are drawn to the work that we can imagine those works can do, the way we are worked upon reading them. Perhaps such attractions initially spoke to the possibility of an edited volume and, combined with the not uncommon rejection of Foucault's name in the wider education discipline, raised our hopes for a different kind of magnetic field.

What we see as fresh in this volume, though, is the complexity of attraction, for an attraction does not always belie a positive or unquestioned uptake or a simplistic "belief in common." The collage that our reading of commentaries and the chapters to follow provides, the invitation to read Foucault differently, and the productive openings that emerge in refusing to demarcate an originary or authentic Foucault are thus what this volume both embodies and illustrates. The chapters are a continuation of the strands in uses of Foucault discussed above and an extension into new domains with new focal points of study that muddy such strands. In Section One, "Coagulations," the papers congeal around the practice of historicization, offering new foci for analysis amid very different senses of methodology for undertaking problematizing histories. There are unique objects of analysis across these chapters that have now been elevated to the threshold of investigation. That is, the topics that appear in this section indicate how some aspects of education can be so taken-for-granted, or so overexposed, that they remain underexposed in their comportment and influence.

In Part One of "Coagulations," the oft-neglected sites of educational studies brought into focus include school uniforms, physical training, and feeling like being a "proper" teacher. Inés Dussel's "Fashioning the Schooled Self Through Uniforms: A Foucauldian Approach to Contemporary School Policies," David Kirk's "Beyond the 'Academic' Curriculum: The Production and Operation of Biopower in the Less-Studied Sites of Schooling," and Erica McWilliam's "What Does It Mean to Feel Like Teaching?" are three very different approaches to the relationship between what the body is made to wear, to do, and to feel—and what might be made of it.

Dussel interrupts the debates on school uniforms and dress codes in public schools, drawing, in unique ways, on the idea of a history of the present. She uses Foucault and the topic of clothing bodies uniformly to problematize the very terms in which we have come to think of schooling, what it raises as a problem, and the limits this sets for solutions. Dussel does not make claims from beyond her "material," arguing that school uniforms are not all-solving policies nor the deadliest of our foes. Instead, they have to be considered as one among many long-standing technologies of the body which, together with other institutional procedures, have produced both conformity and individuality in schools and in larger societies. While régimes of appearance often present themselves as free systems, Dussel argues that the liberty people enjoy to make choices is regulated and that this takes place through complex mechanisms, which include, among other things, patterns of consumption that shape perceptions of self and the very idea of "choice."

Kirk brings to the forefront in his chapter how Foucaultian studies of the regulation of children's bodies in schools often neglect the most obvious and overt sites in a school where such regulation takes place. He examines physical training in the form of late nineteenth-century practices of drilling and exercising and the more mid–twentieth-century shift to games- and sports-based physical education. The shift to team games especially has often been interpreted as a kinder, gentler, freer, more fun, more student-centered and less harsh approach to physical education than military-style drills. Kirk questions the common sense of such interpretations of change through the notion of biopower. Biopower is seen as both a product of such practices *and* as a lens through which to interrogate the "morality" of the shift in practice. He proposes a radical thesis that contradicts positive sentiments about games within the smaller field of physical education, and that operates as radical because it is not or has not been taken on board by those who view the "academic" curriculum as the center of educational study and who do not want to muddy such study with considerations of how bodies are disciplined to move in particular ways. He suggests that within the apparently liberating moment and practice of playing games relative to military drills in both the United Kingdom and Australia, a new form of corporeal regulation emerges. The new forms of regulation refigure both physical education-specific senses of ethics and wider notions of the reconstituted schooled subject.

McWilliam's "What Does It Mean to Feel Like Teaching?" speaks to a different kind of "schooled subject"—the teacher. The chapter questions what constitutes the liberatory, inspirational, or restrictive around the idea of teacher motivation. McWilliam moves away from ideas about motivation as a psychological response and also makes a departure from psychoanalytic ideas about the desire to teach and to learn. In their place, she explores the proposition that "feeling like teaching" does not have its source in some originary interior "personality" or intrinsic or natural calling. Rather, to feel like teaching, to want to teach *well*, is an effect of moral training made possible through disciplinary discourses organized around epistemic rules that exist in a particular time and place. To demonstrate this she contrasts classical constructions of feeling like or being a "good teacher" with more contemporary practices. This is a unique contribution that departs from more formulaic genealogies that make epochal comparisons of "the teacher" over time. In arguing the usefulness of her approach, McWilliam undoes the discursive opposition between pleasure and discipline that is at the heart of humanist assumptions about motivation and desire. She moves the chapter away from the task of advocating "better teaching" in teacher education settings to the "ironic" task of documenting what counts as "proper teaching" at particular points in time.

In Part Two of "Coagulations," Kenneth Hultqvist, Thomas Popkewitz, and Lisa Weems' chapters introduce new topics and reinterpretation of familiar but underexposed ones, coagulating especially around the problematic of the nation and its "ideal subjects." Hultqvist's "The Traveling State, the Nation, and the Subject of Education" offers an historical dimension to studies of educational policy, which, ironically, is rarely undertaken by scholars working out of departments of educational policy. He reads educational policies in Sweden from the nineteenth century into the late twentieth century outside economic foundationalist lenses and within a notion of traveling discourses. The traveling discourses he identifies—interactionism, integrationism, and the cultural child—have transmogrified in different moments within Swedish educational policy, recongealing in the present at overt and frequent references to the desirability of the "autonomous lifelong learner." The nation, the state, and the child are all terms up for grabs here rather than taken-for-granted as easy-to-identify subjects. Hultqvist's chapter is not structured as a formulaic epochal comparison of discourses either—there are both vertical and horizontal lines that cut across and through the narrative. This generates a questioning of current trends in new forms of "qualitative" and historical research that claim to be more "ethical" than their predecessors.

In "The Reason of Reason: Cosmopolitanism and the Governing of Schooling" Popkewitz also offers a new object of historical study that is timely given the turn toward globalization research in the educational field. The idea of having a cosmopolitan reason, a cosmopolitan figure, or a cosmopolitan outlook/morality is not, Popkewitz demonstrates, entirely new. He examines the emergence of cosmopolitanism as a form of reason governing the conduct of citizens in a world no longer ruled by social or theological certainties. A central aim of the chapter is to suggest that the ideal of cosmopolitanism, the hallmark of which is a worldly personhood, is brought into modern schooling as a strategy of governing. Schooling is the site that produces and governs the qualities of a cosmopolitan individual who is to prevail beyond the limits of his or her own locale and at the same time is to fill a specific role in civil society. He argues, however, that such reasoning is not a thing of logic. Rather, it is an amalgamation of cultural practices that historically bring together registers of social administration with narratives of individual freedom, human agency, liberty, and democracy. He takes as his site for this latter argument documents from the United States, overtly avoiding the making of any representational claims as to "the history of American schooling." In addition, rather than "applying" specific "theories" of Foucault, Popkewitz engages in the historical problematics that relate knowledge and power throughout Foucault's work—particularly the idea of governmentality. The chapter concludes with a contemporary revisioning of the cosmopolitan child whose soul is now being administered as a free, self-managed, active, ethical individual who functions as a life-long learner in diverse communities.

Weems' "Troubling Professionalism: Narratives of Family, Race, and Nation in Educational Reform" analyzes the philosophical assumptions associated with the movement to professionalize teachers during the Progressive Era in the United States. Professionalism has long been a sticky issue in education as an insecure field and the topic is not new. What Weems brings to the topic is new, however, constituting an innovation over the same old argument of "We need more professional teachers with a stronger sense of professionalism." Extending a notion of a history of the present to that of "deviant historiography," Weems approaches the topic by asking how professionalism came to be seen as a problem. This includes deconstructing traditional histories of the movement. Attention to the discontinuities and contradictions within discourses of professionalism illuminates the ways in which the emergence of professions, such as teaching, are inscribed in larger narratives of family, race, and nation. Weems argues that educational discourses of professionalism in the United States have historically produced a "teaching" body that is constituted by contingent specifications of whiteness, femininity, and heterosexuality, which while separated for analytical purposes, cannot be understood outside of the meaning that such discourses lent to each other and the fabrication of the "ideal teacher" at different times.

The chapters in "Coagulations" share an historical orientation, some similar nomenclature, such as history of the present, and even somewhat overlapping starting points, such as the current noticeability of a turn toward producing the autonomous, life-long learner, or the flexible cosmopolitan citizen-learner, or the free-thinking games player, or the free-choosing and expressive clothes consumer. They do not, however, travel the same tracks via the same routes to arrive at descriptions, analyses, or explanations of such phenomena that have appeared as taken-for-granted subjects/topics in educational discourse in specific sites. In particular, these chapters collectively constitute a contribution to and departure from previous uses of Foucault in education by offering new topics for study and by complicating, if not problematizing, the more formulaic denaturalizing studies predicated on Foucault's work. They move the terms of debate away from a priori notions of the multiplied but stable and "disciplined" subject into the very conditions of thought for "seeing" a subject as a subject at all.

Section Two of the volume, "Dangers," has two parts, "In Tutelage" and "Inter-views." In both, the quote "Everything is dangerous" appears as a noticeable point of return. This was not a theme of either international conference and is also not the quote from which the title of the book is drawn. It was such a recurrent reference and rationale for the research being undertaken by scholars, however, that we feel coincidence doesn't quite explain it. The frequent appeal to this citation from Foucault might instead suggest something about the conditions of receptivity in educational arenas. If scholars are put on the defensive and dismissed by others who argue that the statement "Everything is dangerous" is proof of Foucault's "relativism," (where relativism is assumed ironically to have only one meaning, i.e., "bad" and to have been *chosen* as a philosophical position), then the systems of reasoning underlying such a reading/rejection are worth considering and/or "correcting," given one's take on it. The chapters in Section Two do just that.[40]

James Marshall's "Michel Foucault: Marxism, Liberation, and Freedom" sets the stage for explaining Foucault's entrance into and reception within leftist educational debates. By contrasting Foucault's meaning of liberation and freedom with Marxist and post-Marxist thought around the two terms, Marshall describes what perhaps underlies some of the critiques that McWhorter (1999) felt compelled to respond to and with which educators are often confronted. Marshall argues that Foucault's ideas about liberation, freedom, and the state (governmentality, not Government-ality) departed from critical theoretical frameworks where different meanings for such terms operated. In giving examples of how Foucault's departures from previous understanding can open new analyses of education, Marshall complicates many of the commentaries on Foucault that are quick to place him in the "evil influence" basket. Without taking an either/or position, his examination of how existing "preferred discourses" in a particular subdiscipline set limits to the reception that "new" ones might offer speaks directly to how the following chapters in the volume play in such places of difference. By refusing a simplifying and superficial reading of Foucault, Marshall's analysis makes the reader consider how being in tutelage, in Foucault's terms, is not necessarily "liberating" nor necessarily a pernicious form of bondage.

The focus shifts from teachers' classrooms and teacher-educators' missions to policymaking of a different kind in the next chapter. Patti Lather's "Foucauldian 'Indiscipline' as a Sort of Application: Qu(e)er(y)ing Research/Policy/Practice" takes the familiar research/ policy/practice trilogy as its starting point—a trilogy that is often the object of debate about how to put the three acts back together. Lather argues that the works of Foucault emphasize the insurrection of subjugated knowledges, articulate a posthumanist subjectivity, and denaturalize the regularities that govern thought in ways that can be useful for rethinking such a nexus. She engages extensively with Foucault's notion of counter-science in *The Order of Things* (1966/1970), with his critics, and further with queer theorists on multiple levels. First, she puts Foucault's concept of positivities to work to help create a more expansive idea of science as counter-science that is appropriate to an era with blurred disciplinary boundaries and the global uprising of the marginalized. Second, she explores what a more expansive science (counter-science) might look like in relation to McGuigan's "the policy turn in cultural studies" and Nietzsche's idea of a Gay Science. Third, she explores what this might mean in relationship to the research/policy/practice nexus through drawing on Sedgwick's notion of queering in order to enact a gay policy analysis in the form of a counter-science. To demonstrate what a counter-science that draws specifically on queer theory might look like, then, Lather provides an example of her own educational policy teaching syllabus and two further examples of policy-inflected research. She concludes that when one operates from a premise of the *impossibility* of satisfactory solutions, this does not mean an "avoidance" of anything nor an assumption to resolve everything, but, instead, it means being prepared to meet problems and obstacles as the very way toward producing different knowledge and producing knowledge differently.

Where Lather challenges received comforts around taken-for-granted notions of "scientific" policymaking, Valerie Harwood and Mary Louise Rasmussen's "Studying Schools with an 'Ethics of Discomfort'" challenges the unwitting attribution of identities to students within schools. They examine the complexities that arise, especially when a researcher, teacher, or policymaker thinks they are most helping. Using a piece by Foucault that is rarely taken up in education, titled "For an Ethics of Discomfort," Harwood and Rasmussen interrogate the "familiar" via research related to the study of people in Australia and the United States who work to support LGBTI-identified (lesbian, gay, bisexual, transsexual, or intersexed identified) students in high school settings. An ethics of discomfort is used to consider a range of materials including newspaper articles, formal policy statements, and interviews. The tendency to conflate LGBTI adolescence with "woundedness" in educational discourses emerges from the survey of literature. The authors discuss how an ethics of discomfort can be applied to an interrogation of "horror stories" surrounding LGBTI adolescence. They introduce readers here to another concept rarely attended to in educational uses of Foucault—the process of thaumaturgy that Foucault describes in *Madness and Civilization* (1961/1965) to explain how some reasonings travel into the domain of truth, disappearing to become part of the fabric of "a poorly known horizon." Their analysis points to the complications around performing an ethics of discomfort, of how a rationale for continuing to do something in identity politics terms might be preferred because of strategic and protective reasons. They suggest that the interstices between the awareness and application of an ethics of discomfort accentuate the necessity of a continuous questioning of certitudes.

The papers in this part of Section Two offer new strategies for rethinking studies of education in a more "sociological" vein that avoids some of the repetitive uses of Foucault that we have found in our survey of the literature. These chapters do not presume that discipline means something negative; they do not presume that liberation is unproblematically positive, and they do not see Foucault's reasonings as standing on their own without context or without peers, allies, and extensions available. In addition, they offer new takes on aspects of Foucault's work that do not commonly appear elsewhere. Marshall's depiction of the problem of tutelage in Foucault's work, Lather's uptake and extension of the notion of counter-science, which has never been drawn on in studies of educational policy before, and Harwood and Rasmussen's introduction of the concept of the poorly known horizon and thaumaturgy to audiences who, even if familiar with Foucault, may not be familiar with these terms or deployments in his writing, indicate the contributions that can emanate from engaging differently with his work.

In Part Two of Section Two, "Inter-views," the chapters play with the productivity of being between views that using Foucault helps to arouse. Elizabeth St.Pierre's "Care of the Self: The Subject and Freedom" begins by stating that her Foucault will be different from everyone else's because her chapter is an introspective examination of how she honors Foucault by "being wary of my attachment to him, by working to get free of the subject he has allowed me to think and be so that I might think and be a different subject." By turning her ethnographic lens homeward, she begins to unravel her subjection by talking with some of the older southern white women in the United States who had taught her how to be a woman. St.Pierre finds four aspects of Foucault's notion of "care of the self" that can help her to understand the different kinds of subjects she experienced, and met the limits of, in the act of interviewing. She not only extends Foucault's varying analytics of the subject to their breaking point but realigns where and what one might see as "educational" or as an institution with educational functions. Her quest to rethink the subject is overlaid by the difficulty she experienced as a researcher, the difficulty of trying to function in the ruins of a particular kind of "qualitative inquiry" after the theoretical move that authorizes its foundation has been interrogated and its limits breached so profoundly that its center can no longer hold.

Dawnene Hammerberg's "Technologies of the Self in Classrooms Designed as 'Learning Environments': (Im)possible Ways of Being in Early Literacy Instruction" draws on the same works of Foucault as does St.Pierre but in a completely different way. As a deployment of Foucault's "technologies of the self" at the classroom level, it is a unique and detailed unpacking of the microphysics of "progressive literacy practices." Hammerberg disentangles the politics of current trends in literacy instruction that make frequent appeal to the terms "authenticity" and "meaningfulness" as key concepts. She notes tensions in new movements in literacy education at the elementary school level. Here especially, spaces formerly known as classrooms are now called "learning environments." Such sites operate on a conception of literacy instruction where individuals are to be made responsible for managing their own behaviors. As such, Hammerberg shows the ways in which literacy learning is not only a problem of teaching, reading, or writing but, more significantly, has become a problem of managing and training technologies of the self. In examining four specific technologies that make classrooms function as learning environments, and which make student selves appear as "independent," she concludes that such techniques of being and becoming "literacy learners" in the learning environment are not only a function of pedagogical practices and discursive constructions rather than innate "cognitive" or "personal" notions of a child's self but lead to a provocative rethinking of ethics around such observations: What is a teacher or teacher educator to do if the above insights are available and yet, if there are injunctions to "not prescribe" action for others?

Cathy Toll and Thomas Crumpler's "Everything Is Dangerous: Pastoral Power and University Researchers Conducting Interviews" is an innovative and thought-provoking piece that interrogates the interrogator, i.e., the researcher-as-interviewer. In challenging what interviews actually tell the researcher, in questioning the notion of data that undergirds a transcription as though it is more special and realistic than other kinds of texts, this chapter undermines one of the most cherished practices in "qualitative" educational studies—taperecording a conversation. The chapter uses Foucault's idea of pastoral power to examine the interview process. It catalogs discrete examples of apparent contradictions between wanting to do good and engaging in activity that might move from the dangerous to the bad or harmful. Toll and Crumpler draw on their own involvement in such interview projects as "the data" itself. Their two different research projects featured moments within and around the practice of interviewing teachers when the procedure had unintended, and what they saw as potentially harmful, consequences. Given the prolific use of interviewing as a research strategy, Toll and Crumpler end by considering how the process might be revisioned. Three new ways of approaching the interview as text, as opposed to the text of the interview, are offered. Their observations and suggestions lead the reader through complex and multilayered issues around reflexivity that are rarely confronted. This includes a response to the presumption that a "proper" use of Foucault reflexively requires "knowing not to offer fixed prescriptions" at the end of the critique, a kind of reflexive knowing and academic monitoring they see as a continuation of pastoral power processes. Moreover, their analysis, they argue, further mobilizes forms of pastoral power through demonstrating the kinds of "ethical reflexivity" that generated their critique of the research interview in the first place.

The chapters in Part Two of this section thus provide new foci for research that moves the study of education to unique sites. Education takes place somewhere other than in rows in front of a blackboard. In St.Pierre's version of inter-views, there is a noticeable shift in the analytics of the "the subject" that she encounters in reflecting on her interviewees and herself. It is an in-betweenness in conceptions of the subject that is so liminal it almost defies articulation. It cannot be spoken in regard to the usual sensation of linear time, and it cannot be retrieved outside of the context of doing the ethnography as though it could be pinned to a wall and held up for analysis later. In Hammerberg, the in-betweenness is articulated as differing senses of how and where the self is. The self of "authentic and progressive literacy practices" is presumed interior, personal, and cognitive—a site that is already there but to be worked upon. The self that Hammerberg identifies is a site that is produced by pedagogy, not revealed by it. It is dispersed and exterior, it is in the microphysics of pedagogical reason before it arrives "inside" and becomes subject to judgments of or as "the child's personality as a learner." Finally, in Toll and Crumpler, the in-betweenness emanates, literally, from the practice of interviewing teachers, and it takes two forms: the being-between of the shepherd-flock game that Foucault's notion of pastoral power makes one notice and an in-betweenness in noticing that to even notice this reflexively is a mobilization of the same.

In sum, the volume's chapters draw on and challenge Foucault's work through their differential engagements with, extensions, criticisms, and deployment of analytical strategies around his name. They do not meet at some central point nor begin from some pure original, even where statements like "technologies of the self" or "everything is dangerous" appear to be in common. Rather, within *how* "the limits" of educational discourse are read *as* limits or *as* "conditions of possibility" they respond, providing insights and springboards to a revisioning of education that might not otherwise have been available.

Conclusion: Your Foucault, My Foucault?

This Introduction and foreshadowing of chapters to come cannot be interpreted as a bland call for a phenomenological "Your Foucault, My Foucault," as a rationale for arguing "See, I knew he said nothing and meant nothing other than whatever you want him to mean!," or as more of the same old Foucault. Foucault's name means something in different places in which it is presenced and his works are made to do work in distinctive, but not infinite, ways. What this Introduction has demonstrated at length, then, is not the impossibility of identifying that but the importance of sensitivity to it, of cognizance of the "dissimilar levels" on which scholars read him and have found him useful, even in the negative. As such, we do not end here with a profound quote from Foucault in order to highlight the authenticity of our approach to him through him but rather with an underscoring of the pleasures of continued close readings and rigorous analyses that take seriously the analytical axes along which he is received, divided, and deployed within the educational field.

Endnotes

1.   We realize the "dangers" in subsuming a variety of settings under the terms
     anglophone and francophone and the implication for identity politics
     issues. Within the specific sites we are speaking of, however, there are
     grounds for noting some commonality in anglophone scholarship. At the
     International Foucault and Education conferences, out of which these
     essays were compiled, presenters who produced scholarship within
     different anglophone contexts commented on the often negative and knee-
     jerk reactions they were met with when citing Michel Foucault. In trying to
     obtain publication, have conference proposals accepted, or receive
     informed reviews on grant applications, scholars frequently referred to
     hostile responses that seemed to come from reviewers who had not read
     Foucault but who were willing to disparage works using his name. A
     convergence of comments and observations appeared, with the dismissals
     often being couched in twofold terms: the dismissal of Foucault as "post,"
     where post equals bad for unexplained reasons, and the dismissal of
     Foucault as one who did not suggest alternatives for "action" in the
     classroom, where actions prescribed from an expert were the only correct
     form of educational critique.

2.   It is important to note that for a significant time the debate around the
     "category" in which Foucault's work should be placed within France, but
     also within eastern Europe, was structuralism. Vitriolic conflict regarding
     this classification emerged especially around the publication of *The Order
     of Things* (1966/1970), and then more widely in relation to his earlier
     Madness and Civilization (1961/1965) and *The Birth of the Clinic*
     (1963/1975). In *The Order of Things*, Foucault states that he and his
     analyses are not structuralist. In *Remarks on Marx* (1978/1991), in
     conversation with Duccio Trombadori, he explains why, again, and
     indicates how subsequent publication of *The Archaeology of Knowledge*
     (1969/1972), was in part a response to critiques of him being a
     "structuralist." The point here is that in anglophone educational scholarship
     which dismisses Foucault as "post" there is sometimes little cognizance of
     how what is being assumed as "poststructural" in the United States,
     Britain, Australia, New Zealand, or Canada, for instance, is actually
     considered *structuralist theory* in Europe and would therefore be labeled
     there as *structuralist*, not as "post." The perceived loss of the primacy of
     the agentive, humanist, and a priori subject, the challenge to dogmatic
     Marxist ideology in the wake of Stalinism, and the emergence of new
     leftist critiques that did not pay homage to purely class-based analyses, saw
     the charge of "Structuralist!" in France in the 1960s as tantamount to being

called "bourgeoisie." For Foucault's understanding of and historicization of such debates and categories, especially in relation to events in eastern Europe, see his responses in chapter 3 of *Remarks on Marx*, "But Structuralism Was Not a French Invention."

3. A rare, recent example of scholars pointing out such differences in debates over educational work appears in an exchange that occurred in *Educational Researcher* in 2000. St.Pierre's and Pillow's response to Wright's critique of postmodern research in education raised to visibility such differences, pointing out how criteria cannot be conflated and how justifications for certain styles of educational research cannot be delivered on the terms of previous styles.

4. Bertrand and Houssaye (1999) provocatively note that the act of quoting sometimes operates in education as a blockage to further thought rather than an extension or deeper consideration.

5. It is possible to see such an enunciation of an "epistemological Foucault" as a demarcation, as a singular point about "multiplicity," as the inevitable use of an unspoken discourse to govern the discourse on difference, as still excluding by stating what it is and giving it a name. Our refusal and acceptance playfully trades on such observations which are by now banal, on how the stating of something as being beyond X requires the naming of the X that it is supposedly beyond. There is a history to this apophatic potential of language that is productive for our purposes here, then. It allows for an orientation to, or perhaps an aporia around, Foucault as an epistemological or traveling discourse without having to see the naming of this orientation as a singular "stance," as a point, or as a firm spot in the ground. The charge of "Reduction!" or "Contradiction!," assumes that no such thing as paradox exists or assumes that every "innovation" can be evolutionarily linked or reduced to charges of "more of the same."

6. Foucaultian and Foucauldian are both adjectival forms used by contributors to this volume. We do not demarcate a consistent use across the volume and have left the matter to each contributor.

7. Foucault's statements are sometimes invoked in commentaries on Foucault to authorize such a position, for example: "If interpretation can never be completed, this is quite simply because there is nothing to interpret. There is nothing absolutely primary to interpret, for after all everything is already interpretation" (Foucault, 1967/1998, p. 275). Or, "If my critics [of *The Order of the Things*] had read the preceding works [*Madness and*

Civilization and *The Birth of the Clinic*], if they hadn't wanted to forget them, they would have recognized that already in them I had proposed a series of problems, explanations, and causes. It's partially the result of the old, well-rooted voice of judging a book as if it were a kind of absolute, perfectly elaborated in each of its elements. But as you know, I write books in progression: the first leaves open problems upon which the second one rests; which, in turn, requires another one. And all of that doesn't happen in linear fashion or continuity; these same texts overlap and criss-cross on another" (Foucault, 1978/1991, pp. 97–98). One does not need to go through such statements to arrive at the sense of impossibility of determining the best sites/cites in regard to Foucault scholarship, however. Any sensitive and close reading will indicate how different criteria operate in specific locales and how even within the apparently "same" locale, such as the educational field, there is no agreement between scholars or even necessarily within the one piece of scholarship.

8.   It follows that we do not think of the naming and citation practices below as any kind of canon or even more selectively as "the best" sites/cites. To determine such unilaterally and cross-temporally is an impossibility and part of the editorial orientation we have taken in this volume.

9.   In African studies (Appiah, 1992; Nagy-Zekmi, 2002; Ray & Lebranche, 2001), African-American studies (Glaude, 2000; Hoem, 2000; West, 1982/2002; Wynter, 1995a), anthropology (Fife, 2001; Melville, 2002; Rabinow, 2002), archaeology (in the traditional sense) (Holtorf & Karlsson, 2000); architecture (Tschumi, 1994), art (Gilbert-Rolfe, 1999), Biblical literary criticism (Moore, 1994), Caribbean studies (Wynter, 1992, 1995a, 1995b, 2002), disability studies (Allan, 1996; Davis, 2002; Erevelles, 2001; Richardson, 1999), East-West studies (Said, 1994; Smith, 1999; Szakolczai, 1994), environmental and planning studies (Palmer, 2001; Ploger, 2001; Raco & Imrie, 2000), family therapy (Besley, 2002), feminist studies (Alexander & Talpade, 1997; Bell, 1999; Hekman, 1996; Kruks, 2001; Langsdorf, Watson, & Smith, 1998; Molinaro & Tusquets, 1991; McNay, 1993; Ramazanoglu, 1993; Sawicki, 1991; Weitz, 1998), gay and lesbian studies (Angelides, 2001; Dow, 2001; Halperin, 1995; McWhorter, 1999; Turner, 2000), geography (Kearnes, 2000; Tamboukou, 2000), history and its subfields, e.g., art history (Crary, 1999; Foti, 1996), histories of the child (Kincaid, 1992; Rose, 1989), histories of the discipline of history (Chartier, 1988; Hacking, 2002; Hamilton, 1996; Megill, 1992; Munslow, 1997; Neubauer, 1999), histories of medicine and science (Deacon, 2002; Peterson & Bunton, 1997; Thiher, 1999), histories of statistics and mathematics (Dear, 1995; Hacking, 1990), the new

disability history (Cocks, Fox, Brogan, & Lee, 1996; Longmore & Umansky, 2001; Rothman, 1971/2002; Stiker, 1999), in Latin American studies (Trigo, 2002; Wynter, 2001), law (Bell, 1993; Hunt & Wickham, 1994; Knafla, 2002; Smart, 1989; Smith, 2000), library and information sciences (Thomas, 2001), nursing (Curtis & Harrison, 2001; Francis, 2001; Riley & Manias, 2002), (non-Biblical) literary criticism (Dougherty, 2001; Kirby, 2001), media studies (Gehrke, 2001), philosophy (Allen, 2002; Gracia, 2001; Owen, 1994; Payne, 1997; Prado, 1992; Scott, 1990), political science (Brigg, 2001; Elden, 2002; Howarth, 2002), postcolonial studies (Bhabha, 1994; Brigg, 2002; Hall & du Gay, 1996; Said & Viswanathan, 2001; Spivak, 1999; Young, 1990, 2001), psychology (Burman, 1994; Danziger, 1990; May, 1993), psychiatry, psychoanalysis (Jones & Porter, 1994; Sedgwick, 1982), social work (Chambon, Irving, & Epstein, 1999; Keenan, 2001; Tsang, 2001), sociology (Biggs & Powell, 2001; Caputo & Yount, 1993; Clifford, 2001; Hacking, 1999; Joyce, 2001; Kendall & Wickham, 1999; Mottier, 2001; Rose, 1999; Russell, 2001; Szakolczai, 1998), and theology (Carrette, 1999, 2000; Gade, 2002; Ray, 1987; Schuld, 2000).

10. In a special edition on "the game of references" in the *International Journal of Applied Semiotics*, Tochon (1999) argues that: "To refer is also to make visible a deed of memory that is congruent with a thought. Approaching a reference around which one's discourse is organized is a poetic act. A reference is a sign of proximity or contrast which demarcates the territory covered by an academic obsession: that of faithfulness to one's sources. A reference is also an internal elsewhere, an edge of meaning, and the allusive, never completed complementarity of dialogue. A reference is inclusion rather than exclusion. Even when rejecting a source, we are taking it into account and thus taking it seriously in its will to mean" (p. 7).

11. Bertrand and Houssaye (1999, p. 16) in their dialogue "Did Derrida Kill Foucault?" examine the different ways in which the politics of the game of referencing is studied and deployed by Derrida and Foucault. Both, they argue, read the authors they choose very closely but take up different styles of quotation and referencing. In Foucault's case: "He analyzes them with very few quotation marks and without any comments. He integrates them into his work because his proposal is theirs. He does not use the authors; he integrates them into his thinking while respecting their thinking. In this way, he avoids looking only at the surface; he escapes from parasitic reading and focuses on the structure of knowledge" (p. 16). We speak to

the issue of "use" and the politics around the interpretation of "uses of Foucault" in Part Three of this Introduction.

12. We are cognizant of how different search engines are available in and through different institutions so we have provided below a summary of how the databases we used gather and explain their sources. We searched both print (hard copy) indices and electronic versions that took over from print. The indices we covered in some cases preceded the period of Foucault's publications, i.e., began before 1954 and in some cases were not in existence until after that year. Thus we have covered as wide a search ground as possible to enable us to compare shifts in citations across the period 1954–2002.

Academic Search
Academic Search is a full-text database of more than 3,000 journals. The *New York Times*, *Wall Street Journal*, and *Christian Science Monitor* are also indexed. It covers many academic areas, including business, social sciences, humanities, general science, and education. A business directory is also included. Academic Search is a newer entity that does not have any direct precursor. It was built by soliciting journals to be included in the database. The start date for different journals varies greatly, e.g., some begin in 1984, others in 2002. However, it includes listings/references that were published before 1984.

Alternative Press Index
The Alternative Press Index, produced by the Alternative Press Center in Baltimore, indexes approximately 300 alternative, radical, and left publications that report and analyze the practices and theories of cultural, economic, political, and social change. Ninety per cent of the publications indexed in API are unique; they are not covered in more mainstream indexes. The print index is available starting with 1969. The electronic database starts in 1991.

Arts and Humanities Citation Index
This is a multidisciplinary index to more than 1,100 journals spanning twenty-five disciplines. It includes articles, reviews, letters, notes, corrections, and editorials. In addition to access by author, title, and institution, it is possible to search by cited authors and to find articles sharing one or more cited references. The print version goes back to 1975. The electronic database covered through the Web of Science starts in 1982.

Education Full Text
The electronic database was preceded by the Education Index, which starts indexing in 1929. Education Full Text indexes more than 400 English-language periodicals, yearbooks, and selected monographic series. It covers all levels of education. Feature articles are indexed as are important editorials and letters to the editor, interviews, reviews of educational films, software reviews, critiques of theses, charts and graphs without text, and book reviews. Abstracts since 1994 are included. Full-text articles have been added beginning with 1996. We found every mention of Foucault in the hard copy of Education Index also to be found in the Education Full Text electronic database. Therefore, this search engine covered the entire period of 1954–2002.

ERIC (Educational Resources Information Center)
ERIC contains citations and abstracts from the international journals and report literature in education and related fields. Subjects include all aspects of education, including child development, classroom techniques, computer education, counseling and testing, administration, higher education, library science, and vocational and adult education. Sources include more than 980 journals, educational reports, project descriptions, curriculum guides, and dissertations. The database has records from 1966 onwards.

Philosopher's Index
Philosopher's Index contains citations and abstracts from books and more than 350 journals of philosophy and related interdisciplinary fields published in the United States and other Western countries. Major philosophy journals in other languages, since 1967, are included. Subject coverage includes aesthetics, epistemology, ethics, logic, and metaphysics, and the philosophy of related disciplines such as education, history, law, religion, and science. The database began in 1940 and therefore made comparison across the entire period of 1954–2002 possible.

Proquest Research Library
ProQuest Research Library indexes more than 2,000 periodicals and provides the full text of nearly 1,000 of these. It has a mix of general interest and academic journals that cover the arts, business, education, health, humanities, psychology, sciences, and social sciences. Some articles contain images, including charts, photos, cartoons, and other illustrations. The database began in 1988 but includes references that were published before then.

Social Sciences Citation Index
This is a multidisciplinary index to more than 1,400 journals spanning fifty
social science disciplines. It lists articles, reviews, letters, notes, correction,
and editorials. It references work from 1956 onwards.

13. The three-volume 1997 publication, *The Essential Works of Michel
Foucault 1954–1984*, is composed out of the longer French compilation
entitled *Dits et Écrits* published by Éditions Gallimard, and edited by
Daniel Defert and François Ewald, who sought to collect all of Foucault's
published texts such as prefaces, introductions, presentations, interviews,
articles, lectures, interventions and so on, not included in his books from
between 1954 and 1988. The French work contains over 3,000 pages of
text, is organized chronologically, and constitutes the base literature from
which the three English-language volumes of the *Essential Works of
Foucault 1954–1984* were composed (Rabinow, 1997b, pp. vii–viii). The
editor of volume 1, Paul Rabinow, explains in the series preface how
commentators on Foucault often feel compelled to use what he is seen as
providing in order to conduct themselves ethically: "Diverse factors shape
the emergence, articulation, and circulation of a work and its effects.
Foucault gave us intellectual tools to understand these phenomena....We
use these very tools to understand his own work." Rabinow also explains
how Foucault was "put together" out of the French putting-together: "What
we have included in this and the following two volumes are the writings
that seemed to us central to the evolution of Foucault's thought. We have
organized them thematically. Selecting from this corpus was a formidable
responsibility and proved to be a challenge and a pleasure....In broad lines,
the organization of the series follows one proposed by Foucault himself
when he wrote: 'My objective has been to create a history of the different
modes by which, in our culture, human beings are made subjects. My work
has dealt with three modes of objectification which transform human
beings into subjects'" (Rabinow, 1997, p. viii). This is a significant
explanation relative to our discussion later on styles of commentary.
Where commentators such as Bernauer have parsed Foucault's research
chronologically along knowledge, power, and then subject lines, reuniting
him in a developmental sense of ethics whose final focus is "the subject,"
Rabinow and Faubion, editors of volumes 2 and 3, parse the entirety of the
"essential works" in regard to the moves they see Foucault making around
the subject all along—the different approaches to studying modes of
objectification of human beings.

14. This represents hits for sites that have the exact wording "Michel
Foucault." It does not refer to or combine sites that have only the words

"Michel" and only the words "Foucault." Therefore, we used a much more restricted search term by using the whole name, and we still came up with over 103,000 hits.

15. The office is composed of Daniel Defert, Arlette Farge, Machiel Karskens, and Pierre Lascoumes, under the presidency of Philippe Artieres. The scientific committee is composed of Maurice Blanchot, Pierre Boulez, Arlette Farge, Pierre Lascoumes, Michelle Perrot, Paul Veyne, François Ewald, and Daniel Defert.

16. IMEC is presently situated at 9, rue Bleue 75009 Paris, France [tel: (33) 1 53 34 23 23; fax: (33) 1 53 34 23 00]. Appointments are necessary due to limited space and no photocopying is allowed (see http://www.qut.edu.au/ edu/cpol/foucault/archives.html). Interested scholars can e-mail or surface mail requests for a study spot. Hours are restricted, e.g., sometimes it is open in the afternoons only, and toward the end of the semester space can be difficult to obtain due to the number of students using the archive.

17. We have made an effort in this Introduction to cite literature in the disciplinary searches that make significant use of Foucault's work rather than those that have just brief or passing references. This does not suggest that the "significant use" or "engagement" necessarily denotes a positive positioning of Foucault. Interested readers will find a range of positions between and among the papers, chapters, and books cited in the literature, virtual, and archival sources.

18. We do not suggest here that it is possible to express anything in English languages outside of a notion of binaries. Rather, it seems more a matter of which binaries one agrees with. In the case of Foucault's name, it seems that binaries have formed but that does not necessarily lock a researcher into anything that cannot be contested or rethought.

19. We are more than aware of the "theory of reading" we are drawing on in the argument here and want to disarticulate our notion of reception and conditions of receptivity of a text from active/passive or producer/receiver constructs. We are not speaking of reception as static and production as originary and full. Furthermore, we question the overreliance on a "framework of production" argument as a theoretical tool and the constant reference, even in our own scholarship, to the use of terms such as "conditions of possibility." Such phrases have become abstracted commonplaces, marking a turn to a "grammar of possibilities" in social

theoretical work that rarely questions the probability reasoning on which
such turns of phrase hang.

20.   The doctoral dissertation was published in 1961 as *Folie et déraison:
       Histoire de la folie à l'âge classique*. In 1964 an abridgement appeared as
       Histoire de la folie, and it was from this that Richard Howard's English
       translation was made, though additional material was included from the
       earlier version. In 1972, *Folie et déraison* was reissued, with minor
       alterations and new appendices, as *Histoire de la folie à l'âge classique,
       siuvi de Mon corps, ce papier, ce feu et La folie, l'absence d'oeuvre*. This
       work is usually referred to as *Histoire de la folie* (See further Still &
       Velody, 1992, pp. 3–5).

21.   The book's three sections consist of a first part in which is reproduced an
       essay published in 1990 by Colin Gordon in *History of the Human
       Sciences* that offered a critique of the mainly English complaints against
       Madness and Civilization, a second part in which scholars were invited to
       respond to Gordon's essay, and a third part in which Gordon responds to
       the responses and Mark Erickson provides a selective bibliography with
       critical notations.

22.   Colin Gordon does not explain the disparate francophone and anglophone
       readings of *Madness and Civilization* by reuniting them around the notion
       of the specific intellectual or a theory/practice binary as Castel does but
       rather begins around the problem of translation. Gordon (1992a) points out
       that well over half of the book has never been translated into English. Two
       hundred thirty-six pages are included in the English edition, with the parts
       omitted from the French version amounting to 299 pages, not including
       appendices. Out of the more than 1,000 footnotes, only 149 are retained in
       the English-language version, and a bibliography comprising over 200
       primary and secondary sources is omitted altogether: "The untranslated
       part of *Folie et déraison* is roughly equivalent in length to (for example)
       the complete text of *Discipline and Punish*" (Gordon, 1992a, p. 19). He
       quotes the French reception of the text in reviews from *Annales E. C. S.*
       published in 1962, indicating how Robert Mandrou and Fernand Braudel
       called it "a very great book" and "a magnificent book" respectively. He
       points out that no English-speaking historian of comparable standing
       within the academic mainstream has subscribed to anything like so cordial
       an assessment of the book. While Gordon goes on to argue that the
       negative assessments of the texts, by English historians in particular, are
       not reducible to simply a lack of familiarity with the fuller version, he also
       complains that the critics whose declared object has been to measure

Foucault's accomplishment as an historian against (unnamed) standards of serious scholarship have nonetheless dispensed with the preliminary task of reading the unabridged text of his book.

23.   For example, "We critical voices, the unwashed and unconverted, are, it seems poor 'defensive' creatures, unwilling to face up to our own 'insecurities'—feebly trying to practise 'normal science...while teetering over an abyss.' Called to account for our failings, we persist in egregious error 'in ways which reveal an unusually drastic economizing of intellectual and scholarly means.' Doubts are even expressed about whether (unspecified) particular individual participants in the debate have 'as a matter of fact, ever managed to find the necessary time to read [*Histoire de la folie*], let alone reread it.' And, in consequence our judgments about the work in question are it seems 'largely a matter of [in?]judicious guesswork'" (Scull, 1992, p. 162; parentheses and quotes in Scull).

24.   For very different discussions of Foucault divided in terms of research trajectory, see Deleuze (1986) and Danaher, Schirato & Webb (2000). For discussions of Foucault divided in terms of teaching, see Bernauer (1990), particularly the introduction. For discussions of Foucault divided in regard to traditional notions of activism, see Still & Velody (1992), Rabinow's (1997a) introduction to the *Essential Works: Vol. 1*, especially under the subheading "Arenas: Iran, Poland, USA," and last, see "Foucault in Tunisia" in *Postcolonialism: An Historical Introduction* (Young, 2001).

25.   Some biographers attribute academic shifts in his work to relationship and/or sexual events in Foucault's life, writing as though they were in the room watching and then in his office afterwards when the discursive shift occurred. Others try somewhat unsuccessfully to avoid one-to-one correlations between current biographical categories and past events by focusing on how his writing retains ambiguities that muddy simplistic correlations.

26.   In literary criticism, for Phillip Barker, consensus over Foucault's writing style has never been reached. Foucault cannot be called a structuralist, for example, because he overtly denied being one in the foreword to the English-language version of *The Order of Things* (1966/1970). He is put together by Barker around a different set of criteria, through a very self-conscious analysis of how "the question of my [Barker's] work can relate to Foucault without freezing other interpretations into a more typically Foucaultian formulation." For Barker, there is an unsettled hesitation that

comes "from acknowledging that to present *my* Foucault...risks congealing that name and eliminating all those other Foucaults already in existence, and yet to come" (Barker, 1998, p. 1). In responding to the question "How is it possible to avoid the trap of commentary while at the same time engaging in a form of critical interaction that is productive, interesting, and useful?" Barker puts Foucault together through juxtaposing certainty and dogmatism with the pleasures of uncertainty, journey, and anxiety: "If Foucault has achieved anything at all that is worthwhile, it is that his work is resistant to all dogmatisms, not only because it problematizes certainties wherever it encounters them, but also because it problematizes the conditions of its own existence....My hope is that...we will be able to leave the drab monotony of modernity behind us and explore Foucault's optimistic and colourful nominalist world, where one is able to delight in the pleasure of the journey and, in those fearful moments of sceptical doubt and anxiety, recall Foucault's thought that the object of intellectual activity is to 'think differently'" (Barker, 1998, p. xiii).

27. For an historical account of the emergence of identity politics in regard to the formation of the welfare state and social security systems, see Eghigian's (2000) *Making Security Social*. It historicizes the first social security system in the Federal Republic of Germany, which was subsequently copied in places such as the United States and Japan, and the specific focus is on the making of a generic disability category.

28. For a chronological bibliography of Foucault's work in French and English see the listing in Bernauer & Keenan's (1988) "The Works of Michel Foucault 1954–1984" in the edited volume by Bernauer & Rasmussen *The Final Foucault*, pp. 119–158. See also the three volumes of the *Essential Works* for available English-language translations of many, but not all, of his publications outside the histories.

29. Philosophy is not the only discipline to demonstrate the developmentalizing tendency. In Privitera (1995), for instance, Foucault is understood from sociological perspectives as someone whose work has been legitimately separated out by commentators into epistemological-structural, vitalistic, and then Heideggerian phases. As a supporter of Foucault's projects, Privitera states that his intent is "not to dispute the strong structuralist and later...genealogical features of Foucault's theory" because "[t]hey are too striking and too universally substantiated for the consensus over them to be questioned seriously" (Privitera, 1995, p. 28). Foucault is subsequently put back together through the work of Gaston Bachelard, showing "that some of Bachelard's intuitions play an important

role as the theoretical background or intellectual habit that shapes the Foucauldian *appropriation* of structuralist, genealogical, and even ethical motifs" (Privitera, 1995, p. 28). A further example of the "developmentalized approach" to Foucault's work exists also in historical sociology. For Mitchell Dean (1994), Foucault's work occupies a third position in a series of historiographies that have emerged in the West. For Dean, these are generally and diachronically evolutionary histories, then progressive histories, and now critical and effective histories, with Foucault's style being exemplary of the latter. Foucault's senses of historical style are also divided into three: archaeology (a term he first uses in *Madness and Civilization*), genealogy, and history of the present. It is the latter, history of the present, that Dean says has been taken by scholars as the solution to problems with the first two senses. The trilogies provide the narrative structure by unifying Foucault's work in the face of qualifying, as Dean overtly acknowledges, the impossibility of reading Foucault in neat boxes. The trilogies indicate through their form, and the argument validates it, that the earlier senses of history occupy positions on a linked developmental scale. A tripartite developmental progression places Foucault's work into the history of the discipline (sociology) and the history of himself (his senses of writing history over his career). Thus, his work is positioned as coherent and interlinked across his life by focusing on a chosen theme—that which is attributed to Foucault as his historical senses.

30. Bernauer gives many examples of how the grid is used to classify commentaries around Foucault. He uses the three axes and four elements to organize Foucault scholarship. First, Bernauer argues that the knowledge axis became the focal point of the Nietzschean treatments of Alan Sheridan (1980) and Gilles Deleuze (1986). The power axis commentaries draw on a different set of scholarship, such as Barry Smart's (1983) commentary, which posits Foucault's contribution to Marxism to consist of his analysis of power. For the subject axis, Bernauer argues that Jeffrey Minson's (1985) commentary focuses on the strengths of Foucault's analytics of the subject in the sense of "its excavation of liberalism and that system's production of the personal" (Bernauer, 1990, p. 22).

Bernauer also considers the second element of Foucault's ethics, its mode of subjection, to be the one domain to have "attracted the interests of other major commentators" besides those already listed. He gives examples of Mark Cousins and Athar Hassain (1985) who have written critically of Foucault's commitment to a genealogical understanding because its concern with the conditions for the emergence of branches of knowledge entails the neglect of a normative assessment of them. Bernauer argues that this criticism, however, leads Cousins and Hassain to a rare appreciation of Foucault's archaeological enterprise of analysis. For Hubert Dreyfus and Paul Rabinow, on the other hand, Foucault's turn to genealogy was a propitious development beyond his archaeological approach, enabling him to found a new project of "interpretive analytics" that they claim represents the "most important contemporary effort both to develop method for the study of human beings and to diagnose the current situation of our society" (Bernauer, 1990, p. 22).

Thirdly, Bernauer suggests that the third and fourth elements of Foucault's ethics, its ascetic project for thinking, is what attracts Karlis Racevskis (1983), Pamela Major-Poetzl (1983), Charles Lemert and Garth Gillan (1982), and John Rajchman (1985). And finally, in regard to the fourth element, aspiration, Bernauer argues that Rajchman describes Foucault as having as his ethical goal an endless "question of freedom," where there is an effort to replace an idealist philosophy of final emancipation with a nominalist philosophy of endless revolt. These examples that Bernauer extends justify our description of his commentary as one of the more self-conscious and elaborated, in regard to its dividing practices, that we have found.

31.   Education poses problems for definition as a field or distinct arena because, in a way, one could controversially claim fundamentality—all publications from all academic arenas and/or disciplinary sites seem to have implicit or explicit educational functions and circulate within educational institutions. We are discussing here, though, a much more delimited sense of education as a professional field that formalized in the late nineteenth century around the emergence of common schooling in particular. Literature referring to formal education with a focus on the (wide) politics of teaching/learning/knowledge in a variety of institutional settings is a notable "Western" delimitation. It follows, in a sense, the patterns of anglophone scholarship that have emerged and an understanding of education through smaller and larger associations such as the Australian Association for Research in Education (AARE), the American Educational Research Association (AERA), the British Educational Research Association (BERA), the Canadian Society for the Study of Education (CSSE), the European Educational Research Association (EERA), and the New Zealand Association for Research in Education (NZARE).

32.   Our reference to 1977 is not fixed and originary in terms of educational uses of Foucault. Rather, a noticeable move was made in that year and that is what we have recorded here.

33. Two exceptions to this are the journals *History of Education Review* (South Pacific, not United States version), chief editor Malcolm Vick and *Paedagogica Historica*, (continental Europe), chief editor Frank Simon.

34. We thank Tom Popkewitz for drawing out and elaborating this insight.

35. An example of this, outside of education, is the very deliberate and deliberative effort of Henri-Jacques Stiker's (1999) *A History of Disability*. Stiker argues that his book goes where Foucault's left off, namely offering suggestions, which he views as different from prescriptions. His Epilogue is a series of assertions as to what could be done differently and better in the present in light of his historical analysis of conceptions and treatment of disability constructs in the previous chapters.

36. For recent exceptions see Alfery (2002) and Erevelles (2002).

37. The term *dispotif* offers a cogent case in point and demonstrates the possibilities. It is translated by Hurley in *The History of Sexuality: Vol. 1* (1976/1978) as "deployment"; by Lemert and Gillan (1982) in *Michel Foucault: Social Theory and Transgression* as "affective mechanism"; by Colin Gordon in *Power/Knowledge* as "apparatus" (Foucault, 1980); by Barry Cooper (1982) in *Michel Foucault: An Introduction to the Study of His Thought* as a "device, disposition of devices etc"; and by McWhorter (1999) in *Bodies and Pleasure* as "a system of relations among heterogeneous elements such as discourses, institutions, laws, architecture, etc, that serves a strategic function." Each provides a different way in which to conceptualize *dispotif*, and in turn, each translation could speak back to, extend, and/or refigure francophone interpretations of the term.

38. There is a further complication to the simplification of originary language arguments. Of late, there is a sense in which Foucault's work has been introduced to French scholars in education where it has not been visible before because of stricter disciplinary boundaries in the French academy; educators read educators, philosophers read philosophers, and so forth. Because of his uptake in anglophone educational literature, Foucault has returned "home," his work taken up in English-language publications on education and then translated back into the French (see the 2001 special edition of *Recherché et Formation*).

39. Penelope Murray (1989) gives some insight into the historicity of interpretative processes in ancient Greek literary criticism relative to the

present. In the early eighteenth century, writers such as Homer and Pindar were rediscovered in Europe. Debates emerged over the worthiness and quality of ancient Greek and Roman writings relative to more recent ones. The ancient works identified as classical, brilliant, or exemplary were being explained in terms of their author's qualities. This was a remarkable reversal from ancient Greek forms of literary criticism where a product, written, sculpted, or built, could never be explained through reference to its maker. In the early eighteenth century, the difficulty of naming the source of creativity in relation to the author's qualities seemed to be compounded by the lack of biographical details available regarding some of the ancient writers. The eighteenth-century fascination with sources of creativity therefore dovetailed with both the lack of personal information available and the belief that such information was necessary to establishing causal connections between a state or quality of mind and a product—a causal connection between the product and a maker's mind that ancient Greeks never posed.

40. Perhaps because historical orientations sometimes compel an analysis to "name" a place specifically, there is a difference between the two sections of the volume in terms of place. The chapters in Section Two of the volume have a sense of place not marked so much by noting the nation/s from which documents are drawn, published, or the research conducted, although some do, but, offer a sense of anglophone educational research that circulates "across nations" as the place or site. In both cases we understand place as discursive before it is "geographical" and "national."

References

Alexander, J., & Mohanty, C. T. (Eds.). (1997). *Feminist genealogies, colonial legacies, democratic futures*. New York: Routledge.

Alfery, C. (2002, April). *The cartography of different spaces in aesthetics: The labyrinth and heterotopia*. Paper presented at the meeting of the American Educational Research Association, New Orleans.

Allan, J. (1996). Foucault and special educational needs: A "box of tools" for analysing children's experiences of mainstreaming. *Disability and Society, 11*(2), 219–233.

Allen, A. (2002). Power, subjectivity, and agency: Between Arendt and Foucault. *International Journal of Philosophical Studies, 10*(2), 131–149.

Angelides, S. (2001). *A history of bisexuality*. Chicago: University of Chicago Press.

Appiah, A. (1992). *In my father's house: Africa in the philosophy of culture*. New York: Oxford University Press.

Atkinson, D. (1998). The production of the pupil as a subject within the art curriculum. *Journal of Curriculum Studies, 30*, 27–42.

Baker, B. (2001). *In perpetual motion: Theories of power, educational history, and the child*. New York: Peter Lang.

Ball, S. (1990). *Foucault and education: Disciplines and knowledge*. London: Routledge.

Barker, P. (1998). *Michel Foucault: An introduction*. Edinburgh: Edinburgh University Press.

Barry, A., Osborne, T., & Rose, N. (1996). *Foucault and political reason: Liberalism, neo-liberalism and rationalities of government*. Chicago: University of Chicago Press.

Bell, V. (1993). *Interrogating incest: Feminism, Foucault, and the law*. New York: Routledge.

Bell, V. (1999). *Feminist imagination*. London: Sage.

Bernauer, J. W., & Keenan, T. (1988). The works of Michel Foucault, 1954–1984. In J. W. Bernauer & D. Rasmussen (Eds.), *The final Foucault*. Cambridge, MA: MIT Press.

Bernauer, J. W. (1990). *Michel Foucault's force of flight: Toward an ethics for thought*. Atlantic Highlands, NJ: Humanities International.

Bertrand, Y., & Houssaye, J. (1999). Reference one. Did Derrida kill Foucault? [Special issue]. *International Journal of Applied Semiotics, 1*, 13–18.

Besley, A. C. T. (2002). Foucault and the turn to narrative therapy. *British Journal of Guidance & Counseling, 30*(2), 125–144.

Bhabha, H. K. (1994). *The location of culture*. New York: Routledge.

Biesta, G. J. J. (1998). Pedagogy without humanism: Foucault and the subject of education. *Interchange, 29*(1), 1–16.

Biggs, S., & Powell, J. L. (2001). A Foucauldian analysis of old age and the power of social welfare. *Journal of Aging & Social Policy, 12*(2), 93–112.

Blades, D. W. (1997). *Procedures of power and curriculum change: Foucault and the quest for possibilities in science education.* New York: Peter Lang.

Bridges, D. (1998, August). Educational research: Pursuit of truth or flight into fancy? Paper presented at the meeting of the *British Educational Research Association,* Belfast, Ireland.

Brigg, M. (2001). Empowering NGOs: The microcredit movement through Foucault's notion of dispotif. *Alternatives: Global, Local, Political, 26*(3), 233–259.

Brigg, M. (2002). Post-development, Foucault, and the colonization metaphor. *Third World Quarterly, 23*(3), 421–437.

Broadhead, L. A., & Howard, S. (1998). "The art of punishing": The research assessment exercise and the ritualisation of power in higher education. *Education Policy Analysis Archives, 6*(8).

Brookfield, S. (2001). Unmasking power: Foucault and adult learning. *Canadian Journal for the Study of Adult Education, 15*(1), 1–23.

Burke, P. (Ed.). (1992). *Critical essays on Michel Foucault.* Brookfield, VT: Ashgate.

Burman, E. (1994). *Deconstructing developmental psychology.* London: Routledge.

Butin, D. W. (2001). If this is resistance, I would hate to see domination: Retrieving Foucault's notion of resistance within educational research. *Educational Studies, 32*(2), 157–176.

Butler, J. (1999). *Gender trouble.* New York: Routledge.

Cannella, G. S. (1997). *Deconstructing early childhood education: Social justice and revolution.* New York: Peter Lang.

Caputo, J., & Yount, M. (1993). *Foucault and the Critique of Institutions.* University Park: Pennsylvania State University Press.

Carrette, J. R. (Ed.). (1999). *Religion and culture by Michel Foucault.* New York: Routledge.

Carrette, J. R. (Ed.). (2000). *Foucault and religion: Spiritual corporality and political spirituality.* New York: Routledge.

Castel, R. (1992). The two readings of *Histoire de la folie* in France. In A. Still & I. Velody (Eds.), *Rewriting the history of madness: Studies in Foucault's Histoire de la folie* (pp. 65–68). New York: Routledge.

Cavanagh, S. (2002, July). The call to matrimony in the shadow of the female homosexual: The changing manifestation of female teacher sexuality in mid-twentieth century Ontario, Canada. Paper presented at the meeting of the *International Standing Conference for the History of Education* XXIV, Paris.

Chambon, A. S., Irving, A., & Epstein, L. (1999). *Reading Foucault for social work.* New York: Columbia University Press.

Chartier, R. (1988). *Cultural history: Between practices and representations.* Ithaca, NY: Cornell University Press.

Cladis, M. S. (Ed.). (1999). *Durkheim and Foucault: Perspectives on education and punishment.* Oxford: Durkheim Press.

Clifford, M. (2001). *Political genealogy after Foucault: Savage identities.* New York: Routledge.

Cocks, E., Fox, C., Brogan, M., & Lee, M. (Eds.). (1996). *Under Blue Skies: The social construction of intellectual disability in Western Australia.* Perth: Edith Cowan University Centre for Disability Research and Development.

Comber, B. (1998, November–December). Literacy, contingency and room to move: Researching "normativity" and "spaces of freedom" in classrooms. Paper presented at the meeting of the *Australian Association for Research in Education*, Adelaide, Australia.

Cooper, B. (1982). *Michel Foucault: An introduction to the study of his thought.* New York: Edwin Mellen.

Cousins, M., & Hussain, A. (1985). *Michel Foucault.* New York: St. Martin's.

Crary, J. (1999). *Suspensions of perception: Attention, spectacle, and modern culture.* Cambridge, MA: MIT Press.

Curtis, J., & Harrison, L. (2001). Beneath the surface: Collaboration in alcohol and other drug treatment: An analysis using Foucault's three modes of objectification. *Journal of Advanced Nursing, 34*(6), 737–744.

Danaher, G., Schirato, T., & Webb, J. (2000). *Understanding Foucault.* St Leonards, New South Wales: Allen & Unwin.

Danforth, S. (2000). Dynamics of discourse: A case study illuminating power relations in mental retardation. *Mental Retardation, 38*(4), 354–362.

Danziger, K. (1990). *Constructing the subject: Historical origins of psychological research.* New York: Cambridge University Press.

Davies, B. (1995). *Poststructural theory and classroom practice.* Geelong, Australia: Deakin University Press.

Davis, L. J. (1995). *Enforcing normalcy: Disability, deafness, and the body.* New York: Verso.

Davis, L. J. (2002). *Bending over backwards: Disability, dismodernism, and other difficult positions.* New York: New York University Press.

Deacon, R. (2002). An analysis of power relations: Foucault on the history of discipline. *History of the Human Sciences, 15*(1), 89–117.

Dean, M. (1994). *Critical and effective histories: Foucault's methods and historical sociology.* New York: Routledge.

Dear, P. R. (1995). *Discipline & experience: The mathematical way in the scientific revolution.* Chicago: University of Chicago Press.

Deleuze, G. (1986). *Foucault.* Paris: Minuit.

Dougherty, S. (2001). Foucault in the house of Usher: Some historical permutations in Poe's gothic. *Papers on Language & Literature, 37*(1), 3–24.

Dow, B. J. (2001). Ellen, television, and the politics of gay and lesbian visibility. *Critical Studies in Media Communication, 18*(2), 123–140.

Drummond, J. (2000). Foucault for students of education. *Journal of Philosophy of Education, 34*(4), 709–719.

Dumm, T. L. (1996). *Michel Foucault and the politics of freedom.* Thousand Oaks, CA: Sage.

Duncan, J. (1999). New Zealand kindergarten teachers and sexual abuse protection policies. *Teaching and Teacher Education, 15*(3), 243–252.

Eghigian, G. (2000). *Making security social: Disability, insurance, and the birth of the social entitlement state in Germany.* Ann Arbor: University of Michigan Press.

Elden, S. (2002). The war of races and the constitution of the state: Foucault's "Il faut défendre la société" and the politics of calculation. *Boundary 2, 29*(1), 125–152.

Elliott, A. (2001). Technologies of the self: Foucault, new technologies, new selves. In *Concepts of the self.* Malden, MA: Polity.

Erevelles, N. (2001). In search of the disabled subject. In J. C. Wilson & C. Lewiecki-Wilson (Eds.), *Embodied rhetorics: Disability in language and culture* (pp. 92–111). Carbondale: Southern Illinois University Press.

Erevelles, N. (2002). Voices of silence: Foucault, disability, and the question of self-determination. *Studies in Philosophy & Education, 21*(1), 17–36.

Eribon, D. (1991). *Michel Foucault.* Cambridge: Harvard University Press.

Falzon, C. (1998). *Foucault and social dialogue: Beyond fragmentation.* New York: Routledge.

Faust, M. A. (1998). Foucault on care of the self: Connecting writing with life-long learning. *International Journal of Leadership in Education, 1*(2), 181–193.

Fendler, L. (1998). What is it impossible to think? A genealogy of the educated subject. In T. S. Popkewitz & M. Brennan (Eds.), *Foucault's challenge, discourse, knowledge and power in education* (pp. 39–63). New York: Teachers College Press.

Fife, W. (2001). Creating the moral body: Missionaries and the technology of power in early Papua New Guinea. *Ethnology, 40*(3), 251–269.

Flecha, R. (1999). Modern and postmodern racism in Europe dialogic approach and anti-racist pedagogies. *Harvard Educational Review, 69*(2), 150–171.

Foti, V. M. (1996). Representation represented: Foucault, Velazquez, Descartes. *Postmodern Culture, 71*(1), 1–23.

Foucault, M. (1965). *Madness and civilization: A history of insanity in the age of reason* (R. Howard, Trans.). New York: Pantheon. (Original work published 1961)

Foucault, M. (1970). *The order of things: An archaeology of the human sciences* (Unidentified collective, Trans.). New York: Vintage. (Original work published 1966)

Foucault, M. (1972). *The archaeology of knowledge & The discourse on language* (A. M. Sheridan Smith, Trans.). New York: Pantheon. (Original works published 1969 and 1971)

Foucault, M. (1975). *The birth of the clinic: An archaeology of medical perception* (A. M. Sheridan Smith, Trans.). New York: Vintage. (Original work published 1963)

Foucault, M. (1977). Nietzsche, genealogy, history (D. F. Bouchard & S. Simon, Trans.). In D. F. Bouchard (Ed.), *Language, counter-memory, practice: Selected essays and interviews* (pp. 139–164). Ithaca, NY: Cornell University Press. (Original work published 1971)

Foucault, M. (1978). *The history of sexuality I: An introduction* (R. Hurley, Trans.). New York: Pantheon. (Original work published 1976)

Foucault, M. (1980). *Power/knowledge: Selected interviews and other writings, 1972–1977* (C. Gordon, Ed. and Trans.). New York: Pantheon.

Foucault, M. (Ed.). (1982). *I, Pierre Rivière, having slaughtered my mother, my sister, and my brother: a case of parricide in the nineteenth century* (F. Jellinik, Trans.). Lincoln: University of Nebraska Press. (Original work published 1973)

Foucault, M. (1983). *This is not a pipe* (J. Harkness, Ed. and Trans.). Berkeley: University of California Press. (Original work published 1968)

Foucault, M. (1985). *The use of pleasure: The history of sexuality: Vol. 2.* (R. Hurley, Trans.). New York: Pantheon Books. (Original work published 1984)

Foucault, M. (1986). *The care of the self: The history of sexuality: Vol. 3.* (R. Hurley, Trans.). New York: Pantheon Books. (Original work published 1984)

Foucault, M. (1989). *Foucault live: (Interviews, 1966–84)* (S. Lotringer, Ed; J. Johnston, Trans.). New York: Semiotext(e).

Foucault, M. (1991). *Remarks on Marx: Conversations with Duccio Trombadori* (J. Goldstein & J. Cascaito, Trans.). New York: Semiotext(e). (Original work published 1978)

Foucault, M. (1995). *Discipline and punish: The birth of the prison* (A. Sheridan, Trans.). New York: Vintage Books. (Original work published 1975)

Foucault, M. (1997). *The essential works of Foucault 1954–1984: Vol. 1. Ethics: Subjectivity and truth* (P. Rabinow, Series Ed. and Ed.) New York: New Press. (Original work published 1994)

Foucault, M. (1998). Nietzsche, Freud, Marx. In *The essential works of Michel Foucault, 1954–1984: Vol. 2. Aesthetics, method, and epistemology*

(P. Rabinow, Series Ed., J. D. Faubion, Ed.; R. Hurley and others Trans.). (pp. 269–278). New York: New Press. (Original work published 1967)

Foucault, M. (1998a). *The essential works of Michel Foucault, 1954–1984: Vol. 2. Aesthetics, method, and epistemology* (P. Rabinow, Series Ed., J. D. Faubion, Ed.; R. Hurley and others Trans.). New York: New Press. (Original work published 1994)

Foucault, M. (1998b). *The essential works of Michel Foucault, 1954–1984: Vol. 3. Power* (P. Rabinow, Series Ed., J. D. Faubion, Ed.; R. Hurley and others Trans.). New York: New Press. (Original work published 1994)

Francis, K. (2001). Service to the poor: The foundations of community nursing in England, Ireland, and New South Wales. *International Journal of Nursing Practice, 7*(3), 169–176.

Franklin, B. (1994). *From "backwardness" to "at-risk": Childhood learning difficulties and the contradictions of school reform*. Albany: State University of New York.

Gade, A. M. (2002). Taste, talent, and the problem of internalization: A qur'anic study in religious musicality from Southeast Asia. *History of Religions, 41*(4), 328–368.

Gehrke, P. J. (2001). Deviant subjects in Foucault and *A Clockwork Orange*: Congruent critiques of criminological constructions of subjectivity. *Critical Studies in Media Communication 18*, 270–284.

Gilbert-Rolfe, J. (1999). Nietzschean critique and the Hegelian commodity, or the French have landed. *Critical Inquiry, 26*(Autumn), 70–84.

Glaude, E. S. (2000). *Exodus! Religion, race, and nation in early nineteenth-century black America*. Chicago: University of Chicago Press.

Goldhill, S. (1995). *Foucault's virginity: Ancient erotic fiction and the history of sexuality*. Cambridge: Cambridge University Press.

Goldstein, J. (1992). 'The lively sensibility of the Frenchman': Some reflections on the place of France in Foucault's *Histoire de la folie*. In A. Still & I. Velody (Eds.). *Rewriting the History of Madness: Studies in Foucault's* Histoire de la folie. New York: Routledge.

Gordon, C. (1992a). *Histoire de la folie:* An unknown book by Michel Foucault. In A. Still & I. Velody (Eds.), *Rewriting the History of Madness: Studies in Foucault's* Histoire de la folie. New York: Routledge.

Gordon, C. (1992b). Rewriting history of misreading. In A. Still & I. Velody (Eds.), *Rewriting the History of Madness: Studies in Foucault's* Histoire de la folie (pp. 167–184). New York: Routledge.

Gore, J. (1994). Enticing challenges: An introduction to Foucault and educational discourses. In R. A. Martusewicz & W. M. Reynolds (Eds.), *Inside/out: Contemporary critical perspectives in education* (pp. 109–120). New York: St. Martin's Press.

Gore, J. (1998). Disciplining bodies: On the continuity of power relations in pedagogy. In T. S. Popkewitz & M. Brennan (Eds.), *Foucault's challenge:*

Discourse, knowledge, and power in education (pp. 231–254). New York: Teachers College Press.

Gracia, J. J. E. (2001). Are categories invented or discovered? A response to Foucault. *Review of Metaphysics, 55*(1), 3–20.

Gray-Rosendale, L. (1999). Investigating our discursive history: "JBW" and the construction of the "basic writer's" identity. *Journal of Basic Writing, 18*(2), 108–135.

Hacking, I. (1990). *The taming of chance.* Cambridge, MA: Cambridge University Press.

Hacking, I. (1999). *The social construction of what?* Cambridge, MA: Harvard University Press.

Hacking, I. (2002). *Historical ontology.* Cambridge, MA: Harvard University Press.

Hall, S., & du Gay, P. (1996). *Questions of cultural identity.* London: Sage.

Halperin, D. M. (1995). *Saint=Foucault: Towards a gay hagiography.* New York: Oxford University Press.

Hamilton, P. (1996). *Historicism.* New York: Routledge.

Hekman, S. J. (1996). *Feminist interpretations of Michel Foucault.* University Park: Pennsylvania State University Press.

Hennon, L. (1999, April). *From "school house" to "school-as-community": Governmentality and the space of the school.* Paper presented at the Annual Meeting of the American Educational Research Association, Montreal, Quebec, Canada.

Heyning, K. (2000). The early childhood teacher as professional: An archaeology of university reform. In J. Jipson & R. Johnson (Eds.), *Resistance and representation: Rethinking childhood education* (pp. 77–105). New York: Peter Lang.

Heyning, K. (2001). Teacher education reform in the shadow of state-university links: The cultural politics of texts. In T. S. Popkewitz, B. M. Franklin & M. Pereyra (Eds.), *Cultural history and education: Critical essays on knowledge and schooling* (pp. 289–312). New York: Routledge.

Hoem, S. I. (2000). "Shifting spirits": Ancestral constructs in the postmodern writing of John Edgar Wideman. *African American Review, 34*(2), 249–262.

Holligan, C. (1999). Discipline and normalisation in the nursery: The Foucauldian gaze. *Scottish Educational Review, 31*(2), 137–148.

Holtorf, C., & Karlsson, H. (2000). *Philosophy and archaeological practice: Perspectives for the 21st century.* Göteborg, Sweden: Bricoleur.

Howarth, D. (2002). An archaeology of political discourse? Evaluating Michel Foucault's explanation and critique of ideology. *Political Studies, 50*(1), 117–136.

Hoy, D. C. (Ed.). (1996). *Foucault: A critical reader.* Cambridge, MA: Blackwell. (Original work published 1986)

Hunt, A., & Wickham, G. (1994). *Foucault and law: Toward a sociology of law as governance*. London: Pluto.

Hunter, I. (1994). *Rethinking the school: Subjectivity, bureaucracy, criticism*. New York: St. Martin's.

Hyatt, V. L., Nettleford, R. M., & Smithsonian Institution. (1995). *Race, discourse, and the origin of the Americas: A new world view*. Washington: Smithsonian Institution Press.

Jones, C., & Porter, R. (1994). *Reassessing Foucault: Power, medicine, and the body*. New York: Routledge.

Jones, D., & Ball, S. (1995). Michel Foucault and the discourse of education. In P. McLaren & J. Giarelli (Eds.), *Critical theory and educational research* (pp. 39–52). Albany: State University of New York Press.

Joyce, P. (2001). Governmentality and risk: Setting priorities in the new NHS. *Sociology of Health & Illness, 23*(5), 594–614.

Karagiannis, A. (2000). Soft disability in schools: Assisting or confining at risk children and youth? *Journal of Educational Thought, 34*(2), 113–134.

Kearnes, M. B. (2000). Seeing is believing is knowing: Towards a critique of pure vision. *Australian Geographical Studies, 38*(3), 332–340.

Keenan, E. K. (2001). Using Foucault's "disciplinary power" and "resistance" in cross-cultural psychotherapy. *Clinical Social Work Journal, 29*(3), 211–227.

Kendall, G., & Wickham, G. (1999). *Using Foucault's methods*. London: Sage.

Kerr, L. K. (2001, March). Foucault and the care of the self: Educating for moral action and mental illness. Paper presented at the meeting of the *Philosophy of Education*, Chicago, IL.

Kincaid, J. R. (1992). *Child-loving: The erotic child and Victorian culture*. New York: Routledge.

Kirby, V. (2001). Writing and skin. *Hecate, 27*(2), 174–186.

Kirk, D. (1998). *Schooling bodies: School practice and public discourse, 1880–1950*. London: Leicester University Press.

Kivinen, I., & Rinne, R. (1998). State, governmentality, and education: The Nordic experience. *British Journal of Sociology of Education, 19*(1), 39–52.

Knafla, L. A. (2002). *Crime, gender, and sexuality in criminal prosecutions*. Westport, CT: Greenwood.

Kruks, S. (2001). *Retrieving experience: Subjectivity and recognition in feminist politics*. Ithaca, NY: Cornell University Press.

Langsdorf, L., Watson, S. H., & Smith, K. A. (1998). *Reinterpreting the political: Continental philosophy and political theory*. Albany: State University of New York Press.

Larmour, D. H. J., Miller, P. A., & Platter, C. (1998). *Rethinking sexuality: Foucault and classical antiquity*. Princeton, NJ: Princeton University Press.

Lather, P. (1996). Postcolonial feminism in an international frame: From mapping the researched to interrogating mapping. In R. Paulston (Ed.), *Social cartography: Mapping ways of seeing education and social change* (pp. 357–373). New York: Garland.

Lechner, D. (2001). The dangerous right to human education. *Studies in Philosophy and Education, 20*(3), 279–281.

Lemert, C. C., & Gillan, G. (1982). *Michel Foucault: Social theory and transgression.* New York: Columbia University Press.

Lesko, N. (2001). *Act your age: A cultural construction of adolescence.* New York: Routledge.

Longmore, P. K., & Umansky, L. (2001). *The new disability history: American perspectives.* New York: New York University Press.

Macey, D. (1993). *The lives of Michel Foucault: A biography.* New York: Pantheon.

Major-Poetzl, P. (1983). *Michel Foucault's archaeology of Western culture: Toward a new science of history.* Chapel Hill: University of North Carolina Press.

Marshall, J. D. (1996). *Michel Foucault: Personal autonomy and education*: Vol. 7. Dordrecht and Boston: Kluwer Academic.

Marshall, J. D. (2001). A critical theory of the self: Wittgenstein, Nietzsche, Foucault. *Studies in Philosophy & Education, 20*(1), 75–91.

Maxcy, S. J. (1977). A structural view of American educational history. *Paedagogica Historica: International Journal of the History of Education, XVII*, 333–346.

May, T. (1993). *Between genealogy and epistemology: Psychology, politics, and knowledge in the thought of Michel Foucault.* University Park: Pennsylvania State University Press.

Mayo, C. (2000). The uses of Foucault. *Educational Theory, 50*(1), 103–126.

McLeod, J. (2001). Foucault forever. *Discourse: Studies in the Cultural Politics of Education, 22*(1), 95–104.

McNay, L. (1993). *Foucault and feminism: Power, gender, and the self.* Boston: Northeastern University Press.

McWhorter, L. (1999). *Bodies and pleasures: Foucault and the politics of sexual normalization.* Bloomington: Indiana University Press.

McWilliam, E. (1999). *Pedagogical pleasures.* New York: Peter Lang.

Megill, A. (1992). Foucault, ambiguity, and the rhetoric of historiography. In A. Still & I. Velody (Eds.), *Rewriting the history of madness* (pp. 86–104). New York: Routledge.

Melville, P. (2002). Kant's dinner party: Anthropology from a Foucauldian point of view. *Mosaic: A Journal for the Interdisciplinary Study of Literature, 35*(2), 93–107.

Merquoir, J. G. (1986). *Foucault.* London: Fontana/Collins.

Midelfort, H. C. E. (1980). Madness and civilization in early modern Europe: A reappraisal of Michel Foucault. In B. C. Malament (Ed.), *After the Reformation: Essays in honor of J. H. Hexter* (pp. 247–65). Philadelphia: University of Pennsylvania Press.

Middleton, S. (1998). *Disciplining sexuality: Foucault, life histories, and education.* New York: Teachers College Press.

Middleton, S. (2001, April). *Researching pleasures: Care of the scholarly self.* Paper presented at the meeting of the American Educational Research Association, Seattle, WA.

Miguel-Alfonso, R., & Caporale-Bizzini, S. (Eds.). (1994). *Reconstructing Foucault: Essays in the wake of the 80s.* Atlanta, GA: Rodopi.

Miller, J. (1993). *The passion of Michel Foucault.* New York: Simon and Schuster.

Minson, J. (1985). *Genealogies of morals: Nietzsche, Foucault, Donzelot, and the eccentricity of ethics.* New York: St. Martin's.

Moi, T. (1985). Power, sex, and subjectivity: Feminist reflections on Foucault. *Paragraph, 5,* 95–102.

Molinaro, N. L., & Tusquets, E. (1991). *Foucault, feminism, and power: Reading Esther Tusquets.* Lewisburg, PA: Bucknell University Press.

Moore, S. D. (1994). *Poststructural-ism and the New Testament: Derrida and Foucault at the foot of the Cross.* Minneapolis, MN: Fortress.

Moss, J. (1998). *The later Foucault: Politics and philosophy.* London: Sage.

Mottier, V. (2001). Foucault revisited: Recent assessments of the legacy. *Acta Sociologica, 44*(4), 329–336.

Mourad, R. (2001). Education after Foucault: The question of civility. *Journal of Urban Design, 6*(3), 297–316.

Munslow, A. (1997). *Deconstructing history.* New York: Routledge.

Murray, P. (Ed.). (1989). *Genius: The history of an idea.* Oxford: Basil Blackwell.

Nagy-Zekmi, S. (2002). Tradition and transgression in the novels of Assia Djebar and Aycha Lemsine. *Research in African Literatures, 33*(3), 1–13.

Neubauer, J. (1999). *Cultural history after Foucault.* New York: Aldine de Gruyter.

O'Farrell, C. (1997). Introduction. In C. O'Farrell (Ed.), *Foucault: The legacy.* Brisbane, Australia: QUT.

Olssen, M. (1999). *Michel Foucault: Materialism and education.* Westport, CT: Bergin & Garvey.

Opfer, V. D. (2001). Charter schools and the panoptic effect of accountability. *Education and Urban Society, 33*(2), 201–215.

Owen D. (1994). *Maturity and modernity: Nietzsche, Weber, Foucault and the ambivalence of reason.* New York: Routledge.

Palmer, C. (2001). Taming the wild profusion of existing things? A study of Foucault, power, and human/animal. *Environmental Ethics, 23*(4), 339–358.

Papastephanou, M. (2001). Reformulating reason for philosophy of education. *Educational Theory, 51*(3), 293–313.

Payne, M. (1997). *Reading knowledge: An introduction to Barthes, Foucault, and Althusser*. Malden, MA: Blackwell.

Peters, M. (2000). Writing the self: Wittgenstein, confession and pedagogy. *Journal of Philosophy of Education, 34*(2), 353–368.

Peterson, A. & R. Bunton, (Eds.). (1997). *Foucault, health & medicine*. New York: Routledge.

Pignatelli, F. (2002). Mapping the terrain of a Foucauldian ethics: A response to the surveillance of schooling. *Studies in Philosophy & Education, 21*(2), 157–180.

Pillow, W. S. (2000). Deciphering attempts to decipher postmodern educational research. *Educational Researcher, 29*(5), 21–24.

Ploger, J. (2001). Public participation and the art of governance. *Environment & Planning B: Planning & Design, 28*(2), 219–241.

Popkewitz, T. S. (1998). The sociology of knowledge and the sociology of education: Michel Foucault and critical traditions. In C. A. Torres (Ed.), *Sociology of education: Emerging perspectives* (pp. 47–89). Albany: SUNY Series on Urban Public Policy.

Popkewitz, T. S., & Brennan, M. (1998a). *Foucault's challenge: Discourse, knowledge and power in education*. New York: Teachers College Press.

Popkewitz, T. S., & Brennan, M. (1998b). Introduction. In T. S. Popkewitz & M. Brennan (Eds.), *Foucault's challenge: Discourse, knowledge, and power in education* (pp. xiii–xvi). New York: Teachers College Press.

Popkewitz, T. S., Franklin, B. & Pereyra, M. (Eds.). (2001). *Cultural history and education: Critical essays on knowledge and schooling*. New York: RoutledgeFalmer.

Prado, C. G. (1992). *Descartes and Foucault: A contrastive introduction to philosophy*. Ottawa, Canada: University of Ottawa Press.

Privitera, W. (1995). *Problems of style: Michel Foucault's epistemology*. Albany: State University of New York Press.

Qi, J. (1998, April). The reasoning of teaching and schooling in Japan: Using Foucault to explicate discourse. Paper presented at the annual meeting of the *American Educational Research Association*, San Diego, CA.

Rabinow, P. (1997a). Introduction. In P. Rabinow, (Ed.), *Essential works of Michel Foucault: Vol. 1: Ethics: Subjectivity and truth* (pp. xi–xii). London: Allen Lane.

Rabinow, P. (1997b). Series Preface. In P. Rabinow, (Ed.), *Essential works of Michel Foucault: Vol. 1: Ethics: Subjectivity and truth* (pp. vii–viii). London: Allen Lane.

Rabinow, P. (2002). Midst anthropologist's problems. *Cultural Anthropology, 17*(2), 135–149.

Racevskis, K. (1983). *Michel Foucault and the subversion of intellect*. Ithaca, NY: Cornell University Press.

Racevskis, K. (1999). *Critical essays on Michel Foucault*. New York: G. K. Hall.

Raco, M., & Imrie, R. (2000). Governmentality and rights and responsibilities in urban policy. *Environment & Planning A, 32*(12), 2187–2204.

Rajchman, J. (1985). *Michel Foucault: The freedom of philosophy*. New York: Columbia University Press.

Ramazanoglu, C. (1993). *Up against Foucault: Explorations of some tensions between Foucault and feminism*. New York: Routledge.

Ray, D. I., & Labranche, S. (2001). Foucault's chiefs: Legitimacy and cultural discourse in chief-state relations in Ghana. *Review of International Affairs, 1*(2), 62–82.

Ray, S. A. (1987). *The modern soul: Michel Foucault and the theological discourse of Gordon Kaufman and David Tracy*. Philadelphia: Fortress.

Richardson, J. (1999). *Common, delinquent and special: The institutional shape of special education*. New York: Falmer.

Riley, R., & Manias, E. (2002). Foucault could have been an operating room nurse. *Journal of Advanced Nursing, 39*(4), 316–324.

Rose, N. (1989). *Governing the soul: The shaping of the private self*. New York: Routledge.

Rose, N. (1999). *Powers of freedom: Reframing political thought*. Cambridge, MA: Cambridge University Press.

Rothman, D. J. (2002). *The discovery of the asylum: Social order and disorder in the new republic* (Rev. 2nd ed.). Boston: Little Brown. (Original work published 1971)

Russell, S. (2001). Witchcraft, genealogy, Foucault. *British Journal of Sociology, 52*(1), 121–137.

Ryan, J. (1998). Critical leadership for education in a postmodern world: Emancipation, resistance and communal action. *International Journal of Leadership in Education, 1*(3), 257–278.

Sackney, L., Walker, K., & Mitchell, C. (1999). Postmodern conceptions of power for educational leadership. *Journal of Educational Administration and Foundations, 14*(1), 33–57.

Said, E. W. (1994). *Culture and imperialism*. New York: Vintage.

Said, E. W., & Viswanathan, G. (2001). *Power, politics, and culture: Interviews with Edward W. Said*. New York: Pantheon.

Sawicki, J. (1991). *Disciplining Foucault: Feminism, power, and the body*. New York: Routledge.

Schrag, F. (1999). Why Foucault now? *Journal of Curriculum Studies, 31*(4), 375–383.

Schuld, J. J. (2000). Augustine, Foucault, and the politics of imperfection. *Journal of Religion, 80*(1), 1–22.

Scott, C. E. (1990). *The question of ethics: Nietzsche, Foucault, Heidegger.* Bloomington: Indiana University Press.

Scull, A. (1992). A failure to communicate? On the reception of Foucault's *Histoire de la folie* by Anglo-American historians. In A. Still & I. Velody (Eds.), *Rewriting the history of madness: Studies in* Foucault's Histoire de la folie (pp.150–163). New York: Routledge.

Seals, G. (1998). Objectively yours, Michel Foucault. *Educational Theory, 48*(1), 59–66.

Sedgwick, P. (1982). *Psycho politics: Laing, Foucault, Goffman, Szasz, and the future of mass psychiatry.* New York: Harper & Row.

Sheridan, A. (1980). *Michel Foucault: The will to truth.* New York: Tavistock.

Skrtic, T. M. (1995). *Disability and democracy: Reconstructing (special) education for postmodernity.* New York: Teachers College Press.

Smart, B. (1983). *Foucault, Marxism, and critique.* Boston: Routledge.

Smart, B. (Ed.). (1994). *Michel Foucault: Critical assessments.* New York: Routledge.

Smart, C. (1989). *Feminism and the power of law.* New York: Routledge.

Smith, C. (2000). The sovereign state v Foucault: Law and disciplinary power. *Sociological Review, 48*(2), 283–306.

Smith, D. G. (1999). *Pedagon: Interdisciplinary essays in the human sciences, pedagogy, and culture.* New York: Peter Lang.

Spencer, B. L. (2001, April). The seduction of the subject/citizen: Governmentality and school governance policy. Paper presented at the meeting of the *American Educational Research Association*, Seattle, WA.

Spivak, G. C. (1999). *A critique of postcolonial reason: Toward a history of the vanishing present.* Cambridge, MA: Harvard University Press.

Stiker, H. J. (1999). *A history of disability.* Ann Arbor: University of Michigan Press.

Still, A., & Velody, I. (Eds.). (1992). *Rewriting the history of madness: Studies in Foucault's* Histoire de la folie. New York: Routledge.

Stoler, A. L. (1995). *Race and the education of desire: Foucault's* History of Sexuality *and the colonial order of things.* Durham, NC: Duke University Press.

Stone, L. (1982, December 16). Review of *Madness and civilization.* In *New York Review of Books* (pp. 28–36).

Stone, L. (1983, March 31). Letter. In *New York Review of Books* (pp. 42–44).

Stone, L. (2002, April). Notes on Foucault's philosophy of history. Paper presented at the meeting of the *American Educational Research Association*, New Orleans, LA.

St.Pierre, E. A. (2000). The call for intelligibility in postmodern educational research. *Educational Researcher, 29*(5), 25–28.

Szakolczai, Á. (1994). Thinking beyond the East-West divide: Patocka, Foucault, Hamvas, Elias, and the care of the self. *Social Research, 61*(2), 297–324.

Szakolczai, Á. (1998). *Max Weber and Michel Foucault: Parallel life-works.* New York: Routledge.

Tamboukou, M. (1999). Writing genealogies: An exploration of Foucault's strategies for doing research. *Discourse: Studies in the cultural politics of education, 20*(2), 201–217.

Tamboukou, M. (2000). Of other spaces: Women's colleges at the turn of the nineteenth century. *Gender, Place and Culture, 7*(3), 247–264.

Thiher, A. (1999). *Revels in madness: Insanity in medicine and literature.* Ann Arbor: University of Michigan Press.

Thomas, G. & Glenny, G. (2000). Emotional and behavioural difficulties: Bogus needs in a false category. *Discourse: Studies in the Cultural Politics of Education, 21*(3), 283–298.

Thomas, N. P. (2001). Unpacking library posters. *Journal of Education for Library & Information Science, 42*(1), 42–36.

Tochon, F. V. (1999). Metareference. A Bakhtinian view of academic dialogue. [Special issue] *International Journal of Applied Semiotics, 1*, 5–12.

Torres, C. A., Mitchell, T. R., & NetLibrary Inc. (1998). *Sociology of education emerging perspectives.* Albany: State University of New York Press.

Trigo, B. (2002). *Foucault and Latin America: Appropriations and deployments of discursive analysis.* New York: Routledge.

Tsang, A. K. T. (2001). Representation of ethnic identity in North American social work literature: A dossier of the Chinese people. *Social Work, 46*(3), 229–243.

Tschumi, B. (1994). *Architecture and disjunction.* Cambridge, MA: MIT Press.

Turner, W. B. (2000). *A genealogy of queer theory.* Philadelphia: Temple University Press.

Veri, M. J. (1999). Homophobic discourse surrounding the female athlete. *Quest, 51*(4), 355–368.

Vinson, K. D. (1999). National curriculum standards and social studies education: Dewey, Freire, Foucault, and the construction of a radical critique. *Theory and Research in Social Education, 27*(3), 296–328.

Walkerdine, V. (1984). Developmental psychology and the child-centered pedagogy: the insertion of Piaget into early education. In J. Henriques, W. Hollway, C. Urwin, C. Venn & V. Walkerdine (Eds.), *Changing the subject* (pp. 153–202.). London: Methuen.

Walshaw, M. (1999). An unlikely alliance: Mathematics education, poststructuralism and potential affirmation. *Mathematics Teacher Education and Development, 1*, 94–105.

Weitz, R. (1998). *The politics of women's bodies: Sexuality, appearance, and behavior.* New York: Oxford University Press.

West, C. (2002). A genealogy of modern racism. In P. Essed & D. T. Goldberg (Eds.), *Race critical theories: Text and context* (pp. 90–112). Malden, MA: Blackwell. (Original work published 1982)

Willis, A. I. (2002). Literacy at Calhoun colored school 1892–1945. *Reading Research Quarterly, 37*(1), 8–44.

Wright, H. K. (2000). Nailing Jell-O to the wall. *Educational Researcher, 29*(5), 4–13.

Wynter, S. (1992). Beyond the categories of the master conception. In H. Paget & P. Buhle (Eds.), *C. L. R. James' Caribbean* (pp. 63–91). Durham, NC: Duke University Press.

Wynter, S. (1995a). 1492: A new world view. In V. L. Hyatt & R. M. Nettleford (Eds.), *Race, discourse, and the origin of the Americas: A new world view* (pp. 5–57). Washington: Smithsonian Institution Press.

Wynter, S. (1995b). "The pope must have been drunk, the king of Castile a madman": Culture as actuality and the Caribbean rethinking "modernity." In A. Ruprecht (Ed.), *Culture and development: Rethinking modernity* (pp. 17–42). Ottawa, Canada: Carleton University Press.

Wynter, S. (2001). Towards the sociogenic principle: Fanon, identity, the puzzle of conscious experience, and what it is like to be "black." In M. F. Durán-Cogan & A. Gómez-Moriana (Eds.), *National identities and sociopolitical changes in Latin America* (pp. 33–66). New York: Routledge.

Wynter, S. (2002). A different kind o' creature: Caribbean literature, the Cyclops factor, and the second poetics of the *Propter nos*. In K. Braithwaite & T. J. Reiss (Eds.), *Sisyphus and Eldorado: Magical and other realisms in Caribbean literature* (pp. 153–172). Trenton, NJ: African World Press.

Young, R. J. C. (1990). *White mythologies: Writing, history and the West.* New York: Routledge.

Young, R. J. C. (1995). Foucault on race and colonialism. *New Formations, 25*, 57–65.

Young, R. J. C. (2001). *Postcolonialism: An historical introduction.* Malden, MA: Blackwell.

SECTION ONE:
COAGULATIONS

PART ONE:
Schooling's Marginalia in Historical Perspective

Fashioning the Schooled Self Through Uniforms: A Foucauldian Approach to Contemporary School Policies

Inés Dussel

The practice of wearing school uniforms in public schools has been ongoing for centuries in most modern educational systems, a fact that is not unrelated to the politics and history of colonialism that contributed to its spreading over the world. In several U.S. cities, however, it has been only recently that uniforms have been adopted as school policy, in a movement that goes against the grain of an international trend of "flexibilization" of dress codes. First started in Long Beach, California, Baltimore, and Cleveland as a measure against indiscipline, dress codes became popular after President Clinton endorsed the idea in his 1996 presidential campaign. Since then, many large urban districts, including Washington, D.C., New York City, Chicago, and Houston have begun to set policies so that their students wear "casual uniforms" (khaki pants, blue shirts) or even scrubs that can be worn over their clothes, to the point that it is becoming a "national phenomenon" (Wingert, 1999).

The implementation of school uniform policies has been surrounded with widespread debate and opposition (cf. Bruchey, 1998; Cruz, 2001; DaCosta, 1999; Wilkins, 1999). These debates have centered on the opposition of individualism versus conformity, or freedom versus discipline. Uniforms appear as an attack to the quintessential character of American life, individual freedom and creativity, or as the solution to the multifaceted problems confronted by contemporary schools: violence, crisis of authority, and loss of focus on educational tasks.[1] They were made into a "pro/con" issue (a controversial topic that supposedly divides public opinion, as the title of a series stresses, Cruz, 2001), in a move that constructed particular discursive equivalences and oppositions and that put political and moral charges on each term.

In this chapter, I will disentangle the discursive constructions around school uniforms through a history of the regulation of school bodies. I hope that this history will help us to distinguish the scaffolding of meanings that have become attached to uniforms and make the politics of this contemporary construction more visible.[2] Using as a foundation the work of Michel Foucault and the work of historians of the body and clothing, I will consider uniforms and dress codes as part of long-standing technologies of the body that, together with other institutional procedures, have produced both conformity and individuality in schools and in the larger societies (cf. Foucault, 1977, 1988, 1991; McWilliam, 1996; Perrot, 1987, 1994; Roche, 1989, 1994; Rose, 1999; Symes & Meadmore, 1996). From this hindsight, individualism is not to be pitted against society or collective selves: quite on the contrary, as Foucault convincingly argued, individuals were produced along with other social institutions as part of the governmentalization of society. This production involved the deployment of specific technologies that shaped both the body and the soul of modern selves and can be traced in what I will call the "régime of appearances," a system that regulates how people and things should look that combines aesthetic, scientific, political, and moral discourses. This notion will be dealt with more extensively in the first and second sections of this chapter, while the third and fourth parts will focus on contemporary debates about school uniforms in the United States.

To claim that Foucault can be used to produce an intervention in contemporary policy issues is in explicit contrast with some critical appraisals of his work as being "apolitical" or "too theoretical" (e.g., Schrag, 1999). I acknowledge that there are as many Foucaults as there are readers of Foucault, who have to live with the fact that, Foucault being such an unorthodox authority, none of them can argue consistently in favor of legitimacy or faithfulness of their own readings. Thus, I will produce my own Foucault through a gesture of politicizing what we think is true and virtuous, defamiliarizing what we take for granted, and questioning the belief that the present is in a seamless line of continuity with the past. From this point of view, I find that few other contemporary theorists give us so many hints as to how we might think and act politically about schools today.

1. Clothing as a Technology of the Body

Bodies are fashionable topics in contemporary social theory (McWilliam, 1996) and have recently been reappraised as a preeminent material upon which inscriptions of culture and its discourses become embedded (Grumet, 1988). For example, identity, a central issue to today's politics and theories, has been conceptualized as a material practice that is located primarily in the body (Butler, 1993). It has been said that the identity scripts for African Americans, Latinas/Latinos, women, and LGBTI individuals (lesbian, gay, bisexual, transgendered, intersexed) imply significant differences in the bodily conducts that are set as "normal" for each of these groups (Donald & Rattansi, 1992). Bodies then are seen as privileged sites for the construction of the social, and great attention has been paid to the bodily practices that function as regulatory ideas of the self.

These theoretical and political shifts owe a great deal to Michel Foucault's work on bodies and power. For the French philosopher, subjectification takes place primarily through the body and the material practices[3] that shape our behavior. Thus, the regulation of social life is first and foremost the regulation of bodies: "Now the phenomenon of the social body is the effect not of a consensus but of the materiality of power operating on the very bodies of the individuals" (Foucault, 1980: 55). Inverting the traditional duality of mind/body, which thinks of the soul as the site of freedom and the body as the boundary that constrains the soul. Foucault once said that "the soul is the prison of the body," implying that the way we feel and act is already regulated by the disciplinarian techniques that have constituted our "soul" (Foucault, 1977: 30; Popkewitz, 1998; Rose, 1990).

The centrality of the history of the body for his historico-political project cannot be overlooked. Foucault said that the history of the last centuries should be read not as that of the "enlightenment of the masses" but as that of a ritualized body-inscription that was no less painful or more "humane" than previous experiences. Instead of thinking of history as a progressive and totalizing teleology, the genealogy of modernity[4] should recognize that the normalization of bodies is never done once and forever but is the object of a permanent struggle. Arguing against the Marxist notion of class conflict, he made it explicit that "the coherence of such a [genealogical] history does not derive from the revelation of a project but from a logic of opposing strategies" (Foucault, 1980: 61). This struggle is indefinite, because for each move by the adversary there is an answer by the other. This conflict is not the unfolding of a transcendental immanence; instead, it is a contingent and unpredictable movement that involves many polarities. In relation to the history of the body, Foucault argued that from the eighteenth to the twentieth century, control over the body was heavy, ponderous, meticulous, and constant, and thus formidable disciplinary régimes emerged, such as schools, hospitals, barracks, factories, cities, families (Foucault, 1977, 1980). The so-called "sexual revolution" in the 1960s posed more flexible forms of control over the body, but that did not mean that it implied fewer constraints or regulations than Victorian morality. Foucault, who was suspicious of this revolution, and whose project on the history of sexuality can be seen as a direct attack on the romanticism and essentialism of its discourses, warned us about the fact that power can retreat here, but only to "reorganize its forces, invest itself elsewhere...and so the battle continues" (Foucault, 1980: 57).

As an example of how power reorganizes itself and how "the battle continues," a Brazilian historian has said that Foucault reminds us that "the body does not cease to be (re)fabricated over time" (Bernuzzi de Sant'Anna, 1995: 12). The body is a "mutant memory," in the sense that it has been produced by mutations of the laws and codes of a culture and by a privileged record of the scientific and technological limits and solutions of a historical period. One cannot take it for granted, limiting its history to the study of how representations change or are distorted over time, as if there were a zero degree of culture where one could find a body uncontaminated by culture. If bodies are caught up in a system of moral and political classifications and categories, it is important to identify the problematizations that made it possible for a series of bodily practices and representations to emerge and to be systematized and set to work in social life.

The history of bodies and bodily practices, then, becomes the genealogy of the *problematizations* and of the *technologies* that organize what appears as "the body." Foucault said in *The Use of Pleasure* that *problematization* is a kind of history that intends "to define the conditions in which human beings 'problematize' what they are, what they do, and the world in which they live" (Foucault, 1990: 10). It "develops the conditions in which possible responses can be given; it defines the elements that will constitute what the different solutions attempt to respond to" (Foucault, quoted in Campbell, 1998: x). Problematization questions thoughts, gestures, and attitudes that seem natural and tries to rewrite them as part of the transformations of a practice that faces difficulties and obstacles and for which diverse practical solutions appear as reasonable and feasible. It is not a rhetorical trope or a topic but a way of conceiving a subject, of looking at a problem, and of defining codes and discourses that are appropriate to deal with it.

The history of *technologies* pays special attention to "the analysis of the activity of ruling...the actual mechanisms through which authorities of various sorts have sought to shape, normalize and instrumentalise the conduct, thought, decisions and aspirations of others in order to achieve the objectives they consider desirable...the humble and mundane mechanisms which appear to make it possible to govern" (Miller and Rose, quoted in McWilliam, 1996: 15). Technology is an assemblage of heterogeneous elements: knowledges, types of authority, vocabularies, practices of calculation, and architectural forms, and thus cannot be reduced to a "single will to govern" (Rose, 1999: 52–53). The schoolroom can be looked at as a technology that combines different techniques (timetables, registers of students and teachers, moralizing aspirations, professional ethos, drills and exercises, architectural dispositions, among others) in order to shape the conduct of children in precise ways. Dress codes and uniforms are part of these technologies of the body that shape individuals in their relationships to themselves and to others.

I will claim, then, that clothing is a very powerful way in which social regulation is enacted: It turns bodies into "readable" signs, making the observer recognize patterns of docility and transgression as well as social positioning. Elizabeth Grosz remarks that clothes mark the subject's body as deeply as a surgical incision, binding individuals to systems of significance in which they become signs to be read, both by others and by themselves (Grosz, 1995). Arguing along the same line, Michel de Certeau (1984) says that clothing is one of the two ways through which the body is inscribed in the text of law. The first wants to eliminate that which is excessive, diseased, or unaesthetic from the body; the second proceeds through adding to the body what it lacks. Cutting, tearing up, extracting, removing, inserting, covering up, assembling, and articulating are the main operations that take place on the body. They are carried out by references to a code, keeping bodies within the limits of a norm. "[C]lothes themselves can be regarded as instruments through which a social law maintains its hold on bodies and its members, regulates them and exercises them" (De Certeau, 1984: 147). They have the effect of making the body tell the code: They realize a social language, they recount a law that has been "historied and historicized" (*histoirée* and *historicisée*) and thus are made more effective.

2. Dress Codes and the "Régime of Appearances" in Schools

As will be shown across this section, the importance of clothing within school experience has not been overlooked although it has rarely been theorized on the level of investigation I propose here. It is relevant to my argument to draw a distinction between dress codes and uniforms—dress codes include all the regulations effected in the realm of clothing practices, while uniforms involve a more strict and rigid code, which mandates the use of particular pieces of clothing. Also, while dress codes generally act through banning some clothes (for example, brand-name clothing, oversized or baggy clothes, hats, baseball caps or bandanas, particular hairstyles or facial hair), uniforms make it compulsory to wear particular attire. Thus, even though all dress codes "restrict" the possibilities of choosing what to wear, uniforms constitute a singular case in this restriction.

A good example of the significance of clothing for schooling is the description of one of the outstanding teachers in Gloria Ladson-Billings' study of successful teachers of African Americans:

> Dupree is a slender, attractive African-American woman. She is always dressed in a style that reminds one of a corporate executive. Her outfits are coordinated: she seems to have a different pair of shoes for each. During our first interview, she said that the girls in her class sometimes peek around the classroom door in the morning to see what she is wearing. When one of her students asked why she was always "so dressed up," Dupree replied that she dressed the way she did because she was coming to work and she worked with very important people, so she wanted to look good. (Ladson-Billings, 1994: 35)

Ms. Dupree's looks are an important part of the statement she wants to make clear to her students: Schooling is a serious matter. Dressed up as an executive, the teacher conveys a sense of mission, of a collective endeavor that intends to instill the ethics of hard work and progress in her students.

Madeleine Grumet recalls a different relationship to clothes, which contrasts with Ms. Dupree's mission-ethics. Talking about rituals and ceremonies, the feminist scholar remembers the white blouse with green ties she used to wear to the assembly days, with its puffed sleeves and pearly buttons that made that day a special one:

> I am a little embarrassed by the prominence of clothing in all these memories, fictive and actual. Was I, at the age of eight or nine, fixated on presentation, on style? Am I now? I would rather think it is about texture, about feeling a new skin. I think the gathered cap, the Mexican costume, and the blouse are tactile memories of moments when music, event, and ensemble performance extended the boundaries of my daily world. (Grumet, 1997: 41)

Clothes marked the public ceremonies that filled the school with joy and pride and made her feel special and unique. They were a relevant feature in the performance of schooling, a subtle yet pervasive text and texture of meanings that enhanced the construction of identities and differences in particular ways. Besides those of Ladson-Billings and Grumet, other examples could be provided that would show the vividness of these memories of clothing and the impact they seem to have had on the experience of schooling (Corrigan, 1988; Davidson, 1990).

Compared to the puffed sleeves and the executive suits, uniforms appear as a standardized and flat dress code. Yet this dull appearance should not cloud the fact that uniforms also produce differences and distinctions. School uniforms are signs and signifying practices that carry meanings about identity and difference and that enact the disciplining of the body through a power that subjects and subjectifies (produces subjectivities) (cf. Symes & Meadmore, 1996). They are supposed to represent inward qualities such as decency and sexual probity (see Vavrus, 1998, ch. 6, for the case of Tanzania). However, according to Synott and Symes, uniforms are not just external "screens" on which meanings are reflected but are part of technologies of power that "govern and regulate both the outward and inward disposition of the pupil" (Synott & Symes, 1995: 140). I propose that moving beyond the idea of "external screens" which reflect a transcendental essence is important in order to begin to understand discourse as producing objects and reality. Synott and Symes go on to say that uniforms are "sets of habiliments in the moral economy of schools" that manifest the kinds of subjectivities valued by educational institutions. They produce moral characters, relationships to the self and to others, that go far beyond the external look. Furthermore, they do so in peculiar ways, through the imposition of minute details and the constant surveillance of transgression.

According to cultural critic Marjorie Garber, author of a fascinating study about cross-dressing, "dress codes function in the social world and the world of social hierarchy as structures that simultaneously regulate and critique normative categories like rank (or its civilian counterpart, class) and gender" (Garber, 1997: 25). That they regulate is probably clear to the reader by now. But the critique that they encompass has to be read as a sign that boundaries need to be established; in doing so, they acknowledge, and sometimes stretch and push forward, the distinctions among ranks, genders, or races. Garber states that dress codes in the nineteenth and twentieth centuries also tried to enhance an upward mobility; in contrast to sumptuary laws in the sixteenth and seventeenth centuries, which were aimed at preventing people from "dressing up," contemporary dress codes generally require a higher standard of dress for particular groups of people (workers, students, spectators) in specific situations (Garber, 1997: 22–25). Garber refers to schools in low-income neighborhoods that have adopted a more formal dress code, e.g., neckties and shirts, which supposedly gives the students an enhanced discipline and self-respect—apparently needed by "at-risk" kids (Garber, 1997: 22). Uniforms, on the other hand, tend to stress the recognizability of a particular hierarchy (in the army, in church); it is a very legible code that has practical consequences for how one is supposed to act and respond to others.

Uniforms and dress codes are part of what I will call, building on the works of the historians of clothing Philippe Perrot and Daniel Roche as well as Michel Foucault, "régimes of appearances." This notion refers to the system of dress codes that regulates the way people dress and that combines aesthetics, hygiene, fashion, and propriety and moral values (Perrot, 1994: 20).[5] These régimes can be more or less restrictive and are protected by a set of sanctions, laws or norms that has "a certain degree of stability or persistence…such that the linkages between its elements become familiar and taken for granted" (Hunt, 2000: 1, speaking about régimes of government). For example, sumptuary laws and vestimentary ordinances were common in medieval Europe and codified textiles and styles in order to produce and maintain social distinctions (Hunt, 1996). In contemporary societies, on the other hand, dress codes are enforced through other mechanisms: consumption, publicity, and health discourses, among others. While this régime presents itself as a free system, the liberty that people enjoy to make their choices is regulated through complex mechanisms that include consumption patterns and perceptions of the self, among others.

The notion of a "régime of appearances" allows me to consider the multiple discourses and "wills to govern" (Rose's term) that inform the regulation of bodies through clothes. I follow Alan Hunt's (1999) and Mariana Valverde's (1998) studies of moral regulation as combining different "repertoires" and kinds of knowledge that conceive of it as "the outcome of a complex of elements of governmental discourses, rationalities and practices" (Hunt, 2000: 1). Hunt argues in favor of speaking of this multiplicity in terms of "hybridity," because it makes it possible "to explore the specific forms of these combinatory elements and to examine the ways they may reinforce each other or, alternatively, set off tensions" (idem).

At which point did uniforms become the "régime of appearances" in schools? Looking back at early modern Europe, one finds school uniforms in two of the first attempts at institutionalizing elementary schools: the Lassallean movement and charity schools. Children wore colored smocks, sometimes with badges from the donors' families, that distinguished them as orphans or poor people. I have claimed elsewhere that the charity schools' uniforms were located at the overlapping of the workings of sumptuary laws, the emergence of disciplinary power and individuation, the transformation of the public and private spheres, and the reorganization of the urban space (cf. Dussel, 2001). As indicated above, sumptuary laws prevented people from dressing up; uniforms were, in that respect, a negative distinction, a marker of poverty and orphanage.

It was the French Revolution that established an equivalence between uniformity, homogeneity, and democracy and made the uniform the symbol of plebeian equality. The utopian children's uniforms of the French Revolution emphasized the production of a homogeneous and equal social body that supposedly erased all differences, but at the same time produced an increased individualization and autonomization. The uniforms were effected within a power régime that thought of the body as a social property and the outcast as a traitor or unfaithful citizen as detailed by Foucault in *Discipline and Punish*. But we can find some parallels in contemporary practices of the enforcement of uniforms, which construct similar associations. Phillip Corrigan's memories of being the only child in a 600-student school wearing a gray blazer instead of the required blue or black jacket inform us of analogous effects: The breaking of a dress code made oneself stand as an outcast, immediately recognizable, humiliated, and separated (Corrigan, 1988). Also, Guacira Lopes Louro's comments on her experience as a schoolgirl in Brazil point to the collective appropriation of the body: Dressed in school uniforms, the girls were made responsible for "representing the school" to the whole society. The uniform carried with it the duty of behaving well, appropriately and respectfully, at any place and at any time (Lopes Louro, 1999: 19). The construction of the body as a social property, and of transgression as betrayal, has shaped the ways in which uniforms and dress codes were and still are enforced in schools, and in that respect, it goes against the modern conception of the possessive individual who "has"/"owns" a body (Duden, 1991). This coexistence between homogeneity, democracy, and authority over people's bodies has been persistent in many Republican ideals (cf. Bleibtreu-Ehrenberg, 1978, for the French case).

Following the revolutionary impulse, and all throughout the nineteenth century, Western European societies, as well as their colonies, saw the construction of a regime of appearances based on the notion of "Republican elegance" that placed austerity and decorum as central tenets of the presentation of the body, and particularly of children's bodies, instead of ostentation and baroque display (Perrot, 1987, who also traces its Calvinist links). To be austere—to wear black, for example—was not only a stylish outfit but the only virtuous one (Harvey, 1995). Uniforms also provided ways in which people and social functions could be recognized easily; it is not by chance that police officers, firefighters, and train guards all started donning uniforms at that time. There was a more general change from the classification of people according to their differential positions in a scale of deviance to a uniformizing norm, which stressed similarities and homologies (Valiente, 1996).

The Republican austerity was rewritten by the irruption of hygienist discourses, mass immigration, and the nationalizing impulse of the late nineteenth century, and these dynamics played a significant role in the adoption of uniforms as the public school's dress code at the beginning of the twentieth century. From smocks to blazers and gray pants, children in most Western educational systems lived through the experience of uniformation in schools (cf. Corrigan, 1988). The United States, however, remained a different case, on whose peculiarities I will dwell in the next section.

3. The Paradoxes of Casual Uniforms in the United States

The emergence of school uniforms in public schools in the United States is certainly a puzzling event. In an educational system traditionally proud of its decentralization and its focus on the individual, and also in a country where to say "liberal" is not equated with right-wing politics but quite the contrary,[6] nothing seems more foreign than uniforms. An example might help clarify this belief:

Clothes symbolize who a person is as an individual and I do not feel that there should be dress codes enforced in schools or any other public facility. This is America and we have a choice to express ourselves in any fashion we feel comfortable portraying as long as it does not violate any laws. Clothing makes us different and unique and more aware of the diverse cultures of our nation. Dress codes seem to eliminate this awareness. (a teenager, in Cruz, 2001: 32)

The opinion of this teenager quite sharply expresses what most people feel is at stake in debates around school uniforms: freedom of expression and multiculturalism versus discipline and homogeneity. Not surprisingly, the American Civil Liberties Union has been one of the strongest opponents of the adoption of dress codes, and it runs a website that offers legal advice to parents and children who want to fight against them.[7]

Despite the widespread view that school uniforms have never existed in American schools, there have been several experiences of uniformation policies in both public and private schools prior to current policies, although they were never as universal as their European and South American counterparts.[8] From early on, the uniformation policies were tied to the disciplining of unruly bodies, of the bodies of those who were positioned as not able to perform self-regulation or self-government: women, blacks, Native Americans, poor classes, immigrants, children. These histories make it evident that the technologies of the body do not operate neutrally or blindly in relation to race, class, gender, and age differences; quite on the contrary, they help to construct these differences, to, paraphrasing Judith Butler (1993), shape them, contour them, stabilize their boundaries and fix their meanings.

It is not surprising, then, that, in the Unites States in the nineteenth and early twentieth centuries, Native Americans and blacks were the privileged targets of a close surveillance in terms of what to wear and when to wear it (White & White, 1998). In particular, the introduction of uniforms in federal Indian boarding schools meant that tribal attire and moccasins were forbidden, and strict measures were enforced to ensure that children wore "civilized" Western clothes, including underwear. Tsiamina Lomawaima (1994), for example, has written a fascinating study that analyzes the struggle around feminine underwear in these schools, as have Archuleta, Child, and Lomawaima, (2000). Further examples include the ways in which white women were subjected to strict regulation, in which first-wave feminists joined doctors and social reformers to produce a hygienic, virtuous body (see Donzelot, 1997).

Even the story of trousers can be read as a result of this alliance: the use of bloomers, the first trousers used by suffragette women, was advocated by feminists and doctors alike on the basis of the comfort, healthiness, and austerity they represented (Banner, 1983; Flower, 1891/2000; Luck, 1992). The only exceptions to this type of regulation were sports uniforms, which have been tied to the production of a pious and energetic body and which were related to the organization of a mass society (the "invention of the social," as Jacques Donzelot [1984] calls it) (cf. Campbell Warner, 1993; Mrozek, 1983)

To analyze the relations of dress codes and the "invention of the social" in early twentieth-century America, I will refer to the work of Jean-Jacques Courtine, who wrote a marvelous history of body-building in the United States.[9] Courtine states that the articulation of religion, health, and consumerism is a remarkably persistent feature in Americans' relationship to their bodies, which are indebted to Puritan themes and the construction of the nation. The "American body," produced by particular technologies, holds, according to Courtine, specific features:

> the belief, with religious and proselytizing overtones, that a corporal metamorphosis is possible; the idea that individual salvation and the regeneration of the nation are simultaneously dependent on this metamorphosis; a rejection of the medical institution, emphasized by the will to have full responsibility over one's body's health; and finally a sharp commercial sense, which perceived quite early that the body was also a market place. It is on this genealogy *religion-health-commerce* that the rationality of contemporary practices of the American body have to be inscribed. (Courtine, 1995: 89, emphasis in the original)

Courtine accentuates the distance of Americans from European physical models. While in the 1830s the English were seduced by the Byronic ethereal, pale, and thin male, the Americans quickly moved to the muscular body. Andrew Jackson, soldier and pioneer, was the robust and strong man of the frontier. Calisthenics for women gained more acceptance, although athletic women would not receive wide support as models of beauty until the 1860s (Banner, 1983). The Civil War was a turning point in relation to body culture: shaping one's body was not only possible; it was also one's duty to the nation and to oneself. Courtine remarks that the movement of "Muscular Christianity," initiated in England in the early nineteenth century but influential in the United States in the second half of the century, had enormous importance in spreading the model of a virtuous body. "The pastoral of sweat," the ingenious name coined by Courtine to speak of this movement, was central to the establishment of the Young Men's Christian Association, to the Boy Scouts movement, and to many other outdoors and sporting institutions in the United States.

> They enlisted physical culture to the service of God, favoring habits of order, discipline, exactitude, essential to the good functioning of an industrial and bureaucratic society. Puritan thought played a central part in the construction of this society. The care of the body was included among the moral obligations, in the way of a Christian duty....The pleasure that is obtained from exercising comes...from the work done upon the body that tends to be perceived as a public virtue. (Courtine, 1995: 93, 101)

Instead of being related to an increased hedonism and secularization of the body, for Courtine the "obsession with the body" has to be linked to an intensification of controls and a repuritanization of behaviors.

While these moral, political, religious, and scientific discourses were central to the production of bodies in twentieth-century America and thus provide the scaffolding upon which school dress codes and uniforms were built, there are other threads that come from different directions but are nonetheless quite relevant to understanding contemporary policies on school uniforms. In particular, I would like to refer to the "preppy look"—generally considered a symbol of the upper classes (Birnbach, 1980)—which has been brought to the fore in current debates both as the model to be imitated and the goal of the transformation. That students show up clean and "properly dressed" was always part of what the school was supposed to accomplish. But, going back to Marjorie Garber's argument about recent dress codes, the preppy look has been turned into the standard for upward mobility, and the symbol of "dressing up" (Garber, 1997). More recently, miniskirts, makeup, earrings, bareness of limbs or abdomen, and bright or flashy colors are among the many pieces of clothing and vestimentary practices that have been subjected to regulation and debate in American schools (Cruz, 2001; Holloman, La Point, Alleyne, Palmer, & Sanders-Phillips, 1996).

Despite this trend toward increased regulation of dress codes in schools, I would like to argue that the introduction of school uniforms during the late 1980s and early 1990s in several school districts introduced a disruption in educational discourses based on freedom and autonomy of the individual, and this disruption has to be acknowledged as an event—an event that speaks of a reorganization of the technologies of the body. First implemented in Baltimore, Cleveland, and Long Beach, California, uniforms that imitated the practice of Catholic schools and English schools became a common practice in American public schools. They went almost unnoticed in the national press until January 1996, when President Clinton endorsed their use while he was campaigning for reelection. The year 1996 was a turning point in the diffusion of uniform policies. Clinton stressed that they would help to promote security in schools and would be a safe attire for children. It has to be remarked that the issue of safety was important and carried a dramatic burden, because some days before his speech a teenager had been killed in New Jersey while somebody was trying to rob him of his Nike shoes. Clinton's speech put together the extended condemnation of the crime with a feasible solution: Had he not been wearing his Nike shoes, this kid would still have been alive. The school uniform could protect children from exterior violence.

As simplistic as it may seem, the argument was effective in propagandizing uniforms in public schools. The secretary of education, under express orders from the president, published a booklet with recommendations for schools and started a national campaign for their use (U.S. Department of Education, 1996). The recommendations, which emphasize the need for consensus and participation of the community in adopting uniforms, do not have the status of law but have been followed in several school districts nonetheless. Most of the initial publicity was based on the success of the pioneer experience in Long Beach. In the *Congressional Bulletin* that published the recommendations, uniforms in the Long Beach school district were given credit for an astonishing 36% drop in school crime and a 51% decrease in school violence. Support for the uniforms grew. A survey of 5,500 principals conducted by the National Association of Secondary School Principals in 1996 showed that 70% were in favor of school uniforms. Also, according to a Gallup Poll of public's attitudes toward the public schools in the same year, more than 50% of the parents supported the initiative. This percentage rose to 70% for parents with children at nonpublic schools (Elam, Rose, & Gallup, 1996). It is not surprising that, given this wide popular approval, most of the largest school districts (Los Angeles, Chicago, New York City, Philadelphia, Baltimore, Boston, Miami, Cleveland, New Orleans, and Washington, D.C., among others), have since adopted uniforms as the dress code for their schools (Cruz, 2001). Most of them have opt-out clauses and consist of casual clothes (khaki pants or blue skirts, blue or white shirts).

What kind of reorganization of technologies and targets of power is implied in the introduction of school uniforms as the régime of appearances in American schools? In order to scrutinize this transformation, I will analyze the confluence and overlapping of multiple discourses that support the spread of school uniforms and that exceed the frames of liberal pedagogies and neoconservative moral fables that monopolize public debates.

The rhetoric of reform has stressed three themes: *discipline, anti-consumerism,* and *social equality.* The emphasis on *discipline* and *social equality* is not new in relation to school uniforms, as discussed in the previous section. Perhaps what has changed in its American version is that social equality is no longer the articulating axis of other discourses; in fact, social issues appear relatively weak when compared to anti-violence and disciplinary discourses. This can be seen in the following justification for the use of uniforms provided in the *Manual on School Uniforms*: "In response to growing levels of violence in our schools, many parents, teachers, and school officials have come to see school uniforms as one positive and creative way to reduce discipline problems and increase school safety. The potential benefits of school uniforms include: decreasing violence and theft...helping prevent gang members from wearing gang colors and insignia at school; [and] instilling students with discipline" (U.S. Department of Education, 1996). The rhetoric of "restoration" is revealing of the moral and political implications of the reform, on which I will comment below, but I would like to underline that the notion of promoting social equality is significantly absent— although, as it will be said later on, it is not unproblematic.

Another discourse that has been central to the spread of uniforms is *anti-consumerism.* The argument says that kids put too much energy and too many resources into their looks, and that they have to be refocused into what "really" matters: study, career progress, and values. As President Clinton put it, "[uniforms] slowly teach our young people one of life's most important lessons: that what really counts is what you are and what you can become on the inside, not what you are wearing on the outside" (quoted in: Cruz, 2001: 41). Paradoxically, children and young people will be able to develop their "insides" through a change in their "outsides," i.e., the wearing of uniforms.

This kind of reasoning related to anti-consumerism and anti-violence has been criticized for putting too much faith on a single measure, and while I might agree with it on some level, the criticism does not address the core of this reasoning—which might be much more problematic in the long run. Clinton's speech is inverting a traditional way of thinking about clothes, which argues that they are the true expression of one's self (that is why uniforms have to be opposed as an obstacle to self-expression). Clinton's argument suggests something different: Work has to be done on the self so that our true selves can develop. The self is the result of an ethical and aesthetic work from the outside to the inside that has to be continually monitored and supervised.

This kind of work upon the self picks up old and new themes—lines of continuity can be established with Courtine's "pastoral of sweat" and the repuritanization of the bodies. But I will argue that this work upon the self emerges out of a very different constellation of technologies and discourses. I will build on Nikolas Rose's (1999) analysis of current patterns of governing the self:

> Today, perhaps, the problem is not so much the government of society as the governability of the passions of self-identified individuals and collectivities: individuals and pluralities shaped not by the citizen-forming devices of church, school and public broadcasting, but by commercial consumption regimes and the politics of lifestyle, the individual identified by allegiance with one of a plurality of cultural communities. Hence the problem posed by contemporary neo-conservatives and communitarians alike: how can one govern virtue in a free society? It is here that we can locate our contemporary "wars of subjectivity." (Rose, 1999: 46)

Rose's formulations are rich in implications, and I find them very helpful for moving the arguments about school uniforms to a different level. In the first place, this quotation speaks about a more general problem faced by schools: As Rose (and many others, Hannah Arendt among them) says, the ascendancy of the school over the constitution of subjectivities has been undermined by other institutions and dynamics. Quite evidently, uniforms constitute an attempt on the part of the school system to regain authority. Advocates for uniforms emphasize that the use of a common and strict dress code will provide an image of respectability and order much needed within schools and also in the schools' relationships to the larger society. Even those who do not think that there is a connection between uniforms and increased academic achievement find that uniforms have some impact on the authority of the school over the community, providing a symbol of commitment to the goals of the school (Brunsma & Rockquemore, 1998). In the rhetoric of reform, the school has to intervene against gang clothing as well as against "fashion slaves" (i.e., middle-class kids who worry "too much" about what to wear).[10] Moreover, uniforms help establish an authority that does not need to be explained or framed in terms of pedagogical theories—in fact, pedagogical arguments for uniforms have been weak and unconvincing, a fact that is not surprising, given the heavy reliance of pedagogical theories on the psychology of the individual and child-centeredness in the United States. It is an authority that emphasizes the common good over the child's interests; it reinstates adult authority conceived as a unidirectional relationship from adults to children and from school to parents, despite the nuances of and appeals to participation done in most districts.

In the second place, the education of "passions" through intervention in people's lifestyles is a substantial change in the way power is effected and the technologies it brings into play. The very idea of "lifestyle" points in a different direction than the liberal technologies of the self and introduces new practices of identity formation through "the active and practical shaping by individuals of the daily practices of their own lives in the name of their own pleasures, contentments, or fulfilments" (Rose, 1999: 178–179). I will illustrate this change through other dress codes that are quite different from uniforms: "hip" or "cool" attire. As it has been stated throuhghout this chapter, the regulation of clothing has continually played a role in the workings of power; there is, however, a difference between the ethical formation of the self through régimes of appearance of "austerity and decorum," whose models were the urban bourgeois families (a unified model), and the ones that are centered around "hipness" or "coolness" which integrate informality and transgression and which pose an ever-changing work upon the self to keep up to date. "Hipness" is by definition an ever-vanishing target; as soon as it becomes popular, it disappears and turns into something else ("that is *SO* yesterday," says an ad for a new hair product). One can be "hip" in a variety of ways; actually, to be "hip" is to be original. To master the techniques of being cool or appearing cool then is a complex learning process.[11] These techniques, on the other hand, are homologous to the ones involved in the reorganization of the workplace and the military, which focus on competency, flexibility, adaptability, and a reeducation of the will ("the entrepreneurial self," as Popkewitz and Bloch [2001] define it). The individual is responsible for self-actualization, in a continual work upon the self, in order to fully develop his/her potentialities.

Uniforms have an ambiguous, paradoxical place in this context.[12] They are clearly related to the efforts to restore "virtue" in a "free society," although the word "virtue" rarely appears in the rhetoric that supports uniforms, and they are related to governing individuals through the adoption of common patterns of consumption and behavior that will reduce the threats to society. School uniforms have repeatedly been praised for the curbing of irrational consumption and transgressive lifestyles, epitomized by gangs' styles and their preferred clothing: low-cut and baggy jeans, bandannas and baseball caps worn backwards. It is believed that through stricter dress codes a change in moral behavior will take place.

But uniforms can seldom be spoken of in terms of "self-help" and even less often as part of the quest of "coolness" or "hipness"—except for the fact, not irrelevant, that most school districts chose khaki pants and shirts as the required outfit, following a trend already established by "hip" brands (cf. Gladwell, 2000). In both respects, they appear to diverge from today's dominant lifestyles. In the adoption of uniforms in the United States, autonomy does indeed appear as a threat; it is the impossibility or inefficiency of the individual to govern his/her passions and to adopt the lifestyle/s that would accommodate his/her interests and those of society simultaneously that calls for an external intervention. This intervention has a different quality: It is direct and continuous and is not effected through "expert knowledge" (pedagogy or psychology) but through other forms (disciplinary measures, peer and community control). Of course, the change is neither total nor definitive; enforcing strict dress codes and instituting a small range of choices for students, one hopes, will result in the adoption of a lifestyle and patterns and dispositions of consumption and behavior that will not need direct intervention (the "slowly teaching" of which Clinton spoke). This teaching/ethical work will allow the individual to regulate his/her passions and interests adequately, to learn from experience, and to institute the kind of relationship to his/her self that is valued and praised in contemporary society.

4. Implications:
Uniforms and the Deployment of Contemporary "Wills to Govern"

I would like to point out four possible implications of my reading of Foucault for contemporary debates on school uniforms. First, Foucault helps me to interrupt a reliance on the opposition of freedom and con-formity and to disclose what this opposition precludes us from seeing. I have tried to show that all dress codes, whether flexible or strict, are technologies of the body that shape children's perceptions of themselves and of others in particular ways. Dress codes participate in the regulatory workings of schooling that "require ways of conducting oneself that are experienced in powerfully and profoundly physical ways by children" (Kirk, 1998: 7). They contribute to the technical realization of the will to govern, translating in practical and technical senses the desires to shape the conduct of people, "in the hope of producing certain desired effects and averting certain undesired effects" (Rose, 1999: 52). In that context, uniforms play a particular role, instituting a top-to-bottom authority that establishes strict boundaries between the normal and the abnormal, the decent and the indecent, and accepted lifestyles and condemnable lifestyles. They are based on the idea that an external regulation is needed, given that the bodies in question are not able to govern themselves either because they are lawless bodies or because they do not yet know how to self-regulate their conduct. "Lawless" or "immature" bodies are generally those of the disadvantaged groups (the poor and orphans in early modern Europe, and blacks, Native Americans, women, and immature children in the case of the United States).

The second point of current debates in which I would like to intervene is to challenge the equivalence articulated between uniformity and democracy, an equivalence that is particularly powerful in the European countries but is also present in progressive advocators of uniforms in the United States. It is important to look at the exclusions performed by this equivalence. Since the eighteenth century, uniforms have been used in attempts to politically erase the marks of difference, as Lynn Hunt (1998) has said, and because of this, they have been articulated to broader practices of citizenship that appear as homogeneous, gender- and race-neutral, indifferent to social and cultural distinctions. In that respect, uniforms have to be understood as part of the construction of a modern democratic polity that has relied on declarations of equality based on the abstraction of difference (Scott, 1997). The works of feminists and postcolonial scholars (Fraser & Gordon, 1998; Gilroy, 2000; Scott, 1997; Spivak, 1999) show that more complex notions of equality have to be construed, notions that need to take into account the paradoxical inclusion of difference and that continually strive for more justice. While these discussions have had wide impact on debates on multicultural education, the discussion over uniforms has rarely taken them into account. I hope my project helps to bring these perspectives into current debates and to analyze both topics as surfaces in which similar strategies about difference and inequality are being deployed.

There is a third line of implications to be drawn from this study, and it has to do with the history of technologies and techniques of government. What is particularly interesting about uniforms is that, having emerged as part of disciplinary techniques "designed to hierarchize and normalize populations" through the regulation of bodies (Meadmore & Symes, 1997: 182), they were not abandoned, as were other contemporaneous disciplinary techniques such as corporal punishment and means for correcting the body's posture. To the contrary, they knew a considerable success, a success that challenges us to rethink theoretically the ways societies and schools change and the relationship between different régimes of power. Alan Hunt advances an explanation for the changes and continuities of sumptuary laws that I find useful for dealing with uniforms as well. For him, it is rare that social change is affected by the displacement of one discursive formation by another; instead, there are always processes of recombination, of coupling and uncoupling, that explain the dynamics of change. In the case of sumptuary laws, "the different discursive elements were present from the beginning; what changes is their respective 'weight' and the combinatory repertoires" (Hunt, 1996: 41). In regard to school dress codes, it can be said that medical discourses, moral and economic regulations, and political discourses of autonomy and obedience reemerge in somewhat different contexts and with diverse arrangements, in a movement that allows for transformation but maintains links with previous formations. It is important to note that techniques have their own historicity and that the school's material culture remains a field of unquestionable value for understanding that specificity.

The fourth line of implications has to do with the title of this section, and leads us to changing the way we think about government and technologies of the self more generally. The changes I have been talking about have been referred to as a restorative or neoconservative movement in recent literature. For example, David Wagner (1997) speaks of "new temperance" when referring to the increased regulation of behavior in contemporary America, including the case against smoking and the renewed Puritanism that arises from time to time in the cultural arena.

But I have been trying to argue that much will be gained if we moved beyond the rhetorics of neoconservativism and look instead at the complex "wills to govern" that are present in contemporary societies. Mariana Valverde's work on the regulation of alcoholism stresses the coexistence of different discourses at the same time and argues that power is to be seen not as evolving unidirectionally or unidimensionally but rather as unfolding (my verb) diverse rationalities and technologies at the same time. She takes as an example the success and persistence of the twelve-step program of Alcoholics Anonymous (AA) and its current influence in other self-help practices:

> Taking a Calvinist view of the will, the twelve steps proclaim that the essence of alcoholism is the mistaken feeling that we do have willpower, that we do have control; and they go on to suggest that the solution to the problem of codependence is not asserting one's willpower even more but rather acknowledging one's profound weakness, one's powerlessness. The tremendous success of AA and its offshoots in the present day is remarkable among other reasons because the Calvinist doctrine of the essential fallenness and frailty of human nature is at odds with the neoliberal belief in the ability of every individual to empower him/herself to any extent that they choose. Codependence is the neoliberal mutation of the Protestant ethic and the spirit of capitalism, whereas AA represents classic Weberian capitalism, in which the Protestant ethic had more to do with self-control than with self-fulfilment. (Valverde, 1998: 34)

Contemporary uniforms then can be read as part of the same Calvinist technologies of the self of AA described by Valverde that promote self-control based on a notion of perpetual threat and weakness by our nature. The goal is not to fulfill one's ambitions, to express oneself truly and completely, but rather to govern our passions—our passions to consume, to display, and to transgress. Once again, I underline that some bodies appear as more in need of/susceptible to government than others: It is not by chance that the school districts that have adopted school dress codes based on uniforms are the ones with the largest minority population (the "urban" schools; on the construction of "urban," see Popkewitz, 1998). But it is important to keep in mind that this government is not a direct domination on people's minds or bodies but that it proceeds through specific operations on our thoughts, bodies, and souls that produce our beings. Foucault writes, "Governing people, in the broad meaning of the word...is not a way to force people to do what the governor wants; it is always a versatile equilibrium, with complementarity and conflicts between techniques which impose coercion and processes through which the self is constructed or modified by himself." (Foucault, 1997a: 182).

5. Concluding Thoughts:
Why Care About School Uniform Debates?

The importance of considering uniforms is, from my point of view, that the paradoxes they encompass help to illustrate the complex workings of power in contemporary societies. Some cases, such as uniforms in Indian boarding schools or uniforms in sports, seem to be simpler, relatively "easy" to read and "decipher." But uniforms in today's public schools still puzzle us, introducing discomfort and uneasiness. School discipline, discourses on lifestyles, new gender politics, racial relations, religious assumptions, and consumption practices all come together to produce particular effects on children's bodies. I suggest that we have to look at them in order to produce new accounts of the reforms that consider the inclusions and exclusions that are being performed. Once again, I would like to quote Valverde's sharp argument, this time talking about the usefulness of these paradoxes for the study of governmentality:

> Governing through alcohol is everywhere an ad hoc, unsystematic, non-professionalized "minor" practice that takes very different forms and is articulated with all manner of extraneous objectives and habits of governance. Its study may be informative, therefore, for those who are interested in complicating the picture painted by many contemporary sociologists of living in an expert-dominated risk-society. That risks have been managed without expert knowledges, that disciplinary control over minute details coexists with hedonistic consumption, that regulation is not necessarily the opposite of prohibition, and that governing through an object such as alcohol may involve governing all sorts of activities, spaces, and identities without doing much to govern drinking itself, are conclusions arising from this specific study of liquor laws but potentially useful across a wide range of fields. (Valverde, 1998: 169)

Governing children's bodies through school uniforms can be analyzed through a lens similar to the one used by Foucault, Perrot, Valverde, and Hunt among others, a lens that cuts across fields and disciplines and interrogates their continuities and discontinuities. Uniforms have emerged in a scaffolding of discourses that were as disparate as sumptuary laws, Republican democracy, health disciplines, and the policing of unruly bodies and that constituted a particular régime of appearance—austere and homogeneous. Moreover, they have been part of the consolidation of modern forms of power that enhance autonomy while simultaneously intensifying techniques of ruling and control. And that is still the case today: A new pattern of authority is being constructed, made of a combination of health discourses, bodily practices, marketing strategies, and cultural assumptions about the body that are built into particular technologies and strategies. I hope it is by now clear why I think that contemporary debates on school uniform policies that keep focused on an antagonistic and irreducible opposition between individualism and conformity are misleading and unproductive. As the Brazilian historian Denise Bernuzzi de Sant'Anna says, it is important to think beyond the opposition that distinguishes freedom and repression, natural body and artificial body, society and individual, not to deny their existence but to analyze them where they have always been: inscribed in history and thus datable, provisional, plural, and most of all, closely intertwined.

Foucault's work is useful for dismantling both the romantic/essentialist view of the body as the ultimate site of resistance, pleasure, and desire, as well as the one that sees it as a direct, univocal effect of repressive power. The history of the problematization of the body as I have tried to write it, inspired by Foucault, within the history of school uniforms and dress codes, should make it evident that the liberties of the body (e.g., the hip or cool style) are also the product of a pedagogical experience, of a regulative operation, and thus always imply coercions and responsibilities. But it should also stress that the control of bodies, created with scientific and technical supports, like the ones present in Indian boarding schools or charity schools, occurred parallel to the discovery of new coercions to be outsmarted and new zones in which to lose control as well as new mysteries and risks. In other words, the history should show that power is not monolithic or unified but plural and contradictory. For Foucault, to point simultaneously in both directions was as much a political statement as it was a theoretical position. He was an heir and a subverter of the emancipatory tradition that always dwells around the same question (Foucault, 1997b): the question of not to be governed quite so much, not to be governed at that cost. This, I find, still reverberates as a central question of our flexible, casual, self-help, hip-and-cool times.

Endnotes

1. For example, the 1996 Phi Delta Kappa/Gallup Poll of the public's attitudes toward the public schools included a question about school uniforms inside the section of measures to maintain order and security in schools (Elam, Rose, & Gallup, 1996).

2. I take the notion of scaffolding from Popkewitz (1998). He uses it to argue that teaching was shaped through a variety of discourses that contributed with heterogeneous statements to its definition as a pastoral work involving the salvation of the soul through scientific and professional knowledge.

3. It is useful to refer to Judith Butler's discussion about the materiality of bodies in order to avoid a commonsensical notion of material practices. "What I would propose…is a return to the notion of matter, not as a site or surface, but as a process of materialization that stabilizes over time to produce the effect of boundary, fixity, and surface we call matter" (Butler, 1993: 9).

4. "Genealogy," as a political project of writing history, was a gray, meticulous task that demanded relentless erudition in order to find the "myriad of events through which—thanks to which, against which—they were formed" (Foucault, 1984: 81). This approach would reestablish the singularity of the event, its disruptive power, and cut across our knowledge, interrupting the continuity of the administration of our future in order to shake it and destabilize it.

5. Philippe Perrot speaks of "systems of appearances" and Daniel Roche of "culture of appearances." I treat appearances as a discourse and thus construct the notion of "régime of appearances," borrowing Foucault's conceptualization of "discursive régimes."

6. On the uniqueness of Americans' sense of liberalism as "common sense," and not as a particular vision of the self and society, I find Patricia Williams' prose very powerful. She writes: "This last summer…I drove across the country with a friend of mine who had never visited the United States before. His conclusion was that "Free is a magic word in America." At that moment we were on the highway just outside Las Vegas. He pointed to a sign on a roadside diner: "Free! All you can eat, only $7.99." The sign was more than a joke. It symbolized the degree to which much of what we call "freedom" is either contradictory or meaningless" (Williams,

1991: 29). That the irony of the sign is lost for most Americans is revealing of its common-sense statute.

7. The coalitions that support and oppose school uniforms are, however, diverse and pluralistic. For example, there might be conservatives who find it hard to support uniforms as they imply an increased intervention by the state on people's lives, and libertarians who believe that avoiding market brands will develop more freedom (cf. Bruchey, 1998; Wilkins, 1999).

8. An exception was the utopian community established by the Welsh Robert Owen (1771–1858) in New Harmony, Indiana. As in the New Lanark colony in Scotland, children had to wear uniforms made of white cotton cloth, shaped as Roman tunics, reaching to the knee in the case of boys and to the ankle in that of girls (Silver, 1969: 152). Women wore pantaloons under a long skirt in order to have freedom of movement (Pitzer, 1997: 119), in an earlier version of the Bloomer attire designed by feminists in 1850.

9. The title of his essay, published in French and Portuguese, is "The Stakhanovists of Narcissism: Body-building and Ostentatious Puritanism in American Body Culture." Alexis Stakhanov was a miner from the USSR, who reportedly extracted 102 tons of carbon in 6 hours, multiplying by 14 the normal average. Stakhanov appears in the biography of the body builder Sam Fussel as his role model. One can see how industry, ascetics with its religious bearings, and constructions of masculinity were put together in the construction of body-building.

10. Both targets of intervention have their peculiarities, and they can be traced back to older practices of regulation of clothes, as it has been said before. But there are some new practices as well. Gunilla Holm (1994), studying the portrayal of schooling in *Seventeen* magazine, stresses that it was by the end of the 1970s that what to wear in schools became an important part of the magazine. Coincidentally with what Frank (1997) describes for "coolness" in advertising and male fashion, the post-1960s period seems to be the time when contemporary images and practices related to the appearance of the body took their actual shape.

11. It could be argued that the mastery of "hipness" is not important to most people and that it is restricted to some social groups—urban middle-class males and females who aspire to social mobility and careers. But I believe that hipness is much more extended than that: it constitutes a lifestyle that

is advertised and imposed as valid for everyone, through fashion trends (The Gap being its symbol) and through advertisement (see Frank, 1997). Also, its importance might be even more significant for teenagers, due to their dependence on fashion and exterior marks for establishing a sense of identity (see, for example, *New York Times Magazine*'s article on the "tyranny of cool" for female teenagers [Le Blanc, 1999] or the PBS show *Merchants of Cool* [2000]).

12.   Joan W. Scott defines paradox in the following way: "Technically, logicians define it as an unresolvable proposition that is true and false at the same time. (*Robert's dictionary* offers as an example the liar's statement: 'I am lying.') In rhetorical and aesthetical theory, paradox is a sign of the capacity to balance complexly contrary thoughts and feelings and, by extension, poetic creativity. Ordinary usage carries traces of these formal and aesthetic meanings, but it most often employs 'paradox' to mean an opinion that challenges prevailing orthodoxy (literally, it goes against the doxa), that is contrary to received tradition. Paradox marks a position at odds with the dominant one by stressing its difference from it" (Scott, 1997: 4). She then goes on to examine the "paradoxical" position of feminism in face of democratic politics, stressing that paradox is not an opposition strategy but a constitutive element of its identity. It is this latter meaning, paradox as the ambiguity that brings together contradictory positions that I will use in this chapter.

References

Archuleta, M., Child, B., & Lomawaima, K. T. (Eds.). (2000). *Away from Home: American Indian Boarding School Experiences, 1879–2000.* Phoenix, AZ: Heard Museum.

Banner, L. W. (1983). *American Beauty.* Chicago: University of Chicago Press.

Bernuzzi de Sant'Anna, D. (1995). Apresentaçao (Introduction). In D. Bernuzzi de Sant'Anna (Ed.), *Políticas do Corpo: Elementos para uma história das práticas corporais* (Politics of the Body: Towards a History of Bodily Practices) (pp. 11–20). Sao Paulo: Estaçao Liberdade.

Birnbach, L. (Ed.). (1980). *The Official Preppy Handbook.* New York: Workman.

Bleibtreu-Ehrenberg, G. (1978). *Tabu Homosexualität: Die Geschichte eines Voruteils.* Frankfurt am Main: S. Fisher.

Bruchey, S. (1998). Out of uniform. The Board of Education Ballyhooed School Dress Code May Not Be So Smart. *Village Voice, 43* (38), 27–32.

Brunsma, D. L., & Rockquemore, K. A. (1998). Effects of Student Uniforms on Attendance, Behavior Problems, Substance Use, and Academic Achievement. *Journal of Educational Research 92,* (1), 53–62.

Butler, J. (1993). *Bodies That Matter: On the Discursive Limits of "Sex."* New York: Routledge.

Campbell, D. (1998). *National Deconstruction: Violence, Identity, and Justice in Bosnia.* Minneapolis: University of Minnesota Press.

Campbell Warner, P. (1993). The Gym Suit: Freedom at Last. In P. Cunningham & S. Voso Lab (Eds.), *Dress in American Culture* (pp. 140–179). Bowling Green, OH: Bowling Green State University Popular Press.

Corrigan, P. (1988). The Making of the Boy: Meditations on what Grammar School Did with, to, and for My Body. *Journal of Education, 170* (3), 142–161.

Courtine, J. J. (1995). Os Stakhanovistas do narcissismo: Body-bulding e puritanismo ostentatório na cultura americana do corpo (The Stakhanovists of Narcissism: Body-building and Ostenatory Puritanism in American Body Culture). In D. Bernuzzi de Sant'Anna (Ed.), *Políticas do Corpo: Elementos para uma história das práticas corporais* (Politics of the Body: Towards a History of Bodily Practices) (pp. 81–114). Sao Paulo: Estaçao Liberdade.

Cruz, B. C. (2001). *School Dress Code: A Pro/Con Issue.* Berkeley Heights, NJ: Enslow Publishers, Inc.

DaCosta, K. (1999). Exploring Urban Adolescents' Reactions to a Public High School Uniform Policy. Paper Presented to the 107th Annual Convention of the *American Psychological Association.* Boston, MA.

Davidson, A. (1990). *Blazers, Badgers and Boaters: A Pictorial History of the School Uniform.* Horndean, UK: Scope Books.

De Certeau, M. (1984). *The Practice of Everyday Life.* Berkeley: University of California Press.

Donald, J., & Rattansi, A. (Eds.). (1992). *"Race," Culture and Difference.* London: Sage/Open University Press.

Donzelot, J. (1984). *L'invention du social. Essai sur le déclin des passions politiques* (The Invention of the Social: Essay on the Decline of Political Passions). Paris: Fayard.

Donzelot, J. (1997). *The Policing of Families.* Baltimore, MD: Johns Hopkins University Press.

Duden, B. (1991). *The Woman Beneath the Skin: A Doctor's Patients in Eighteenth-Century Germany.* Cambridge, MA: Harvard University Press.

Dussel, I. (2001). *School Uniforms and the Disciplining of Appearances: Towards a Comparative History of the Regulation of Bodies in Early Modern France, Argentina, and the United States.* Ph.D. dissertation, Department of Curriculum & Instruction. Madison, WI: University of Wisconsin-Madison, 311.

Elam, S. M., Rose, L. C., & Gallup, A. M. (1996). The 28th Annual Phi Delta Kappa/Gallup Poll of the Public's Attitudes Toward the Public Schools. *Phi Delta Kappan, 78* (1), 41–59.

Flower, B. O. (1891/2000). Fashion's Slaves. In S. H. Smith & M. Dawson (Eds.), *The American 1890s: A Cultural Reader* (pp. 273–288). Durham, NC: Duke University Press.

Foucault, M. (1977). *Discipline and Punish. The Birth of the Prison.* New York: Vintage.

Foucault, M. (1980). Body/Power. In C. Gordon (Ed.), *Power/Knowledge: Selected Interviews and Other Writings, 1972–1977* (pp. 52–62). New York: Pantheon.

Foucault, M. (1984). Nietzsche, Genealogy, History. In P. Rabinow (Ed.), *The Foucault Reader* (pp. 76–100). New York: Pantheon.

Foucault, M. (1988). Technologies of the Self. In L. Martin, H. Gutman & P. Hutton (Eds.), *Technologies of the Self: A Seminar with Michel Foucault* (pp. 16–49). Amherst: University of Massachusetts Press.

Foucault, M. (1990). *The History of Sexuality, Vol. 2: The Use of Pleasure.* New York: Vintage.

Foucault, M. (1991). Governmentality. In G. Burchell, C. Gordon, & P. Miller (Eds.), *The Foucault Effect: Studies in Governmentality* (pp. 87–104). Chicago: University of Chicago Press.

Foucault, M. (1997a). Subjectivity and Truth. In S. Lotringer (Ed.), *The Politics of Truth* (pp. 171–197). New York: Semiotext(e).

Foucault, M. (1997b). What Is Critique? In S. Lotringer (Ed.), *The Politics of Truth* (pp. 23–82). New York: Semiotext(e).

Frank, T. (1997). *The Conquest of Cool: Business Culture, Counterculture, and the Rise of Hip Consumerism*. Chicago: University of Chicago Press.

Fraser, N., & Gordon, L. (1998). Contract versus Charity: Why Is There No Social Citizenship in the United States? In G. Shafir (Ed.), *The Citizenship Debates* (pp. 113–127). Minneapolis: University of Minnesota Press.

Garber, M. (1997). *Vested Interests: Cross Dressing and Cultural Anxiety*. New York: Routledge.

Gilroy, P. (2000). *Against Race: Imagining Political Culture Beyond the Color Line*. Cambridge, MA: The Belknap Press of Harvard University Press.

Gladwell, M. (2000). Listening to Khakis: What America's Most Popular Pants Tell Us about the Way Guys Think. In J. Scanlon (Ed.), *The Gender and Consumer Culture Reader* (pp. 179–191). New York: New York University Press.

Grosz, E. (1995). *Space, Time and Perversion: Essays on the Politics of Bodies*. New York: Routledge.

Grumet, M. (1988). *Bitter Milk: Women and Teaching*. Amherst: University of Massachusetts Press.

Grumet, M. (1997). Restaging the Civic Ceremonies of Schooling. *The Review of Education/Pedagogy/Cultural Studies, 19* (1), 39–54.

Harvey, J. (1995). *Men in Black*. Chicago: University of Chicago Press.

Holloman, L., La Point, V., Alleyne, S., Palmer, R., & Sanders-Phillips, K. (1996). Dress-Related Behavioral Problems and Violence in the Public School Setting: Prevention, Intervention, and Policy—A Holistic Approach. *The Journal of Negro Education 65* (3), 267–281.

Holm, G. (1994). Learning in Style: The Portrayal of Schooling in *Seventeen* Magazine. In P. Farber, E. Provenzo Jr., & G. Holm (Eds.), *Schooling in the Light of Popular Culture* (pp. 59–79). Albany: State University of New York Press.

Hunt, A. (1996). *Governance of the Consuming Passions: A History of Sumptuary Regulation*. London: Macmillan.

Hunt, A. (1999). *Governing Morals: A Social History of Moral Regulation*. Cambridge, UK: Cambridge University Press.

Hunt, A. (2000). Notes on school uniforms. Personal Communication.

Hunt, L. (1998). Freedom of Dress in Revolutionary France. In S. Melzer & K. Norberg (Eds.), *From the Royal to the Republican Body: Incorporating the Political in Seventeenth- and Eighteenth-Century France* (pp. 224–249). Berkeley: University of California Press.

Kirk, D. (1998). *Schooling Bodies: School Practice and Public Discourse, 1880–1950*. London: Leicester University Press.

Ladson-Billings, G. (1994). *The Dreamkeepers: Successful Teachers of African American Children*. San Francisco: Jossey-Bass.

Le Blanc, A. N. (1999, November 14). The Tyranny of Cool. *New York Times Magazine*, 94–96.

Lomawaima, K. T. (1994). *They Called it Prairie Light: The Story of Chilocco Indian School*. Lincoln: University of Nebraska Press.

Lopes Louro, G. (1999). Pedagogias da sexualidade. In G. Lopes Louro (Ed.), *O corpo educado: Pedagogias da Sexualidade* (pp. 7–34). Belo Horizonte: Autêntica Editora.

Luck, K. (1992). Trouble in Eden, Trouble with Eve: Women, Trousers & Utopian Socialism in Nineteenth-Century America. In J. Ash & E. Wilson (Eds.), *Chic Thrills: A Fashion Reader* (pp. 200–224). Berkeley: University of California Press.

McWilliam, E. (1996). Pedagogies, Technologies, Bodies. In E. McWilliam & P. Taylor (Eds.), *Pedagogy, Technology and the Body* (pp. 1–22). New York: Peter Lang.

McWilliam, E. (1999). *Pedagogical Pleasures*. New York: Peter Lang.

Meadmore, D., & Symes, C. (1997). Keeping Up Appearances: Uniform Policy for School Diversity? *British Journal of Educational Studies, 45* (2), 174–186.

Mrozek, D. (1983). *Sport and American Mentality, 1880–1910*. Knoxville: University of Tennessee Press.

Perrot, P. (1987). La richesse cachée: Pour une génealogie de l'austerité des apparences (Hidden Wealth: Towards a Genealogy of the Austerity of Appearances). *Communications 46*, 157–179.

Perrot, P. (1994). *Fashioning the Bourgeoisie: A History of Clothing in the Nineteenth Century*. Princeton, NJ: Princeton University Press.

Pitzer, D. (1997). The New Moral World of Robert Owen and New Harmony. In D. Pitzer (Ed.), *America's Communal Utopias* (pp. 88–134). Chapel Hill: University of North Carolina Press.

Popkewitz, T. (1998). *Struggling for the Soul: The Politics of Schooling and the Construction of the Teacher*. New York: Teachers College Press.

Popkewitz, T., & Bloch, M. (2001). Administering Freedom: A History of the Present—Rescuing the Parent to Rescue the Child for Society. In K. Hultqvist & G. Dahlberg (Eds.), *Governing the Child in the New Millennium* (pp. 85–118). London: Routledge.

Roche, D. (1989). Postface: Apparences révolutionnaires ou révolution des apparences? (Postscript: Revolutionary Appearences or Appearences of a Revolution?) In N. Pellegrin (Ed.), *Les vêtements de la liberté: Abécédaire des pratiques vestimentaires en France de 1780 à 1800* (The Clothes of

Freedom: An Alphabet of Vestimentary Practices in France From 1780 To 1800) (pp. 193–201). Aix-en-Provence, France: Ed. Alinea.

Roche, D. (1994). *The Culture of Clothing: Dress and Fashion in the Ancien Regime.* Cambridge, UK: Cambridge University Press.

Rose, N. (1990). *Governing the Soul: The Shaping of the Private Self.* London: Routledge.

Rose, N. (1999). *Powers of Freedom: Reframing Political Thought.* Cambridge, UK: Cambridge University Press.

Salvatori, M. R. (1996). *Pedagogy: Disturbing History, 1819–1929.* Pittsburgh, PA: University of Pittsburgh Press.

Schrag, F. (1999). "Why Foucault Now?" *Journal of Curriculum Studies, 31* (4), 375–383.

Scott, J. (1997). "La Querelle des Femmes" in the Late Twentieth Century. *New Left Review, 226,* 3–19.

Silver, H. (Ed.). (1969). *Robert Owen on Education.* London: Cambridge University Press.

Spivak, G. C. (1999). *A Critique of Postcolonial Reason: Toward a History of the Vanishing Present.* Cambridge, MA: Harvard University Press.

Symes, C., & Meadmore, D. (1996). Force of Habit: The School Uniform as a Body of Knowledge. In E. McWilliam & P. Taylor (Eds.), *Pedagogy, Technology, and the Body* (pp. 171–191). New York: Peter Lang.

Synott, J., & Symes, C. (1995). The Genealogy of the School: An Iconography of Badges and Mottoes. *British Journal of Sociology of Education, 16* (2), 139–153.

U.S. Department of Education. (1996). *Manual on School Uniforms.* Updates on Legislation, Budget and Activities. www.ed.gov/updates/uniforms.html

Valiente, E. (1996). Anorexia y bulimia: El corsé de la autodisciplina (Anorexia Nervosa and Bulimic Disorders: The Corset of Self-discipline). In M. Margulis (Ed.), *La juventud es más que una palabra: Ensayos sobre cultura y juventud* (Youth Is More Than Just a Word: Essays on Culture and Youth) (pp. 69–83). Buenos Aires: Editorial Biblos.

Valverde, M. (1998). *Diseases of the Will: Alcohol and the Dilemmas of Freedom.* Cambridge, UK: Cambridge University Press.

Vavrus, F. (1998). *Schooling, Fertility, and the Discourse of Development: A Study of the Kilimanjaro Region of Tanzania.* Ph.D. Dissertation, Department of Curriculum & Instruction. Madison: University of Wisconsin-Madison, 413.

Wagner, D. (1997). *The New Temperance: The American Obsession with Sin and Vice.* Boulder, CO: Westview.

White, S., & White, G. (1998). *Stylin': African American Expressive Culture from Its Beginnings to the Zoot Suit.* Ithaca, NY: Cornell University Press.

Wilkins, J. (1999). School Uniforms: The Answer to Violence in American Schools or a Cheap Educational Reform? *Humanist, 59* (2), 19–23.

Williams, P. (1991). *The Alchemy of Race & Rights: Diary of a Law Professor.* Cambridge: Harvard University Press.

Wingert, P. (1999, October 4). Uniforms Rule. *Newsweek, 134,* 72–73.

Beyond the "Academic" Curriculum: The Production and Operation of Biopower in the Less-Studied Sites of Schooling

David Kirk

Introduction

In *Schooling Bodies* (Kirk, 1998), I argue along with Philip Corrigan (1988) that bodies matter in schooling. Indeed, the regulation of children's bodies has been of such major significance, I suggest, that it may be viewed legitimately as a defining characteristic of schooling since the inauguration of compulsory mass elementary education. Many forms of school practice contribute to the process of schooling bodies, but there are some practices that have a more specific relationship to this process than others. My study explored the emergence and interrelationships between the 1880s and the 1950s of three of these practices in Australian and British education, physical training, medical inspection, and school sports. In this chapter, I will be concerned with two of these practices, physical training (in the form of drilling and exercising) and games and sports-based physical education.

I want to show how Foucault's (1984, 1980, 1977) work opened up for me insights into the historical record and permitted me to deal with some of the tensions and apparent contradictions in this record. Reading the historical record alongside Foucault's work, I was struck by Foucault's notion that there had been, over time, a shift in forms of biopower from the 'heavy, ponderous and meticulous' to 'a looser form of power over the body' (Foucault, 1980, p. 58). I wanted to explore the idea that shifts in forms of school practices aimed at schooling bodies signaled shifts more generally in biopower. Biopower for Foucault is the integration of two forms of power over life, the first centred on the material body and its capabilities, the second focused on 'the species body' (Dreyfus & Rabinow, 1982). The first form of power, an anatomo-politics of the human body, developed from the beginning of the seventeenth century, and the second, a biopolitics of population, began to emerge later, towards the end of the eighteenth century. It is towards the end of the nineteenth century that we find these two forms of biopower reaching a stage of close integration in a variety of institutions such as schools and through a range of specialised practices such as rational gymnastics. I was interested to know to what extent these shifts might be understood to represent a break from, or merely another iteration of, the disciplinary practices that constitute biopower.

The process of schooling bodies had two moments in late-nineteenth-century Australia and Britain. The first was regulative, in which population reproduction and racial hygiene were of utmost concern to physical culturists. This interest found expression in the school curriculum for the Australian and British working classes through a form of schooling bodies based on drilling and exercising or calisthenics. The second moment emerged from among the bourgeoisie in particular. Here, schooling bodies in the form of participation in games and sports was viewed as more productive than other forms of disciplinary practice on several grounds. It was viewed as a way not only of redirecting homosexual desire but also of producing new desire to be part of a team and by extension part of the collective, such as a social class or ethnic group or a nation. My argument is that by the 1950s, games and sports as a kind of 'sport-based physical education' (Kirk, 1992), had taken the place of drilling and exercising in the education of the masses. This shift took place on the basis of the perceived potential of games to 'liberate' bodies from what came to be regarded as the oppressive regime of drilling and exercising. I suggest, however, with the help of Foucault, that we can see that within this apparently liberating moment, a form of corporeal regulation is retained. Corporeal regulation may be 'looser' in games than it was in drilling and exercising, but participation in games nevertheless enmeshes bodies in matrices of power.

Disciplined Bodies:
Drilling and Exercising as Disciplinary Technology

In arranging a scheme of drill at assembly, care must be taken that no class shall interfere with the drill of the other classes in the front, rear or flank; therefore, the school will probably have to be arranged in two columns. The classes in each column must be placed at least at column distance (the depth of the class), and the movements, confined almost to this limited area, should be so arranged that, at the close, the class will be on the line of the original formation. For concerted movements, classes will require to move to the same flank; whether left or right will depend on the arrangement of the drill ground....The infants should be drilled separately, and, for the junior classes, easier movements should be substituted for the diagonal march, squad marching in file, and forming up into squad. (Education Department of Victoria, 1903, p. 31)

Writing in the *Education Gazette* of 1903, Head Teacher Mr. Carter described for his readers the way in which morning assembly was organised at Maryborough State School, a government elementary school located in the northwest of the newly founded Australian state of Victoria. He commented that once the school had been arranged in space, each class and each child in their rightful place, the timing of events could be detailed.

At 9am the first bell announced the commencement of the school day, followed by a second bell at 9.15am that signaled the beginning of assembly, which should cease ringing at precisely 9.16am, at which point, as children turned towards the flagpole and stood to attention, a first whistle was blown signaling the beginning of drill, then a second, third, fourth and fifth, each requiring specific actions on the part of children and teachers. Mr. Carter carefully set out the exact movements to be accomplished by the classes, and the order in which these should be performed. A sixth whistle, blown at precisely 9.20am, indicated that assembly was over and the children should return to the classroom. Once inside

Children march to their places, halt, and remain standing in file.
Right (left) turn.
Cover files.
First signal–"Step."
Second Signal–"In."
Caution–"Hats."
First Signal–Right incline.
(Hats are passed by numbers.)
Second Signal–First desk to second desk.
Third Signal–Second desk to third desk.
Fourth Signal–Third desk to fourth desk.
Fifth Signal–Hats hung up.
Sixth Signal–Left incline.
Double Signal–Hands folded behind.
The teacher commences the first lesson.
(Education Department of Victoria, 1903, p. 31)

And so a day in the life of Maryborough State School would begin.

Almost forty years before Mr. Carter's advice to his fellow teachers was published, Gustav Techow wrote in his 1866 volume, *Manual of*

Gymnastic Exercises for the Use of Schools and at Home, that only a 'systematic culture of the muscles' could 'counter-balance the pernicious influences of civilised life'. Techow was a leading physical culturist of the day, of Prussian extraction and resident in the colony of Victoria. What he meant by the phrase 'a systematic culture of the muscles' is outlined in intricate detail in terms of the spacing, alignment, and subdivision of groups of bodies from each other, with minute descriptions of the exercises to be performed.

Perhaps one example from Techow's manual, a description of the 'fundamental position' of the gymnast from which all exercises start and finish, may suffice to show why school administrators such as Mr. Carter, some forty years later, could seem convinced that corporeal regulation was part of the core business of schooling. According to Techow, the fundamental position of the gymnast required 'the shoulders and body' to be 'square to the front',

> the heels in line and closed, the knees straight and firmly braced back; the feet turned out so as to form an angle of sixty degrees, the arms straight down from the shoulders, the elbows turned in and close to the sides so as to bring the palms of the hands full to the front, the five fingers close together, the hips and shoulders drawn back, the chest advanced, the body straight and inclining forward so as to have its weight bearing on the fore part of the feet, the head erect without being thrown back, the eyes straight to the front. (Techow, 1866, p. xii)

It is worth taking a few moments to try to follow these instructions and to adopt Techow's fundamental position of the gymnast, just to feel what it is like to stand in this way. Then begin to imagine this as the root position of a whole range of flexion and extension exercises of the head and neck, trunk, arms, and legs. As in all other aspects of his work as a gymnast, Techow was quite precise in what he meant by the phrase 'a systematic culture of the muscles'. He meant that the development of corporeal regulation through a system of physical culture was a central, essential, indeed, constitutive, element of a well-ordered society.

In using the notion of discipline to describe power-knowledge combinations aimed at producing compliant and yet productive bodies, Foucault (1977) was able to conjoin the ideas of social regulation and knowledge. In so doing, he was able to provide a means of locating educational practices as one dimension of disciplinary technology that, together with other sets of 'little practices' within domains like the military, medicine, and so on, made up the infrastructure of disciplinary society. Foucault developed the concept of 'disciplinary technology' to explain how this detailed attention to bodies instantiated new forms of what he called biopower (Foucault, 1984, pp.140–144). Foucault suggested that as disciplinary technology diffused through a range of social practices during the eighteenth and nineteenth centuries in Western Europe, new forms of corporeal power produced new knowledge. The possible domains of knowledge to which Foucault referred, the anatomo-metaphysical (in science and philosophy) and the technico-political (in military procedures, medicine, penal policy, and education), take the body as their central concern. The aim of each of these domains of knowledge was to know the body intimately and precisely in order to meet the dual purposes of productivity and compliance, or what Foucault called 'docility-utility', which were essential qualities of the urban citizenry in capitalist democracies. The outcome of specific and substantive power-knowledge combinations was not mere subjugation (as in slavery) but, rather, controlled production (Kirk & Spiller, 1994). In *Discipline and Punish*, Foucault (1977, pp. 25–26) usefully suggests that these methods of knowing and controlling the body might be called disciplines; 'discipline produces subjected and practised bodies, docile bodies. Discipline increases the forces of the body (in economic terms of utility) and diminishes the same forces (in political terms of obedience)'. Keith Hoskins (1990) has shown that the examination, originating in the pedagogical practices of the universities of the twelfth century, was the wellspring of other forms of disciplinary technology developed to measure, record, and relate in precise detail the nature of the body and its powers. The notion of disciplinary society itself, as Foucault used this term, rests on educational practices.

The school practices that emerged during the latter part of the nineteenth century provide archetypal examples of disciplinary technology at work. As we can see in the case of Mr. Carter's practices at Maryborough State School, the school operated as a differentiating space. In the classroom, differentiation was evident in the spatial distribution of pupils, allowing close supervision by the teacher. The seating of pupils in rows also made visible a hierarchy of competence and worth depending on where pupils were positioned in relation to the teacher and to each other. Disciplinary time, the division of linear time into marked and measured units, combined with this attention to the differentiation of space to control the ebb and flow of the school day, the timetable specifying the precise periods of time to be spent on particular activities and ordering the sequence of work.

Within this form of schooling that took children's bodies as its subject matter, there emerged, then, a set of practices that had a specific and specialised relationship to schooling bodies. The core business of these drilling and exercising practices was the regulation and normalisation of bodies. As we saw in the case of Techow's work, there was concern for meticulous, detailed, and precise work on the body, not merely its surfaces but its substantive shape, size, and movement capacities. Drilling and exercising was part of a complex matrix of discursive practices that had as their special responsibility the construction of children's bodies as an integral part of the process of social regulation.

Resisting Bodies:
The Failure of Drilling and Exercising as
Micro-technologies of Power

Any system of defence which asks for drill alone or mainly drill as a duty will, whether the appeal is to man or boy, be a failure. Considered even as a preparation for impending battle, drill may quite easily be overvalued. It was not drill that gave the name Anzac its immortal meaning. It was an exceptional moral courage born of sunshine, a free life, education, a fine national pride, but above and beyond all—supreme physical fitness. (Macdonald, 1917)

Formal exercises are artificial, unrelated to life situations, and generally lacking in interest; they also completely ignore the very important influence that the emotions exert on the physical well-being of the individual. Enjoyment and enthusiasm are necessary if the exercise is to have a stimulating and beneficial effect. We therefore insist that every child has the right to play, and that this right must be restored to all children who have lost it. (Dr. Kelly, Chief Medical Officer, Victoria, 1946)

These comments by journalist Donald Macdonald, near the end of the First World War, and by medical officer Dr. Kelly, at the end of the Second World War, capture a sentiment that took hold in Australia during this time. This sentiment was that drilling and exercising was more likely to produce 'resisting' rather than productive bodies. A reading of the historical record through Foucault's work creates, however, the possibility of understanding the changes to school practices of physical training in a different way. First, the shifts in the practices of schooling children's bodies began to take place in relation to broader shifts in public discourse and forms of biopower. And second, perceptions of bodies as either resisting or productive are both functions of biopower. Through Foucault what might be differently understood about the historical record is that resistance and production do not necessarily sit in opposition. This is because what is perceived as resistance is necessarily a response to some new imperatives within a discursive field.

Drilling and exercising children's bodies with precision and obsessive attention to detail seemed appropriate within a form of public discourse concerned, in the late nineteenth and early twentieth century, with the problems of social order and economic productivity, public health and racial deterioration. From a present-day perspective, drilling and exercising children's bodies may appear to be 'heavy, ponderous, meticulous' (Foucault, 1980, p. 58) expressions of power, coercive and unpleasant ways of regulating behavior. It is true that they were explicitly motivated by policy makers' concerns to ensure that there was a sound return for the investment of public money in schooling in the form of healthy, compliant yet productive citizens. Yet Foucault's concept of docility-utility allows us to note that this process of disciplining bodies was not merely and simplistically oppressive. As he noted, discipline produces docile bodies by increasing the body's productive capacities while constraining its potential to be unruly (Foucault, 1977, pp. 25–26).

Thus, the practice of drilling and exercising might also be viewed as an optimistic expression of the idea that schools were key sites for educational interventions that could prevent much human misery before it had a chance to manifest itself, a view that was consistent with the eugenics movement in Australia prior to 1915 (Kirk & Twigg, 1994). Whatever else this project involved, schooling bodies through drilling and exercising, allied to school medical inspection, at least took a positive and hopeful view of itself at the time and of what it saw as Australia's future. But by the end of the First World War, this optimism seems already to have vanished as public discourse shifted to accommodate attempts to make sense of the turmoil that beset Australian society during the war and the peace that followed. Not only did the war expose the social class and religious divides within Australian society, which as historian Michael McKernan (1979) has noted were vividly portrayed by conflict surrounding sport, but it also contributed to a climate of bluntly authoritarian and conservative politics, industrial strife, and economic depression. It seems almost as if the optimism of the prewar era was no longer thought to be worth the effort. The net result of this profound shift in public discourse for the practices that sought to school bodies through drilling and exercising was that such practices produced bodies that were disinclined to be subjected to apparently coercive regimes of regulation.

Through this postwar turmoil, the notion that playing games and sports was a means of both civilising and 'liberating' the bodies of all children began gradually to impress itself on educational policy makers. Policy makers became steadfast in their view that participation in games could have a beneficial civilizing effect on working-class children, even though there was little evidence to support their view that games prevented wealthy young men from engaging in immoral or criminal acts (Kirk & Twigg, 1995). Since these games and sports appeared to be so unlike the 'heavy, ponderous, meticulous' drilling and exercising that was the staple form of physical activity for the majority of working-class children, it may not be too difficult to see why they might also have been viewed by commentators and policy makers such as Donald Macdonald and Dr. Kelly as liberating experiences for these children.

Shifting Ground:
From Drilling and Exercising to Games and Sport

> The development of well-supervised sport among the boys and girls attending our high schools is important, and should show effect at no distant date; for sport has come to stay in the schools. Our boys and girls will go forth physically better equipped and socially more adaptable than in the past, and should take with them ideals that will gradually place sport in the State on a very high level, and it is not unreasonable to hope that they will so influence sporting public opinion that little of the undesirable will be left in popular contests and displays. (Mr. J. H. Warren, Headmaster, 1919)

The rise of sport in mass schooling signals an important shift in the technologies of power employed to school bodies, from the meticulous and ponderous to seemingly looser forms of power over the body. This shift did not happen abruptly. Instead, it spun out over a period of at least forty years, between the end of the nineteenth century to the middle of the twentieth century, as games first took their contemporary form in the educational institutions of the privileged classes (Mangan, 1986) to their emerging prominence in schools for the masses by the end of the Second World War (Kirk, 1992; Kirk & Twigg, 1995). While the competitive team games that made up the bulk of sport in schools marked a sharp contrast to the regimentation of drilling and exercising, they nevertheless need to be viewed as a technology of power and a means of regulating bodies in space and time.

As many historians of sport, chief among them J. A. Mangan (1986, 1981), have now shown convincingly, the games ethic was a powerful educational ideology that was able to transcend otherwise obdurate and impermeable boundaries of class, race, and national identity. For some, the advocates, this robustness was merely confirmation of their belief that games and sports are a form of common currency among all civilized people. No better example of this is Baron De Coubertin's deep admiration for the sporting pursuits of the English public schools that shaped his re-invention of the Olympic Games. For others, the skeptics, the excesses of games and sports confirmed their deep-seated disdain for the merely physical side of human nature and their firm belief that it was dangerous to let the animal passions of young men and women run wild.

Between these extreme positions we can perhaps find another explanation drawing on Foucault's work on disciplinary society. This explanation, I suggest, lies in the forms of embodied public social interaction that games and sports permitted, which were in most other spheres of everyday life repressed or at least denied expression, particularly between males. Apart from the monotony, tedium, and regimentation reportedly felt by many participants in drilling and exercising, gymnastics-based forms of physical training never really became mass recreational pastimes because they were intentionally designed to restrict and delegitimize any public social interaction that involved bodily contact. In Foucault's (1977, p.143) words, these systems of movement sought to minimize 'unusable and dangerous coagulations', perhaps as much for reasons of health and hygiene, or racial integrity, as for compliance with emotional and sexual mores. The obsessive concern to regulate the movement of bodies in space and time that is so clearly evident in systems of drilling and exercising revealed public discourses that were overwhelmingly concerned with problems of social order in all its forms, including theories that children developed in fixed stages (Baker, 2001), and produced solutions in systems of segregation and differentiation. The precise, detailed, and meticulous drilling and examination of children's bodies seemed to present solutions to a perceived need for social order and productivity.

The notable exception to the tendency of Australians to avoid such regimes of the body was, of course, the immense popularity of various forms of 'keep fit' among women. 'Keep fit' activities emerged during the 1920s and 1930s and drew extensively on modifications of

DanoSwedish gymnastics, usually set to music (Matthews, 1987). In considering the apparent contrast between this example and the growing enthusiasm for games and sports among men, we can perhaps speculate that the latter was a means of compensating for the severe restrictions on legitimate bodily contact between men that might take place publicly in a fiercely heterosexual society. Women, on the other hand, may have had less need for the forms of physical contact that games playing permitted, since avenues for various legitimate bodily interactions in public were considered permissible (Fletcher, 1984; Mangan & Park, 1987; McCrone, 1988).

The idea that games playing offered an antidote to homosexual activity among boys in England's public schools was already widespread in elite school circles by the 1880s (McIntosh, 1968). Games offered a cathartic release of emotional energy that, it was held, only with grave consequences could be bottled up in adolescent males. Games seemed to offer some solutions to this problem of the illicit intermingling of male bodies, not by methods of segregation and differentiation, of keeping bodies apart, but by bringing them together in particular, socially sanctioned ways. Competitive team games are above all else public performances in which little or nothing of the performance could be hidden from the gaze of other players or spectators. Male bodies are permitted to make physical contact, but typically this contact is violent, the brutishness merely constrained but not disguised by formally agreed sets of rules. It is not difficult to see how, in the heat of the contest, this rough physical contact between males, in states of high alertness and excitement, might offer an acceptable form of behavior for male relating to male in public. In contrast to the strategy of segregating and outlawing any form of physical contact between males offered by drilling and exercising, games at least gave boys and men one avenue for socially approved bodily contact.

Liberated Bodies as Disciplined Bodies: Games and Sports as Disciplinary Technology

Games and sports came to occupy a dominant role in school and community practices after the 1940s in Australia and Britain (Kirk, 1992; Kirk & Twigg, 1995). To what extent did this emerging force in physical culture offer a means of 'liberating' bodies, as so many commentators at the time believed? Or was it merely a new form of biopower?

Certainly, against drilling and exercising, team games appear to offer quite contrasting experiences of physical activity. There are no words of command, no ranks or files and, most significant of all, in the most popular team sports such as football, cricket, netball, and so on, no need for precise attention to detail in the execution of a movement. Indeed, players are encouraged to be innovative, to employ novel combinations of movements in order to beat an opponent, and particular forms of physical contact are sanctioned. These features of games may indeed seem to suggest a 'looser form of power' over the body.

But this does not suggest that power has ceased to operate on and through bodies. As many game theorists have noted, games are rule-bound activities (Suits, 1967). It is the rules that provide games with their characteristic forms. These rules define the objective of the game, the kinds of movements players might perform, and the ways in which they can conduct themselves in relation to other players. Within the context of these rules, players and coaches devise techniques and strategies that may assist them to win the game. In most games, space is organized explicitly, from the drawing of boundary lines that contain the playing area to markings within the playing area that permit or prohibit actions or players entering or occupying the defined space. Time is also organized explicitly, from the drawing of a temporal boundary that defines when play is to begin and end to the timing of particular actions. Players who learn to play a game well submit themselves to this regulation of their bodies in time and space (MacIntyre, 1985). The repetitive work that is required to achieve some degree of mastery of the techniques of games creates movement patterns that, once learned, tend to stay with the player, and may even influence and at times interfere with other movements, such as the squash player's difficulties with a tennis shot. It is even possible, indeed not uncommon, for highly practiced techniques and strategies of movement to become dominant characteristics of a person's movements outside of the game, such as is often the case, for example, with the posture of ballet dancers.

Biopower, which Foucault saw as the integration of two forms of power over life, the first centred on the material body and its capabilities, the second focused on 'the species body', is clearly operating within these matrices of regulated space and time that constitute games. Power has not disappeared in this new form of physical activity that replaced drilling and exercising. But the manifestation of power has changed. In traditional competitive team games and many more recently developed and popular sports, a level of individualization of movement is tolerated and in some cases encouraged. Individualism would never have been possible in drilling and exercising, where the synchronized execution of movements *en masse* was at the heart of the process of schooling bodies. It is also the case that the new form of biopower involved a shift in the locus of regulation, from a predominantly though not exclusively external source to a predominantly though not exclusively internal source (Kirk, 1994). Drilling and exercising depended heavily on the instructor issuing the words of command, and on prompt obedience to these commands on the part of the child. Calisthenics required little critical interpretation on the part of the child of the instructor's commands or of the environment in which the exercises had to be performed: Obedience was everything.

The games player, in contrast, needs to be able to make sense of patterns of play and to select field or court positions and movements appropriate to the phase of the game and the multiple configurations of other players. While an instructor-centred approach remains common in contemporary school physical education, good games players need to take a level of responsibility for their own learning that was entirely absent in drilling and exercising. In this respect, the locus of corporeal regulation has shifted away from the teacher as an external and coercive source of power over the body to the learner, who, if she is participating wholeheartedly and seriously in playing the game, submits to the regime and regulates her own behavior on its terms (MacIntyre, 1985; Siedentop, 2002).

In the process, a new subject is constructed. Walkerdine (1997) suggests that practices produce 'subjects', which are in the Foucauldian sense discursive constructs rather than actual individuals. The Foucauldian subject describes the delimited range of positions a particular individual might be able to take in relation to other individuals, and the ways in which they can relate to other positions. In other words, as Walkerdine notes, the notion of a subject position not only establishes a measure for normalcy within a practice, but it also inscribes relations of power between subjects.

In addition to the individualization and internalization of biopower attendant on the rise to prominence of games and sports in school and community settings, the massification of physical recreation has led to the greater diffusion of this looser form of power over the body. As ever-increasing numbers of people have experienced sport-based school physical education in Australia and Britain since the 1950s, and as awareness of opportunities for and the desirability of physical recreational activity have become more widespread, so the newer form of biopower is diffused throughout these societies. People need not be actively involved in physical recreation to feel the effects of biopower. Even those who lead sedentary lives may have found it hard to remain unaware of and unaffected by the many campaigns advocating the desirability of an active lifestyle and may have been unable to avoid feelings of guilt and anxiety over sedentariness.

Conclusion

Many other factors may now, in this new century, be implicated in accentuating the individualization, internalization, and diffusion of biopower as public discourse is constituted by debates over globalization and technologization, environmentalism and flexible capital accumulation, healthism and visualcy (Kirk, 1994). The increasing prominence of idealized bodies in the visual media and through advertising may be prominent among these factors as may new dietary regimes and medical practices. Notwithstanding the importance of these recent developments and the need for their careful analysis, I suggest Foucault permits us to view the emergence of games in the postwar era as a new form of schooling bodies signaling, moreover, the imminent arrival of a profound shift in biopower. Competitive team games had formed a central plank in the educational ideologies of socially elite schools for both boys and girls in Australia and Britain since the late nineteenth century. However, it was their incorporation into mass school and community practices after the Second World War, and the various reconstructions of the games ethic to accommodate this change, that heralded a major shift in the form of biopower.

Against the formality of drilling and exercising, games may have seemed to offer a liberating experience for the children able to make the direct comparison or at the very least a freeing up of the processes of schooling bodies. Evidence from a wide and diverse range of sources would suggest that, against this notion, games have been unpleasant experiences for many children, particularly girls and women, which they would go to some lengths to avoid (Bryson, 1990; Deam & Gilroy, 1998). The fact that the vast majority of adults never voluntarily played any form of team game or sport when they had left school would seem to add some weight to this observation (Flintoff & Scraton, 2001; Roberts, 1996).

Yet these uncomfortable truths were scarcely ever acknowledged in the policies and practices of school and community physical educators and educational policy makers. They would, I suspect, have been quite shocked and dismayed to learn, if they were capable of facing this truth, that playing games and sports was a deeply unpopular recreation for many people. Of course, they did accept, as many others with a mission in life do, that there are some people who have yet to come to the light. But their firm conviction was that once given the opportunity to participate in sport, the masses would be won over to the joys and delights of chasing a football around a field or swatting a ball with a racquet. Instead, most of the Australian and British populations who did develop an interest in sport preferred to be entertained by watching others performing rather than by playing themselves. Just as Australians and Britons in the 1920s and 1930s avoided drilling and exercising as popular pastimes, against the hopes of educational and social policy makers, so the large numbers of contemporary Australians and Britons who refuse to participate in games and sports provide an example of the various ways in which individuals can occupy and be positioned within discursive fields.

There are a number of features of games that make them potentially hazardous activities from a participant's point of view. Key among these is that games can be violent, even when this physical aggression is contained within the rules, and injury is always a possibility. Games involve competing, a requirement that can be extremely stressful for some children. And perhaps even more important still is that games can be a humiliating experience, since they demand a public demonstration of physical competence (or incompetence) that, in turn, exposes one's body to the critical scrutiny of others. In fact, it is these features of games playing, the very features that most recommended it to educationists in the first place, that render this activity a potentially hazardous one for so many participants. Some physical educators have recognized this and have attempted through various means to humanize games. Moreover, feminist and pro-feminist physical educators have recognized the overtly masculinist nature of games and their complicity in reproducing heterosexuality among boys and men (Messner & Sabo, 1990). The extent to which these women and men can transform games in ways that make them more attractive to more children and adults and provide a means of challenging rather than reinforcing compulsory heterosexuality remains to be seen.

Through the lens of Foucault's work on biopower and disciplinary society, we can understand the process of schooling bodies to be layered, complex, and contradictory. A necessary constituent of the process of schooling bodies is both their empowerment and their regulation; empowerment in the sense that practices such as physical education provide opportunities for young people to develop and realise particular movement capacities of their bodies; regulation in the sense that the development of some forms of movement expertise inevitably delimits other movement capacities young people might develop. By bringing school practices under detailed examination through Foucault's work, one might begin to address such policy dilemmas. For example, one can seek out the connections between these school practices and other related practices within the wider public domain, take seriously the effects of these practices on young people, and rethink the means by which teachers, policy makers, and the general public are educated about the whole range of consequences of school practices, in particular those physical practices that have been by and large ignored or misunderstood as a component of an otherwise academic school curriculum.

References

Baker, B. (2001). *In perpetual motion: Theories of power, educational history, and the child.* New York: Peter Lang.

Bryson, L. (1990). Challenges to make hegemony in sport. In Messner, M. A. & Sabo, D. F. (Eds.), *Sport, men and the gender order: Critical feminist perspectives.* Champaign, IL: Human Kinetics, pp. 173–184.

Corrigan, P. (1988). The making of the boy: Meditations on what grammar school did with, to, and for my body. *Journal of Education,* 170 (3), 142–61.

Deam, R. & Gilroy, S. (1998). Physical activity, life-long learning and empowerment: Situating sport in women's leisure. *Sport, Education and Society,* 3(1), 89–104.

Dreyfus, H. & Rabinow, P. (1982). *Michel Foucault: Beyond structuralism and Hermeneutics.* Brighton, UK: Harvester.

Education Department of Victoria. (1903). *Education Gazette and Teachers' Aid.* Melbourne, Australia: Government Printer, p. 31.

Fletcher, S. (1984). *Women first: The female tradition in English physical education, 1880–1980.* London: Althone.

Flintoff, A. & Scraton, S. (2001). Stepping into active leisure? Young women's perceptions of active lifestyles and their experiences of school physical education. *Sport, Education and Society,* 6 (1), 5–22.

Foucault, M. (1977). *Discipline and punish.* New York: Allen and Unwin.

Foucault, M. (1980). *Power/knowledge: Selected interviews and other writings.* Brighton, UK: Harvester, Trans. C. Gordon.

Foucault, M. (1984). *The history of sexuality: An introduction.* Harmondsworth, UK: Penguin.

Hoskins, K. (1990). Foucault under examination: The crypto-educationalist unmasked. In Ball, S. J. (Ed.), *Foucault and education.* London: Routledge, pp. 29–56.

Kirk, D. (1992). *Defining physical education: The social construction of a school subject in postwar Britain.* London: Falmer.

Kirk, D. (1994). Physical education and regimes of the body. *Australian and New Zealand Journal of Sociology,* 30 (2), 165–77.

Kirk, D. (1998). *Schooling bodies: School practice and public discourse, 1880–1950.* London: Leicester University Press.

Kirk, D. & Spiller, B. (1994). Schooling the docile body: Physical education, schooling and the myth of oppression. *Australian Journal of Education,* 38 (1), 80–97.

Kirk, D. & Twigg, K. (1994). Regulating the Australian body: Eugenics, anthropometrics and school medical inspection in Victoria, 1909–1915. *History of Education Review,* 23 (1), 19–37.

Kirk, D. & Twigg, K. (1995). Civilising Australian bodies: The games ethic and sport in Australian government schools, 1904–1945. *Sporting Traditions: Journal of the Australian Society for Sport History,* 11 (2), 3–34.

Macdonald, D. (1917). *In the Argus,* 7 April.

Mangan, J. A. (1981). *Athleticism in the Victorian and Edwardian public school.* Cambridge: Cambridge University Press.

Mangan, J. A. (1986). *The games ethic and imperialism: Aspects of the diffusion of an ideal.* Harmondsworth, UK: Viking.

Mangan, J. A. & Park, R. J. (Eds.). (1987). *From 'fair sex' to feminism: Sport and the socialisation of women in the industrial and post-industrial eras.* London: Frank Cass.

Matthews, J. J. (1987). Building the body beautiful. *Australian Feminist Studies,* 5 (Summer), 17–34.

McCrone, K. (1988). *Physical education and the emancipation of English women.* London: Routledge.

McKernan, M. (1979). Sport, war and society: Australia, 1914–1918. In Cashman, R. & McKernan, M. (Eds.), *Sport in History.* St. Lucia: University of Queensland Press, pp. 1–20.

McIntosh, P. C. (1968). *PE in England since 1800.* London: Bell.

MacIntyre, A. (1985). *After virtue: A study in moral theory* (2nd. ed.). London: Duckworth.

Messner, M. A. & Sabo, D. F. (Eds.). (1990). *Sport, men and the gender order: Critical feminist perspectives.* Champaign, IL: Human Kinetics.

Roberts, K. (1996). Young people, schools, sport and government policies. *Sport, Education and Society,* 1 (1), 47–58.

Siedentop, D. (2002). Junior sport and the evolution of sport cultures. *Journal of Teaching in Physical Education,* 21(4), 392–401.

Suits, B. (1967). What is a game? *Journal of Philosophy of Science,* 22, 148–156.

Techow, G. (1866). *Manual of gymnastic exercises for the use of schools and at home.* Melbourne, Australia: George Robertson, p. xii.

Walkerdine, V. (1997). Redefining the subject in situated cognition theory. In Kirshner, D. & Whitson, J. A. (Eds.), *Situated cognition: Social, semiotic and psychological perspectives.* Mahwah, NJ: Lawrence Erlbaum Associates.

Warren, Mr. J. H. (1919). Headmaster of the Horsham High School, in *Victorian Education Department Education Gazette and Teachers' Aid,* August, p. 128.

What Does It Mean to Feel Like Teaching?

Erica McWilliam

There is a narrative about teacher motivation that is cosily familiar to many of us in the teaching profession. I want to begin by presenting an outline of this narrative in order to question its common sense as a story about what and how teachers feel. In doing so, I am seeking to open up a space for thinking otherwise about familiar stories of teacher desire, that is, to understand what we might not be able to say about "the motivation to teach." The narrative that follows is one that I have written for the purpose of telling a recognizable story, not my own story.

A Familiar Story

Teachers generally enter a program of teacher preparation for three reasons. Many are motivated by an inspiring or caring teacher, and this includes all those (and there are many) who "enlist" after seeing popular feature films like *Dead Poet's Society* or *Stand and Deliver*. Others are motivated by their desire to redress some of the "wrongs" that were inflicted on them as students. In her account of "the visceral pleasures" of teaching (Blount, 1998), American schoolteacher Jackie Blount[1] (whose work I shall engage with from time to time throughout this chapter) locates herself among this second group, saying that she knew she would "defy the rule-bound models of [her] past" (p. 85) when she became a teacher. A third group "end up" in teaching by default or by accident—they do not have the grades they needed to enter one of the more prestigious professions, so they settle for teaching. At least this means a secure job with relatively short working hours.

During their training, preservice teachers find the real experiences of school practicum much more valuable than the theory they are given at university or college. If they are lucky enough to work with an inspiring teacher during the practicum, they may feel even more motivated to teach, drawing on that teacher as a role model in crafting their own teaching style. As the course progresses, they become increasingly aware of their inadequacies as professionals, but they are reassured that they are not expected, as beginning teachers, to know how to do everything. They get a feeling for their special strengths as teachers. They spend some time sharing their teaching stories with friends—the good, the bad, and the ugly.

It is as beginning teachers that individuals experience the crunch of "reality shock" (Corcoran, 1981). Despite the years of professional preparation, it seems that nothing has adequately prepared beginning teachers for the sights, smells, sounds, and struggles of the daily work of teaching. It is at this point that they are likely to desert any romantic idealism that is left over from college days and work instead on the custodial management of the children in their care (Fullan, 1982). Some teachers settle for this custodial role long-term. Others like Jackie Blount struggle on to find a more meaningful role as a teacher. They reject the managerial persona that attaches to new systems of accountability and control in favor of working on a better relationship with the children they teach. They are assisted in this goal by educational writers like Nel Noddings (1984), who know that a caring relationship is the basis of all good teaching.

Armed with this understanding, teachers come to know themselves and their students in more ethical and educationally appropriate ways. It is then that they experience the true satisfaction of teaching. They may even feel that they want to spend more time reading theories of teaching and learning, possibly even enrolling in a postgraduate university course for this purpose. Fortunately, their teacher colleagues are there to remind them not to become "just another university professor depicting teachers as compliant non-intellectuals in need of experts to tell them how to do their work" (Blount, 1998, p. 105).

Making the Familiar Strange

Of all the issues that might be taken up to "denaturalize" the above story, the way in which the story insists on constructing "discipline" and "desire" as oppositional ideas is the most compelling to me as a poststructuralist writer in education. Whether as resentment directed against "rule-bound models" or as managerialism spelling the end of romantic idealism or as relational caring as the antidote to managerialism, the desire to teach well is framed throughout as possible only when discipline is removed. I want to move to undo this discursive opposition between desire and discipline and thus to challenge the familiar logic that underpins this story. To do so I make a departure from traditional writing about teaching and teacher education in that I do not draw on the psychological literature about motivation for my understanding of what it means to feel like doing something. My exploration also stands outside Lacanian psychoanalytic understanding of the nature of desire and the desiring subject. It draws instead on the philosophical work of Michel Foucault (1980, 1985) and the literary criticism of Peter Cryle (1994, 1997, 2001), both of whom turn our attention to ways in which desire is produced *through* discipline rather than *in opposition to* discipline. They use the term "discipline" both in the sense of punishment or coercion and also the skills and knowledges (including "disciplines" in the academic sense) that must be mastered in order to achieve success in a particular field of human activity (Danaher, Schirato, & Webb, 2000). Where power is linked to knowledge in this way and where "power-knowledge" in turn is understood as productive of desire, it becomes possible to tell a very different story about the desire to teach!

Desire, Pleasure, Truth

"Desire" is a term that rarely appears in educational research. Where it does occur, it is most likely to be in relation to student-related concerns about sexual harassment (O'Brien, 2000; McWilliam, 1995, 1996) rather than a teacher's desire to teach. As desire for the student, teacher desire is a risk management issue, one that renders teacher desire suspect, a potential problem for all students because the pedagogic economy is one in which the student is "prey" (Deutscher, 1994). The term "motivation" is preferred because it sidesteps *eros* in its framing of the desire to teach and is thus a less problematic term than "desire" for describing those feelings that, when properly nourished, lead to "satisfaction," "psychic rewards," or "psychological fulfillment" (see Woods, 1985). So educational research talks about what *motivates* young people to enter the teaching service rather than speak of their desire. Any talk of "teacher desire" as both erotic and productive is inevitably followed by much throat-clearing, which includes acknowledgment (early and often) of the repressive effects of *eros* in the classroom (Barreca & Morse, 1997). Put simply, the term "motivation" has come to mean "desire without the sex."

Michel Foucault has other reasons for avoiding the term "desire." He says:

That term [desire] has been used as a tool...a calibration in terms of normality. Tell me what your desire is and I will tell you who you are, whether you are normal or not and then I can qualify or disqualify your desire. (Foucault, cited in Macey, 1994, p. 363)

Instead, Foucault's preference is for the term *pleasure*. This is because he understands pleasure to be "almost devoid of meaning," given that there is "no pathology of pleasure"—it is "a notion that is neither ascribed nor ascribable" (p. 363). This very fact may well account for the absence of the term from educational texts—it comes as too much of a wild card in the academic pack, a notion whose boundaries have yet to be policed by academic disciplinary discourses in general and are certainly not amenable to policing within the epistemes of social scientific research.

Both Michel Foucault and Peter Cryle focus on ancient and other premodern social practices to show how pleasures were trained and sustained in a particular time and place. Moreover, they both point to the importance of the idea that pleasure (sexual or otherwise) is not increased by taking it beyond what is "proper." They show how knowing about the right pleasure comes through knowledge about the rules for correct ethical conduct[2] and then disciplining the body to perform according to such rules. These rules are made available in disciplinary discourses that organize "Truth" in any given moment of historical time.

The work of Foucault that is of most relevance here is *The Use of Pleasure: The History of Sexuality, Volume 2* (1985). In it, Foucault attempts to determine how human beings in the West have come to recognize themselves as individual "subject[s] of desire" (p. 6). That is, Foucault attempts to analyze the ways that individuals "were led to focus their attention on themselves, to decipher, recognize, and acknowledge themselves" as sexually desiring persons (p. 5). Foucault turns to ancient Greece to examine notions of sexuality and desire that preceded a Christian tradition of thinking about sexuality and "the flesh," arguing that "one could not very well analyze the formation and development of the experience of sexuality from the eighteenth century onward without undertaking...[such] a genealogy" (p. 5).

In describing his project as a "genealogy" rather than a "history," Foucault indicates that this is an analysis of "games of truth" rather than Truth itself (p. 6). This means that he does not understand human experience as naturally occurring, or as occurring through rational or true fields of learning. Instead, experience is historically constituted out of games of truth and error. This is how we come to believe that "something...can and must be thought" (p. 7). His interest in Greek and Greco-Roman culture is in "how, why and in what form sexuality was constituted as a moral domain," and why such a particular ethical concern "was so persistent despite its varying forms and intensity" (p. 10). In speaking of truth and error as a game, Foucault, like Francois Lyotard (1979), refuses any discursive opposition between "games" and "seriousness," a move that reflects his refusal to see pleasure (of the game) sitting outside the (serious) rules for playing the game. The pleasure of the game is optimal when the game is properly understood and played according to the rules of its conduct.

The method by which Foucault undertakes his project is to inquire into the discursive construction of what he terms "techniques of the self" (Foucault, 1985, p. 11). This does not mean analyses of behaviors or ideas or sociology or ideology but rather of what he terms *problematizations* (the ways "being offers itself to be, necessarily, thought") and the practices on the basis of which such problematizations are formed (p. 11). So Foucault takes as the object of his analysis the manner in which sexual activity is problematized in texts written by philosophers and doctors, focusing on what he terms "prescriptive texts," that is, "texts which elaborate rules, opinions and advice as to how to behave as one should" (p. 12). His understanding is that such texts serve as devices that enable individuals to "question their own conduct, to watch over and give shape to it, and to shape themselves as ethical subjects" (p. 13). In some senses we could see the scholarly disciplines of educational psychology and sociology doing similar work in providing teachers with scripts for becoming "properly professional" in their pedagogical work.

Pleasure as a Disciplinary Product

To analyze pleasure as a product of moral training as Foucault does is clearly a departure from either the idea that pleasure occurs as a spontaneous and sudden outpouring of feeling or the idea that individuals need to be free of constraint, of bodily discipline, to maximize their own gratification. Instead, Foucault demonstrates that texts written by Plato, Aristotle, and others serve as important ways of training a population in knowledge about the limits beyond which certain attitudes or acts may be considered excessive. This knowledge is applied by individuals to themselves (Foucault, 1985, pp. 45–46). It is not therefore a process of overt or "top-down" coercion but one of training the individual in the sort of disciplined relationship with the self that is necessary to the achievement of "proper" pleasure (p. 63). "Proper" pleasure is not achievable by "going for broke," that is, through excessive or immoderate behavior—but in the very exercise of moderation (p. 65). The ethical individual, as a subject of certain discourses of training about how pleasure ought to be taken "properly," "deliberately chooses reasonable principles of action that he is capable of following and applying them" (p. 64). To deliberately choose bad principles and surrender to the weakest desires, thus taking pleasure in "bad conduct," is to produce oneself as a "shameless and incorrigible" individual (p. 65).

Like Foucault, Peter Cryle's work contributes to the undoing of modernist assumptions about a necessary discursive opposition of pleasure and discipline. In *Geometry in the Boudoir: Configurations of a French Erotic Narrative* (1994) and subsequent work (e.g., Cryle, 1995, 2001), he explains that notions of pleasure and the ways of achieving it were, until relatively recently, understood to have to be taught. Classical or premodern understandings of eroticism were learned as a form of postural modeling, an idea that was only supplanted in the late eighteenth century by more modern notions of eroticism as "inner fire" (Cryle, 1995, p. 5). Pre-modern erotica, Cryle explains, had little to do with the sex act, desire, or climax (1994, p. viii). The *Kama Sutra*, for example, is not about sexual spontaneity; rather it is a highly didactic and relentlessly prescriptive text about adopting precise bodily postures. Learning about the pleasure of the erotic, then, was not about "getting in touch with one's inner feelings," or about getting away from constraints through a more fertile imagination or an ability to fantasize, but about adopting the right pose for learning to feel proper pleasure. In adopting a certain posture, the individual would come to feel like adopting it—"feeling like doing it" was not a precursor to doing it (as is true of modernist accounts of desire) but a product of the highly disciplined postural act itself.

Disciplinary Desire and the Teacher

The idea of teaching "properly" is one that makes trouble for the idea that our prescriptions of good teaching are the result of the progress we have made in understanding pedagogical work as a complex and multifaceted endeavor. The terms "effective teaching" or "excellence in teaching" or "quality teaching," as sociohistorical inventions of our times, are much more familiar to us than "proper teaching," which sounds at once too prescriptive, puritanical, and/or mundane to be worthy of investigation. In Jackie Blount's (1998) account of her teaching, she describes herself as making a breakthrough when she finds a script for resisting "reliance on fixed rules and eternal principles of right and wrong" (p. 104). She comes to see that a "proper" teacher is a "caring educator" (p. 104), one whose caring, in Nel Noddings' terms, is "grounded in relatedness, receptivity, and responsiveness, find[ing] expression in individual relationships where each person strives to meet the other morally" (p. 103). Where once she saw herself engaging in "the delicate daily navigation of the tricky terrain between authoritarianism and permissiveness" (p. 103), Jackie comes to invest in "caring relationships" (p. 104) with her students, which "increase...levels of mutual trust" leading to "the emergence of both planned and spontaneous democratic processes" through which it is possible to "work out agreeable improvements together" (p. 105).

It is clear that Jackie experiences more pleasure/satisfaction as a teacher when she feels that she is doing her job "properly," that is, when she is working more democratically and more collaboratively with her students, whether or not the "institutional structure" (p. 104) of the school is entirely supportive of her conduct; although it is clear that, when the school principal appears to endorse her belief, her satisfaction is increased. Put another way, the conviction shared by Jackie Blount and Nel Noddings that a good teacher is one who has a caring relationship with a student is an idea that is crucial to the discursive organization of the "good (ethical) teacher" at this point in time. Teaching pleasure is optimized where the possibility of caring relationships is optimized, and pleasure is diminished when pedagogical work cannot be thought of as "caring" or "relational" work. It now goes without saying for many, indeed most, educators that a teacher teaches best and a student learns best when they both engage with each other in a caring relationship.

Thinking Otherwise

Proper teaching has not always been constructed around notions of mutual caring as it is understood today. Indeed, it is interesting to note how far the notion of the proper teacher as a "relational caregiver" is from the idea of the proper teacher in ancient times. The measure of virtue (i.e., proper teaching) for the sophists of ancient Greece was the ability of the teacher to overcome all physical and intellectual passions, including the "distraction" of student relationships, by focusing entirely on the pursuit of wisdom and virtue for its own sake. Untersteiner cites

Georgias as one Sophist who apparently achieved this state in his 109 years:

> [Georgias] explained his longevity as being due to "never having done anything for the sake of giving pleasure to another"...he did not allow himself to be deflected by anything which might injure his health...but also refused to be troubled by other people's praise or blame or by the intervention of a fact which might disturb his thought....His moral character and his genius attracted to him such affection that he was followed by many disciples. (p. 94)

The idea that the moral fitness[3] of a teacher is bound up with "never having done anything for the sake of giving pleasure to others" looks to the "progressive teacher"[4] more like selfishness than ethical high ground. "Indifference at its best" was the goal here; the teacher was not to be lured away from "proper teaching" by responding to student needs. That a teacher teaches best when *not* distracted by thinking about the relational needs of any individual student or group of students is the antithesis of what is held by Jackie Blount and others to be a proper enactment of an ethic of care and of pedagogical responsibility. My argument here is not that Jackie is wrong to privilege the caring relationship nor that the Sophists were wrong to value "indifference at its best." Rather it is to note that neither Jackie nor Georgias are free to decide what makes for proper teaching. What these good teachers share is that they are constituted as proper or ethical through the power-knowledge available to them, and they experience their satisfactions as the precise products of such power-knowledge. This way of understanding the desire to teach is a departure from the idea of a continuous history of improvement within teaching. Interest is on how teaching is discursively organized from era to era and place to place rather than on a breakthrough moment in which a teacher "sees the light."

In moving to practices that are more focused on caring relationships with her students, Jackie shares with many other progressive educators a view that the purpose of education is "to save the child for (democratic) society and to rescue the society through the child" (Popkewitz, 1997, p. 91). Under this logic, it follows that "proper" teachers need to understand themselves as "redemptive agent[s] in the name of progress and...populism" (p. 91). By implication, teacher education in all its forms becomes "a redemptive project to save the teacher who rescues the child" (p. 97).

The idea that the student/child is in need of saving and that the teacher is the one to do it is not new. Nor is the idea of the progressive teacher as liberator of the oppressed. Such a progressive vision of teaching parallels that found in many nineteenth-century novels, where teaching (as preaching) apparently leads to "the reversal of the movement toward corruption and to the eventual redemption of...an initially corrupting force" (De Jean, 1982, p. 100). As evangelist, the teacher can feel both anguish for the badly behaving child as a lost soul, and elation at the transformative moment when she detects the first positive signs of a soul saved. Like evangelists, however, redemptive teachers must remain vigilant at all times. Ideally, they should have a personal relationship with every individual student, but the boundaries of that personal relationship must be constantly policed by the individual-as-teacher. This is so because the power differential that is presumed to exist in any pedagogical relationship privileges the teacher over the student.

Given the extent to which, as indicated earlier, the teacher/student relationship is also believed to be an economy in which the student is prey, good teachers need to be carefully trained in how to have proper relationships with their students. Teachers may come to express this knowledge as a matter of personal conscience, or what feels right, or what they know to be right from professional ethics, or simply because of their "natural" understanding as mature and caring human beings. Nevertheless, however this professional understanding is arrived at, the proper pleasure that attends this understanding is likewise a product of moral and ethical training. That is, we are trained as teachers not simply to engage with students in a particular way but *to feel like doing so*. Just as many teachers in past times felt like hitting kids because they knew it was right to do so (to beat the devil out of them), so we, understanding that kids are not devils but "angelic being[s], overflowing with goodness and an impeccable moral sense of rightness" (Symes & Sheahan-Bright, 1998, p. 3), don't hit, nor do we feel like hitting.

From Emancipation to Irony[5]

To probe the ways in which "proper teaching" is constituted differently from one time and place to another is to "'re-describe' practice" (Rorty, 1989) as part of the larger game of truth and falsity we could call pedagogical power-knowledge. Richard Rorty terms this sort of thinking "ironic scholarship," in that it is a project that refuses a final vocabulary of explanation (Rorty, 1989, p. 73). Thinking ironically does not tidy up nor provide a vision splendid, nor condemn, nor redeem. Rather, it works in the same way that blasphemy does to keep the faith in a liberal humanist order of things. As Haraway (1991) puts it, irony functions in a liberal social order in the same way that blasphemy functions in relation to religion:

> Blasphemy protects one from the moral majority within, while still insisting on the need for community. Blasphemy is not apostasy. Irony is about contradictions that do not resolve into larger wholes, even dialectically, about the tension of holding incompatible things together because both or all are necessary and true. (p. 149)

Ironic texts do not produce formulae and visions and truths for making ourselves into "quality professionals," or "relational caregivers," or "excellent teachers" or "reflective practitioners" or "facilitators of learning" or "transformative intellectuals" or "lifelong learners." The sort of knowledge produced by ironic research is instead "self-referential knowledge" (Baert, 1998), that is, knowledge that cuts across traditional consensus to create distance from our most familiar categories, treating them as contingent and strange. Used in this way, self-referential knowledge is not specifically knowledge that informs one about oneself (e.g., a caring educator) but rather asks about those taken-for-granted knowledges through which we produce our selves as works of art (e.g., as "relational caregiver").

For some, insisting on the historical contingency of all modes of human conduct seems to put us on a very slippery slide into a relativism that refuses any moral center and thus any position from which to advocate one set of pedagogical values or strategies. The concept of pedagogy as progress—the idea that we know better now—is more seductive. We are no longer trapped by false assumptions and practices born of ignorance, well-intentioned though they might have been. We like being the heroes of the progress story, the enlightened ones who, when confronted by a recalcitrant student, know to reach for the evaluation instrument rather than the dunce's hat. We know that it is wrong to use the sarcastic or derogatory expressions that once peppered teachers' talk. We know not to use literary or Latin quotes to intimidate and alienate. Whatever our grasp of Shakespeare or Latin, we know that such practices are demeaning and unethical, that they lower student self-esteem, and that they have a detrimental effect on student learning. So *we don't use them and we don't feel like using them*, whether or not these language practices are familiar to us.

Pleasure *as* Discipline

Not all teachers accept the naturalness of their practices without question. Some re-interrogate their teaching by rethinking the naturalness of the pleasure/disciplinary dichotomy through reflecting on events in their classrooms. In his compellingly titled paper "Kama Sutra and Curriculum" (1997), Peter Cryle engages in such a rethinking. He reflects on a pedagogical "mistake" he made in refusing to undo the discursive opposition of discipline and pleasure (i.e., discipline as denial of or antithetical to pleasure) that is so well embedded in antimanagerial accounts of good pedagogy, including that of Jackie Blount. Cryle describes two attempts he made to teach a lesson in French language skills to undergraduate students, a lesson in which a relaxation exercise was the first activity. The first time he taught the lesson, Cryle "began...with a tackily permissive preamble...You can lie on the floor if you want to, I said...or you can just sit comfortably in your chair, or you can stretch across a couple of chairs etc...."(p. 3). The result was that "nobody quite knew what to do in order to be properly relaxed—or properly prepared for relaxation" (p. 3). Cryle understands that he was at fault "although the fault wasn't narrowly personal or psychological" (p. 4). It was, as he came to see it, "the fault of a certain discourse, and a certain way of thinking about teaching" (p. 4). He describes himself as "baulk[ing]...at   the   pedagogical   practices   involved   [for relaxing]...because they disturbed my notion of the liberal teacher inviting students to forms of self-relaxation" (p. 4). There was a discipline involved for his students here, just as much as if he were asking them to sit up straight and watch him. The next year he said, "When we do this, we find it is best to lie on the floor. Lie on the floor" (p. 4).

What Cryle draws attention to here is the extent to which bodies are subjected to, and shaped by, disciplinary discourses in pedagogical events, including those very moments when we are being invited to cast aside our inhibitions. He goes on to say:

> The basis of my teaching mistake...[was] the refusal to discipline or train my students too closely, for fear that their learning would then be aligned against pleasure and spontaneity. I might have faltered less if I had been able to undo this dichotomy by thinking of desire and pleasure as being themselves the subjects of discipline. (p. 6)

Peter Cryle is not the only scholar who reminds us of the need to undo the pleasure/discipline dichotomy. Jane Gallop (1986) also breaks with humanistic accounts of the good teacher as "anti-discipline" or "anti-authority" when she observes cryptically:

> School presents us with a world of numbers: grades, curves, credit hours, course numbers, class hours, and room numbers. I suppose not all teachers experience as I do a diffuse yet unmistakable pleasure when calculating grades at the end of the term. (p. 128).

Gallop's story about her pleasure in grading makes it clear that, for her, certain pleasures arise *through* discipline. This is an unusual and troubling story about teacher desire, one that is unavailable to be told—to be thought—through the mainstream texts on "effective" teaching.

Making Demands

The above examples suggest that good teachers conduct themselves according to prescriptions of good teaching that are available to be thought—and felt. To speak of proper feelings is to draw attention to the fact that probities around our desires and our pleasures are not natural but trained. This fact is rendered invisible by the very appearance of good pedagogy as "natural." It is natural that a good teacher should care about the student. It is natural that a teacher should want to get to know the student. It is easy to forget, as Peter Cryle (1997) points out, that "naturalness" is itself a modern construct, a means of organizing language in such a way that certain ideas about what is proper come to be thinkable. So how we come to feel like teaching, how we come to desire the particular pleasures it affords, can be understood as a domain that is governed rather than spontaneous. The pleasures we have as good teachers are not unlimited because they are themselves the products of disciplinary discourses. We maximize our pedagogical pleasures by working within the discursive rules of "proper teaching." If those rules point to a caring relationship as the right way to teach, then this is what we feel like having.

Jackie Blount is not wrong or hoodwinked or naïve. She feels more like teaching when she can have more caring relationships with her students, and she feels less like teaching when she feels "constrained" by management processes. The point that needs to be made here is that *what enables also constrains*. Caring relationships do not sit outside power-knowledge; they make their own demands. That is, they constitute certain pedagogical identities with their own preferred forms of engagement, forms that are made available through disciplinary discourses for the shaping of conduct. So caring relationships are not innocent—they *require* something from teachers and also from students. Students must be trained (morally) to desire caring just as teachers need to learn to feel like caring. They need to know the sorts of bodily conduct (thoughts, feelings, attitudes, language, behaviors) that are necessary to constituting themselves as properly relational and caring.

The desire to teach, or teacher motivation, or the pleasure of teaching, is, as Foucault reminds us, not a spontaneous inner feeling (though it is often held or felt to be so), but a product of training individuals in particular ways of thinking, speaking, and doing as a "proper" teacher. The idea that it is right to be a student-centered and caring teacher rather than a self-centered teacher is one that, while strongly held at this point in time, is as contingent as any other idea about good teaching in any other historical time. Thus, there can be no safety in pedagogical work—no pure place from which to do the labor of teaching and feel the feelings of the good (emancipatory) teacher. Good teachers will one day feel differently about progressive teaching, just as they have done in other times and places. However they conduct themselves, whatever they feel and think and say, they will be drawing on power-knowledge to discipline themselves and others—it is impossible to do otherwise.

Endnotes

1. Jackie Blount is an American high school teacher who provides, in a published account of her teaching (see Blount, 1998), her reflections on being a former public school teacher in the southern United States. She is now working as a professor. Her reflection is useful because it is constituted in ways that are familiar to many who work in teacher education and in teaching.

2. Ethical conduct covers the widest spectrum of human activity. It means deliberately conducting oneself as one should in every area of activity, not simply in the area of sexuality or human relations. This is more than avoidance of criminal acts, it is a deep commitment to the highest ideals of human conduct as understood and enacted in a particular historical time and place.

3. Moral fitness here means the extent to which the teacher possesses the right (i.e., approved) attitudes to students and to the work of educating them. Persons who believed in severely punishing children to "help them learn," for example, would no longer be regarded as "morally fit" to teach, as they were in former times and places.

4. By "progressive" teachers, I mean those teachers who seek to understand and utilize the very best methods of teaching as defined by the norms and standards of their time and place.

5. Irony here is not to be confused with sarcasm or satire. While it can be fun to work ironically, and while sarcasm and/or satire may even be involved at times, there is a deeper level of significance. Irony is insistence upon the doubleness of propositions about (educational) truth. Thus, ironic research allows educators to examine the enabling and constraining of human conduct as simultaneous occurrences rather than as an "either-or" binary. Irony is therefore not useful for those seeking a quick solution to a problem or a breakthrough moment for the researcher. But it is very useful for asking questions about how educational problems are framed.

References

Baert, P. (1998). Foucault's history of the present as self-referential knowledge acquisition. *Philosophy and Social Criticism*, 24 (6), 111–126.

Barreca, R., and Morse, D. D. (Eds.). (1997). *The erotics of instruction*. Hanover, NH: University Press of New England.

Blount, J. (1998). The visceral pleasures of the well-worn rut: Internal barriers to changing the social relations of American classrooms. In R. Butchart and B. McEwan (Eds.), *Classroom Discipline in American Schools: The Democratic and Emancipatory Potential of Public Education*. Albany, NY: State University of New York Press, pp. 85–107.

Corcoran, E. (1981). Transition shock: The beginning teacher's paradox, *Journal of Teacher Education*, 32 (3), 19–23.

Cryle, P. (1994). *Geometry in the boudoir: Configurations of a French erotic narrative*. Ithaca, NY: Cornell University Press.

Cryle, P. (1995). Marble and fire: The thematic metamorphosis of sculpture in French erotic literature. Invited lecture, School of Language and Linguistics, University of Melbourne, Australia.

Cryle, P. (1997). Kama Sutra and curriculum. Invited paper presented at the Pedagogy and the Body Conference, Queensland University of Technology, Brisbane, Australia, 29 November.

Cryle, P. (2001). *The telling of the act: Sexuality as narrative in eighteenth- and nineteenth-century France*. London: Associated University Presses.

Danaher, G., Schirato, T., and Webb, J. (2000). *Understanding Foucault*. St Leonards, Australia: Allen and Unwin.

De Jean, J. (1982). La nouvelle Heloise, or the case for pedagogical deviation. *Yale French Studies*, Special issue, The pedagogical imperative: Teaching as a literary genre, 63: 98–116.

Deutscher, P. (1994). Eating the words of the other: Ethics, erotics and cannibalism in pedagogy. In J. J. Matthews (Ed.), *Jane Gallop seminar papers, proceedings of the Jane Gallop seminar and public lecture 'The teacher's breasts,'* June 1993. Canberra, Australia: The Humanities Research Centre, pp. 31–46.

Foucault, M. (1980). *Power/knowledge: Selected interviews and other writings 1972–1977*. New York: Pantheon.

Foucault, M. (1985). *The use of pleasure: The history of sexuality, volume 2*. (trans. Robert Hurley). London: Penguin.

Fullan, M. (1982). *The meaning of educational change*. Toronto, Ontario: The Ontario Institute for Studies in Education.

Gallop, J. (1986). The immoral teachers, The pedagogical imperative: Teaching as a literary genre, *Yale French Studies*, No. 63, 117–128.

Haraway, D. (1991). *Simians, cyborgs and women: The reinvention of nature.* London: Free Association Books.

Lyotard, J. (1979). *The postmodern condition: A report on knowledge.* London: Vintage.

Macey, D. (1994). *The lives of Michel Foucault.* London: Vintage.

McWilliam, E. (1995). (S)education: A risky inquiry into pleasurable teaching. *Education and Society,* 13 (1), 15–24.

McWilliam, E. (1996). Touchy subjects: A risky inquiry into pedagogical pleasure. *British Educational Research Journal,* 22 (3), 305–316.

Noddings, N. (1984) *Caring: A feminine approach to ethics and moral education.* Berkeley: University of California Press.

O'Brien, S. (2000). The lecherous professor: "An explosive thriller about lust, perverted justice and obsession beyond control." In C. O'Farrell, D. Meadmore, E. McWilliam, and C. Symes (Eds.), *Taught bodies.* New York: Peter Lang, pp. 39–56.

Popkewitz, T. (1997). Educational sciences and the normalisations of the teacher and the child: Some historical notes on current USA pedagogical reforms. In I. Nilsson and L. Lundahl (Eds.), *Teachers, curriculum and policy.* Umea, Sweden: Umea University, pp. 91–114.

Rorty, R. (1989). *Contingency, irony, and solidarity.* New York: Cambridge University Press.

Symes, C., and Sheahan-Bright, R. (1998). *School's out! Learning to be a writer in Queensland: An anthology in six lessons.* Brisbane, Australia: Queensland University of Technology.

Untersteiner, M. (1954). *The sophists.* (trans. Kathleen Freeman). Oxford: Basil Blackwell.

Woods, P. (1985). Sociology, ethnography and teacher practice. *Teaching and Teacher Education,* 2, 51–62.

PART TWO:
Nations and Subjects
in Historical Perspective

In Memory of

KENNETH HULTQVIST

—friend, colleague, avant-garde intellectual—

The Traveling State, the Nation, and the Subject of Education

Kenneth Hultqvist

Introduction

The nineteenth and twentieth centuries saw the emergence of the self-governing liberal and autonomous subject in the Swedish educational context. The inscription of this subject was not restricted to the popular school but appeared in other contexts like programs for the making of civil societies and the new welfare practices that were invented at the time. The popular school, like other inventions, served the purpose of making the Nation and the subject of citizenship in the emerging modern Swedish society. The liberal subject is still with us, but the twentieth century saw a series of transformations and mutations both in educational discourse and the discourses that inscribed the subject in other institutional settings.

Today, a new-ish liberal subject has emerged in the rhetoric of educational reform. It is reminiscent of previous versions, but it has also acquired attributes and characteristics that distinguish it from the subjects of the past. That subject is presupposed in strategies for a decentralized school, and it is inscribed in the national curricula as well as in the methods of teaching and instruction. It is not even confined within the school proper but can be found almost everywhere, in the public arenas as well as in the private sector of the economy, and it plays a significant role in the context of today's discussions about citizenship and democracy. It is not even restricted to the Swedish national borders but crosses countries and nations. It's what I will call a *traveling concept*.

The emergence of this subject in the context of schooling has interesting points of articulation. Perhaps the most salient is its link to changing notions of the Nation. The Nation, or the national heritage, is mentioned now and then in curricula and other public documents, but for the most part the Nation seems to have receded into the past. A second allied effect is the reinvention of the notion of the educational State. Since the 1980s and 1990s there has been a shift in the notion of the State. The State is no longer conceived of as a bureaucratic organization that governs citizens in the name of rules and prescriptions. Rather, the role of the State is to stimulate and nurture the activities of participatory, flexible, and autonomous players on the local stage, which now has become the center of attention. The construction of Skolverket, the Swedish Agency for School, is an interesting example in this context. The agency is constructed in the image of the autonomous subject (individual or collective) that governs itself through the use of knowledge.

The autonomous player who appears in recent reform documents is, then, part of a larger pattern of change. The purpose of this chapter is to explore how the autonomous subject is linked with the new notions about the State/Nation and knowledge. My primary focus will be on the current changes, but the analysis will begin with an overview of nineteenth- and twentieth-century Swedish thought about the school. The ways of reasoning that governed thought about the subject during this period of time are reminiscent of today's discourses, and I believe that it is quite instructive to use them as a points of departure for reflections about the autonomous subject in today's school reforms.

Specifically, I will examine Torsten Rudenschöld's and Fridtjuv Berg's political thoughts about the school. They were two of the most prominent men in the Swedish educational thought of their times. The school policy thinking that they developed represented a great breakthrough in the discussion of the Swedish popular school. The popular school was intended to be for all the children, for the children of the rich as well as for the children of the poor, for the children of those who occupied leading positions in society as well as for those who were to be led or governed. These ideas eventually had a great impact on the so-called Skolkommissionen in the 1940s, when plans were being made to construct the Swedish comprehensive school (Grundskola).

In this chapter, I examine three key discourses that help to highlight continuities and discontinuities between older and newer versions of educational subjects in Sweden. In unpacking discourses that produce faith in the cultural subject (that is, a child who is explained by constant reference to its culture), interactionism, and integrationism, I provide a map of how today's educational reforms are remobilized and reconstructing images of the individual, the Nation, and the State under new conditions.

My theoretical perspective relies on a variety of sources but mainly on Michel Foucault's notions about governmentality, which he developed at the end of his career (see Foucault, 1979). Foucault argued (1991) that the governing of subjects in modern societies relies, to an increasing extent, on knowledge and particularly on scientific knowledge. His second argument claimed that knowledge is based on historical preconceptions or what he called historical a prioris. The historical a priori is the product of a reversal of the metaphysics in Kant's thought. The possibility of knowing, Foucault claimed, was neither in the inherent structures of the brain nor in Kant's transcendental categories but in the historical archives of knowledge. For example, we are used to thinking of the State, the Nation, and the subject as fixed entities with certain localization and as distributed in time. The concept of governmentality enables us to take another route. Instead of asking about the essential character of things and people, we might ask how such conceptions emerged, where and in which contexts, and what effects they have on ourselves and on other people. Using this line of reasoning, the State is a changing epistemological pattern of assumptions about government, e.g., the normative and theoretical assumptions behind the art of governing, as well as assumptions about the who and the what of government: Who has the right to govern in the name of the State and who has not, and what are the relations between the governors and the governed?

Under this view, government in the name of the State presupposes some assumptions about that which is to be governed. If it's a child, the child must be governed in accordance with the assumptions we make about children, e.g., that they have a nature, which is still a common belief, or that they develop in accordance with this or that pattern. Whatever the object, some assumptions are always involved, and it makes no difference should government rely, as it does today, on "scientific knowledge." All knowledge rests on assumptions, or as I call them, historical epistemologies.

Finally, I believe that this line of thought might account for the presence of the autonomous subject on the international stage. The epistemology of the self-governing individual, I will argue, makes possible the modern State and the Nation. I will explore this argument in the final part of the chapter, where I consider some of the implications of the continuities and discontinuities in present-day versions of the flexible, participatory, and autonomous subject of educational discourse. A particular focus in my discussion will be on the divide between nature and culture. This divide organizes much thought about the school even today in spite of its rather weak intellectual foundation. Nature/culture are not stable categories but are the product of (cultural) thought and have no existence outside the particular discourse where they are used. I use the language of nature/culture in this chapter not to reproduce an "empty history" but to identify and analyze shifts and discontinuities.[1]

Analytics of the State

In drawing on Foucault's notion of governmentality, it is more useful to think of the State less as a discrete entity, centralized power, or pure bureaucracy. If States are not primarily substances or things, we might conceive of the State as a traveling agency. States travel like their citizens, e.g., in the shape of the epistemological patterns that construct the subject, such as the autonomous, participatory, and flexible version of the subject favored in educational reforms today. The autonomous subject as well as the epistemologies that construct the notion of the State in the 2000s are parts of wider patterns of discourse that move between Nations. When crossing the "borders" of singular Nations they intersect with locally and historically produced imaginaries and ways of reasoning (see Popkewitz, 2000, 2001a). The State might also be seen instead as a diagnostic approach to the conditions of governing in society much like the role of the doctor with respect to his or her patient. Bernadette Baker (2001a) uses this line of thought to play with the double meaning of "state" in English. On the one hand "state" could mean condition or existence; on the other it could refer to the State as a ruling entity. Foucault notes that certain questions arose more persistently from the 1600s onwards in Europe in the wake of the Reformation, the dissolution of monarchies, and the emergence of civil society: How do we need to govern ourselves, which are the proper normative conditions of a "truly sound" society, and how do we deal with those subjects that deviate from the normal conditions of life, in schools, in the workplace, or in other places?

It becomes noticeable through such heuristics and lists of questions that the State is as much about *epistemology* as it is about physical power and localization. Today, the Swedish State, like States in most countries, is being inscribed and problematized in new ways. New languages emerge that stimulate new conceptions of the relationship between the State and educational subjects. The following section provides some historical examples of such shifts.

**Part One: The Mobilization of Life
in the Name of Discourses on Organicism and Circulation**

When reading Rudenschöld and Berg one realizes that they saw the construction of the popular school or the folkskola as part of a much broader agenda than just the school. They tried in their work to sketch a program for government in a liberal society. To accomplish this end, they had to invent and reinvent both the notions of society and the subject. Of course, they did not accomplish this by themselves. The ground was prepared, and when they invented the program for a popular school, they did so in the prevailing discourse of their times.

I will argue that their program for a popular school is a mobilization program. On the one hand it served the purpose of mobilizing human and material resources, and on the other it was a means to create the Nation or the bonds between people in a modern and increasingly, as they saw it, fragmented society. Like today's thought on the school, they focused on life itself. It is life that is at the center of the mobilization efforts. In the second part of my chapter, I will try to show that the mobilization of life in the early 1800s and the early 1900s was governed by a set of epistemologies and discourses that were akin to today's discourses. Like today, the mobilization of the autonomous or self-ruled subject of the nineteenth and early twentieth century also presupposed a certain notion of the State and the Nation. The differences between now and then, I argue, are in the way these discourses and epistemologies are constructed and put to use.

Rudenschöld's thought was part of a liberal project that he called the ståndscirkulationen, or, in English, class-circulation (social mobility). The ståndscirkulationen was a tool to create greater social mobility in society, and thus a tool to replace the old hierarchical society with its fixed obligations and positions with the more flexible, liberal, and democratic society. The construction of the popular school was one of the techniques of this project. Another was the invention of liberal associations or societies that would limit the exercise of power by the sovereign State of his times. Rudenschöld believed in the power of society to act as a self-governing entity, and he saw the school as a tool to spread the new mentalities or attitudes that were needed in modern society.

There is a background to the ståndscirkulationen in the Swedish context. In the eighteenth century there was a debate about education for citizenship and a school in which subjects from different corners of the social strata would be able to compete for social positions. The idea of liberal freedom organized this debate. In the latter part of the eighteenth century the idea of the People, much stimulated by the French and the American revolutions, became influential and during this period of time the name Folkskola or popular school also appeared in the discussions (see Sjöstrand, 1961). In Rudenschöld's work this rather extensive debate was organized into a coherent program for the reshaping of society, the Nation, and the subject. His major pieces, *Tankar om Ståndscirkulationen* (*Thoughts About Social Mobility*) and *Tankar om Ståndscirkulationens Verkställighet* (*Thoughts About the Realization of Social Mobility*), to which I will refer in this section, were written in 1845 and 1846.[2] Rudenschöld's work coincided with an intensive period of reforms of the school and other major institutions. The popular school was developed in 1842, and Rudenschöld soon became one of the main figures in this context, not only as a writer but also as a highly regarded practitioner and organizer of the emerging modern Swedish school system.

Ståndscirkulationen and the Visions about Nature

The ståndscirkulationen was certainly not only about the equality of the classes[3] and individuals' life-possibilities. First of all it was a means to release the collective forces of the Nation and in the process this very Nation was invented.[4] When Rudenschöld looked around in the nineteenth-century Sweden, he saw a society in decay. The overall national performance was declining and the inefficiency of the ruling classes, he argued, was the major cause of this state of affairs. Social positions were inherited, and many of the individuals who occupied the leading positions in society were not fit for the job. The ståndscirkulationen was a means to change that unfortunate situation by inviting members from all social classes to engage in a competition about status positions. According to Rudenschöld, this would increase performance in society, and it would also lead to greater brotherhood between the classes, since all members of the classes would now have equal opportunities to promote their welfare. Rudenschöld's idea of brotherhood was a version of Christian brotherhood, and many of the ideas he brought to use in his reform thought derive from religious sources. He believed, in fact, that the Ståndscirkulationen was an act of providence and the inevitable result of a natural process that would finally inaugurate the Christian State on earth.

Although religious thought played an essential role in this context, the word of God now spoke from another ground. The word was to be found in life itself and in the earthly existence of men and women (especially men). The historian Carl Becker wrote a beautiful book in the 1930s, *The Heavenly City of the Eighteenth-century Philosophers*. In the book, Becker shows how the city of God in previous religious thought was inscribed in Enlightenment thought as the city of man and nature. This transfer predates the welfare policies of the twentieth century and the political ambitions to create the heavens on Earth. Rudenschöld expressed this line of thought in the following way: "Is the life of mankind in this world forever to be seen as a vale of tears and is all reliable joy of men to be postponed until the after-life? Or would it be possible to create a life on earth that is truly and to its kernel a joyful life" (Rudenschöld, 1920a, p. 7). The heavens in previous religious discourse were thus inscribed in the temporal dimension as the time that is ahead of us, the Future. "Future" in this context is not an object of contemplation or revelation; it is about making productive use of time with the purpose of creating a more humane world. This second reformation (Popkewitz & Pitman, 1986) furnished the word of God with a new basis. It became the *living word* that spoke in nature and society.

Such organic and circulatory discourses traveled beyond Rudenschöld's Sweden of the 1840s and found their place, reworked, in general and philosophical and child study literature. For example, the pedagogies of Maria Montessori[5] reflect Carl Becker's more general observation that future/heavens is inscribed in the soul and nature of the child. Let me illustrate this shift with three quotations from her work:

> We make a false diagnosis when we state that the intellect reigns in our times. On the contrary, it is clouded, and we must return to reason. Let us return to the child, this inspiring creature, that renewer of race and society. We must extinguish our self and let us be filled by this faith. Let us approach the child as the Wise Men, loaded with gifts and led by the star of hope. (Montessori, quoted in *Barnträdgården*, 1934, p. 60)

In another of Montessori's texts, faith in the heavens/future is inscribed in the scientific endeavor:

> The fundamental principle of scientific pedagogy must be, indeed, the liberty of the pupil—such liberty as shall permit a development of the individual spontaneous manifestation of the child's nature. If a new and scientific pedagogy is to arise from the study of the individual such a study must occupy itself with the observation of free children. (Montessori, 1912, p. 69)

And finally, she concludes that the child:

is almost like an unexplored landscape. We do not know very much about it, but what we know indicates that there is more to gain knowledge of. The question is, however, how it is possible to know that there is a nature of the child when we are so ignorant of its existence. (Montessori, 1936, p. 124)

The mutation of thought that is illustrated with my three examples linked the child's nature and its liberties with scientific observation. Research "reads" the signs of nature. Liberty plays a dual role in this scheme. From the point of view of observation, it makes this reading possible. From the political point of view, it is the means to make the future. Liberty will release the (human) forces and powers that are inherent in the child. Thus, the religious hope that was announced in the first quotation now becomes the conditions of possibility for the realization of the future of mankind—the child. The mission of pedagogy is to realize the historical telos inscribed in the nature of the child, a telos that has always been governed by the same purpose and that always sought to realize itself in history but encountered insurmountable obstacles on its way to realization. The paradox is, of course, that pedagogy itself is the product of the same evolutionary process that it serves.[6]

The State and the Powers of Nature

The idea of ståndscirkulationen is set in this kind of evolutionary thought. Ståndscirkulationen is a technology to promote the evolutionary process and thus a technology to mobilize the natural resources of mankind (the child). In the opening part of one of Rudenschöld's major works, he turns directly to the issue of freedom:

> It is our opinion that this movement (the ståndscirkulationen) cannot emerge and remain without the free will of individual members of society and the question of freedom cannot be the object of the power of the State. In general we might expect that those rather extensive movements in society must be based on a free and self-driven power in the wombs of the people. (Rudenschöld, 1920a, pp. 74–75)

Subjects must be ruled differently from the past. They must be freed from the restraints of elderly forms of governing, that is, those embodied in the bureaucratic State. Rudenschöld's almost poetic vision of the possibilities of government points to what Foucault describes as the governmentalization of the State (see Foucault, 1991). The State in Rudenschöld's work is the target of problematization. The State cannot guarantee the freedom of individuals; it must be the task of the individuals themselves. It takes some special skills to decipher the movements of nature and freedom, and it cannot be taken for granted that individuals or collectives are able to grasp their true freedom or needs. The program of ståndscirkulationen provides a map over the possible routes of natural freedom, and it is also a technology that can be used to construct those agencies that will enhance the evolutionary process, e.g., the school, liberal societies, and other agencies of freedom.

When reasoning about the forces of freedom, Rudenschöld turned to the medical model of the body, the blood circulation. This model enabled him to diagnose the state of affairs in Swedish society in the mid-1850s:

> If we now return to our main subject, it should be apparent to us that social mobility will bring and maintain a healthy circulation, just as natural and indeed necessary as the circulation of blood in the human. The opposite, however, which we can call social stagnation, threatens social life with a very pernicious unnaturalness. (Rudenschöld, 1920a, pp. 19–20)

A sound and healthy society, according to this medical model for social life, means that the (blood) circulation:

> "will maintain healthy movement" and not clog the blood vessels but could be let from the sick society's head to cure and cool the suffocating stoppage that causes feverishness in the upper classes. Over the centuries they have become overfull, long past the need for positions of intelligence. (Rudenschöld, 1920a, p. 17)

The keystone of class circulation in Rudenschöld's thought is natural selection. Each individual has a natural power[7] that regulates the opportunities of the individual, and these natural powers would be the solid ground from which an individual's proper place in society could be determined (see Rudenschöld, 1920a; Rudenschöld, 1920b). It is obvious that Rudenschöld's main concern was about economy.[8] Using the medical model, he came to the conclusion that the world of human resources was split into two halves, each with their separate localization. There were the governors and there were the governed. The governors were the heads while the governed was the body. The governors prescribed the rules of discourse, while the body was free to obey and exercise the order. This version of freedom might seem odd, but it was a logical conclusion of Rudenschöld's discourse. Freedom was about the powers distributed in nature, and each and all should be governed in the name of their share of these natural powers. Some were born to be rulers and some were born to be ruled. Freedom was just another word for the ability or power to rule or to be ruled. It is obvious that the problem

Rudenschöld was dealing with here was about finding new means to unite the elite with the masses. This was considered to be an urgent problem, and Rudenschöld, as well as many of his contemporaries, feared the rise of democracy and the possibility that the future would be ruled not by reason but by unreason in the shape of the irrationality of the masses, the mob. The theme was raised not only in the party politics but also in the discourses of the nascent social sciences in the 1800s (see, for example, Le Bon, 1968). This particular debate is still part of our present, for example, as the relationship between theory and practice.

These are the pieces of thought that laid the ground for the emergence of the liberal society that he envisioned. The former hierarchical society with its inherited positions should be replaced with a liberal meritocratic order, where positions were distributed in accordance with natures. Thus a hierarchy of positions based on the natures of individuals replaced the previous hierarchy. It is important to maintain, that the order and distribution of natures not only mirror the natural order of things, it also corresponds, to use Becker's words, to the order of heavens. There were still rulers and ruled, but from now on rulers ought to be selected by their natural powers and not by social and cultural inheritance. The latter did not always reflect the order of nature, i.e., God, and could not ground any idea of liberty and justice.

Where did the popular school enter in this argument? There was also a second argument. Although there is a natural determinism, it is not apparent until everyone is offered equal opportunities to develop their natural talents. Rudenschöld develops his argument in the following way:

> Always concealed is some precious—we can call it—metal, which in its original State is combined with several binding ingredients. Providence, which with its all-seeing eye unmasks everyone's self-acquired, noninherited constituents, and understands which solution will best and most safely purify the precious heart metal from slag and bring it out to be used, each in its kind. (Rudenschöld, 1920a, p. 11)

Although the work of nature is governed by strict rules, there is a principle of indeterminacy involved here. We know for sure that each individual is granted a certain power, but this power is not visible at the time of his or her birth. Therefore, the school has a dual task; to discover each child's natural abilities and to promote the development of these abilities in the name of knowledge. Thus, the school is both a laboratory where nature becomes visible and a place to nurture and stimulate natural development. To be fair and just such a laboratory must be a laboratory for each and all. Powers are not distributed in accordance with social status or rank, and every individual must regarded as a species of nature without any consideration of social or cultural inheritance. The school must be a popular school, then. There is another reason why the school must be popular. When children interact with each other in the school, they also learn to respect the foundations of the ståndscirkulationen, which is about the relationship between the rulers and the ruled. An ethos of brotherhood will emerge that unites the governors with the governed.

The Nation

The evolutionary process points toward the future, and the ståndscirkulationen in this particular sense is a goal-governed project. We know where we came from and we know where we are going. But as the evolutionary process needs a technology to promote itself, the ståndscirkulationen also needs some framework to guide the process. Nature is part of the framework, so is brotherhood or interaction between the social classes, but there is a third, namely, the Nation. The Nation, in Rudenschöld's scheme, is about the formation of a mentality that will steer the activities of individuals and collectives to certain goals that will promote and increase the communal human and material resources and thus enable "a life on earth [that] is truly and to its kernel a joyful life" (Rudenschöld, 1920a, p. 7).

The mentality in question is "freedom from vanity" or modesty. Individuals and collectives should regulate themselves in accordance with idea of freedom from vanity. They should be diligent and strive toward the future, and they shouldn't make unreasonable claims on the common resources. Rudenschöld also used the idea of modesty to construct a kind of Swedish exceptionalism. In one of his publications he made Sweden the origin of this particular ethos: "From the head of the earth which is in Scandinavia there have emerged great and refreshing human powers...the origin of which is the poor but modest and proud Nordic countries" (Rudenschöld, 1920a, pp. 73–74). The idea of modesty is everywhere in Rudenschöld's work, not only when he deals explicitly with the issue of the Nation but also when he reflects on the tasks of different topics in school, e.g., the role of art and poetry in education. The idea of modesty is a regulator not only of collectives but also of the soul of the child. The child is the Nation seen from another angle and vice versa.

One could claim that this puritan attitude is the product of Lutheranism in the interest of accumulating capital. It would be a reasonable conclusion in view of the context of Rudenschöld's work. But modesty was not invented by either Luther or Rudenschöld, even Plato considered the idea of modesty to be part of a good life (see Platon, 1969). Modesty is a floating currency, and in Rudenschöld's work and that of his contemporaries it was used to shape the imaginaries of the new Swedish Nation.

The Epistemologies of the Ståndscirkulationen

To briefly summarize: Rudenschöld's thought is based on three epistemologies. One is about the *powers of natures*, which afford each man or women with energies and capabilities that direct them to their proper position in society. Rudenschöld was probably not familiar with the work of Darwin, although they were contemporaries. Rudenschöld's conception of Society is a version of social Darwinism, and had he been familiar with Darwin's work, he probably would have subscribed to a notion of the survival of the fittest. The link to Darwinism is made more explicit in Fridtjuv Berg's work, which I will describe in the next section. The second epistemology is *interactionism* and is about social interaction. Interaction is the means to create solidarity between the classes. The third is *integrationism* or social integration. Integrationism resembles interactionism, but the difference is that it is goal directed and makes no distinctions between human and material forces. It is heading toward the future. In Rudenschöld's scheme, integrationism is about the National framework. The Nation collects and integrates the human and material forces in the name of the future.

The basic issues in Rudenschöld's thought are about power and knowledge. The subjects must be governed not in the name of their inherited social positions but in the name of whom they are—their natures. But then, there is no natural route to the subjects' knowledge of themselves, nature, and society. Knowledge must be thought and practiced, and this is the task of school and other agencies. School must also distinguish individuals' capabilities and aptitudes to profit from knowledge. Individuals must be distinguished, ranked, and distributed in social space with regard to their abilities, whether these are about cognitive capacities, moral aptitudes and judgments, or emotional capabilities, that is, the ability to create and maintain bonds with other people. The latter ability, the ability to move the hearts of people, Rudenschöld named the *fire soul*.

Now, the emergence of knowledge created a new space for government that I would like to call the "lateral tower of observation." Why do I call it lateral instead of hierarchical? The reason is that observation is based on the notion of *freedom*. Freedom is, as I tried to show with the example of Maria Montessori, the key to visualizing the nature of the subject. This reversal also introduces a new and more interactive relationship between the authorities and those who are to be governed in schools or in other places. Rudenschöld and his contemporaries put these parameters of governing in place well before the early psychologists and pedagogues of the twentieth century explored them empirically. It is my belief that we are repeating this set of epistemologies even today, but it is done differently from the past. I will return to this subject in the second part.

I have also argued that Rudenschöld's pioneer work is reminiscent of the pragmatic thought that was developed in the United States in the late 1800s (see Hultqvist, in press).[9] The teleological character of his thought as well as his antidemocratic stance would disqualify him as a pragmatist, but there are other and more pragmatic features to his thought. His program for a school is a social one. The school should be useful and serve the purposes of the individual and society. School is a school for life. There is also an experimental attitude in Rudenschöld's work that is reminiscent of Dewey's, for example, when he reasons about the child's nature. Children are different when they enter the school, he says, but school cannot know in advance which will become leaders and which will be led. School must experiment and improvise to find out the secrets that are known only to God.

John Dewey's work appeared in the Swedish context in 1902.[10] It was the first of Dewey's articles published outside of the United States. This is probably no coincidence. Pragmatism in the broad sense of the word was already a "reality" in the Swedish context when Dewey's texts were brought to Sweden. If we regard Dewey as an epistemic subject (see Deleuze & Guatteri, 1994), and not as the author Dewey, it is obvious that Dewey was present in the Swedish context as early as the 1850s or even before. To understand the impact of his work in Sweden in the early 1900s and later, I believe we must regard the issues that it dealt with and that he shared with his Swedish contemporaries. Both parties were concerned with the problem of uniting the elite with the masses in a world ruled by the contingency, where norms and values no longer could be upheld by religious thought and established institutions.[11] The epistemologies that were inscribed in Dewey's work could travel and cross Nations and continents because these were about issues of governing that were of wider concern at the time (see Popkewitz, 2001a).

Fridtjuv Berg

The next important figure in the Swedish context was Fridtjuv Berg. He was the head of the teacher's union in the early part of the twentieth century, and he was also a minister of education on two occasions.

Berg repeated the framework of Rudenschöld's thought. It was still about the ståndscirkulationen, the nature of the subject/child. His work then, is a continuation of the effort to establish the more just and interactive "laboratory" that I named "the lateral tower of observation." A close reading of his work, however, reveals a major shift—especially in his work from the twentieth century. There is no longer a mention of a telos of nature, and thus, the possibility of a common future can no longer, as with Rudenschöld, be taken for granted:

> More than one believe that the people of the white race and generally the Culture of the Western people hardly have any future to count on. These people have had—they say—its heyday, is withering away and only death remains. This is not because the Nations are natural individuals that obey their laws or that they follow the blind necessity in recapitulating one stage after another childhood, youth, manhood, and old age until they finally disappear from the chains of living beings. No, if humanity has a common derivation, it derives from a common root. It cannot thus be nature that puts the one Nation in front of the other in decay. No, it is culture....But cultures emerge and vanish and one might ask oneself: What is the point of all of it?
>
> ...Choice is not open to us. And we do not want to choose. The road points toward the future, not backwards. We wish to increase and deepen Culture. Let it shape and make our material existence more safe and richer, our emotional life more subtle and intimate. Open our eyes to greater and more clear breadth of vision through the subordination of all these sides of human life to the kernel of human life and existence: striving, willing and action. (Berg, 1922, p. 39)

This is an important shift. There is still a telos, but a different register than that of Rudenschöld organizes Berg's thought. It is as if Culture and Nature are moving apart and become two different but interactive registers. Nature has no other telos than the will and the desire to act. It is about the release of energies and desires. As such, culture and civilization become the only route to the Future, for individuals as well as for collectives.

Berg's thought is clearly influenced by pragmatism and is revealed by the many articles he wrote about John Dewey and other U.S. pragmatists. There is, however, an undercurrent to Berg's pragmatism, and it is revealed when he writes about normality and abnormality. In several of these texts he is concerned with the issue of the deviant child, that is, the child who cannot be coped with by teachers and other authorities. There are children who can be saved, for example, the children of the poor. Poor living conditions might trigger deviant behavior and attitudes, even among children with good natural heritage, Berg argues, but then there are those children who "are born with a heritage of evil tendencies [energies] and when left to themselves they are prone to become morally declined" (Berg, 1921b, p. 171).

The latter argument was developed in accordance with the then widespread theory of recapitulation. The theory of recapitulation states that the child repeats the developmental tracks of humanity. But there are exceptions in the shape of the abnormal child. This child was arrested on a lower level of maturity. As Nancy Lesko (2001) shows, the theory of recapitulation is part of the colonial thought that sought to understand the difference between "us" and the "other." The metaphor used to express difference was the great chains of being (notice that this same terminology was used by Berg in the quote on page 162). The barbarians like the abnormal child were at the lower end of the chain while the white middle-class man embodied the achievements of civilization. It is worth noticing, however, that Berg's conception of the recapitulation theory is different from many of the versions that circulated in other national contexts at this period of time.[12] For example, in Stanley Hall's work in the United States or Maria Montessori's in Italy, the theory of recapitulation was tied to natural evolution and progress. Berg's thought operates with two registers; one is Nature and the other is Culture, and the link between them is "purely" contingent. This is the reason why Berg can raise questions like the one in the quote on the previous page: *What is the point of all of it?* There is no point, but we cannot go back. Why? Because the contingencies of our present situation made us the kind of people we are. There is still progress, but it is not natural! The problem with Berg's view from the perspective of this chapter is that it naturalized contingency.

There is a natural zero point in Berg's Nature/Culture spectacle, though, that no *reasonable* Culture can go beyond; it consists of the masses of abnormal energy that emerge from beneath, as it were, ordinary human biology. What are at stake here are reason and the ability to govern the future. In Berg's work, the opposite of reason is desire and the impulse to go against reason. The figure of the abnormal is the embodiment of desire, evil desire. But there are other figures as well, for example, the desire for pure aesthetics, extravagant consumption of goods, be they mental or material, and other activities that are related to the waste of communal energy. For Berg as well as for Rudenschöld, desire can only be meaningful in the context of the Nation, which is about freedom from vanity. It is also interesting to note that Berg's conception of democracy is shaped by his conception of desire. Like Rudenschöld, he feared the imaginary figure of the mob, the masses (meaningless energy). In the work of both men there is thus a way of organizing and selecting the kinds[13] of entities that go together and make up the world of action, to use a phrase of Nelson Goodman (1978). Freedom from vanity in poetry, art, sexuality, and democracy are linked in chains to make up the normal citizen. Mention of the one "entity" in the string automatically triggers the other entities. This world making also organizes that which does not belong to normality and reason; for example, aestheticism in art and poetry, promiscuous sexual behavior are linked with unreason, and in Berg's work, with an antidemocratic attitude and with the annihilation of the future.

Thus in Berg's writing, the theory of recapitulation replaced Rudenschöld's teleological notion. There is still an overarching goal, progress, but the goal is now inscribed in another register, culture, and it is also open to the "forces" of contingency. This is an important distinction in the context of today's educational thought. Both Berg and Rudenschöld were concerned with the management (and production) of difference, and both men subscribed to a version of Social Darwinism in dealing with such matters.[14] But Berg's disconnection of nature from the register of culture and the rejoining of them in a new register opened new avenues to govern difference. Power did not only derive from nature (Rudenschöld) but had a dual origin; it was located both in nature (as energy) and in Culture as tools and collective intentions (goals and directions). Berg and Rudenschöld were dealing with the nation and natural culture. Today the task of governing difference is even more complex when "the local" and local cultures have become main issues in thought about government. Which version of "difference" will govern difference? After this long detour, I will now turn to the "subject of the present."

**Part Two: The Cultural Biology of the
Advanced Liberal Subject, Interactionism and Integrationism**

The period that came after Berg saw the emergence of the Swedish Welfare State. It is difficult to describe in a few sentences the quality of the changes that appeared in educational thought from the 1920s to the 1950s, but I would like to suggest that the one significant change is about the replacement of cultural thought with psychology and the nascent social sciences (see Hultqvist, 1990, 1998; also see Sävström, 1999). Government was centralized in the name of the State, and it was assumed that the school and other institutions could be governed in accordance with universal rules. This idea is part of the new conception of the Nation, the so-called People's Home,[15] which appeared in the late 1920s. The People's Home is a home or Nation for each and all, and there should be no exceptions to this rule. The rulers and the ruled were supposed to be treated equally. This conception of government was repeated in educational thought in the shape of assumptions of universal laws of learning. It's obvious that the contract between the governed and the governors has now been redefined and shaped by modernist ideas. Educational thought becomes part of the so-called "social engineering" (see Hultqvist, 1998). But ideas keep coming back. One is the belief in science's ability to ground objective judgement, which is akin to the word of God in Rudenschöld's scheme. Another is the view of the State (the centralized State, and the notions of sovereignty that historically have been inscribed in the conception of the State). The third would be a slightly disguised version of the ståndscirkulationen, now called the "reserve of talents." This latter concept was used in the post–World War II period to calculate the potentials for higher education among the lower classes (see Boalt & Husén, 1964; Härnqvist, 1958; Husén, 1951).

The idea of the ståndscirkulationen continued to fascinate educational and social thought. In the 1980s it appeared in another disguise as the so-called "class-journey."[16] Now, the medium of thought had changed. It was no longer the discourse of nature but Culture. Cultural thought thus regained its privileged place in educational thought. The new discourse of the ståndscirkulationen dealt with the individual's life experiences and the ethical and existential conflicts that people endured during their class-journey as they moved up the social ladder. And more importantly, the focus was now on the individuals themselves. They were in the foreground while the Nation or the social hierarchy served as the more or less dark background to the individual's journey through social and cultural space. This change in the fabrication of knowledge is significant. It is my belief that the way this subject is positioned is akin to the way the subject is positioned in the School reforms of the 1990s and after.

In this part of my chapter I will explore the epistemologies that carry the subject of the class-journey in the school reform of the 1990s. I will suggest that the new subject presupposes a new conception of the State and the Nation. This renewal of thought about the State and the Nation relies on new conceptions of knowledge. I argue that the basic set of issues that the pioneers of the nineteenth and twentieth centuries dealt with are still with us, but they are used differently from the past.

The Home We Inherited

In 1994 the Swedish author Jan Larsson published *The Home We Inherited*. The title refers to the Swedish People's Home concept that I referred to earlier. Larsson is not the only Swedish author who is concerned with the People's Home construct. The 1980s and the 1990s saw a tidal wave of books about the People's Home, and the list of publications grew quickly. The fascinating part of this endeavor is that it is concerned with the reinterpretation of this part of Swedish history and particularly with the task of forwarding a new and more liberal conception of the subject. For instance:

> The creation of the People's Home became a search for grandeur in the universal mechanisms of human action. The goal was to predict, decide and distribute resources in accordance with the need of the modern democratic citizen and this goal in turn, became a National principle of order for the growing bureaucracies. However, we now realize that the rational conviction, translated into a project to subordinate human beings to a science-based National project to build the modern society, has lost sight of the needs of human beings in its eagerness to guide and govern in accordance with standardized system solutions. The human being cannot be reduced to an economic or social partial being. She is a culturally whole being with unique genetic characteristics, with her own reason and creativity....To grow as a citizen means, in accordance with this line of thought, to live at one's own risk, to be active and exercise one's responsibilities without endangering the freedom of others. (Larsson, 1994, p. 254)

The subject we are dealing with here is different from post–World War II thought about the subject and the Nation. Like so many authors, Larsson declares that the subjects enjoy living their lives at their own risk. We might even assume from Larsson's statements that the subjects detest hierarchical orders, whether these are in the shape of a Nation, a State, or the persona of the patriarch. Thus, the individual is moved to the foreground and the Nation or the collective context resides in the background.

The turn to cultural thought is very significant, but there is more to it than just culture.[17] The individual is a cultural-biological whole entity, and the one cannot be separated from the other. This operation of thought is akin to Berg's efforts to integrate the register of nature with the register of culture. But there are differences. The subject has been given new powers, and these are inscribed in the biological heritage of the individual subject. It is almost as if biology has become more liberal. This rethinking of the relationship between culture and biology/nature creates new challenges for government. The task is no longer to govern individuals through measures that are alien to the qualities of the subject, for example, external rules or detailed instructions. The objective is to stimulate and to enhance the natural resources of the subject. This notion of the subject is akin to the thought of the pioneers and the people's home concept, but the difference is that the nature of the subject is no longer contained in the hierarchical image of the Nation.

I believe that this shift accounts for the amazing popularity of cultural thought in educational circles and elsewhere during the last two decades. Cultural thought is everywhere. An example of this is the increasing popularity of Vygotsky's thought in educational corners. Of course it is not Vygotsky the Marxist who is the popular hero, but those features of his thought that fit the new mobilizing epistemologies.[18] Today's educational thought is very much concerned with the task of stimulating, so to speak, what is already there, namely, the powers that are presupposed in the child and other learners. The child is, as Larsson told us, empowered with an active cultural biology, and the task is to release what is already present. Vygotsky's thought, especially his ideas about the proximal zone of development, suits this agenda of government very well. The child may not be able to do all the tasks by himself or herself, but he or she certainly can manage them in the presence of the skilled educator. No need, as in postwar psychological thought, to wait for nature to do the job (natural development). Here the mobilization of the child's resources is optimized through the skilled assistance of the educator.

The point here is what I would like to call the superpragmatic attitude that governs today's use of theories. Anything that can be used to facilitate and mobilize the child's competencies and capacities is brought to use.

Another example of a similar trend is the recent reintroduction in the Swedish context of the German concept of Bildung (see Broady, 1992). Originally, Bildung was about free education and to make something of oneself that could not be predicted in advance (Broady, 1992). Practically, it functioned in the context of an elite education as a preparation for services in the State (see Hunter, 1988). In the nineteenth century, Bildung was inscribed in the notion of a popular school. Rudenschöld and Berg referred to the concept frequently as a Bildung for Citizenship. The fate of the concept in the Swedish context is tied to the changing epistemologies of government in the twentieth century. It played an important role in the educational context in the first and more "liberal" decades of the twentieth century, but it disappeared during the postwar period in connection with the construction of the People's Home and the centralized welfare State (see Hultqvist, 2001a). As in the past, today's use of the concept is about mobilizing all of the individual's faculties, cognition, emotion, and will, but today's Bildungsjourney is different from past versions. It is reminiscent of Berg's way of reasoning in the early twentieth century (Bildung for Citizenship), but the journey itself has changed; it is now governed by those contingences of the present that I coined superpragmatism. This change is tied to a new notion of the future. Future is still the most important concept in Education, but future in today's educational context is governed differently. It is governed not in the name of society or the nation but in the name of the autonomous and flexible subject (Rose, 1996; Wagner, 1994).

Finally, there is a particularly interesting example that provides a bridge between the thought of the pioneers of Swedish school and today's school reforms. In Sweden there is a figure of thought called the Eldsjälen; in English it would be the fire soul. The fire soul, or Eldsjälen is a person who is driven by the romantic ideal to be committed to community without receiving any economic compensation for his or her services. Wherever he or she appears they ignite the soul of other people, much like the Vygotskian tutor. I have met this figure while I was studying local projects in the south of Sweden. The local authorities who paid for the project were continuously referring to the importance of Eldsjälen for the success of local projects of this kind. The figure of Eldsjälen is widely distributed in the current discourse about the school; it appears in government reports, in educational literature, and it is also part of the common parlance in schools. It appears that the Eldsjälen is a descendant of the discourse about nature and religion. The Eldsjälen is a person with particular natural powers in his or her soul. In Rudenschöld's scheme, the Eldsjälen is a natural governor. It is triggered to inspire other people to govern themselves (people with less power), and in a sense, it is also the savior of souls.[19] The setting has changed, but the Eldsjälen continues to perform its duties.

To summarize: I have argued that the cultural thought is used to mobilize the subject under new conditions. The cultural child in the shape of Vygotsky's subject is one of many examples of this change. As I have tried to indicate, this mobilization of the subject relies on historical figures of thought, for example, local subjects like the fire-soul, as well as international and globalizing figures like Vygotsky or the subject of Bildung. The conditions are also set for reappearance other historical figures. I will revert to these in the final part.

Interactionism and Integrationism

Let me now turn to the two other dominant epistemologies of our present, *Interactionism* and *Integrationism.* A version of these was, as we saw, already present in the work of Rudenschöld and Berg. These two epistemologies work as a pair, but I would like to make a difference between them. Interactionism refers to patterns of human communication, while integration is about bringing parts together without any consideration of whether these are things or people. When brought together for particular purposes, they facilitate the use of available sources as discussed earlier. The mentality that brings them together is what I previously called superpragmatism. Anything might be related to anything as long as it increases resources and wealth. For example:

> Lifelong or, more aptly, life-spanning learning involves a shifting of the responsibility for education and teaching from the public sphere to the private. The public education monopoly is terminated and replaced by a variety of learning environments, players, and principals. This in turn requires a distribution of responsibility and assignments between different educational and learning environments. The subsystems must be seen in relation to each other. The formal educational system's goals and responsibility should be judged in relation to the learning that occurs in other environments....But lifelong learning also involves a shifting of responsibility from the State to the individual. The implementation of the principles of lifelong and life-spanning learning depends on the individual and on the individual's motivation and

ability to seek out and utilize opportunities in the educational
environment....The implementation of the lifelong learning project depends on
the individual, and it is the government's responsibility to create good prior
conditions. The individual's attitude is crucial to his/her own need of further
education. Subject-specific knowledge must be complemented with the desire
to learn, self-confidence, and the ability to master change and feel secure in
spite of uncertainty. (Skolverket, 2000, p. 11)

The quotation illustrates that the subject replaces the Nation. This
replacement also changes the mentalities that govern the conception of
the State. While the postwar conception of the State was modeled on the
notion of the Sovereign, e.g., the State as a rule-governing entity (see
Lindensjö & Lundgren, 1986), recent problematizations focus on the
State as a medium of interaction through which power and agency
become redistributed. In the rhetoric of today's school reforms, power is
"coming from below." This tendency is very pronounced, and if we look
around, for example, in Swedish government reports and steering
documents, the patriarchal image of the State is replaced with the image
of the counselor, and the relationship between the State and the subject is
constructed in the shape of partnership and dialogue. Another example
would be the personalization or perhaps the privatization of public
documents like government reports. During the postwar years, these
documents spoke in the name of the Nation, but now they tend to speak
in the name of the individual authors who contribute.

The third dominant element, integrationism, is also contained in the
quotation—in two ways. First, it appears as if lifelong learning and all of
the resources of the individual should be accounted for, both now and
continuously on a lifelong scale. Second, the quotation stresses the
importance of taking into account all available institutional resources,
both with regard to the formal educational resources as well as the
informal ones. This work is well under way in the Swedish context, and I
believe that we are now witnessing the rise of a completely new *political
educational sector*. This sector is comprised not only of the school and
the traditional educational system, to use a loose phrase, but of political
areas and institutions that were not previously conceived to be
educational, for example, libraries, the criminal sector and the prison
system, and the museums, to mention a few. It is interesting to note that
the curriculum of the prison system speaks roughly the same language as
the curriculum for the preschool (see Hultqvist, Popkewitz, Petersson, &
Andersson, 2001). The current tendency to loosen the borderlines of the
school and integrate it with community is part of this shift.

Implications of Past Discourses in Present Educational Work:
Traveling Discourses and Knowledge Production

I will consider briefly here a few examples of how the discourse that I have called interactionism is organizing systems of reasoning in educational work in the present. The purpose of my examples is to point to similarities between the past and the present but also to show the distinctively new qualities of today's reasoning.

In the historiography of the present, past research efforts were pursued in the image of the ivory tower. The researcher was a detached observer, and the tower was an apt position to get the right overview of things and people. Arnold Gesell's laboratory is a proper example of this figure of the researcher. But this image is probably highly mythical. A closer look at the past reveals another and perhaps more typical quality. The notion of nature and freedom guided Maria Montessori, G. Stanley Hall, and even Arnold Gesell, introducing a new and more interactive quality between the adult and the child. Gesell's own laboratory even reproduced this quality. The pioneers of the Swedish school invented a version of this kind of laboratory (see Part One). To understand the nature of the child and to respect his or her freedom, the adult had to step back. But this withdrawal was part of a new pattern of interaction. The lateral tower of observation was constructed in this image. The lateral tower is still part of the present, *but now even the act of observation* has become interactional. The researcher and his subjects are engaged in an interaction where both parties observe each other in a continuous stream of mutual interaction. This trend is reflected in the increasing popularity of all sorts of qualitative research, such as action research or ethnographic research, where the researcher is involved with the subject in exploring his or her everyday life in schools or in other local places. Its possible to argue that the new practices of knowledge and reasoning are part of an emancipatory process, but then it is not clear what the emancipation is about or how the new voices of freedom differ from those of the past. Could it be that the new qualitative researcher, while exploring the local and particular, is himself or herself involved in the very production of the kind of superpragmatic liberal subject that he or she might feel inclined to criticize on other occasions?

This shift in the production of knowledge implies and promotes a new notion of the conditions of the State as government and a nation-ness. The hierarchies are withdrawn, and the subject engages with research and knowledge in what seems to be a horizontal relationship.

Thus it promotes the conception of the State as a counselor or adviser rather than the image of the State as a patriarch. A common theme in the Swedish school context is that "power comes from below" (see Carlgren & Hörnqvist, 1999; Carlgren & Marton, 2001). It's the teachers, parents, the local politicians and others who *possess* their own projects. The schemes of power are turned upside down, it seems, and power now comes from the depth of the body,[20] to use the imaginaries of Rudenschöld. The counterpart of the new conception of the State is the subject of the new cultural biology. This link is particularly evident in the research that is promoted by the Swedish Agency for school,[21] but similar ways of reasoning are distributed widely in and outside of educational research. Before "we" accept this version of power from underneath, however, one important question probably remains to be answered: *What regimes of power construct those subjects that will govern themselves in the name of themselves?*

Conclusions

In summary: The political epistemologies of culturalism/nature, interactionism, and integrationism are linked to produce the schools' new mission, that is, to shape the autonomous, flexible, and self-reliant subject. This shift presupposes that the State is problematized in new ways, and it also presupposes a shift in the production of knowledge, toward what I called the lateral tower of observation

I have raised three questions in this chapter:

1. Where is the Nation in today's schools' National mission?

2. What are the discourses that organize the imaginaries about the subject, the social differentiation or inclusion/exclusion, that determine who is normal and who is not?

3. What can be said about history and the recurrent patterns of thought in today's governmentalities?

Let me start with my first question. I am not sure how to answer it, but I do not believe that the Nation has disappeared from the Swedish National context or from any other National context. The Nation is still there, but it has become decentralized, and it is the figure of the flexible, autonomous, and self-reliant individual that now embodies the Nation. The autonomous individual is just another name for the Nation. Current political strategies operate under this label when they mobilize the Nation's resources. These strategies rely on the superpragmatic epistemologies that I labeled interactionism, integrationism, and the cultural child. One can view the autonomous individual as the Nation under new international and globalizing conditions. Compare with Rudenschöld's or Berg's time. In their days, the Nation was in the foreground while the subject was in the background. This was due to the possibility of stabilizing the figure of the Nation State at this period in time. It was this stabilization of the "nation" that made it reasonable to mobilize human and material resources in the seemingly fixed space of a National territory, as in Rudenschöld's model of blood-circulation or as in Berg's organic vision of Society.[22]

The emergence of the liberal figure of the autonomous, flexible, and self-reliant individual[23] in the politics of schooling is a sign that the previous configuration of the Nation has changed.[24] School's role is still National, but the Nation has become more interactionistic and flexible and its borders much more fluid than in Berg's or Rudenschöld's days. The autonomous individual is the formula to realize the Nation's resources under such conditions, and it is a way to problematize and govern those conditions. By itself, the figure of the autonomous individual has no National home; it's a traveling discourse that moves between countries. It's a matrix for the construction of Nations that enables the interactions between them under new National and international conditions. These new notions of the subject, the Nation, and the State, are inscribed in the epistemes of globalizing discourse that are named: Dewey, Vygotsky, and, of course, Foucault, to mention of few of them (see Popkewitz, 2001a on this subject).

The autonomous liberal individual of the early twenty-first century is different from the past, but it is not, as I have tried to show with my historical examples, a completely new construct. The subjects of the nineteenth and early twentieth centuries were mobilized as participants in the liberal and collective endeavor to create welfare Society. The orientation to the future remains in today's educational settings. A whole set of historical practices and discourses are reused to mobilize this subject and to direct and redirect his or her energy with regard to different and increasingly shifting ends (see Fendler, 2001). The supportive State, for example, is based on pastoral images, the enlightenment discourses are everywhere and are used to visualize opportunities of mobilization and thus to create the needed resources. Religious thought still has a hold on the present, for example, in all sorts of practices to save the child's soul under postmodern or late-modern conditions and so on. In today's context, religious discourse travels under names like emancipation or empowerment.

Now I turn to my second question about differentiation or inclusion and exclusion. A school for each and all has been the major credo for the popular school in Sweden since its start in the mid-1800s. Both Rudenschöld and Berg were committed to this idea, and it still is the most important idea in the context of the Swedish school. It is important to remember, however, how the pioneers originally constructed this idea. To start with, "all" had a special meaning attached to it. All should have the same opportunities to develop their natural resources. Inscribed in the "all," then was a principal of selection that was based on the idea of *natural justice* (see Hultqvist & Petersson, 2000). This is, however, only the beginning of a huge theoretical and social problem. Neither Rudenschöld nor Berg or their followers reflected on the construction of nature. It was taken for granted, and consequently the justice that followed from governing in the name of nature depended on how "nature" was constructed, that is, it depended on which historical a prioris, to use Foucault's terminology, governed the use of this concept.

This heritage is, I believe, still with us. And this is the third question I have covered in this chapter. Human beings are now endowed with all the capacities and powers they need to "conquer" modern life at the turn of the new century. The new images of the subject are, as I have tried to show, differently configured than those images that were held by pioneers of the Swedish school. They belong to different registers, and there is thus no evolutionary scheme that ties the one register to the other. Still there obviously are certain similarities in the way the subject is "produced." In all of the cases that I reviewed in this chapter, human powers are firmly located within the subject. As in the mid-1800s and the early 1900s, the role of knowledge is to gain access to and visualize that which is already present in the subject's natural makeup. Larsson's conception of the subject, which I described in the second part, is no mistake; it is part of a dominant way of reasoning. Other examples are the recent Swedish government reports on Democracy, the so-called Demokratiutredningen (2000): "Compared with other ideas about the organization of society, the vantage point of democracy is that we are all different and that we shall remain so. We shall not be forced to be different from what we are" (p. 240). The statement is somewhat opaque, but it does tend to reinforce the conception that power is internal to the individual's biological makeup. It thus underestimates the power of knowledge and other artifacts (like the school and other technologies) to make up and shape subjects as well as produce the differences that are taken for granted in the modernist scheme about nature, culture, and society (see Latour, 1999).

It is easy to imagine that today's governmentalities, which are in the service of extended forms of mobilization discourses, might well actualize past differentiation discourses, such as Social Darwinist discourses, to account for so-called human inadequacies. But one should not search after identity between past and present. The 150 years that divide the present from the past saw a series of shifts in the Social Darwinist-like discourse of Rudenschöld and Berg and from these shifts today's cultural/biological subject eventually emerged. It is an open question whether and how Social Darwinism discourses operate in today's educational settings, but if they do, then they probably travel in the medium of "cultural" discourse. Perhaps choice and the ability to choose will be the candidates of today's policy of differentiation.

According to common opinion, the nineteenth and twentieth centuries were the ages of the *social* (see Donzelot, 1980). New social technologies, minor as well as large-scale technologies, were invented to govern subjects, institutions, and society. There is no reason to challenge this view. When reading "the past," however, one is immediately aware that "the social" is not the final term but is a part of larger projects which are concerned with the means to govern and control the future—to make the heavens on earth, to use a phrase of Becker (1932). In that sense, but only in that particular sense, there is a strong continuity between the projects of the nineteenth and twentieth centuries and today's projects. The difference is perhaps that in our era, the art of governing is increasingly subsumed under the category of the subject. The Nation is governed in the name of the (autonomous) subject instead of the other way around. Nietzsche once made the claim that every one of us contains parts of each of us. The autonomous and self-reliant subject is a very good illustration of his statement. In a sense, it certainly is the all of us in each of us, but it is not easy to recognize how this "us" is constructed when we are supposed to carry the burden of the Nation in the name of our singular selves. There is no Nation or society to blame should we not realize our natures.

Endnotes

Acknowledgments: This chapter is based on my forthcoming book: *Governing the Subject in the Name of the Past, the Present and the Future: Reforms of the Swedish School as Reforms of the Conception of Time.* My study is promoted by the Skolverket (The Swedish Agency of School). Several colleagues have read this chapter. A special thanks to Bernadette Baker, who raised questions which helped me resolve important historical issues, and Thomas S. Popkewitz for his careful reading and insightful comments. I would also like to thank both of the editors, Bernadette Baker and Katharina Heyning, for doing a brilliant job with the manuscript. I also appreciated the comments I received from members of the Wednesday group at the department of Curriculum and Instruction, University of Wisconsin, Madison. Finally, I want to thank Per-Johan Ödman, Kenneth Petersson, Ulf Olsson, Dan Andersson, and other members of my research group (Genoped) at the Stockholm Institute of Education.

1. There is a nice discussion of this problematic in the introduction to *Cultural History and Education* (see Popkewitz, Franklin, & Pereyra, 2001).

2. I use the editions of Rudenschöld's work that were published in *Pedagogiska Skrifter* in 1920. *Pedagogiska Skrifter* is a journal of the Sveriges allmänna folkskolelärarförenings litteratursällskap (The Literary Society of Teachers of the Swedish Popular School).

3. Rudenschöld talked about classes, e.g., the class of workers and the class of nobility, but his use of "class" is not a modern one. "Class," for Rudenschöld, is defined by one's positions in a complex moral/natural/economic cosmology that differentiates groups of people according to their ability to exercise leadership, that is, the power or ability to rule oneself and other people.

4. It's important to note that the construction of the nation or a local belonging is also part of universalizing tendencies. In Rudenschöld's work, the Swedish national identity is consistently worked out in relation to what he called the European and American conditions. Thomas S. Popkewitz pointed out to me in a personal correspondence that the interplay between the universal/global and the local is not an invention of the eighteenth century. It had already occurred in ninth-century England and France in the eleventh century, when a literary culture was formed that was local and particular as well as universal and cosmopolitan.

5. The reason I mention Montessori in this context is that she became a rather influential figure in Sweden in the early twentieth century. But the favorable reception of her work was only partial. The part that was accepted in Swedish educational circles was her view of the child's nature, but there were fewer acceptances with regard to her natural teleology. In the early-twentieth-century Swedish context, nature and culture became two different registers, and the development of the child was due to the interaction between those registers. I will explain this in my next section. In a sense, then, Montessori was born too late to be fully accepted in the Swedish context. Had she been born in Rudenschöld's Sweden, her work probably would have made a greater impact.

6. Foucault explores this way of reasoning and concludes that in modern thought, the limits of knowledge become the very foundation of the possibility to gain knowledge. See Foucault, 1970.

7. The idea that there are individual capabilities/abilities/capacities is taken for granted in much educational discourse. But the belief that power exists is an arbitrary one and culturally specific. Bernadette Baker (2001b) makes a very detailed study of this belief and how it moves between different registers of discourse in the U.S. context, from theological obsession with power-as-potential to mechanized notion of power as force to biologized notions of power-as-energy/capability. Also see Nikolas Rose (1989), where he describes how the surface of the child's body was made to demonstrate the discourses of the early twentieth century's psychological thought on the child.

8. "Economy" in Rudenschöld's work is based on the model of the moral economy of the household. On this subject, see Foucault (1991).

9. See Menand (2001) for an interesting discussion of the emergence of pragmatic thought in the U.S. context.

10. See Hartman & Lundgren (1980).

11. See Popkewitz, T. S. (2001b).

12. Bernadette Baker made me aware of the different uses of the theory of recapitulation. It is a very keen observation and I believe that differences in this respect indicate differences in the way the subject is constructed and governed in various national contexts.

13. On the conception of "kinds," see Hacking (1999).

14. Berg's Darwinistic views are clearly present in several of his pieces. In one of his most famous articles, "Folkskolan som Bottenskola" (1882) he writes: "For the educational system to act on behalf of the welfare of society, it may not hinder the talents of anyone, independent of their social class, from finding their right place in society. The educational system diverts from its mission, if it should in an arbitrary way intervene in the course of natural development" (Berg in *Pedagogiska Skrifter*, 1921a, p. 50). His separation of nature from culture made this task (the promotion of natural justice) even more efficient. Cultural tools could now be used in a more rational way to promote the natural abilities of the child (energy, which was not considered to be arbitrary).

15. It is worth mentioning in this context that Rudenschöld's notion of the home was modeled on the idea of the household, the leading figure of which was the sovereign-governor-father. Another and more decentralized version of the nation/home appeared in conservative circles at the turn of the nineteenth century. At the end of the 1920s the social democratic party adopted the home idea to envision belonging and identity in large-scale (Gesellschaft in the sense of Ferdinand Tönnies) industrial society. In an interesting article, Bo Stråth (2000), a Swedish historian, describes this construction as a marriage between a Lutheran-like notion of the State and ideas of personal freedom that were embodied in Swedish popular movements, especially those that emerged in the late nineteenth century and the early twentieth century. As we have seen, such or similar imaginaries also governed the construction of a popular school in the work of Rudenschöld and Berg.

16. See e.g. Åström (1991); Frykman (1991); Löfgren (1991); Trondman (1993).

17. When reading current texts about education, it seems to me that those texts are using "culture" in much the same way as in Fridtjuv Berg's work, i.e. in a rather broad sense that includes both the material and symbolic/linguistic dimensions of culture. The difference is, I believe, that culture penetrates the "natural dimension" more thoroughly than it did in the early twentieth century (on this subject, see Rose, 2000).

18. Here I like to refer to Thomas S. Popkewitz's article, "Dewey and Vygotsky: Ideas in Historical Spaces" (2001a), which I consider to be the most elegant piece of work on this particular subject.

19. Rudenschöld often returns to the issue of the fire soul, and he sees it as the natural/divine power that would join men and women in their common task to fight for a better society and to conquer the "dark forces" of his times (Rudenschöld, 1920a, *Tankar om Ståndscirkulationen*, p. 40). Sometimes he uses words like "enthusiasm." Today we would use the language of motivation to talk about the forces or powers that trigger men's and women's actions.

20. It is interesting that "body" in Rudenschöld's thought referred to the popular classes or, as he also called them, the community. One might wonder about the genealogical ties between today's community school movement and nineteenth-century thought about the body/community.

21. See Carlgren & Marton, 2001.

22. National imaginaries are not about fixed territories but appear in a relational field. The Nation/national is the outcome of struggles to stabilize and harmonize its governmentalization. On this subject, see Meyer, Kamens, & Benavot (1992).

23. The formation of the European Union is, of course, part of this major revision of identity and globalization, regionalization in which particular discourses are sanctified.

24. The new subject emerged quite recently. In the post-World War II popular educational literature, the child was still governed by the imaginaries of Rudenschöld and Berg, i.e., freedom from vanity. Every schoolchild in Sweden, from the 1950s until the 1970s, met this particular child in the shape of two diametrically opposed literary figures. The one figure was Slösa (spend money and energy) and the other was Spara (save money and energy). This literature was produced and distributed by the so-called Sparbanken (a common bank agency in Sweden).

References

Baker, B. (2001a). State-formation, teaching techniques, and the management of desire. *Recherche et Formation: Special edition on reconstructing the teacher*, no. 38, 47–62. T. S. Popkewitz & A. Nóvoa (Eds.).

Baker, B. (2001b). *In perpetual motion: Theories of power, educational history, and the child.* New York: Peter Lang.

Becker, C. (1932). *The heavenly city of the eighteenth-century philosophers.* New Haven: Yale University Press.

Berg, F. (1921a). Folkskolan som bottenskola (The people's school as a basic school). *Pedagogiska Skrifter.* Stockholm.

Berg, F. (1921b). Den sedliga förvildningen av de unga (The demoralization of youth). *Pedagogiska Skrifter.* Stockholm.

Berg, F. (1922). Kulturen och Nationerna (Culture and Nations). *Pedagogiska Skrifter.* Stockholm.

Boalt, G., & Husén, T. (1964). *Skolans sociologi* (The sociology of school). Stockholm: Almqvist & Wiksell.

Broady, D. (1992). Bildningstraditioner och Läroplaner (Traditions of bildung and curricula). In "Skola för Bildning." Betänkande av läroplanskommittén, Stockholm: SOU (Government reports on social issues), 94, 347–370.

Carlgren, I., & Hörnqvist, B. (1999). *När inget facit finns. Om skolutveckling i en decentraliserad skola* (When there were no final answers. About school development in a decentralized school). Stockholm: Skolverket.

Carlgren, I., & Marton, F. (2001). *Lärare för en ny tid* (Teachers for a new time). Stockholm: Lärarförbundet.

Cronon, W. (Ed.). (1995). *Uncommon ground: Rethinking the human place in nature.* New York: W. W. Norton & Company.

Demokratiutredningen. (2000). *En uthållig demokrati! Politik för folkstyret på 2000-talet* (A durable democracy). Stockholm: Statens Offentliga Utredningar.

Deleuze, G., & Guatteri, F. (1994). *What is philosophy?* London: Verso.

Donzelot, J. (1980). *The policing of families.* London: Hutchinson.

Fendler, L. (2001). Educating flexible souls: The construction of subjectivity through developmentality and interaction. In K. Hultqvist & G. Dahlberg (Eds.), *Governing the child in the new millennium* (pp. 119–142). New York: RoutledgeFalmer.

Foucault, M. (1970). *The order of things: An archaeology of the human sciences.* New York: Vintage Books.

Foucault, M. (1979). *Discipline and punish: The birth of the prison.* New York: Vintage Books.

Foucault, M. (1991). Governmentality. In G. Burchell, C. Gordon, & P. Miller (Eds.), *The Foucault effect: Studies in governmentality* (pp. 87–104). London: Harvester Wheatsheaf.

Frykman, J. (1991). *Social mobility and national character, natural culture as process* (Papers from a Hungarian-Swedish Symposium presented in honour of Tamás Hofer on his 60th birthday), reprinted from *Ethnologica Europaea* XIX, i, 1989.

Goodman, N. (1978). *Ways of worldmaking*. Indianapolis: Hackett.

Hacking, I. (1999). *The social construction of what?* London: Harvard University Press.

Härnqvist, K. (1958). Beräkning av reserver för högre utbildning (Measuring the reserves for higher education), SOU (Government reports on social issues), 11, 7–92, Stockholm: Eckliastikdepartementet.

Hartman, S., & Lundgren, U. P. (1980). *Individ, skola och samhälle. Pedagogiska texter av John Dewey* (Individual, school, and society. Pedagogical texts about John Dewey). Stockholm: Natur och Kultur.

Hultqvist, K. (1990). *Förskolebarnen: En konstruktion för gemenskapen och den individuella frigörelsen* (The pre-school child. A construction for community and the liberation of individuals). Stehag/Stockholm: Symposion förlag.

Hultqvist, K. (1998). A history of the present on children's welfare in Sweden: From Fröbel to present-day decentralization projects. In T. S. Popkewitz & M. Brennan (Eds.), *Foucault's challenge: Discourse, knowledge, and power in education* (pp. 91–116). New York: Teachers College Press.

Hultqvist, K. (2001a). From the people's home to the pupil's home? The cultural child, the enabling state and the lateral tower of observation. In *Tidskrift for Börne & Ungdomskultur*, no. 43, 101–142. Odense Universitetsforlag, Odense, Denmark.

Hultqvist, K. (2001b). Bringing the gods and the angels back? In K. Hultqvist & G. Dahlberg (Eds.), *Governing the child in the new millennium* (pp.143–171). New York: RoutledgeFalmer.

Hultqvist, K. (in press). *Governing the subject in the name of the past, the present and the future: Reforms of the Swedish school as reforms of the conception of time and space* (the study is supported by the Swedish Agency for School [Skolverket]).

Hultqvist, K., & Petersson, K. (2000). Iscensättningen av samhället som skola. Konstruktionen av nya nordiska människotyper mot slutet av det tjugonde århundradet (The deployment of society as school. Constructions of new Nordic human types towards the end of the 1900s). In J. Bjerg (Ed.), *Grundbog i pedagogik* (pp. 517–549). Stockholm: Liber.

Hultqvist, K., Popkewitz, T., Petersson, K., & Andersson, D. (2001). *The state, the subject, and pedagogical technology: A history of the present of political epistemologies and governmentalities at the beginning of the twenty-first century.* Project proposal funded by the Swedish Council for Scientific Research.

Hunter, I. (1988). *Culture and government: The emergence of literary education.* London: Macmillan.

Husén, T. (1951). *Begåvning och miljö.* Stockholm: Gebers.

Larsson, J. (1994). *Hemmet vi ärvde: Om folkhemmet, identiteten och den gemensamma framtiden* (The home we inherited: About the people's home and the common future). Stockholm: Arena.

Latour, B. (1999). *Pandora's hope: Essays on the reality of science studies.* London: Harvard University Press.

Le Bon, G. (1968). *The crowd.* Dunwood, GA: N. S. Berg.

Lesko, N. (2001). *Act your age: A cultural construction of adolescence.* New York: RoutledgeFalmer.

Lindensjö, B., & Lundgren, U. P. (1986). *Politisk styrning och utbildningsreformer* (Political steering and educational reforms). Stockholm: Skolöverstyrelsen/Liber Förlag.

Löfgren, O. (1991). Officiellt är vi alla lika (Officially we are all alike). In K. Molin & B. Ågren (Eds.), *Klassresan* (pp. 24–35). Malmö: Alfabeta Bokförlag.

Menand, L. (2001). *The metaphysical club.* New York: Farrar, Straus and Giroux.

Meyer, J., Kamens, D., & Benavot, A. (1992). *School knowledge for the masses: World models and national primary curricular categories in the twentieth century.* Washington, D.C.: RoutledgeFalmer.

Montessori, M. (1912). *The Montessori method.* London: Heinemann.

Montessori, M. (1934). *Barnträdgården* (Kindergarten), no. 4, p. 60.

Montessori, M. (1936). *The secret of childhood.* Bombay: Orient Longman.

Platon. (1969). *Staten* (M. Dalsjö & D. Tabachowitz, Trans.). Stockholm: Wahlström & Widstrand.

Popkewitz, T. S. (1998). *Struggling for the soul: The politics of schooling and the construction of the teacher.* New York: Teachers College Press.

Popkewitz, T. S. (2000). *Educational knowledge: Changing relationships between the state, civil society and the educational community.* Albany: State University of New York Press.

Popkewitz, T. S. (2001a). Dewey and Vygotsky: Ideas in historical spaces. In T. S. Popkewitz, B. M. Franklin, & M. A. Peyreyra, (Eds.), *Cultural history and education: Critical essays on knowledge and schooling* (pp. 313–349). New York: RoutledgeFalmer.

Popkewitz, T. S. (2001b). Cultural productions and the new expertise of science: Constituting the nation-ness and the citizen in the practices of schooling: Toward a political sociology of schooling. *Revista Brasileira de História* (the publisher is Associaçno Nacional de História– ANPUH [*The Brazilian Journal of the History of Education*]) (pp. 59–78). Brazil: Revista.

Popkewitz, T. S., Franklin, B. M., & Pereyra, M. A. (2001). History, the problem of knowledge, and the new cultural history of schooling: An introduction. In T. S. Popkewitz, B. M. Franklin, & M. A. Peyreyra (Eds.), *Cultural history and education: Critical essays on knowledge and schooling* (pp. 3–42). New York: RoutledgeFalmer.

Popkewitz, T. S., & Pitman, A. (1986). The idea of progress and the legitimation of state agendas: American proposals for school reform. *Curriculum and Teaching, 1*, (1–2), 11–23.

Rose, N. (1989). *Governing the soul: The shaping of the private self.* New York: Routledge.

Rose, N. (1996). The death of the social? Refiguring the territory of government. *Economy and Society, 25*, (3), 327–356.

Rose, N. (1999). *Powers of freedom: Reframing political thought.* Cambridge: Cambridge University Press.

Rose, N. (2000). The politics of life itself: Bio-sociality, genetics and the government of the human vital order. Paper presented at an open lecture at the Stockholm Institute of Education, February 8.

Rudenschöld, T. (1920a). *Tankar om ståndscirkulationen* (Thoughts about social mobility). *Pedagogiska Skrifter*, vol. 89. Stockholm. (Original work published 1845)

Rudenschöld, T. (1920b). *Tankar om ståndscirkulationens verkställighet* (Thoughts about the realization of social mobility). *Pedagogiska Skrifter.* Stockholm. (Original work published 1846)

Sävström, C. A. (1999). Educational psychology in the Swedish welfare state: A model for knowledge production in liberal democracy. *Rapporter från Institutionen för Lärutbildning*, no. 13, Uppsala Universitet.

Sjöstrand, W. (1961). *Pedagogikens historia. 3:1. Sverige och de nordiska grannländerna under frihetstiden och gustavianska tiden* (The history of pedagogy. 3:1. Sweden and the neighboring Nordic countries during the enlightenment and the Gustavianic era). Lund: Gleerup.

Skolverket. (2000). *Det livslånga och livsvida lärandet* (The lifelong and life wide learning). Stockholm: Liber.

Stråth, B. (2000). The Swedish image of Europé as the other. In B. Stråth (Ed.), *Europé and the other and Europe as the other* (pp. 359–383). Bruxelles: PIE Lang.

Trondman, M. (1993). *Bilden av en klassresa. Sexton arbetarbarn på väg till högskolan* (The image of a social class traveled. Sixteen working class children on their way to high school). Stockholm: Carlson.

Wagner, J. (1994). *The sociology of modernity.* New York: Routledge.

Åström, L. (1991). Klassresenärernas arv (The heritage of class travelers). In K. Molin & B. Ågren (Eds.), *Klassresan* (pp. 134–137). Malmö: Alfabeta Bokförlag.

The Reason of Reason: Cosmopolitanism and the Governing of Schooling

Thomas S. Popkewitz

Introduction

Cosmopolitanism can be thought of as a particular theme that recurs and mutates from the European Enlightenment to the present.[1] The Enlightenment's cosmopolitan was an urbane individual who used the reason of science for development that promoted universal values of progress and humanity. But the reason of a cosmopolitan individual was never universal, an ideal, a thing of logic, or a "description" of individual thought. "Cosmopolitan reason" was the will to empower, to borrow from Cruikshank (1999), that inscribed a relation between the "freedom and will of the individual" and the "political liberty and will of the nation" (p. 70). Cosmopolitanism was a political object of social administration to fabricate the child and family as self-governing actors who were simultaneously responsible for social progress and the personal fulfillment of their own lives. The discipline of cosmopolitan reason was the cornerstone of liberty but also the limit and object of government. Today Cosmopolitanism is still talked about as the global citizen freed from provincialism and tradition, who rules by principles of human rights rather than social or theological certainties (see, e.g., Beck, 2000; Castells, 2000). Cosmopolitanism circulates in the projects of pedagogy that are to produce the moral, self-responsible and self-governing child. Its values are in *topoi* of "the knowledge" and "communication" society and the child who is a "life-long learner" who continually recreates his or her self through *being* a problem solver.

The title of this essay, "The Reason of Reason," is intended to historicize the universality and particularity of cosmopolitan reason by working through Foucault's (1991) notion of governmentality in the study of schooling.[2] Foucault argued that it is possible to think about the principles of reason as an inscription device in which different cultural practices come together to govern, shape, and fashion the conduct of conduct. By the eighteenth century, he argues, there is a new complex of relations in the exercise of power in European settings. The hierarchical and sovereign power residing in God, the king, and the queen moved downward to a horizontal notion of power. Power was not so much a negative power that imposed constraints upon the citizen but one that fabricated a subject disciplined through rules of conduct. This new individuality is captured, I believe, in the notion of "cosmopolitanism." Cosmopolitanism makes possible the conditions of the modern state, its citizens, and the pedagogy of the school by bringing together the scientific ordering of reason and the individual who reasoned through science.[3] But the freedom and liberty of the cosmopolitan individual simultaneously embodied distinctions that divided the characteristics of the "civilized" from those who were "noncivilized"—those who were called savages and barbarians and who nineteenth-century United States' pedagogics wanted expelled from the gates of the Republic.[4]

The chapter is concerned with the normalizing and dividing practices in which the cosmopolitan child is fabricated. It travels in uneven historical patterns that give form to eighteenth- and nineteenth-century schooling in the United States. The first section considers cosmopolitan "reason" with an amalgamation of cultural practices to join the registers of social administration with the ordering of the inner characteristics of individual liberty and freedom. I speak of this as a governing of *the soul*.[5] This soul is one not of salvation in an afterlife but one where the reason of the individual is disciplined to order progress and salvation in this world. The governing of the soul, I argue, is made possible through theories of the actor and agency and through notions of community. The calculation and administration of reason connect the intimate relations of the child and family with the collective "home" that constitutes the cosmopolitanism of a nation-ness. The second section explores the new sciences of pedagogy as inscription devices. Intellectual techniques of studying behavior or the processes of the mind produce a type of mapping that renders the characteristics of the child and teacher visible and amenable to government (see Latour, 1986; Rose, 1999). The inscription of cosmopolitan reason was to regulate uncertainty and tame change in the new political/social spaces of the republic and democracy. The third section considers the alchemy of school subjects, that is, the translation and transformation of academic fields into normalizing pedagogies of governing the soul which embodied and did not embody the capabilities of freedom and liberty.[6] In the fourth and final section, I examine briefly the contemporary revisioning of the cosmopolitan child. Whereas the soul of the child at the turn of the twentieth century was socialized to practice a freedom in a collective social entity, today's child is an unfinished cosmopolitan whose soul is administered as a free, self-managed, life-long learner.[7]

I speak of the governing principles of cosmopolitanism as a field of cultural practices or as coagulation, to use the title of this present book. To speak of a *field* of cultural practices is to consider the amalgamation of institutions, authority relations, stories, analogies, memories, and images at different times/spaces that order and classify the objects of reflection and action (see, e.g., Popkewitz, 1991; Popkewitz & Bloch, 2001). My choice of the United States as a site of study is methodological. I focus on the historical materials of American social science and curriculums, but I make no claim to the exceptionality of that history.[8] Finally, my strategy, like that suggested by Cryle (2001), is not to insert Foucault as an author and "look" for the instantiation of concepts as an interpretative shortcut through naming, finding, and consolidating a supposed universal. My approach is to consider the broad contours of different cultural practices that construct the objects of reflection and action and that order what is true and false.

Cosmopolitanism: Fabricating the Soul for Liberty and Freedom

Reason, as a regulating device, can be thought of as a governing practice prior to the European Enlightenment. Greek cosmopolitanism embodied a particularism while preaching universalism, such as in the writings of Stoics who thought of themselves as citizens of the world "due to the fact they were able to transform the *kosmos* into their *polis*...to transform *orbis* into their *urbs*, the world into their own city" (Pollock, 2002, pp. 26–27). The notion of cosmopolitan reason was also embedded in the Church's claim to universality. St. Augustine and Erasmus made reason proof that the individual had a soul and thus could be saved through the Church. Reason was given by God and thus could be used to distinguish the civilized and Christian from the infidels and nonhumans. Further, debates over slavery and colonialization involved the question of whether indigenous groups had the faculty of reason and thus could take part in a civil life that recognized the sovereignty of God and his earthly ministries (see, e.g., Fredrickson, 2002; Menand, 2001).

My interest in cosmopolitanism is related to the European Enlightenment as elite notions of reason moved downward to order the principles of action and participation of individuals. Narrated as a story of the evolution of a universal humanity, the European and American

Enlightenment sought the perfection of man and woman through the "reasoned" actions that brought progress to a secular, earthly paradise. The individual's possession of reason, whether conceptualized as innate to the individual or as socially produced, gave perfection to the individual and to the progress of society (see, e.g., Bell, 2001; Ferguson, 1997). The cosmopolitan was an urbane traveler who moved from city to city in which there was no particular home except the "home" of intellect. But the fabrication of that urbane and cosmopolitan individual embodied different cultural practices that, to borrow from Comte (1827/1975), brought together "order and progress," social administration, and individual freedom.

Fabricating the Child as an Actor with Agency

While current social and educational theories often decry the loss of the actor as part of a dehumanizing approach to research, there has been little acknowledgment that actor and agency are historical inventions.[9] Theories of the actor and agency embody narratives of cosmopolitanism in registers that join social administration with those of the individual's freedom. As Wagner (1994) writes, "The history of modernity cannot simply be written in terms of increasing autonomy and democracy, but rather in terms of changing notions of the substantive foundations of a self-realization and of shifting emphases between individualized enablements and public/collective capabilities" (p. xiv).

Theories of actors and agency make possible "reason" as a calculable object that joins individual enablement and public capabilities. Meyer (1986) argues, for example, that there was the progressive discovery of human personality in the eighteenth and nineteenth centuries—that each person carries a whole system of motives and perceptions that reflect different biological and social forces through which the individual self is integrated. Theories of action and actors/agency were central to the international spread of mass education in the construction of the modern nation in the late nineteenth and early twentieth centuries (Meyer, Boli, Thomas, & Ramirez, 1997). Modern pedagogical theories, for example, focus on practices to make the child a self-regulated actor whose agency is inscribed in being a "learner," a problem solver, or member of a "community" who participates in civic life. Modern theories of the family, as well, order the home to make the parent and child actors whose agencies produce their own self-development and social progress. Such theories of the family, domestic life, and childhood were embodied in the radical assumption that human progress was possible through a rational intervention of individuals in social affairs.

Theories of actors and self-conscious agency are regulatory norms of participation. An individual is produced as an actor who has a perceived natural development of the self that can be rationally managed for individual and social ends. "The competent actor builds the good society....The American individual is free and empowered only within this constraining scheme, and within it freedom is compulsory" (Meyer, 1986, p. 211; see also Meyer & Jepperson, 2000). By the end of the nineteenth century, for example, cosmopolitanism embodied an individuality in which there was a deliberate intention to order one's life. For the middle classes, life was to be organized from one sphere of life to another as if life was a planned workshop that had a value in and of itself (Berger, Berger, & Kellner, 1974). The continued calculations of one's professional decisions inscribed one's identity, one's self-image, and one's material prospects in an expanding universe (Bledstein, 1976, p. 159). The individual calculated one's future so that one's life was not to be taken for granted.

The calculations of freedom and liberty embodied in theories of the actor are historically understood in relation to Foucault's consideration of productive power rather than that of a control system (see, for example, Foucault, 1966/1973, 1975/1979, 1988). Theories of the agentive individual constitute persons as moral subjects of their own actions. The new knowledges of individuality function as disciplining technologies that shape and fashion what it means to act, think, and feel as a responsible and autonomous person. Society became an entity in which to think about individual actors whose agency secured progress.[10] This productive power directs attention in pedagogy to "reasoning" itself as providing governing principles that order who we are and discipline our action and participation in the everyday world.

Central to the theories of the agentive individual was an American Exceptionalism.[11] This Exceptionalism brought "the Chosen People of God" into the imagery of the nation, producing a radical "otherness" in which the nation's citizens were inscribed in terms of "racially elect" conceptions (Glaude, 2000, passim).[12] The early American sociologist, Charles Horton Cooley, thought the family was an administrative practice that brought love and sympathy into the ordering and classifying practices of science in an industrial world. Evoking an Exceptionalism, Cooley wrote that "the new industrial modernity" of America was close to being the first real democracy that is "totally different from anything before it" because it places "a greater emphasis on individuality and innovation and does not inherit the class culture of Europe" (quoted in Ross, 1972, p. 245).

This Exceptionalism was embodied in pedagogy and social science (see, e.g., Ross, 1991). The Exceptionalism was no longer explained in relation to the place of the nation unencumbered by the harmful European traditions from which the New World could be free. The American Exceptionalism of the nineteenth century was perceived as escaping the burden of historical time by fabricating a future cosmopolitan citizen who would be truly universal and a model to the world. Cooley expressed this American Exceptionalism when he saw the United States as "nearer, perhaps, to the spirit of the coming order" that was totally different from anything before it (Cooley, 1909, p. 167).

Pedagogy embodied the exceptionalism of the nation in transporting and translating individual intentionality into the child's freedom. The child's *being* was to develop a liberal, cosmopolitan sense of self-reliance and control to become a citizen of the future who acted with liberty and freedom. One's individual life had an organization and calculable trajectory through life-long career planning. The idea of individual character and biography as having a career was made into an element of individuality. Charles Eliot, an important educational leader in the late nineteenth century, saw education as a civilizing of the child through the learning of a disciplined reason that produced progress toward the unity of the nation. Eliot argued that democratic institutions required that children be educated in the systematic use of reason that could train them "for the duties of life" (Eliot, 1892–1893, p. 417). Eliot continues that "this systematic training could work almost a revolution in human society in two or three generations if wisely and faithfully conducted" (idem). Education is to teach children the "reasoning power and general rationality which are needed for the wise conduct of life" and which differentiate the cosmopolitan and modern child from that of "the savage" who does not use the rules of observation and the correct methods of recording to collaborate and verify one's observations (Eliot, 1892–1893, p. 418).

But the science of observation and the rationally managed "self" were never merely those of rationality alone. The disenchantments of science were never without religious and moral concerns but were remade and (re)visioned into a secular, moral disciplining of the inner characteristics and capabilities of the child.[13] G. Stanley Hall asserted, for example, that

The new psychology [of the child], which brings simply a new method and a new standpoint to philosophy, is I believe Christian to its root and centre; and its final mission in the world is not merely to trace petty harmonies and small adjustments between science and religion, but to flood and transfuse the new and vaster conceptions of the universe and of man's place in it...with the old Scriptural sense of unity, rationality, and love beneath and above all, with all its wide consequences. (Hall quoted in Ross, 1972, p. 140)

Ross continued,

Concepts of adolescence and natural education of children were first worked in the context of religious feeling, and...[were meant] to describe the newer experience of intellectual doubt and return a confirmation of one's place not in a religious universe but in the natural world. (Ross, 1972, pp. 334–335)

The relation of religious and secular narratives travel in pedagogy. The Puritan's notion of pedagogy as "converting ordinances," or evangelizing works that were written with a calculated design on the souls of their readers, was transferred to the development of the child. G. Stanley Hall, for example, brought together discourses of a nation-ness, science, and religion in the production of a cosmopolitan child (Hall, 1905/1969). Hall, as did other social scientists, spoke of *the soul* in describing the focus of psychology and the relation of psychology to pedagogy. For Hall, psychology was a way of reconciling faith and reason, Christian belief and "Enlightenment empiricism" in the making of an *American* society. "The bible is being slowly re-revealed as man's great text-book in psychology" (quoted in O'Donnell, 1985, p. 119; also see Bloch, 1987). Hall's (1893/1924) studies of the adolescent embodied a liberal and democratic image of shaping and improving the nation through the child.

Hall's synthetic transformation of these earlier ideas of youth into the modern concept of adolescence clearly owed much to the social setting of the 1890s in America. The decade was rife with fear of the new urban, industrial society and its destruction of the older rural and village ways that most Americans still knew firsthand. It was also beginning to spawn a more optimistic desire to find new sources of vitality and new norms for the emerging society. Conservatives and liberals looked to nature, to a nostalgic image of the rural past, or to a confident image of the dynamism and intelligence ever present in the nature of man and society. There was a romantic desire to build organic values into an increasingly specialized and mechanized urban, industrial, and scientific civilization (Ross, 1972, pp. 335–337).

The inscription of the soul to bring the past, present, and future into a determinant relation through a disciplining of reason is a problematic of the Enlightenment. Foucault's (1984) "What Is Enlightenment? *Was ist Aufklärung?*" focuses on an attitude and experience that situates the individual as object and subject of reflection in a conditional world. There is no longer a transcendental or universal structure of all knowledge but an individuality that emerges "from the contingence that has made us what we are, the possibility of no longer being, doing, or thinking what we are, do, or think" (p. 46). This contingency is embodied in the notion of the agentive individual who interiorizes the norms or patterns of action as the rules and standards of individuality. The future is marked by the conditionality of citizen participation that is stabilized and harmonized through the rules of reason and the "reasonable" citizen. The agent is the cosmopolitan child who is also to become the future citizen.

In sum, *the soul* of the child inscribed a universal notion of reason that in fact was a local and particular amalgamation of American and European bourgeois norms, Protestant religious notions of salvation, and political rationalities of a Republic that entailed colonialization and slavery. Revelation is transferred to the inscriptions of a cosmopolitan reason that administers development, self-reflection, and inner, self-guided moral growth of individual personality and character (see, e.g., Hirst, 1994). Outwardly, European Enlightenment notions of cosmopolitanism were to radically separate the norms of progress of humanity from the transcendence norms of the Church and the parochialism of the nation. But in fact, they continually overlapped as evident in the phrases "New World" and "Manifest Destiny" in the construction of the imaginaries of the American nation. American cosmopolitanism remained powerfully shaped by the missionary and salvation heritage of a Protestant Christianity reinscribed in the images of a new sovereign nation as shaped by a cosmopolitan political "will" (see, e.g., Bell, 2001).

Community, the Family, and the "Home" of the Nation: Ordering Intimate Relations

Theories of the child, family, and community are inscriptions that govern agentive individuals who manage their lives and carry responsibilities that are not only for self-development and growth but also for standardized public virtues that enable the conferring of that agency

(Rose, 1999). The notion of community brought the images and narratives of the nation into the intimate relations that fabricated the child as the citizen of the future. Community and family were the intermediary sites at which "a home" was to be established that connected collective obligations and intimate relations. Community and family are still regulated sites for moral agency as a basis and product of a mode of life today.

Community is a concept that overlaps spiritual and religious traditions and the processes of secularization (Cronon, 1996). It is a site in which the cosmopolitan travels to establish a home that links individuality with the collective "home" of the nation.[14] As Hennon (2002) argues, there is a more precise telescopic pinpointing of the individual citizen within towns as the normative place of the local community which brought segments of a national population into tighter social, civic, moral, and economic relations. In the early American colonial situation, for example, authority and liberty flowed from the structure of personal relations and not from the political organization of the society (Wood, 1991). The family or household was the basic institution in society on which all rights and obligations were centered (see, e.g., Foucault, 1991). Puritans called the family a little commonwealth. It was the fundamental source of community and continuity, the place where most work was done, and the primary institution for teaching the young, disciplining the wayward, and caring for the poor and insane. The family was the model for describing most political and social relationships, not only between the king and subjects but also between superiors and subordinates.

But by the end of the eighteenth century, the family ceased to be simply an institution for the transmission of a name and an estate. The family, the school, and the town (community) were places where freedom and liberty were problematized and technologized to constitute and shape moral agency.[15] The new expertise of the social sciences was to regulate and discipline reason that ordered the rules and standards of an individual's participation. Theories of the family, child, and learning ordered the dispositions and sensitivities of the liberty of the citizen. Whereas children formerly had mixed freely in adult society, the elites of society now "saw" the child as a person with distinctive attributes—impressionability, vulnerability, and innocence—which required a new pattern of governing that protected and prolonged the period of nurture and regulated development (see Ariès, 1960/1962; Steedman, 1995).

The invention of a range of technologies enabled the family to inscribe the norms of public duty while not destroying its private authority. The family and community were transformed into particular spaces that would move the adult away from public vices and impose a duty of responsibility on the home, the child, and the desire for bettering one's own condition. Rose (1999) refers to these as technologies of *responsibilization.*

> The government of freedom, here, may be analyzed in terms of the deployment of technologies of *responsibilization.* The home was to be transformed into a purified, cleansed, moralized, domestic space. It was to undertake the moral training of its children. It was to domesticate and familiarize the dangerous passions of adults, tearing them away from public vice, the gin palace and the gambling hall, imposing a duty of responsibility to each other, to home, and to children, and a wish to better their own condition. The family, from then on, has a key role in strategies for the government of freedom. It links public objectives for good health and good order of the social body with the desire of individuals for personal health and well-being. A "private" ethic of good health and morality can thus be articulated on to a "public" ethic of social order and public hygiene, yet without destroying the autonomy of the family—indeed by promising to enhance it. (Rose, 1999, p. 74)

The school had a particular place in this new governing that related the family, childhood, and communities. The affection, sympathy, and cognition of the family were redeployed as an explicit problem of the school's pedagogy. The school was narrated in the image of the family yet had to supersede its norms and cultural values in order to produce the citizen who would guarantee the future of American progress. A document by the American Superintendents of Schools (1874) for an international meeting in Vienna argues that "The existence of a republic, unless all its citizens are educated, is an admitted impossibility" (p. 6). The education in the school was then differentiated as a phase of education lying between the earliest period of family-nurture (which was still a concomitant and powerful auxiliary), on the one hand, and the necessary initiation into the specialities of a vocation in practical life on the other.

> In America, the peculiarities of civil society and the political organization drew the child out of the influence of family nurture earlier than was common in other countries. The frequent separation of the younger branches of the family from the old stock renders family influence less powerful in molding character. The consequence of this is the increased importance of the school as an ethical point of view. (The American Superintendents of Schools, 1874, p. 13)

The family was a way to deal with the threat to cultural production and dissemination tied up with the American identity. Some early political scientists, for example, spoke about "race suicide" as a national problem produced through immigration—but they understood and represented the threat as a challenge, literally and metaphorically, to the American family (Wald, 1995). MIT President Francis Amasa Walker, a statistician involved in the censuses in 1870 and 1880, saw the outcome of immigration as the destruction of the American family. John R. Commons, a prominent progressive economist, raised the question of race suicide through the analogy of the family and gender, heeding Theodore Roosevelt's warning that "if the men of the nation are not anxious...to be fathers of families, and if the women do not recognize that the greatest thing for any woman is to be a good wife and mother...that nation has cause to be alarmed about its future" (quoted in Wald, 1995, p. 245).

The teacher was analogous to the mother, but her tasks were to fabricate the child as an actor who disregarded the traditions of familiar provincialism to embody the rules and standards of a cosmopolitan "reason." Teacher education, for example, was to select self-motivated and morally devoted candidates who would shape the character of the child.[16] "The real end of all education is to produce morally trained *men* and *women*," an educator wrote in 1898, "rather than, except in special cases, scholars. Unless this point is kept in mind by the teacher throughout his school-life experience, the professional element of his chosen vocation fails utterly of its chief end, and the pedagogue places himself in the same class as the mechanic, producing things instead of creating characters" (quoted in Mattingly, 1977, p. 44).

The school was a site for the extension of the universal (primary) ideals that underlay democracy and Christianity, but these ideals were not to be achieved in a large school but through interpersonal communication and the development of personality that regulated action and participation. Theories of growth, development, and progress embodied narratives of the nation and its people as the guardian and exemplar of the moral, social, and economic qualities of an industrious people who brought progress to humanity (see Ross, 1991). Progress in government was not simply an education to accommodate society but needed to "be in the direction of acquainting every member of society more thoroughly with the special nature of the institution, and awakening him to a more vivid conception of his personal interest in its management" (Ward, 1883, p. 243). The cosmopolitanism of the child rationally ordered options, placed development into linear sequences, and saw progress as a synchronized relation between individual action, family practices, and national destinies. The discipline and freedom embodied a universal humanity—the social/psychological laws and indeterminacy constituted the unique development of democratic values and a cosmopolitan outlook.

Social Sciences as Inscription Devices

If the discipline of the reason of the child and family were the cornerstone of liberty, the social sciences were the inscription devices. Into the nineteenth century, science was a rather vague notion of rationality to order progress and the cosmopolitanism of the individual. Science at the end of the century was more focused, systematic, and empirically oriented.[17]

The new expertise of the sciences of the child and family tamed and regularized irregularities and conditionality of the social world.[18] The individual was no longer to conform to the exercise of political will but to the active production of a rationally managed individuality whose agency secured progress and social ends. Control was transformed into processes mediated through a social-psychological language (Ross, 1991, pp. 230–239). Sociological theories moved into a plane of a social psychology and psychology at the University of Chicago, for example, to focus on the processes of intersubjective mediation for self-realization (see, e.g., Franklin, 1986; Kliebard, 1986). George Herbert Mead and his colleague at the University of Chicago, John Dewey, pursued concepts of social mediation and self-realization through ordering individual actions in the domains of community.

The initial focus of the social sciences was on environmental conditions that produced poverty and thus prevented participation. The foci of social science in relation to education were transmogrified into the individual personal and psychological characteristics of the child and family that made for unhappiness. This soul required pastoral care. Measurement theories, psychological testing, and norms of child development established a hierarchy of an evolutionary racial history of "The Great Chain of Being," a term that circulated in the nineteenth century (Lesko, 2001).[19] For some of the early social scientists and social reformers, the Old World cultures had to be destroyed through resocializing the immigrant family and child. But for other social scientists and reformers, the immigrant groups of the city embodied elements of culture that could be integrated to produce the ideal of a future American Exceptionalism.

A major focus was on the planning of the new society and reforming of its citizenry. The early sociological theories by founders of American sociology such as Frank Lester Ward, Albion Small, and Charles Horton Cooley accepted the uncertainties of a democracy but also sought to tame change through the making of the child. New and finer distinctions of the mind, social interaction, and community emerged through surveys and qualitative studies of urban planning, the domestic sciences, the social psychologies of the mind, and child development. The sciences provided calculations that were descriptive of the actors and the social spaces of the nation. The theories of family and community fabricated the rules and standards of action and participation. Albion Small combined the social with psychological notions of agentive actors. Pedagogy was "the science of assisting youth to organize their contacts with reality" that was concerned "for both thought and action" (Small, 1896, p. 178). The progress of the nation, Small continued, was in the teacher who was "a maker of society...[and] making a better future" (Small, 1896, p. 184).

Cooley exemplifies the emergence of a new expertise of social and psychological sciences in the shaping a new form of affiliation and belonging in which the life trajectories of the family and the child in the nation could be produced (Baker, 2001; Bell, 2001, p. 19; see also Bloch, Holmlund, Moqvist, & Popkewitz, 2003; Hultqvist & Dahlberg, 2001). Cooley deployed the concept of community as a regulatory principle to fabricate the active agent of an American democracy through ordering the characteristics of family and childhood (see, e.g., Franklin, 1986). Cooley's community articulated a romantic liberalism given shape by a national exceptionalism in which the American spirit was an embodiment of "a more general spirit of human nature" (quoted in Ross, 1991, p. 245).

A dual vision emerged. Community was a romantic model of escape that could capture the nostalgia of times prior to modernity; but at the same time, the notion of community located the individual *in* modernity by making the social interactions of individuals and groups sites for social planning. It was believed that lost in modernity was what Tönnies called *Gemeinschaft*, the image of a rural and pastoral vision of community that functions as the sublime, where the home of God is found and where neighbors prior to modernity come closest to nature. While the word *community* was used by the Puritans to talk about "communities of believers," it assumed a different set of connections as an organizing concept of the new social sciences. Community was to serve as a corrective of the alienation produced in the urbanization and industrialization of modernity, what Tönnies (1887/1957) called *Gesellschaft*. One's participation in civic life and cosmopolitanism in a "community" was to regain what was "lost" in urbanization and industrialization. Community was a site for reestablishing allegiances of close, emotional, face-to-face ties, and the attachments of homogeneous regulated traditions and customs. The new cathedral of science was to calculate and engineer the forms of conduct through which individuals engaged in face-to-face relation of "communities" through the systems of reason and rationalities of modernity. The notions of nature and the innate qualities of childhood embodied in the social and psychological sciences, for example, embodied romantic, pastoral images of community that were translated and transported from the writings of Rousseau, Pestalozzi, Thoreau, and Emerson into the sciences of pedagogy of the United States curriculum (see Baker, 2001).

The family and community were sites visioned (revisioned) to a belonging and "a home" in which the distancing of modernity was brought into a relation to the intimate relations of the face-to-face interactions. The family was no longer a hindrance to developing a universal "reason" and reasonable person but one that linked the individual and community (*Gemeinschaft*) with the conditions of modernity (*Gesellschaft*). The community sociology developed at the University of Chicago during the first decades of the nineteenth century reinscribed the importance of interaction and connections of *Gemeinschaft* as calculable practices (see, e.g., Franklin, 1986; Lindner, 1990/1996). Connections between the family, marriage, urban conditions and, in some instances, women's issues were studied to consider the new problems of socialization and identity formation. The family was visualized as the cradle from which civilization was produced where a child learns to be civilized and of civilization. Parents, under the guidance of new social theories of health, would develop altruistic instincts that expressed self-obligation and self-responsibility in their children. Images of Protestant moral and ethical life were overlaid with the categories of science to humanize and personalize individual disciplines (see, e.g., Greek, 1992).

The "primary group" was a notion of the community sociology to create new senses of belonging and "home." The primary group was an intellectual tool to link the familiar face-to-face relations (*Gemeinschaft*) with the conditions of modernity (*Gesellschaft*) (Popkewitz & Bloch,

2001). Cooley (1909) saw the family as *a primary group* where a child learns of civilization through face-to-face interaction—an assumption that persists in various forms in contemporary social and psychological thought. Cooley thought that proper socialization by the family and the neighborhood would enable the child to lose the innate greed, lust, and pride of power that was innate to the infant and thus to become fit for civilized society. The communication systems of the family would, according to Cooley, establish the family on Christian principles that stressed a moral imperative to live and self-sacrifice for the good of the group (also see Lasch, 1977).

The Alchemy of School Subjects: Normalizing Pedagogies

The governing practices of sociology and psychology were constitutive in the formation of school subjects. If we compare teaching during the early decades of the nineteenth century with that of the early twentieth century, the primer books of the classroom that organized teaching were replaced by textbooks designed for school subjects (see Popkewitz, 1987). The school subjects, to borrow a phrase from Hunter (1988), were normalizing pedagogies. School subjects were to shape or fashion particular subjectivities of the child who was to become the future citizen. It is not that reading or music were not taught before this time or that children did not previously learn about a moral history of the nation but that school subjects now stood in the new pedagogies as particular strategies to fabricate the child's moral agency as a mode of life. The classifications of school subjects were to govern the inner dispositions and sensitivities of the children and teachers and were not pedagogies of the academic disciplines.

I speak of school subjects in this context of governing as "an alchemy." Pedagogy transports, translates, and transmogrifies the spaces of academic disciplines as academic disciplines move into the spaces of school subjects. The alchemy transforms school subjects into sites to order the child, family, and community, as I discussed previously. Like the sorcerer of the Middle Ages who sought to turn lead into gold, pedagogy magically transforms sciences, social sciences, and humanities into pedagogical psychologies and social psychologies of the child. The significance of the alchemy in governing is in its double sense: School subjects embody representations that engage the child with the objects that stand as part of the real world, and school subjects fabricate the child and teacher as subjects whose agencies act on the representations embodied in school subjects.

The formation of school subjects was not about the particular grammars and styles of expressions that inhere in the knowledge of mathematics, physics, and linguistics. Nor was it about the network and relations that form and give order to the norms of participation, truth, and recognition in the various academic fields associated with school subjects. School subjects were to calculate the "proper" dispositions and sensitivities of reason so that children would become "reasonable" citizens of the future. The school was to inscribe the maps that order the freedom of the child; learning of arithmetic and reading was "to acquire the feelings, sentiments, and ideas of mankind" as government was "charged with the interests of civil society, and thus directly concerned in the creation and distribution of wealth and the personal well-being of the individual in the community" (The American Superintendents of Schools, 1874, p. 11). Pedagogy is to enable "the completion of the individual" that involved "the individual cooperation and perfecting the development of that individuality" (Small, 1896, p. 175). In this alchemy, concepts and generalizations of academic knowledge are treated as logical, non-temporal structures that function as foundations from which learning occurs. The social mooring of the disciplinary knowledge that orders relations and constructs identities in science or social science is denied.[20]

The alchemy is related to a broader shift in what Hamilton (1999) has called "the instructional turn." The development of syllabi, curriculum, and method occurred in the sixteenth and seventeenth centuries. These developments placed an emphasis on teaching rather than on learning. Prior to this, the medieval teacher was to give a faithful representation and transmission of the inherited teaching or doctrine. A new pedagogical literature directed at schoolteachers emerged. It mapped a knowledge that gave rise to the notion of curriculum (the course of modern schooling); knowledge was organized around a set of principles related to upbringing or "content" and ordered through the notion of method (delivery of instruction) (Hamilton, 1999, p. 139).

The alchemy of school subjects is related to a progressivism that tied the rationality of planning to the interior of the child's mind, thought, and problem-solving. Progressivism embodied new relations of time and space as the child's interior was opened and was given a history of "development" that related the past and present to the future. The Report of the Committee of Ten (National Education Association, 1892/1969), for example, recommended modern, high school academic subjects be designed to impose greater standardization on the pattern of college admissions (Krug, 1972). The high school was to replace school subjects tied to church concerns of literacy with a secularization and rationalization of knowledge. The Committee proposed that the training of the child was not only of the mind, but that it also was to fabricate an individual character who planned life through the rationality of science. Charles Eliot, the chair of the Report of the Committee of Ten and the President of Harvard University, argued that each of the conferences of the Committee, had "shown how every subject which they recommend can be made a serous subject of instruction, well fitted to train the pupil's powers of observation, expression, and reasoning" (National Education Association, 1892/1969, p. 43).

The Report of the Committee of Ten embodied a differentiated high school with different tracks for students organized through school subjects. The Report differentiated between those going to college and those who did not prepare for college:

> Their main function is to prepare for the duties of life that small proportion of all the children in the country—a proportion small in number, but very important to the welfare of the nation—who show themselves able to profit by an education prolonged to the eighteenth year, and whose parents are able to support them while they remain so long at school....A secondary school programme intended for national use must therefore be made for those children whose education is not to be pursued beyond the secondary school. (National Education Association, 1892/1969, p. 51)

The organization of school subjects in the report can also be read as bringing into the school a particular cosmopolitan individuality. The interior of the child was open to scrutiny and to rational, ordered development that embodied an American Exceptionalism and its exclusions.[21] For example, the writer of the report argued that

> One is fortified against the acceptance of unreasonable propositions only by skill in determining facts through observation and experience, by practice in comparing facts or groups of facts, and by the unvarying habit of questioning and verifying allegations, and of distinguishing between facts and inferences from facts, and between a true cause and an antecedent event. One must have direct training and practice in logical speech and writing before he can be quite safe against specious rhetoric and imaginative oratory. (Eliot, 1892–1893, p. 424)

The student of the school embodied a particular trajectory of time in which self-realization, personal fulfillment, and individual destinies were rationally ordered options of a synchronized relation. Each school subject was to teach a universal reason that tamed passions, desires, and sentiments through an ordering of human subjectivity. Psychology of the child was implicit in the report but later was given an explicit role in the reform of schooling. Eliot (1892–1893), the chair of the Report, took criticisms of the Report as not taking into consideration the knowledge of child study by arguing that there is a need to consider the "bodily changes in childhood and youth...to mark off the years between birth and maturity into distinct, sharply defined periods, bearing separate names like childhood and adolescence, and to prescribe appropriate pedagogical treatment for each period" in the formation of the curriculum (Eliot, 1905, pp. 342–343). Curriculum, Eliot continued, needs to be pay attention to a relation between "the idea of individual differences and a scientific educational theory" (p. 343).

Psychology became the major discourse in the alchemy of school subjects. Its intellectual mapping provided a practical set of skills for making the individual child an object of administration. This administration of the inner characteristics of the child's soul involved competing ideological agendas. The curriculum was to develop labor market skills, leisure time activity of the middle class, moral character and aesthetic taste, and a healthful and creative self-expression (Freedman, 1987; Stanic, 1987).

The alchemy of academic knowledge provided a concrete set of strategies in normalizing and governing *the soul* of the child. The school subject of mathematics, for example, was ordered through the psychology of Edward Thorndike and his students. Mathematics gave focus to the administration of the child who worked on his or her self to become self-directed and self-governed. The high school mathematics curriculum initially was a form of character training through its methods to mentally exercise and train the mind. By the early decades of the nineteenth century, mathematics education was to train the individual in observation, experimentation, and reflection through relevancy to the practical problems of children. The standards of development and learning were to order thought, the mind, and the social interactions of children to produce "higher emotions and [the] giving [of] mental pleasure" (Stanic, 1987, p. 155).

The psychological and social psychological practices were particular translation and transportation devices in the governing of the child. Theories of the child as actor and agent mobilized distinctions of inner characteristics that could be supervised, planned for, and judged. In this context, the systems of knowledge in mathematics were sites in which to effect this normalization of reason and "the reasonable" child. School subjects were represented as stable "entities" for children to reflect on and to order the possibilities of their worlds. Pedagogy ordered and cataloged the "reason" of the child in using the representations of school subjects.

Transmogrification of Cosmopolitanism: Some Comments about the New Millennium

I began this discussion with an observation about today's cosmopolitanism, which celebrates a global citizen who organizes life through the reason of science, is committed to a universal humanity, and whose freedom is enacted by a citizen of a world society (rather than of the nation). But globalization is not new. And the cosmopolitan continually involves a particularism with its universalism. My focus on cosmopolitanism has been on a word (and attitude) that has changing cultural configurations which traveled globally in the making of the nation and the school from the nineteenth century onward (Meyer, Boli, Thomas, & Ramirez, 1997). The distinctions and differentiations of the cosmopolitan mutated from those of elites to the governing of populations. The disciplining of reason was central to the governing practices. And while today there is talk of a globalized economy and information society with the withering of the state, I argue that there is no withering but rather new fields of cultural practices that fabricate the child, family, community, and teacher. The redemptive project appeals to terms such as democracy and freedom in remaking the capabilities and characteristics of the cosmopolitan child.

Who is the cosmopolitan citizen whose reason is to secure today's "freedom and national survival"? Whereas one can think of the child of the pedagogical world of the early nineteenth century as producing a subject who embodied the collective social narratives of the nation, today's child is an *unfinished cosmopolitan.* This unfinished cosmopolitanism is captured in the phrase, "life-long learner." The life-long learner is flexible, continuously active, and a person who works collaboratively in a decentralized world.

The inner characteristics are cosmopolitan in the sense of an individuality that can chase desire and work in a global world in which there is no finishing line. The child is someone who can choose to refuse allegiance to any one of the infinite choices on display, except the choice of choosing. The unfinished cosmopolitan is an individual in a perpetual intervention in one's life through working actively in "communities" of learning. Life becomes a continuous course of personal responsibility and self-management of one's risks and destiny (see Hammerberg in this volume).

Today's salvation stories are of an active sense of "self" whose emotional bonds and self-responsibility are circumscribed through networks of other individuals—the family and the community. The self-management of the early part of the nineteenth century was a *socialized* individual ordered through universalized laws of child development and the scientifically organized family that expressed an American Exceptionalism. Current reforms no longer seem guided by externally validated social morals and obligations. American Exceptionalism, in contemporary reforms, is a freedom of empowered individuals whose ethical selves are tied to continually constructing and reconstructing their own practices and ways of life in multiple communities.

The embodiment of the unfinished cosmopolitanism is the problem solver. Problem solving is not a natural process found in the child but a fabrication that responds to a humanitarian impulse of schooling. Problem solving is a fabrication just the same. It functions as both a "fiction" and a "making" of kinds of people. The category of problem solving is *fiction that responds to things* occurring in the world. It inscribes particular psychologies of the mind and social interaction of the child into pedagogy.

But the fabrication of the child as a problem solver "makes" a human/kind, that is, "makes" a determinate classification that has distinct chronological, physiological, and psychological characteristics that can be applied to the governing of many people. The location of responsibility is no longer sedimented in the range of social practices directed toward a single public sphere but instead traverses diverse and plural "communities" to constitute the common good. The struggle for the soul is now in the "autonomous learners" who are continuously involved in "self-improvement" and ready for the uncertainties through working actively in "communities of learning" (see, e.g., The National Council of Teachers of Mathematics, 2000). Reason is no longer for the perfection of the Republic through making multiple communities into the collective embodiment of the social good. Change, contingency, and uncertainty in daily life are tamed through the rules and standards that place the problem-solving child in diverse communities where the common good is formed.

The home and collective belonging of earlier times are realigned in the internments and enclosures of *community* as sites for the development of life-long learners. The school remains a site of school/family connections to recalibrate political aspirations of the individual. Children work in "learning communities" or "communities of discourse." New forms of differentiating and calculating the child as a site of governing are produced in "the community." Children construct knowledge while teachers work as partners and collaborators who are governed through communication systems and networks (discourse communities) of the reformed curriculum.

The cosmopolitanism of the new millennium involves a different construction of the parent. The parent is pedagogicalized (Popkewitz, 2003). The domestic sciences at the turn of the century sought to provide parents with technologies to calculate proper child development and health. The school took on the role of the family in teaching moral agency through learning a professionalized knowledge. Contemporary research and policy proposals remake parenting in the image of pedagogies. Parents (mothers) are no longer the "primary group" to effect child-rearing strategies that ensure the growth and health of the child. These responsibilities are broadened into teaching the conduct that produces school achievement and learning. The cultural patterns of the classroom operate as the rules and classifications for the actions of the parent. The family governs the soul of the child in the images and narratives of learning the skills of the school (Bloch & Popkewitz, 2000).

The unfinished cosmopolitanism of the child is also that of the teacher who is similarly classified as a life-long learner. The teacher is self-actualized by remaking his or her own biography. That biography is continually calculated through researching the self as the teacher. The "reflective teacher," for example, assesses the child through life histories or portfolios and makes and remakes his or her own biography through personal assessment of self-development and self-management (see Fendler, 2003). Teachers are now asked to go into the "community," to become part of communities to "better know" their pupils and their families, to become trusted, or to "know" what they should include in their classrooms from "community knowledge" (Bloch & Tabachnick, 1994; Borman, 1998; Delpit, 1995).

Today, the alchemy of school subjects is the curriculum as an instructional device "*regulating* the interaction among children rather than just regulating the individual action" (emphasis added) (Cazden, 1986, p. 450). Mathematics curriculum, for example, is to have children "construct their mathematical knowledge" so that there is not only mastery of content but supervision of the "sense-making activities" of children. The mapping of "sense making" of the child is the target of pedagogical action to remodel the child's thought processes. Children explain their solutions verbally so teachers can have them revise (see, e.g., Nelson, Warfield & Wood, 2001; for analysis of the alchemy in mathematics, see Popkewitz, in press). But *the sense making* is no longer the child's but that of the pedagogical system of reason that classifies and divides the child's inner characteristics. Change is ordered and stabilized via the sense making by which the child becomes a "life-long learner"— a child who is able to embody particular rules of conduct for reflecting on how a problem was solved.

The alchemy of school subjects in contemporary curriculum also calls for greater participation and collaboration by children and teachers. But the self-management of choice and the autonomous conduct of life is about less. Let me provide an example. If we look at school science, it has moved dramatically to include greater student participation (McEneaney, 2003). Instruction is about greater personal relevance and emotional accessibility. The curriculum imbues the child with an expert status. But the child's expert status is not at the expense of the knowledge of the professional expert. The social and physical/biological worlds stand as representations about wider claims of the natural world as ordered and manageable through science. The child's participation is in relation to a world of science that has a double task. Science provides the authoritative knowledge about broader and broader elements of the world. The rules of science that express the representations of science are given as the methods for telling the truth. The new expertise of the child is not to assess truth but to learn its Elysian mysteries. The teacher is a coach/facilitator of the child's internalization of the rules of interpretation and expertise of science to order conduct in the world.

The fears of social-cultural disintegration and moral disorganization permeate questions of globalization, nation, and cultural identity. The fear is that the school will not prepare the child adequately for globalization. Today, talk is of the natural *birthright* of the child, whose freedom transcends the family and school but whose family and school have responsibility for development and discipline. No longer is the school to socialize the child to become an adult in a community whose belonging is imagined through the singular standards of a nation-ness. The child stands as a fabrication who has his or her own rights, obligations, and responsibilities that the teacher nurtures. Progress is embodied in a universal political philosophy about the natural, inalienable *birthright of the child*, who now has the independent rights of the citizen (see, e.g., Moqvist-Lindberg, 2003). But that *birthright* is shaped and fashioned through the qualities and characteristics described earlier as the life-long learner. The taming of change is now embodied in the processes in which the child makes and remakes his or her soul as a self-actualized individuality.

The exclusions appear as a quest for greater inclusion. Research and reform proposals are about *all* children as seen in *No Child Left Behind*, the title of United States legislation for the new millennium. Everyone is to have the possibility of being cosmopolitan and free! But the clarion call for teaching reform is not only a call to meet future economic progress. It is also a warning about the threats of moral and cultural disorganization as embodied in the characteristics of the child who is placed outside of the values that order the composite of the *all* children, the child who does not choose, chase desire, and become a life-long learner. Inserted into policy and research reports about "all children" are references to children who do not fit the universalized characteristics: children "who live in poverty, students who are not native speakers of English, students with disabilities, females, and many nonwhite students [who] have traditionally been far more likely than their counterparts in other demographic groups to be victims of low expectations" (National Council of Teachers of Mathematics, 2000, p. 13). Today's deviant child is to be rescued through finer and finer distinctions that order and classify the wayward child; the child is one who does not yet have the "problem-solving skills" and is not a flexible learner.

As Foucault (1984) stated in "What Is Enlightenment?" my argument is not against reason, community, or even problem solving. My strategy is to interrogate the field of cultural practices in which reason, community, and problem solving are historically constituted. My movement between the past and the present notions of cosmopolitanism is to explore the (re)formation of schooling as fields of cultural practices that order who the child is, should be, and is not to be. Reason is a governing practice that stands as a salvation narrative in the administration of freedom and liberty in an indeterminate future. But reason is also a historical practice that generates distinctions and divisions about action and participation. Making thought and reason a subject of inquiry is a critical engagement in knowledge as a productive practice and thus part of the materiality of schooling. There is no *a priori* philosophical structure or *ahistorical* subject to shape and fashion the meanings and images of the subject of schooling.

Endnotes

Acknowledgments: The discussion relates to a broader analysis that I am writing, and the references are selective so as not to overload the paper with these citations. At the same time, I owe a lot to a number of people for conversations that have raised questions regarding the historical themes that I pursue here. These people have continually pushed my thinking and sent me on intellectual odysseys that are reflected here although probably not as adequately as they have hoped. Among them are Lynn Fendler, Kenneth Hultqvist, Mirian Warde, Miguel Pereyra, Ruth Gustafson, Dar Weyenberg, Amy Sossnoski, the Wednesday Group seminar, and the editors of this book, Bernadette Baker and Katharina Heyning.

1. This is not to say that an image of the individual as a cosmopolitan miraculously appears in the Enlightenment or that there were not multiple cosmopolitanisms before or during the Northern European Enlightenment (see, e.g., Breckenridge, Pollock, Bhaba, & Chakrabarty, 2002). Rather, one needs a point of entrance, and the national projects, secularization, individualization, and imposition of science in the ordering of reason make a convenient place to begin my story. For example, there is a Catholic Counter-Reformation use of cosmopolitanism in education that was in opposition to that of northern Europe. Miguel Pereyra and his colleagues are working on the use of cosmopolitanism in Spain during the nineteenth century. My focus is in relation to the Protestant movements as they circulated in Europe and in the American Enlightenment (see Ferguson, 1997).

2. Foucault and political reason are discussed in Barry, Osborne, and Rose (1996). I discuss this in, for example, Popkewitz (1991, 1998), Popkewitz and Brennan (1998), and Popkewitz, Franklin, and Pereyra (2001).

3. The notion of the modern is used hesitantly here. My concern is not to engage in the periodization that occupies many historians and sociologists. Rather it is to explore the slow and uneven changes in the categories, epistemologies, and distinctions that make possible the institutional developments of the state, industrialization, and urbanization, among others, that are often associated with modernity. The inscription of reason as a cultural practice to administer the universal/particularities of a cosmopolitanism is one strategy in which to consider how the modern is constituted and mutates.

4. In one sense, the idea of the republic and the historical instantiation of democracy overlap with multiple historical practices that include capitalism. My focus, however, is on the cultural patterns that travel along overlapping paths rather than any normative principle of democracy or republicanism. Further, my reading across different national sites suggests that there are global discourses of reform that circulate as universal cosmopolitan values in the making of the "educated" child. But this globalizing also requires particular and differentiated historicizations (see, e.g., Popkewitz, 2001; Fendler, 2003; Lindblad & Popkewitz, 2002; also Popkewitz, Franklin & Pereyra, 2001).

5. The governing of the soul is initially discussed in Foucault (1975/1977), and in Rose (1989).

6. Historically, the notions of freedom and liberty were used interchangeably in the American context (see, e.g., Foner, 1998).

7. This notion came out of a conversation with Ruth Gustafson. I appreciate her thinking through with me some of the intellectual and historical questions raised in this paper.

8. Later in this discussion, I talk historically about an American Exceptionalism embedded in the narrative of schooling. The former should not be confused with this use of the word "exceptionalism" as differentiating a methodological strategy. See footnote thirteen.

9. This way of thinking of theories of actors can be inferred in the discussions of feminist cultural theory and postcolonial historical writers (see, e.g., Butler, 1993; Chakrabarty, 2000).

10. The notion of society emerged in the Enlightenment and made possible the notion of the individual, as the two stand in relation to each other historically. The changes that occurred involved multiple historical trajectories; among others are the Protestant Reformation and economic changes related to early capitalism embedded in the notion of cosmopolitanism. But my concern here is not with an institutional history of such changes. The invention of "the social" is a hybrid space that makes possible the space of the social economy and the new relations of the private and public in which the family is located (see Baker, 1994; Deleuze, 1977/1979).

11. American Exceptionalism is not a static notion, nor is the notion of exceptionalism confined to the United States. It is revisioned throughout the nineteenth and twentieth centuries as the modern nation was embedded in world system that continually made/remade the imaginaries in which the "exceptionalism" of the nation was positioned.

12. This racially elect had multiple meanings that accounted for cultural and physical difference among people. That led to a classification and judgment of the inferiority of African people (see Glaude, 2000, pp. 63–65).

13. Early schoolmen and schoolwomen in the United States did speak directly about this problem, although today it is more coded as when reforms in teacher education are "to provide the teacher with the appropriate dispositions and cognitive skills" (see Popkewitz, 2001).

14. "Natio" initially meant the local community, domicile, family, and conditions of belonging.

15. The translation and transportation of Locke and Rousseau can be read in this field of cultural practices of the home and child rearing in North America. Translation and transportation are metaphors to think about the circulation of ideas as they move from one field of cultural practices to another (Popkewitz, 2000b).

16. While not discussed as such in the history of the European teacher, its images and narratives can be understood in relation to cosmopolitanism (see, e.g., Nóvoa, 2000).

17. I use the nineteenth century to mark the emergence of the human sciences as formalized academic disciplines by receiving institutional homes and also as a time when the social sciences established a closeness to the governing patterns forming with the modern welfare state concerned with the care of populations. For discussions of its prior history, see the *Sociology of Sciences* yearbooks (Heilbron, Magnusson, & Wittrock, 1998; Wagner, Wittrock, & Whitley, 1991).

18. I borrow this phrase from Hacking's (1990) study of statistics in which he talked about chance and processes of normalizing populations. I am using "taming" to talk about the administration of change in relation to different but overlapping historical registers.

19.   This also requires understanding social Darwinism, which is beyond the scope of this discussion (see, e.g., Hawkins 1997; Hofstadter, 1955; Kazamias, 1966).

20.   I discuss this in Popkewitz (2000a).

21.   The Report of the Committee of Ten also involved eugenic notions to differentiate working-class children. I am grateful to Bernadette Baker for having brought this to my attention.

References

The American Superintendents of Schools (1874). *A statement of the theory of education in the United States of America as approved by many leading educators.* Washington, DC: Government Printing Office.

Ariès, P. (1962). *Centuries of childhood: A social history of family life* (R. Baldick, Trans.). New York: Vintage Books. (Original work published 1960)

Baker, K. (1994). Enlightenment and the institution of society: Notes for a conceptual history. In W. Melching & W. Velma (Eds.), *Main trends in cultural history* (pp. 95–120). Amsterdam: Rodopi.

Baker, B. (2001). *In perpetual motion: Theories of power, educational history, and the child.* New York: Peter Lang.

Barry, A., Osborne, T., & Rose, N. (1996). *Foucault and political reason: Liberalism, neo-liberalism and rationalities of government.* Chicago: University of Chicago Press.

Beck, U. (2000). The cosmopolitan perspective: Sociology of the second age of modernity. *British Journal of Sociology* 51, (1), 79–105.

Bell, D. A. (2001). *The cult of the nation in France: Inventing nationalism, 1680–1800.* Cambridge, MA: Harvard University Press.

Berger, P., Berger, B., & Kellner, H. (1974). *The homeless mind: Modernization and consciousness.* New York: Vintage.

Bledstein, B. (1976). *The culture of professionalism: The middle class and the development of higher education in America.* New York: Norton.

Bloch, M. (1987). Becoming scientific and professional: An historical perspective on the aims and effects of early education. In T. S. Popkewitz (Ed.), *The formation of school subjects: The struggle for creating an American institution* (pp. 25–62). New York: Falmer.

Bloch, M., Holmlund, K., Moqvist, I., & Popkewitz, T. S. (Eds.). (2003). *Restructuring the welfare state through new patterns of governing children, families, and education/schooling.* New York: Palgrave.

Bloch, M., & Popkewitz, T. S. (2000). Constructing the parent, teacher, and child: Discourses of development. In L. D. Soto (Ed.), *The politics of early childhood education* (pp. 7–32). New York: Peter Lang.

Bloch, M., & Tabachnick, B. R. (1994). Improving parent involvement as school reform: Rhetoric or reality? In K. M. Borman & N. P. Greenman (Eds.), *Changing American education: Recapturing the past or inventing the future* (pp. 291–296). Albany: State University of New York Press.

Borman, K., (Ed.). (1998). *Ethnic diversity in community and schools.* Norwood, NJ: Ablex.

Breckenridge, C., Pollock, S., Bhaba, H., Chakrabarty, D. (Eds.). (2002). *Cosmopolitanism.* Durham, NC: Duke University Press.

Bush, G. W. (2001). *No child left behind.* Washington, D.C.: U.S. Government Printing Office.

Butler, J. (1993). *Bodies that matter: On the discourse limits of "sex."* New York: Routledge.

Castells, M. (2000). Materials for an exploratory theory of the network society. *British Journal of Sociology 51,* (1), 5–24.

Cazden, C. (1986). Classroom discourse. In M. Wittrock (Ed.), *Handbook of research on teaching* (pp. 432–463). New York: Macmillan.

Chakrabarty, D. (2000). *Provincializing Europe: Postcolonial thought and historical difference.* Princeton, NJ: Princeton University Press.

Comte, A. (1975). *Auguste Comte and positivism: The essential writings.* G. Lenzer (Ed.). New York: Harper & Row. (Original work published 1827)

Cooley, C. H. (1909). *Social organization: A study of the larger mind.* New York: C. Scribner's Sons.

Cronon, W. (1996). The trouble with wildernesses or getting back to the wrong nature. In W. Cronon (Ed.), *Uncommon ground: Rethinking the human place in nature* (pp. 69–90). New York: W. W. Norton.

Cruikshank, B. (1999). *The will to empower: Democratic citizens and other subjects.* Ithaca, NY: Cornell University Press.

Cryle, P. (2001). *The telling of the act: Sexuality as narrative in eighteenth- and nineteenth-century France.* Newark, DE: University of Delaware Press.

Deleuze, G. (1979). Foreword: The rise of the social (R. Hurley, Trans.). In J. Donzelot (Ed.), *The Policing of families* (ix–xix). Baltimore, MD: Johns Hopkins University Press. (Original work published 1977)

Delpit, L. (1995). *Other people's children.* New York: New Press.

Eliot, C. (1892–1893). Wherein popular education has failed. *The Forum 14,* 411–428.

Eliot, C. (1905). The fundamental assumptions in the report of the Committee of Ten (1893). *Educational Review,* 325–343.

Fendler, L. (2003). Teacher reflection in a hall of mirrors: Epistemological and political reverberations. *Educational Researcher 32,* (3), 16–25.

Ferguson, R. A. (1997). *The American Enlightenment, 1750–1820.* Cambridge, MA: Harvard University Press.

Foner, E. (1998). *The story of American freedom.* New York: W. W. Norton.

Foucault, M. (1973). *The order of things: An archaeology of the human sciences.* New York: Vintage. (Original work published 1966)

Foucault, M. (1979). *Discipline and punish: The birth of the prison* (A. Sheridan, Trans.). New York: Vintage. (Original work published 1975)

Foucault, M. (1984). "What Is Enlightenment? *Was ist Aufklärung?"* In P. Rabinow (Ed.), *The Foucault Reader* (pp. 32–51). New York: Pantheon.

Foucault, M. (1988). The political technologies of the individual. In L. Martin, H. Gutman, & P. Hutton (Eds.), *Technologies of the self* (pp. 145–162). Amherst: University of Massachusetts Press.

Foucault, M. (1991). Governmentality. In G. Burchell, C. Gordon, & P. Miller (Eds.), *The Foucault effect: Studies in governmentality* (pp. 87–104). Chicago: University of Chicago Press.

Franklin, B. (1986). *Building the American community: The school curriculum and the search for social control.* New York: Falmer.

Fredrickson, G. (2002). *Racism: A short history.* Princeton, NJ: Princeton University Press.

Freedman, K. (1987). Art education as social production: Culture, society and politics in the formation of the curriculum. In T. S. Popkewitz (Ed.), *The formation of school subjects: The struggle for creating an American institution* (pp. 63–84). London: Falmer.

Glaude, E. Jr. (2000). *Exodus! Religion, race, and nation in early nineteenth-century Black America.* Chicago: University of Chicago Press.

Gramsci, A. (1971). In Q. Hoare & G. Smith (Ed. & Trans.), *Selections from the prison notebooks.* New York: International.

Greek, C. (1992). *The religious roots of American sociology.* New York: Garland.

Hacking, I. (1990). *The taming of chance.* Cambridge, MA: Cambridge University Press.

Hall, G. S. (1924). Aspects of child life and education: The contents of children's minds on entering school. *The Princeton Review II,* 249–272 (Original work published 1893)

Hall, G. S. (1969). *Adolescence: Its psychology and its relation to physiology, anthropology, sociology, sex, crime, religion, and education.* New York: Arno and The New York Times. (Original work published 1905)

Hamilton, D. (1999). The pedagogic paradox (or why no didactics in England?). *Pedagogy, Culture, and Society 7,* (1), 135–152.

Hawkins, M. (1997). *Social Darwinism in European and American thought, 1860–1945: Nature as model and nature as threat.* Cambridge, England: Cambridge University Press.

Heilbron, J., Magnusson, L., & Wittrock, B. (Eds.). (1998). *The rise of the social sciences and the formation of modernity: Conceptual change in context, 1750–1805. Sociology of Science 1996 Yearbook.* Dordrecht, The Netherlands: Kluwer Academic.

Hennon, L. (2002). Inclusionary education in the U.S.A.: A genealogy of schooling, governance, and urbanism. Unpublished doctoral dissertation. University of Wisconsin, Madison.

Hirst, P. (1994). The evolution of consciousness: Identity and personality in historical perspective. *Economy and Society 23,* (1), 47–65.

Hofstadter, R. (1955). *Social Darwinism in American thought 1860–1915 revised.* Boston: Beacon Press.

Hultqvist, K. & Dahlberg, G., (Eds.). (2001). *Governing the child in the new millennium.* New York: RoutledgeFalmer.

Hunter, I. (1988). *Culture and government: The emergence of literary education.* Hampshire, England: Macmillan.

Kazamias, A., (Ed.). (1966). *Herbert Spencer on education.* New York: Columbia University Press.

Kliebard, H. (1986). *Struggle for the American curriculum.* London: Routledge and Kegan Paul.

Krug, E. (1972). *The shaping of the American high school. Vol. 2. 1920–1941.* Madison, WI: University of Wisconsin Press.

Lasch, C. (1977). *Haven in a heartless world: The family besieged.* New York: Basic.

Latour, B. (1986). Visualization and cognition: Thinking with eyes and hands. *Knowledge and society: Studies in the sociology of culture past and present 6,* 1–40.

Lesko, N. (2001). *Act your age: A cultural construction of adolescence.* New York: Routledge.

Lindblad, S., & Popkewitz, T. S. (Eds.). (2002). *Statistical data and inclusion & exclusion.* Uppsala Reports on Education. Uppsala, Sweden: University of Uppsala.

Lindner, R. (1996). *The reportage of urban culture: Robert Park and the Chicago school* (A. Morris, J. Gaines, & M. Chalmers, Trans.). Cambridge, England: Cambridge University Press. (Original work published 1990)

Mattingly, P. (1977). *The classless profession: American schoolmen in the nineteenth century.* New York: New York University Press.

McEneaney, E. (2003). Elements of a contemporary primary school science. In G. Dori, J. Meyer, F. Ramirez, & E. Schofer (Eds.), *Science in the modern world polity: Institutionalization and globalization* (pp. 136–154). Stanford: Stanford University Press.

Menand, L. (2001). *The metaphysical club.* New York: Farrar, Straus, & Giroux.

Meyer, J. W. (1986). Myths of socialization and of personality. In T. C. Heller, M. Sosna, & D. E. Wellbery (Eds.), *Reconstructing individualism: Autonomy, individuality, and the self in Western thought* (pp. 208–221). Stanford, CA: Stanford University Press.

Meyer, J., Boli, J., Thomas, G., & Ramirez, F. (1997). World society and the nation-state. *American Journal of Sociology 103,* (1), 144–181.

Meyer, J., & Jepperson, R. (2000). The Actors of modern society: The cultural construction of social agency. *Sociological Theory 18,* (1), 100–120.

Mignolo, W. (2002). The many faces of cosmo-polis: Border thinking and critical cosmopolitanism. In C. Breckenridge, S. Pollock, H. Bhabha, & D. Chakrabarty (Eds.), *Cosmopolitanism* (pp. 157–188). Durham, NC: Duke University Press.

Moqvist-Lindberg, I. (2003). Constructing a parent. In M. Bloch, K. Holmlund, I. Moqvist, & T. Popkewitz (Eds.), *Restructuring the welfare state through*

new patterns of governing children, families, and education/schooling.
New York: Palgrave.

National Council of Teachers of Mathematics. (2000). *Principles and standards for school mathematics.* Reston, VA: Author.

National Education Association. (1969). *Report of the Committee on Secondary School Studies.* New York: Arno and The New York Times. (Original work published 1892)

Nelson, B. S., Warfield, J., & Wood, T. (2001). Introduction. In T. Wood, B. S. Nelson & J. Warfield (Eds.), *Beyond classical pedagogy: Teaching elementary school mathematics* (pp. 5–9). Mahwah, NJ: Lawrence Erlbaum.

Nóvoa, A. (2000). The restructuring of the European space: Changing relationships between states, citizens, and educational communities. In T. S. Popkewitz (Ed.), *Educational knowledge: Changing relationships between the state, civil society and the educational community* (pp. 31–58). Albany, NY: State University of New York Press.

O'Donnell, J. (1985). *The origins of behaviorism: American psychology, 1876–1920.* New York: New York University Press.

Pollock, S. (2002). Cosmopolitan and vernacular in history. In C. Breckenridge, S. Pollock, H. Bhabha & D. Chakrabarty (Eds.), *Cosmopolitanism* (pp. 15–53). Durham, NC: Duke University Press.

Popkewitz, T. S. (in press). The alchemy of school subjects: Standards-based mathematics education research and the fabrications of the child. *American Educational Research Journal.*

Popkewitz, T. S. (2003). Governing the child and pedagogicalization of the parent: A history of the present. In M. Bloch, K. Holmlund, I. Moqvist, & T. Popkewitz (Eds.), *Restructuring the welfare state through new patterns of governing children, families, and education/schooling* (pp. 35–61). New York: Palgrave.

Popkewitz, T. S. (2001). Reconstituindo o professor e a formação de professores: Imaginários nacionais e diferença nas práticas da escolarização [Reconstructing the teacher and teacher education: National Imaginaries and difference in schooling practices]. *Revista Brasilieria de história da Educação,* 59–78.

Popkewitz, T. S. (2000a). The denial of change in the process of change: Systems of ideas and the construction of national evaluations. *The Educational Researcher 29,* (1), 17–30.

Popkewitz, T. S. (2000b). Reform as the social administration of the child: Globalization of knowledge and power. In N. Burbules & C. Torres (Eds.), *Globalization and educational policy* (pp. 157–186). New York: Routledge.

Popkewitz, T. S. (1998). *Struggling for the soul: The politics of schooling and the construction of the teacher.* New York: Teachers College Press.

Popkewitz, T. S. (1991). *A political sociology of educational reform: Power/knowledge in teaching, teacher education, and research.* New York: Teachers College Press.

Popkewitz, T. S. (1987). *The formation of school subjects: The struggle for creating an American institution.* London: Falmer Press.

Popkewitz, T. S. & Bloch, M. (2001). Administering freedom: A history of the present rescuing the parent to rescue the child for society. In K. Hultqvist & G. Dahlberg (Eds.), *Governing the child in the new millennium* (pp. 85–118). New York: RoutledgeFalmer.

Popkewitz, T. S. & Brennan, M. (1998). *Foucault's challenge: Discourse, knowledge and power in education.* New York: Teachers College Press.

Popkewitz, T. S., Franklin, B., & Pereyra, M. (Eds.). (2001). *Cultural history education: Critical essays on knowledge and schooling.* New York: Routledge.

Rice, J. M. (1969). *The public school system of the United States.* New York: Arno and The New York Times. (Original work published 1893)

Rose, N. (1989). *Governing the soul: The shaping of the private self.* New York: Routledge.

Rose, N. (1999). *Powers of freedom: Reframing political thought.* Cambridge, MA: Cambridge University Press.

Ross, D. (1972). *G. Stanley Hall: The psychologist as prophet.* Chicago: University of Chicago Press.

Ross, D. (1991). *The origins of American social science.* New York: Cambridge University Press.

Small, A. W. (1896). *Demands of sociology upon pedagogy.* National Educational Association Thirty-Fifth Annual Meeting. Journal of Proceedings and Addresses. St. Paul: MN.

Stanic, G. (1987). Mathematics education in the United States at the beginning of the twentieth century. In T. S. Popkewitz (Ed.), *The formation of the school subjects: The struggle for creating an American institution* (pp. 145–175). New York: Falmer.

Steedman, C. (1995). *Strange dislocations: Childhood and the idea of human interiority, 1780–1930.* Cambridge, MA: Harvard University Press.

Tönnies, F. (1957). *Community and society.* East Lansing, MI: Michigan State University Press. (Original work published 1887)

Wagner, P. (1994). *The sociology of modernity.* New York: Routledge.

Wagner, P., Wittrock, B., & Whitley, R. (Eds.). (1991). *Discourses on society: The shaping of the social science disciplines. Sociology of Science 1991 Yearbook.* Dordrecht, The Netherlands: Kluwer Academic.

Wald, P. (1995). *Constituting Americans: Cultural anxiety and narrative form.* Durham, NC: Duke University Press.

Ward, L. F. (1883). *Dynamic sociology, or applied social science, as based upon statistical sociology and the less complex sciences.* New York: D. Appleton and Co.

Wood, G. S. (1991). *The radicalism of the American Revolution.* New York: Vintage.

Troubling Professionalism: Narratives of Family, Race, and Nation in Educational Reform

Lisa Weems

This chapter employs the writing of Michel Foucault to analyze the philosophical assumptions and practices associated with the movement to professionalize teaching during the Progressive Era (1900–1930). Although contemporary and historical educational movements take heterogeneous forms, what often connects disparate events and practices is a unifying claim to a broader discourse known as "professionalism." Using Foucault's notion of genealogy, I approach the topic of professionalism by historicizing it, as well as by deconstructing traditional histories of the movement. Attention to the discontinuities and contradictions within discourses of professionalism illuminates the ways in which the emergence of specific subject positions and their relations are inscribed in larger narratives of family, race, and nation in the Progressive Era. Heteronormativity (Butler, 1990) is introduced as a matrix of intelligibility to analyze how narratives of family, race, and nation operate implicitly and explicitly in histories of the development of the professions. My analysis suggests that professionalism is linked to the production of the categories of family (including Butler's preferred notion of sex/gender/desire), race (WASP and not WASP) and nation (American citizenship) that reflect what Foucault refers to as "repro-technology" (1990). In repro-technology, discourses of racialized sexuality, morality, and science converge to produce the "natural" positions of particular bodies and identities within the educational "family." Specifically, in this chapter I investigate the construction of the heteronormative educational family across multiple and disparate sites of education in the Progressive Era: public commentary by educational leaders regarding teacher preparation; higher education for women (including normal schools, female seminaries, and liberal arts institutions); and contemporary histories of American universities. These dispersed and seemingly unrelated locales made use of heteronormative, racialized, and class-based figures of sexuality and citizenship in crystallizing relations of power within and among discourses of education and professionalism. My analysis pulls together documentary evidence to explore the production and circulation of various subject-positions, including "teacher" and "professional," which recuperate "eugenicist" images of the educational family as a model for American citizenship.

Foucault, Genealogy, and the Notion of Deviant Historiography

Among his many contributions to the study of education is Foucault's articulation of a critical methodology for historical inquiry (1972, 1984a, and1991).[1] Writing against the French intellectual tradition of historical materialism, Foucault advocates a mode of critique called genealogy. He characterizes genealogy as:

> a form of history which can account for the constitution of knowledges, discourses, domains of objects, etc. without having to make reference to a subject which is either transcendental in relation to the field of events or runs in its empty sameness throughout the course of history. (1984b, p. 59)

Interested in questions of power and subjectivity, Foucault attempts to move beyond liberal humanist and Marxist constructions of subjectivity. Caught between notions of the Subject constituted by either sovereignty (humanism) or ideology (Marxism), Foucault sought to reconceptualize the Subject as a function of both structure and agency in posthumanist terms.[2] Foucault's conceptualization of genealogy has been associated with the linguistic turn within historical inquiry, given that Foucault's analytics of power and subjectivity are heavily linked to the play of language. Genealogy shifts the problematic (of historical inquiry) from institutions and Subjects (previously theoretically distinct categories) to discursive practices and subject positions. For Foucault, the Subject is constituted by multiple and oftentimes contradictory subject positions inscribed within various historical and cultural discourses. The move is key for Foucault, in that subjectivity is not available outside a discursive position and is never pure, complete, or consistent. This move displaced the role of the historian as an objective, omniscient, passive recorder of historical events. Rather, the historiographer is positioned in a particular time and space, and genealogical inquiry is driven by desires that are themselves produced by sociocultural discourses (1984a, p. 90).

The transformative possibilities of genealogical analysis lie in the malleability of discursive formations. Foucault (1984a) argues that the critical task of the archivist is to bring new narratives into discourse through the careful retracing of familiar discourses. Unlike historical materialists who characterize ideology as teleological, Foucault conceptualizes discourse (in terms of practices and the orders of discourse) as historically and strategically contingent. He notes that a discursive formation "is essentially incomplete, owing to the system of formation, its strategic choices. Hence the fact, that taken up again, placed and interpreted in a new constellation, a given discursive formation may reveal new possibilities" (1972, p. 67).

Unlike traditional history, which emphasizes origins, continuities, and stability of interpretation, genealogy privileges dispersion, discontinuities, and discursive transformations (Foucault, 1972, p. 4). Foucault argues that genealogy "opposes itself to the search for 'origins'" (1984a, p. 77). Indeed, he sees genealogy as an interrogation of the descent of discourses, that is, which epistemological and social forces allowed for their emergence and the forms of their dispersion. Analyzing the discontinuities of discourse, for Foucault, is to attend to the specificity or singularity of events (statements) within a particular discourse. He elaborates, "discontinuity is not a monotonous and unthinkable void between events, which one must hasten to fill with the dim plenitude of cause…but it is a play of specific transformations, each one different from the next" (1991, p. 59). It is this attention to the discontinuities within discourses that allows the researcher/historian to foreground issues of change and transformation, including a transformation of the ways in which certain texts and storylines get monumentalized into dominant narratives that become authoritative "history."

Power-Knowledge

Foucault argues that genealogical analysis of discourse is not merely an analysis of either the content or form of a particular discourse. Rather, it is an investigation of the assumptions or set of rules that govern statements; i.e., what can and cannot be said within a particular domain (1984b, p. 74). In this way, Foucault argues that inter-related discourse-practices (or "ideas-in-action") can be characterized as a "regime of truth."[3]

There is much debate over whether there is historical determinism evident in Foucault's writing. Many scholars read Foucault as deterministic—that we are trapped in the "prison house of language." My reading of Foucault emphasizes the ways in which subjectivity is inscribed through various regulatory systems. In "Truth and Power," Foucault reiterates his analytics of power-knowledge introduced in *Discipline and Punish* and elaborated in *The History of Sexuality, Volume 1*. Power-knowledge refers to the idea that all power references a particular domain of knowledge and that all knowledge entails configurations of power. Challenging the Marxist theory of power as negation, and the Freudian theory of power as repression, power-knowledge is Foucault's insistence on the productive elements of power. He states:

> What makes power hold good, what makes it accepted, is simply the fact that it doesn't only weigh on us as a force that says no, but that it traverses and produces things, it induces pleasure, forms knowledge, produces discourse. It needs to be considered as a productive network which runs through the whole social body. (1984b, p. 61)

Herein lie the nuances of Foucault's rearticulation of power. Regulatory systems and regulation do not equate with determinism. Power circulates throughout and among discourse-practices, such that the taking up of various subject positions allows for the disagreement, resistance, or adaptation of relations of power as always already at play and can represent discursive contradictions as much as "enlightened" or "empowered" action.

Finally, from *Discipline and Punish* (1995) I employ Foucault's notion of "panopticism"—a new technology of the exercise of power that works as an apparatus of self-regulated surveillance. Foucault argues that normativity is produced by discourses (particularly scientific discourses). We conform to and contest normalizing practices by policing ourselves in relation to particular classificatory systems. In the following pages I elaborate how educational reform discourses produced particular subject positions (namely, "the professional"). I utilize Foucault's notion of the panopticon to read the practices associated with the development of professionalism as an apparatus that always already constituted the subject positions "teacher," "student," and "expert" through attempted processes of normalization. In other words, I illustrate the ways in which professionalism produced a notion of the "good professional" that was always already gendered, raced, and sexed. My particular interest is how the formation of discourses of professionalism within education coincided with narratives of family, race, and nation. To bring out this point, I borrow Jennifer Terry's notion of "deviant historiography" (1991, p. 55).

Deviant historiography refers to a "method for mapping the complex discursive and textural operations at play in the historical emergence of subjects who come to be called lesbians and gay men" (Terry, 1991, p. 55). Deviant historiography is not interested in locating gay men and lesbians throughout educational history but rather in tracing "deviant subject formation" (p. 55). Deviant historiography "looks not only for how subjects are produced and policed, but how they are resistant and excessive to the very discourses from which they emerge" (p. 57). Using Foucault's notion of effective history, deviant historiography "exposes not the events and actors elided by traditional history, but instead lays bare the processes and operations by which these elisions occurred" (Terry, 1991, p. 56). Terry argues that effective history "allows us to theorize a counterdiscursive position in history" as we look at practices that disrupted dominant discourses. Deviant historiography is a method of looking at historical events and practices as sites of conflict and negotiation over the contested terrain of professionalism discourse to render visible the assumptions that govern the boundaries of professionalism. Specifically, I deconstruct the production and operation of heteronormativity in discourses of educational professionalism. My desire is to "queer" and "racialize" professionalism by insinuating/ subverting new narratives into an old story.

Troubling Categories: Family, Race, and Nation

Heteronormativity, a term that is widely used in the literatures of queer theory, was made visible by Judith Butler (1990). At its broadest meaning, heteronormativity refers to the discourses around sex, gender, and sexuality that produce certain identities and practices as "normative" and others as "deviant." I prefer the term heteronormativity over the term gender since it foregrounds the interrelated assumptions of biological essentialism (male/female or man/woman), gender polarity (masculinity/femininity), and compulsive heterosexuality. Generally, an analysis that uses heteronormativity as a matrix of intelligibility problematizes essentialism and binaries associated with identity categories, such as gender and race. Following Foucault (1990), Butler argues that racialized and sexed bodies are the effects of socially produced discourses rather than the "truth" of an interior core. Butler's approach is to show how identity categories are more messy than feminist theorizing (Rubin, 1993) has previously considered. Rubin and other feminist theorists (Sklar, 1976; Weis, 1995) make the distinction between sex and gender, arguing that the former is a biological category and the latter a social category. In contrast, Butler argues that a matrix of heteronormativity complicates these distinctions. Both sex and gender are considered culturally constructed and already-loaded terms. Furthermore, they are performative; normative gender performative acts involve not only performing femininity, but also heterosexuality. Thus, identity is overdetermined yet performative as we confuse sexual practice with sexual function with epistemological orientations.[4]

Elsewhere, postcolonial and queer theorists have pointed out how sexual categories are racialized and have historically been linked to nationalist efforts to define normative identity (Pellegrini, 1997; Patton & Sanchez-Eppler, 2000; Sommerville, 2000; Stoler, 1995). This scholarship explores the relations between Western conceptions of race and sexuality and provides documentary evidence of the connections between nineteenth-century scientific racism with the invention of homosexuality in the United States (Sommerville, 2000). Such research resonates with Foucault's argument that science produced race- and class-based sexualities (1990). Foucault contends that science played a key role in positioning citizen-subjects through discourses of sexuality framed as normative or deviant. As Foucault notes, scientific discourses on sexuality worked in collusions with moral discourses on sex, deviance, and crime during the eighteenth and nineteenth centuries. However, during the nineteenth century, medical science took on a new form of authority: that of truth. Medical science, according to Foucault:

> set itself up as the supreme authority in matters of hygienic necessity, taking up the old fears of venereal affliction and combining them with the new themes of asepsis, and the great evolutionist myths with the recent institutions of public health; it claimed to ensure the physical vigor and the moral cleanliness of the social body; it promised to eliminate defective individuals, degenerate and bastardized populations. In the name of a biological and historical urgency, it justified the racisms of the state, which at the time were on the horizon. It grounded them in "truth." (1990, p. 54)

In Foucault's terms, sexuality became a regime of truth, a set of rules for thinking and talking about oneself and others that presupposed sexual practice as indicative of a citizen's moral and social worth. While constructions of "the good society" were morally, socially, and politically derived, it was science that supported an authoritative methodology for this eugenicist project. Science (with its claims to objectivity, skill, and precision) would become the backbone of a whole network of institutions (medicine, education, law, etc.) whose primary aims were to create a "democratic" form of power and discipline (panopticism)—to actively seek out knowledge and evaluation of one's behaviors and identities in relation to normative ideals of good citizenship.

The (scientifically based) association between knowledge and truth, coupled with the new technology of power or democratic discipline, fueled an explosion of institutions, organizations, and agencies specifically designed to do their part in creating a good society. Some examples include social-service agencies, schools, and community-health programs. In *The Order of Things*, Foucault (1994) explicitly discusses the range of disciplinary fields associated with the deployment of this new technology of power. In that text, Foucault (1994) provides an archaeology of the human sciences and their methodologies for gaining knowledge and evaluation of human behavior, ranging from psychoanalysis to economics to ethnology and natural history. Foucault, however, foregrounds psychology and sociology as two methodologies (themselves regimes of truth) that became part of authoritative knowledge in constructing "the good society." It is not simply that the fields of psychology and sociology were popular fields of study for young professionals. It is also that the specific techniques and methods of inquiry from psychology and sociology were embraced within existing "professions" such as business, medicine, and law. Perhaps most important is that psychology (i.e., human development and behaviorism) and sociology (i.e., demography and social efficiency) formed the epistemological foundation for structuring education and schooling in the twentieth century. I turn now to the problematic of professionalism, as traditionally conceptualized by historians of education. After a brief introduction to the traditional histories of professionalism, I then offer an analysis of the rules that govern these traditional histories by exploring the transformations and discontinuities within discourses of professionalism.

The Problematic of Professionalism

Professionalism is, of course, a concept with a history. Rather than providing a definitive idealized set of characteristics or practices, my interest is to trace the historical effects of the practices associated with the concept of professionalism. Like other fields considered "semi-professions" (Etzioni, 1969), educational reform currently entails further efforts to professionalize the field of education. Within colleges of education, plans of action are filled with professionalism talk, including creating "master" or "expert" teachers, post-certification "residency," etc., all framed within the aim of increasing the efficiency and status of the field. While talk of professionalism circulates in many educational sites, there is a disjunction between meanings around professionalism. In other words, there are multiple sites and practices that operate under the sign "professionalism."[5] However, for the remainder of this paper, I use the term "professionalism" to refer to a historically contingent discourse that emerged during the mid-Victorian period in the United States and continued through the Progressive Era: roughly between 1900 and 1930. While I will return to contemporary practices and implications, the primary focus below is to investigate the historical formation of educational professionalism with particular attention to the roles of family, race, and nation in its production.

(Traditional) Histories of Professionalism in Education

The work of Burton Bledstein (1978), David Labaree (1992, 1995, 1996, and 1997) and Thomas Popkewitz (1993, 1994, and 2000) is helpful in situating the current movement to professionalize teaching within its historical contexts. However, in the present analysis, these historical texts are not viewed as the "true history of professionalism." In contrast, these texts become part of the discursive archive of "professionalism" texts, which, in turn, become part of the field (or object) of inquiry. I underscore this point since the distinction between primary and secondary sources is one of the taken-for-granted assumptions and practices within historical inquiry. My choice to analyze these texts across historical time frames, then, suggests my commitment to the epistemological, methodological, and ontological challenges posed by genealogical analysis.[6]

The first of these histories of professionalism comes from Burton Bledstein's "classic" text, *The Culture of Professionalism*. Bledstein (1978) analyzes the relations between the development of higher education and the middle class in America. Bledstein argues that the relationship is symbiotic in that a growing middle class provided both the impetus for professionalization and that professionalization, in turn, solidified the myth of the United States as a middle-class society embedded in American cultural imaginary. The middle-class person was an ideal candidate as a professional for two related reasons. First, the middle-class person possessed the "correct" character: a belief in perseverance and a commitment to self-glory. The middle-class person could establish and model "universal standards for moral and civil behavior" (Bledstein, 1978, p. 27). According to Bledstein, the middle-class person was considered a "democrat incarnate"; he transcended the egoistic desire in the pursuit of wealth and channeled natural competitiveness into the betterment of the social body. The second characteristic of the middle class that fed into professionalism was the notion of career (Bledstein, 1978). Professionalism became associated with social mobility and careerism, encouraging individuals to consider their stations in life and work as mobile. The effects for a growing professional class were the links between higher education and specialization of work. In other words, higher education served as a preparation for the professional's future life, which would include moving from specialized job to specialized job to form a "career."

While Bledstein's analysis offers a modernist history of the development of the professions, more recent scholarship theorizing professionalism adopts a more genealogical approach to the subject. Using a Foucaultian analytics, the research of both Popkewitz and Labaree investigates the movement to professionalize teaching through unpacking its historical crystallization and political implications. Popkewitz's scholarship is particularly insightful for its elaboration on how, historically, educational reform discourses have been linked to a "culture of redemption." Popkewitz (1994, 2000) shows how the burgeoning field of teacher education at the beginning of the twentieth century linked the development of the teacher to the development of the child through an ideological focus on "governing the soul" and the "administration of freedom." In his analyses, Popkewitz utilizes some of the central insights of critical theories of teaching as a profession (Apple, 1987; 1994; Lather, 1987) including schooling as a site of social and economic reproduction, knowledge as a function of relations of power, and educational reform as an apparatus of regulation and surveillance of both teachers and students alike.

The work of David Labaree constitutes a third body of scholarship that has contributed greatly to histories of professionalism. Like that of Popkewitz, Labaree's work builds upon critical research regarding the culture of professionalism and the professionalization of teaching as a field. Labaree (1997) documents how the professionalization of teaching, historically, has resulted in changes for teachers and schools that have both reduced and augmented social inequalities. For example, in his analysis of the career ladder of the early schoolteacher, Labaree illustrates how the model of teacher professionalism (including standardization of training and credentials) was beneficial to some teachers (particularly urban, male, secondary schoolteachers) but marginalized others, including those serving rural and/or working-class student populations. Labaree's work suggests that there are multiple dynamics that contribute to organization and effects of various movements to professionalize teaching, which cannot be subsumed into a metanarrative of progress in educational reform from the eighteenth century to the twentieth century. Similarly, Labaree argues that the contemporary movement to professionalize teaching is a product of several heterogeneous forces. Among these influences are the shift from "equity" to "excellence" in educational philosophies and policy formation, rising disenchantment with bureaucratic reform efforts, Reagan-era shifts from state to market solutions, and feminist critiques of women's work (Labaree, 1992, p. 132).

Most germane to my project is Labaree's discussion of gender and professionalization. Labaree contends that the rise of feminism has led to an increased awareness of gender relations within educational contexts. Feminist scholarship has called attention to how gender plays a role in the field of teaching (Lather, 1987; Weiler, 1988), educational administration (Blount, 1999), and even educational reform policies (Weis, 1995). For example, educational philosopher Mary Leach argues that professionalization initiatives do not take into account the lived experiences of women. Leach problematizes the use of the term "commitment" in describing women's relationships to teaching historically: "Glossing over the ideology of domesticity in addition to ignoring the practical constraints of women who have children, the responsibilities they bear for the maintenance and socialization, as well as biological reproduction, severely limits any understanding of what operates as an 'incentive' for women's paid work" (1988, p. 281). In assessing the Holmes Group Forum, Leach makes this observation:

> There is, in fact, no recognition that in all likelihood, relations of gender will be a prime factor in determining who decides to become a teacher or why they will make that decision. Thus, there is no acknowledgement of the differential, culture-bound modes of self-understanding, lived experiences or forms of expression that males and females develop in our society and which they will necessarily bring to this new teacher education and their "career" in teaching. (1988, p. 276)

However, as Labaree (1992) notes, such critiques have not been integrated successfully into the teacher professionalization movement.

This oversight, he claims, can be seen in the problematic appropriation of the medical field as the ideal professional model. Labaree refers to this as the problem of attempting to reshape the female schoolteacher in the image of a male physician (1992, p. 132). Labaree's analysis, while insightful, stops short of explaining why and how it is possible that this image, despite its failures to be achieved materially, continues to hold promise as a possible solution.

One of the factors that contributes to the relatively low status of the field of teaching may be the status of the populations served by the "domestic professions," e.g., immigrants and children (Glazer & Slater, 1987; Heyning, 2001; Labaree, 1992). Early childhood education in the United States was closely linked to immigrant and/or settlement programs at the turn of the twentieth century. As Heyning (notes, definitions of the early childhood profession revolve around two poles, scientism and welfarism, to authorize (in the Foucaultian sense) its legitimacy as a profession (2001, p. 82). Scientism included teaching and learning scientific methodologies to affiliate early childhood studies with other university-based educational studies. Welfarism refers to the idea that women have a natural calling to teach young children, based on their commitment to "nurture, care and child advocacy" (Heyning, 2001, p. 82). Similar to other professional educational programs, appeals to scientism and the use of expert knowledge to supervise, evaluate, and "correct" young children were more prevalent (thus perhaps effective) than appeals to welfarism. In other words, caring for and advocating for the young are less affiliated with measures of professionalism than technical expertise.

In a parallel argument, my historical analysis investigates the *paradoxes* inherent in the movement to professionalize teaching by investigating some "strange" or "queer" statements that are also part of the discourse of professionalism but which typically are erased from traditional histories of professionalism. By insinuating analytic terms of the present (such as heteronormativity and racialization), I hope to invoke Foucault's notion of history as a practice of "cutting" (1984b, p. 88) rather than understanding. Specifically, I wish to interrogate heteronormativity and whiteness (read Anglo-Protestant) as significant constitutive elements in the problematic of professionalism. The construct of heteronormativity and its related signifiers (the family, femininity, the female body, and desire) are discursively produced and negotiated in the writings and practices in the historical movement known as professionalism. As I argue below, the terms "nation," "race," and "citizen" are interrelated systems of thought that further situate the constructs of "woman" and "femininity" as always already inscribed in terms of white, middle-class Anglo-American Protestantism.

The figure or metaphor of the family takes center stage in this analysis under the view that educational reform has implicitly and explicitly utilized the nuclear model to think about the role of educational institutions in establishing and maintaining boundaries of American citizenship (i.e., Who gets to be a citizen, and by doing what?). A good example is how heteronormative ideologies became institutionalized in high schools and industrial training in the Progressive Era. Educational historian Karen Graves documents how the logic of the "twin pillars of citizenship and work" combined to make "domesticated citizenship" the goal of differentiated curriculum for females (1998, p. 227). Domesticated citizenship conveyed to schoolgirls that to be a good citizen (as a white, middle-class woman) was to learn the arts and sciences of (heterosexual) marriage and motherhood.

My theoretical interest is in how the image of the heteronormative family has historically figured into discourses of professionalism. In my discussion below I isolate various signifiers that are interrelated to heteronormative subject positions crystallized in the image of the "family" within discourses of professionalism (e.g., "female," "femininity," "women," "race," and "nation"). For example, I use the term "female" when writing about either actual female bodies or the figure of the feminine body as they appear in various scientific, literary, and cultural constructions of the family. I use the term "women" when referring to the constructed attributes assigned to the category of women—namely, femininity. I differentiate between these signifiers for analytic clarity. In doing so, I hope to show the complex relations of power articulated through the heteronormative and racialized construct of the family within discourses of professionalism and education. Thus, I use these terms as subcategories of the umbrella term family. Furthermore, I investigate their shifting implications for what such terms might suggest about the historical development of professionalism. In other words, just as the discourse practices of professionalism have evolved and vary greatly from context to context, the constitutive elements and regulation of heteronormative and racialized constructs also shift from context to context. What is relatively stable, I argue, is the continuing association between normative ideals of sexuality and professionalism and the role of the educational professional in their surveillance.

Constructing a (Professional) Expert

Scientific and moral discourses were significant in the constitution of professionalism between the 1850s and the 1930s. My choice to focus on these two bodies of discourse is informed by Foucault's analysis in *The History of Sexuality, Volume 1* (1990). Foucault argues that scientific discourses emerged during the Progressive Era as a new form of power-knowledge in understanding identity in general and sexuality specifically. Scientific discourses (the technology of medicine and the biology of reproduction) operated alongside existing moral discourses (the notion of the confession in Western Christianity) that both contradicted and coincided to produce the "truth of sex." Similarly, I suggest that scientific discourses (the professional as technical expert) operated alongside moral discourses (Republican motherhood) to produce the family of education professionals. Moral and scientific discourses during the Progressive Era became intertwined in establishing educational reform as well as larger conceptions of professionalism. The distinction between moral and scientific discourses is arbitrary. Prior to the Progressive Era, these two domains were held separate by Enlightenment distinctions between the empirical and the divine world. During the Progressive Era, however, science lost its status as immoral or amoral to become the very path to morality by reforms articulated by advocates of social reform, such as John Dewey.

Moral Discourses:
Republican Motherhood, Domesticity and Female Bodies

The idea of Republican motherhood is perhaps the most pervasive in contemporary analyses of heteronormativity and professionalism. Republican motherhood is a metaphor to describe the relations between women's domestic responsibilities and a larger moral, political, and cultural role. The notion of Republican motherhood was advanced in the writing of Catherine Beecher and implemented through the Common School era, approximately between the 1830s and the 1870s (Sklar, 1976). Beecher appealed to discourses of morality to articulate a "national" agenda and women's roles within it. Utilizing the doctrine of "separate spheres," Beecher argued for the education of women or for what is called "domestic education." She, like other founders of female seminaries, predicated the education of women on their natural role to become the bearers of American culture as well as the development of the science of domesticity. Included in this science of domesticity were developing spiritual, maternal and nurturing characteristics among white women who could afford higher education. Beecher (and other educational reformers of the period) glosses the racialized and class-based constructions of motherhood in that she is not including the kind of maternal, spiritual and nurturing activities conducted by working-class immigrant and/or enslaved African American women who provided the bulk of domestic service from the 1850s to the 1920s (Graves, 1998, p. 54).

Despite this narrow construction of the domestic, separate spheres provided multiple opportunities for (middle-class and/or white) women to become "domestic professionals":

> It was a positive sign of power, independence, and respectability in Mid-Victorian life that women no longer worked alongside their husbands, that they were mistresses of a special space and class called children, and they participated in their own cultural rituals and ceremonies. (Bledstein, 1978, p. 118)

What Bledstein is arguing here is that the practices of professionalism mapped onto the doctrines of natural law and separate spheres, which constituted professionalism as an already masculine enterprise. Blount (1999) concurs with this association between professionalism and masculinity. According to Blount, the development of school administration in the United States depended on a presumed gendered division of labor by recruiting "manly men" into administration as well as creating social organizations with men in business and government (1999, p. 66). Both practices effectively maintained distinctions between men and women as well as their proper roles in the field of education.

The idea of Republican motherhood found much favor within a growing field of education. During the mid-nineteenth century, Horace Mann appropriated Beecher's arguments of women's natural role as culture bearers (coupled with Pestalozzi's pedagogy of love) to argue for women as the "natural" candidates for teaching as a profession.[7] Educational reform in the mid-nineteenth century mobilized (and helped to invent) moral discourses on sex/gender/desire with citizenship to produce a figure of the educational professional that modeled "feminine" characteristics for the good of students, schools, and the emerging American nation.

Employing the rhetoric of domesticity to describe the educational profession (specifically, to the work of teaching), however, had its costs. That teaching was constructed as an extension of "mothering" was used to justify (or "rationalize" if you will) lower pay for female teachers as well as the need for male supervision (Tyack & Hansot, 1982). Bledstein states:

> Educational standards for proficiency and certification rose throughout the later nineteenth century; and such fields of female employment as librarianship and nursing attempted to acquire the schooling, the status, and the independence (without the income) of a profession. (1978, p. 39)

Despite the growth of normal school attendance and teacher education in the early twentieth century, teachers saw their work as their moral duty to serve America by nurturing its children. Given this construction, it is of little surprise that the status of teaching as a "domestic" (read white, middle-class female) profession did not accelerate the same as other public (read white, middle-class male) professions (e.g., medicine, law, and clergy).

The (Female) Body and "Women" in Education

Simply put, the female body is a source of contamination within scientific discourses of professionalism, both in terms of participation in "expert" communities and the larger social body. From G. Stanley Hall's claim that coeducation would feminize schooling (Graves, 1998) to the development of the social services profession (Glazer & Slater, 1987) to Eliot's coding of the city as a site of female licentiousness, female bodies were seen as polluted objects that teased and tainted the experiences and minds of young men and experts-in-the-making.

While the female body had a visible place within scientific discourses of professionalism, "women" did not. Here I am referring to histories of the professions, such as those of Veysey and Rudolph and Bledstein. These texts are considered "seminal" historical accounts of the university and its role in professionalism discursive practices. Certainly the works of Beecher, Cooper (1988), and others that advocate higher education for women beginning in the nineteenth century make mention of "women," but these writers are consistently written out of "the grand narrative" of the development of the professions. Self-proclaimed scientific educational leader G. Stanley Hall made clear his views about the role of women in higher education:

> From the available data it seems, however, that the more scholastic the education of women, the fewer children and the harder, more dangerous and more dreaded is parturition, and the less the ability to nurse children.[8]

Taken from his 1903 two-volume treatise on adolescence, Hall concludes (from what "data" is unclear) that higher education (a necessary component of professional development) is "dangerous" not only to women's reproductive health but also to women's "ability to nurse children." Thus, only those women who wanted to forfeit their credentials as good mothers would traverse the road of professionalism. Hall's above comments appear to be aimed at protecting women's individual reproductive health. However, in his address to the 1903 NEA conference, Hall articulates his view that much more was at stake in debating women's participation in higher education:

> savagery women and men are more alike in their physical structure and in their occupations, but with real progress the sexes diverge and draw apart, and the diversities always present are multiplied and accentuated.[9]

In this passage, Hall inscribes women's education into a larger narrative about sexual difference at the societal level. He suggests that only the "savage" woman would aspire to be "more alike" men in their occupations. An ardent proponent of the view that America was the world leader in a march towards civilizational progress, Hall frequently argues that social progress is equated with sexual difference. Thus, the practices of professionalism during the Progressive Era were to admit women in small numbers to higher education but also to place upon their bodies the dangerous negotiation between "savagery" and "civilization."

The distinction between female bodies, femininity, and women signals the complexities of heteronormativity and professionalism. The female body as the referent for the "feminine" is a site of both comfort and contamination, its valence determined in its strategic deployment. However, women as a category were either absent or written out of traditional histories of professionalism. This is in contrast to the typical lack of distinction between "male," "masculinity," and "men" within discourses of professionalism. I read this slippage as a sign of the typical elisions made in the subject position of the professional. Drawing on humanist notions of subjectivity, the professional is assumed to be a universal position despite its specific historical constitution as white, Anglo-Saxon, Protestant, and male.

Scientific Discourses—
An "Objective" Crusade for Civilization

A new hope in the promise of democracy, science, and progress ushered educational reform into the twentieth century and the Progressive Era

(Kliebard, 1995). The democratic contribution by professionals was their increasingly specialized knowledge. Unlike empirical scientists, the professional grasped the concept behind functional activity. Professionals created their role and identity as a growing class of experts who could identify, diagnose, and offer solutions to contentious depictions of American social problems. As Bledstein states:

> The culture of professionalism incarnated the radical idea of the independent democrat, a liberated person seeking to free the power of nature within every worldly sphere, a self-governing individual exercising this trained judgment in an open society. The Mid-Victorian as a professional person strove to achieve a level of autonomous individualism, a position of unchallenged authority before unknown in American life. (1978, p. 88)

It was the professionals' ability to apprehend the theoretical rules of "nature" that differentiated them from practitioners' emphasis on "mechanics" and "tradition." Bledstein notes:

> As professionals, they attempted to define a total coherent system of necessary knowledge within a precise territory, to control the intrinsic relationship of their subject by making it a scholarly as well as an applied science, to root social existence in the inner needs and possibilities of documentable worldly processes. (1978, p. 88)

Traditional histories of education reiterate Bledstein's assessment of the role of higher education and discourses of professionalism in the Progressive Era (Rudolph, 1990; Veysey, 1965). First, there was a public dependency upon a professional class of experts charged with the "administration" of society. The human sciences proliferated and circulated their mandates to classify, diagnose, and regulate American citizens for the good of the person and the nation (Foucault, 1994). Scientific studies announced social problems and solutions from emerging disciplines such as social work, psychology, sociology, urban studies, and economics. A second effect of Progressive Era professionalism was an "ideology of autonomy" (Readings, 1996). Operating within scientific narratives of precision, mastery, and control, the work of professionals was to isolate elements, including themselves, from a larger social context. Perhaps more visible is how professionals utilized scientific method for establishing social policy (Bledstein, 1978, p. 122). The work of professionals was to identify, with precision, the specific (natural) laws that determined social behavior (p. 110). The effect of this method was to isolate problems from the social contexts in which they were located.[10]

A key point here is the public's voluntary submission to the authority of the "expert." Educational historians (Bledstein, 1978) refer to this phenomenon as the "cult of the expert"—that functional social living required the assistance of the specialized knowledge created and disseminated by these new professionals.[11] The authority of this burgeoning class of professionals derived from an order of merit. Bledstein argues that this created a dependency on a professional class and a justification for the expansion of higher education programs to become the training centers for this class. Professional organizations and associations policed these growing specialized fields through the regulation of credentials. Bledstein notes that the scientific method (the pursuit of control, efficiency, and progress through objective measures) is evident among multiple layers of professionalism discourse. The authority of experts is produced by meritocracy, which assumes equality of opportunity based on ability, and mirrors the assumptions that govern science (Glazer & Slater, 1987). As Bledstein states, "The public came to accept the middle-class article of faith that the regularly trained professional, however dubious his reputation...was superior to the merely experienced operator. The difference was the role played by the school" (1978, p. 125). Higher education became the model democratic institution—governed by objectivity, meritocracy, and equal opportunity. Thus, in many ways professionalism is characterized by a bureaucratic model of disinterested inquiry. It may appear that professionalism, with its investment in scientific ways of being, is in direct contradiction with a view of education as a project of nurturing students and its religious overtones of teachers as people of God. Quite the contrary, professionalism worked in concert with existing discourses on religion, morality, and a divine order of "natural law." Histories of professionalism are steeped in moral discussions of teachers. Proponents of teacher professionalism, such as Catherine Beecher and Horace Mann, relied heavily on the (constructed) notion of Republican motherhood— the idea that it is the "natural" role of "woman" to lead America (and civilization) by transferring their maternal skills into a pedagogical context.

Professionalism as Moral Science

As I have shown above, professionalism during the Progressive Era was laced with scientific discourses that emphasized objectivity, disinterested inquiry, and autonomous individualism. However, as Popkewitz (2000) notes, we should not overlook the historical importance of moral discourses in shaping the ideas and practices around professionalism. Professionalism, with its emphasis on reproducing professionals as men of high character, reflected Protestant ideals. That the founders of most institutions of higher learning were WASPs is well documented (Rudolph, 1990; Veysey, 1965). More interesting perhaps are the ways in which professionalism utilized religious (particularly Protestant) arguments to advance a particular format for relations among a growing social body. The emphasis on developing character remained constant despite a shift in its constitutive elements. Bledstein notes that the man of high character did not simply possess industrious habits. Rather the man of high character, the budding professional, must be aggressive in mental initiative (Bledstein, 1978, p. 133). Drawing from the tenets of evangelical Protestantism, the professional acts as an agent of "social gospel."[12] Although educational institutions have always served a moral function, the edge of evangelism in the 1880s and 1890s reflected the role of the professional in the great crusade for civilization. Fueled by a historical project of manifest destiny, professionals could put the fruits of scientific inquiry to work in recreating a social order.

Progressive Era educational reform leaders, such as Charles Eliot, conceptualized the role of the professional in advancing eugenics projects. Eliot feared that vice, such as alcoholism and venereal disease, would corrupt the growing American cities. Bledstein articulates Eliot's attitude as a fear that "undesirable races" would overtake the "natural" cultural bearers: white Anglo-Saxon Protestants. Thus, the very idea of the professional was bound to specific projects—not abstracted but grounded—in utopian visions like that of the eugenics movement.[13] As the first president of the American Social Hygiene Association (ASHA), Eliot envisioned the role of the professional to wipe out prostitution and promiscuity. Eliot (and ASHA) utilized scientific discourse to advance a moral project:

> Recent inquiries have demonstrated that more than half of the prostitutes in a modern city, or a rural community, are likely to be feeble-minded women. The effective confinement of feeble-minded women, at least till they are past childbearing is, therefore an indispensable part of the restriction of prostitution and the limitation of venereal disease. (quoted in Bledstein, 1978, p. 157)

It is through statements such as Eliot's concern for the expansion of "licentiousness" that women's bodies are produced as objects in the emergent discourse of professionalism. According to Eliot (white) feeble-minded women, like their immigrant, Native American, and

African American counterparts, constitute a threat to the nation. Considering that such constructions "other" the majority of bodies/persons living in the United States during the time, creating this class of professionals (white, middle-class, educated men) as the born leaders to protect and police those it deemed threatening, crystallized the notion that nationhood or community would be on the backs of the marginalized groups.[14] Put another way, the emerging subject position of the professional was produced as a white, able-bodied, heterosexual, "native-born male," and "sexuality" was construed as a dangerous force, unleashed by racially marked females, and to be contended with and contained by this class of professionals or experts.

Herein lies yet another of the ironies regarding discourses of sexuality, race, and nationhood: The professional needed to be "virile" yet protect against sexual activity. Indeed, it is not just a male body that makes a professional; it is the man of character, with vigilance toward masculinity that achieves the position.[15] As Bledstein notes, "The man of character exuded virility, a physical toughness that had moral consequences" (1978, p. 152). While scientific discourses of professionalism left the male body unproblematized in the construction of an "expert," moral discourses made explicit the connections of gender to the exercise of professional control. I now turn to discussing the role of the racialization of the (heteronormative) educational/American family and professionalization in more detail.

Queering the (Educational) Family:
Dispersed Sites for Constructing Professionalism

Thus far, I have discussed how heteronormativity operated in discourses of professionalism with particular attention to the ideas of educational leaders. I have attempted to demonstrate how the professional educational family consists of the Republican mother (the "natural" teacher) and the educational professional (the "manly" yet objective expert). Yet the "mysterious" force (located in the nexus of sex/gender/desire), that differentiates the professional from the teacher, remains uninvestigated. In the following paragraphs, I explore the notion that female sexuality is the "stuff" of the educational Subject that must be regulated via discourses of professionalism. Specifically, I suggest that masculinity and participation in all-male environments (the residential college and professional associations) played an active role in constructing normal professional development for men. Slipping between homoeroticism and hypermasculinity, men's development as professionals involved putting men in touch with other men and above women (the teacher, the prostitute, etc.).

My discussion returns to the practice of deviant historiography to investigate the regulation of heteronormativity within higher education. Deviant historiography revisits specific discourses and instances that produce normative bodies and identities to illustrate that boundary maintenance is an active process of negotiation and contestation involving multiple actors. The remainder of this chapter therefore addresses the regulation of female sexuality in two emergent spaces of professionalism: "romantic friendships" in Anglo-American women's colleges and constructions of female sexuality within all-male colleges and universities.

Spaces of Racialized Sexuality

Female sexuality is constructed as the vice that young male professionals need to protect and need protection from—both inside and outside of the classroom. For example, Rudolph (1990) outlines the influence of Calvinist notions of expansionism, progress, and virtue with a pastoral imaginary and assumptions about gendered education. He argues that the trend to build colleges in the countryside as a way of maintaining the status of the university as both "outside of" and "leading the way" to civilization. This move to the country was a strategy to avoid the "licentious" activity of urban life that is coded female (prostitution). At the turn of the last century, residential colleges and universities relocated men (future professionals) away from the female body both literally and figuratively. Ironically, however, the female body (at least in fragments) is also used to code the agrarian countryside as an artificial reconstruction of the pedagogical "bosom" in which the student Body is nestled. In addition, the architecture of the prototypical college is, by design, a function of assumptions about cultural geography that display heteronormative and racialized elements. The college dormitory or fraternity house (complete with housemothers) served as a "home away from home" to ease the "critical passage from boyhood to manhood" (Rudoph, 1990, p. 88). The female body represents this complicated and somewhat contradictory position of women's relationship to professionalism in that, at times the female body is used to represent a space of comfort and nurturance and yet at other times is used to signify the potential for dangerous moral transgressions among the student body (coded male and heterosexual).

While Rudolph gives an account of dormitory life as a technique of surveillance to regulate the commingling of male and female bodies (both literally and figuratively), Horowitz (1984) describes the parallel practice in women's education. Her analysis of the design and experience of women's colleges from the nineteenth century to the 1930s illustrates how architecture recirculated power relations. For example, Horowitz argues that female seminaries, such as Mt. Holyoke College, reflected a disciplinary system based on the "family government" hierarchy of authority. Students and faculty shared dwellings modeled like asylums that granted neither privacy nor public access to their female inhabitants.[16] Thus, the potential for same-sex sexuality was limited due to the panoptic layout of the sleeping quarters (Horowitz, 1984, p. 21). However, in the later part of the nineteenth century, Vassar College, Wellesley College, and Smith College *changed* the space from house to asylum to a place of "beautiful luxury" so as to cultivate the ladylike behavior of female students (p. 53). Smith College shared this trend towards developing suites as sleeping quarters. Horowitz notes that this gave rise to a "student culture" that was separate from faculty. Part of the student culture became a practice of "smashing," or crushes between women. Horowitz claims that romantic relations between women were not considered threatening, despite her documentation that students were reassigned suitemates every four weeks so as to prevent excessive intimacy. Horowitz's claim here makes sense that during the late nineteenth century, female same-sex sexuality was inconceivable. At that time, women's desire for academic knowledge was viewed as more of a threat to heteronormativity than were such "romantic friendships," since (Anglo-American) women were constructed as "asexual." This tolerance for romantic friendships, however, *shifted* by the 1920s when female sexuality came into public discourse (largely via Freud and the popular notion of the "new woman") as well as the prevalence of the eugenics-based fear of a diminishing white race. Whereas in previous generations, women's education posed a threat to femininity, women's colleges in the 1920s "threatened the nation with race suicide" (Horowitz, 1984, p. 279).

It is interesting to note that the doctrine of separate spheres, mobilized in preceding decades as an ideology that celebrated female-only spaces as a model unit of nationalist heteronormativity, later became suspect spaces—laden with nationalist anxieties because female fraternization also possessed the potential for female same-sex sexuality.

In this way, images of female education, female sexuality, and nationalist fears about the future of the "American race" comingled to produce some remarkably direct reassertions that a woman's capacity for citizenship was linked to her reproductive duty. Remember that after World War I through the 1920s, debates about sexuality conceded that women were sexually active (Graves, 1998, p. 85). Even Margaret Sanger, a central figure in the development of birth control, was a member of both the American Eugenics Association and the English Eugenics Association. While there is much contemporary debate regarding the extent to which Sanger supported white supremacy, her comments make it clear that the discourses around female sexuality in the 1920s could not be uncoupled from citizenship, nationalism, and women's roles in creating a good society:

> Eugenists imply or insist that a woman's first duty is to the state; we contend that her duty to herself is her first duty to the state. We maintain that a woman possessing an adequate knowledge of her reproductive functions is the best judge of the time and conditions under which her child should be brought into the world. We further maintain that it is her right, regardless of all other considerations, to determine whether she shall bear children or not, and how many children she shall bear if she chooses to become a mother. (Sanger, 1970)

This passage highlights the always already complicated relationship between (female) sexuality and citizenship. As Sanger contends, a "woman" has a duty to her own physical body as well as the national body to which she is to submit. However, Sanger makes no appeal to a "natural" body; rather it is an educated woman (i.e., "a woman possessing an adequate knowledge of her reproductive functions") who should be afforded the right to determine "whether she shall bear children or not, and how many children she shall bear if she chooses to become a mother." While this distinction may be subtle, it reflects the practice of differentiating between worthy and unworthy "women" based on class, racial, religious, educational or sexual status.

A key point here is how conceptions of "women" and womanhood indicate relations of power regarding class and race that are located precisely in the politics of the Progressive Era yet rarely articulated. In her analysis of the field of social work at the turn of the twentieth century, Mary Odem (1995) illustrates how the rhetoric and practices of the time reflect that the term "female" typically refers to "feminine" women. By semiotic association, then, the term female makes a citation reference to the ideology of domesticity in Victorian America. This is important because it is precisely the move that occludes and precludes all the actual women who provided domestic service during the Progressive period (prior and after) but who are not associated with the dominant terminology of the "domestic." Drawing from the work of Hortense Spillers, Eva Cherniavsky makes a similar and compelling argument that "republican motherhood stands as a discourse on femininity which operates only on *condition* of the black woman's exclusion" (1995, p. 3). Cherniavsky refers to this as a double disappearance of black women in discussions of Republican motherhood and liberal discourse. She refers to the "nonequivalence between white women's displacement from the social as origin, and black women's displacement from liminal womanhood as commodity" (Cherniavsky, 1995, p. 5). Spillers (1987) illuminates two important effects of the discourse-practices of slavery; first, black women are positioned as "genderless" persons; and second, black women's sexuality is considered public property under the conditions of white supremacy.

Despite popular belief that discussions of sexuality are absent from educational discourses, histories of the development of the professions demonstrate the overt role of sexuality in the shaping of "the professional" (Bledstein, 1978; Faragher & Howe, 1988; Glazer & Slater, 1987; Rudolph, 1990; Solomon, 1985; Veysey, 1965). This is a good example of Foucault's repressive hypothesis. Contrary to both Freudian and Marxist hypotheses of sexuality as repressed in the Modern era, Foucault argues that discourses of sexuality are not repressed but rather serve as an incitement to discourse, to regulate the boundaries of normal sexuality. These histories make explicit references to female sexual practices in constructing discourses of sexuality in relation to the professions. Specifically, white female (hetero)sexuality is discussed at length as an effort to police the boundaries of heteronormativity within educational contexts.

It was during this time that relations *between* women came under more scrutiny and actions were taken against women who expressed same-sex desire (Horowitz, 1984; Solomon, 1985). Fear of same-sex sexuality led to curricular changes that institutionalized heteronormative relations. For example, colleges that had previously privileged liberal arts and the natural sciences added the "domestic sciences" to the curriculum. In addition, the number of male faculty increased to encourage heterosexual desire and proper moral guidance (Horowitz, 1984). Eugenicist fears, coupled with the growing availability of the category "lesbian," caused an increased effort to direct white female sexuality into its "proper place"—heteronormative relations. If a woman wanted to be educated (toward a professional class) she must now prove her racial and class allegiance (her moral obligation) to marry and reproduce.

This tension between profession and marriage for educated women, and women in education, was a common theme throughout the early accounts of women in the professions (Faragher & Howe, 1988; Hoffman, 1981). Women's participation across the emerging professions before 1900 maintained women's maternal role, yet the consequences of this role varied by discipline. For women in medicine, there was not an option to combine marriage, motherhood, and career (Glazer & Slater, 1987). For a woman to attain a position within medicine she must forego family. This conflict was framed in terms of the need for a doctor to concentrate on performance; marriage and children would be a distraction. In the teaching profession, there was also a tension between marriage and career; however, this conflict was framed as a sexual and moral dilemma. Female teachers were to represent the highest moral character, thus requiring sexual abstinence. For example, teacher contracts from this period indicate that marriage, as well as "keeping the company of men," was grounds for termination (Apple, 1987, p. 73). Despite widespread belief that teaching was an extension of women's maternal role, it was not until the 1950s that the formal policies prohibiting female teachers from childbirth (even within marriage) were challenged. In light of the analyses of Solomon and Horowitz, it seems plausible that shifts in marriage policies for teachers can be linked to eugenicist desires to maintain "the race" and/or the proper heteronormative family as much as feminist desires of removing restrictions against female teachers. The development of the professions (including education) provided a new "technology of sex":

> Through pedagogy, medicine, and economics, it made sex not only a secular concern but a concern of the state as well; to be more exact, sex became a matter that required the social body as a whole, and virtually all of its individuals, to place themselves under surveillance. (Foucault, 1990, p.116)

In this new technology of sex, education serves a primary role in the administration or regulation of the human population. Education provides a physical space for housing and training bodies; the mechanisms for classifying, diagnosing, and treating bodies according to their "natural" abilities, tendencies, or potential; and practices and identities linked to the model American citizen through the family of educational professionals themselves. Heteronormativity, which was key to establishing relations of sex/gender/desire during previous eras (i.e., Common School), took new forms of authority as Science became a "regime of truth" (Foucault, 1984b) during the Progressive Era. As Foucault notes, "the political significance of sex is due to the fact that sex is located at the point of intersection of the discipline of the body and the control of the population" (1984b, p. 67). Thus, projects of professionalism as efforts to discipline bodies and control populations are efforts inscribed within larger historical narratives of family, race, and nation.

WASP as American Family: Sexuality and Citizenship

The positioning of sexual identities mapped onto other "systems of thought" (e.g., racism and/or nationalism, etc.) regarding who and how regulation of sexual practice occurs. Indeed, during the Progressive Era, leaders of political and social reform (including educational leaders) often invoked the term Anglo-Saxon or WASP (white Anglo-Saxon Protestant) to refer to the ideal professional. Speaking about the influx of Italian, Slovakian, Polish, Russian and Jewish immigrants during 1880–1900, Ellwood Cubberly wrote in 1909:

> these southern and eastern Europeans are of a very different type from the north Europeans who preceded them. Illiterate, docile, lacking in self-reliance and initiative, and not possessing the Anglo-Teutonic conceptions of law, order, and government, their coming has served to dilute tremendously our national stock, and to corrupt our civic life....Our task is to break up these groups or settlements, to assimilate and amalgamate these people as part of our American race, and to implant in their children, so far as can be done, the Anglo-Saxon conception of righteousness, law and order, and popular government, and to awaken in them a reverence for our democratic institutions and for those things in our national life which we as a people hold to be of abiding worth. (1974, p. 2162)

Cubberly, a former superintendent and education professor at Stanford, makes explicit the association between education, "health," and politics in nation building prevalent in Progressive-Era reform literature. In this construction, the WASP family serves as a metonym for democratic citizenship, and furthermore, it is the goal of education to both produce and reproduce "healthy" citizens.

This usage of the term Anglo-Saxon, or WASP, racializes the discourse practices of American citizenship during the Progressive Era in three ways. First, writing at this time draws an association between national identity (American) and racial identity (whiteness). In the above passage, although eastern and southern European persons are constructed as potentially "diluting" the "American national stock" or "American race," there is, nevertheless, the possibility of "assimilation" "into our American race." The omission of immigrants from Asia, Africa, and the Americas from Cubberly's laundry list of undesirable immigrants suggests that some groups were impossible candidates for American citizenship altogether. Remember that in 1909, African Americans (as well as Native Americans and white women) had not yet secured the right to vote—thus precluding citizenship in terms of political representation. Moreover, U.S. miscegenation laws, written as early as 1662 and as late as 1925, which made sexual relations between American descendents of European ancestry with persons of African, Latin, Asian, or Native American descent a *federal crime,* reflect how white supremacist attitudes created laws and policies to "protect" the "racial purity" of American citizenry in theory and practice.[17]

Second, conceptions of U.S. citizenship during the Progressive Era highlighted religious diversity and conflated non-Protestant religions with non-white racial categories (such as Catholicism and Judaism). Although anti-Semitism is not limited to the time and location of U.S. Progressive Era reform, anti-Semitic prejudice changed in its shape and form during that time (Young-Bruehl, 1996). Elisabeth Young-Bruehl documents how anti-Semitism in the U.S. shifted from "earlier religiously based Jew hatred" to an "obsessional prejudice" imbued with qualities of a more political and economic tone (1996, p. 28). Popular and academic debates regarding American citizenship during that time utilized racialized constructions of Jewish people to institutionalize anti-Semitic discrimination, through, for example, restricted access to public spaces and participation in professional organizations and institutions (including higher education) as well as immigration policies.

Third, WASP was synonymous with "native-born American"—thus an obvious positioning of the status of indigenous/Native Americans as "outside" while "within." Like African American women during the Progressive Era, Native American women seeking education were encouraged to attend industrial or vocational training to become a "domestic" (housekeeper, nanny and/or maid). This form of domesticity results in servitude of two exponential forms: racial and national servitude—as well as servitude to other females—all in the name of domesticated citizenship (Graves, 1998). Domesticated citizenship involves an interrelated set of racialized and (hetero)sexualized dynamics that are unproblematically upheld when educational positions and *relationships are tied to duties to "the family" and "the nation." Heteronormativity, a technology of gender/sex/desire, crystallized in the images of the family and the nation, both marks and erases the relations of power and contested movements regarding race and nationalism during this period.*

Conclusion

This analysis suggests that Progressive-Era discourses of professionalism appropriated conceptions of sexuality (both scientific and moral) that aligned with racist and xenophobic constructions of citizenship. Furthermore, women's bodies and sexuality—constructed through the lenses of scientific racism and heteronormativity—were a force to be feared, controlled, and educated via discourses of professionalism. The growth of a professional class was linked to a desire to predict, regulate, and control a growing social body constituted by the socio-historical problematics of this era: urbanization, immigration, industrialization, and the rising class of educated women. I have shown how various educational movements within discourses of professionalism represent what Foucault refers to as "repro-technology," where discourses of sexuality and science conflate to produce the "natural" positions of particular bodies and identities within the educational "family." Specifically, Progressive-Era discourses on sexuality simply reconfigured earlier notions of heteronormativity into new positions of WASP women and men as the "managers" of education in a changing society. As the "culture bearers" of a nation, women (read white, middle-class, heterosexual women) would model domesticated citizenship in the form of servitude. As the technical specialists, some men will ensure the proper administration of freedom (both seduced by and in control of female sexuality). We might reduce this to say that Republican motherhood was charged with the management of souls and the educational professional charged with the management of bodies and populations. The limits of the ideal teacher and the ideal expert in education were inscribed differentially, then, around heteronormative notions of the family oriented around reproduction.

This inscription is achieved through the discursive positionings that a Foucaultian analytics of the subject suggests. Foucault's observation that the rise of science as a regime of truth that culminated in the Progressive Era is helpful for theorizing higher education as the apparatus that both creates and maintains the privileged place of the "expert" in education and the wo/man of character in professionalism. As subject positions, expert and teacher are separated out and then brought into union in the form of the heteronormative family of education: the all-knowing, rational father (expert) and in-need-of-guidance mother (teacher). These images take shape as idealized versions of good citizenship. What is curious though, is that both the expert professional and the teacher are granted the authority to oversee and evaluate the behaviors, identities, and practices of noncitizens. In this way, nonwhite and non-Protestant categories are infantilized as the imaginary children/offspring of the democratic father and Republican mother of the American educational family. This analysis has thus demonstrated how discourses of professionalism have been historically situated within sociocultural politics of racism, homophobia, and xenophobia. I suggest that until we address the history of these interrelated images, present-day appeals to professionalism will carry the legacies of discrimination in the guise of providing "caring" and "objective" models (parents) for the yet-to-be-citizens ("nonwhite" Americans).

Endnotes

1. My analysis here may perhaps be better characterized as an "effective history" or "history of the present" rather than a genealogy. A history of the present, according to Dean "may be loosely characterized by its use of historical resources to reflect upon the contingency, singularity, interconnections and potentialities of the diverse trajectories of those elements which compose present social arrangements and experience" (Dean, 1994, p. 21). In contrast, genealogy can be likened more to a materialist historiography that carefully scrutinizes documents across various time periods to elaborate a nonlinear sense of regularities in systems of thought. However, Foucault himself utilized neither/nor and both/and forms of critical analyses without much explication as to his methodological "plan." See Dean (1994) for a discussion of the complexities of Foucault's methodological stances.

2. In *The Order of Things*, Foucault (1994) specifies his use of the term "structure" to mean "systems of thought" or "the rules of reasoning" as opposed to its conceptualization as institutions in French poststructuralism.

3. For Foucault, the separation between symbolic and material domains is a logical fallacy.

4. Butler (1990) uses the term sex/gender/desire to refer to the matrix of intelligibility that constitutes heteronormativity, signaling how this matrix is a system of interarticulated categories that conflate to produce the category of woman, which gets read as "mother." At times, for analytic purposes, I will foreground one aspect of heteronormativity more than another. However, this unraveling of interarticulated terms is not intended to privilege one term over another. This "problem with words" also extends to my discussion of race and nation.

5. There is a significant body of work on the "professionalization" of teaching. See, for example, Gitlin (1996) and Apple (1994). This work emphasizes a critical or Marxist perspective, through a careful analysis of the terms and practices of labor organizations in reshaping the teaching profession. My analysis privileges a cultural history of how the categories of family, race, and nation are inextricably tied to discourses of professionalism rather than to an economic analysis of sex and professionalization. For a good discussion of the terms and implications of the most recent mobilization around "professionalizing teaching," see the

special issue of *Teachers College Record* devoted to the subject: Reforming Teacher Education: A Symposium on the Holmes Group Report. *Teachers College Record*, 88(3).

6. See Rousmaniere (in press) for an overview of various movements and strands within historiography.

7. See Weems (1999) for a discussion of Pestalozzi's pedagogy of love and its centrality in nineteenth- and twentieth-century educational reform conceptions of teaching.

8. G. Stanley Hall, quoted in D. Schneider and C. Schneider (1993, p. 153).

9. Ibid, p. 446.

10. Within educational theory and reform during this time, debates over the role of science were multiple and heated. These debates can be seen in curriculum reform debates that manifested in the dispersion of various curriculum theories. See Kliebard (1995) for an overview of these debates and their implications.

11. Consider, for example, the rise in the production of curricular materials such as child psychology and pediatric brochures created for a popular audience.

12. By evangelical Protestantism I am referring to the Calvinist influence that characterized the Common School Movement (1830s–1880s) advocated by Beecher, Mann and others—education involves the development of the soul. Beecher and others advocated mass education as a form of redemption, thus making way for the prosthelization and spread of educational institutions with a particularly religious zeal.

13. Thanks to Katy Heyning and Bernadette Baker for highlighting this point.

14. See *This Bridge Called My Back*, Moraga and Anzaldua (Eds.), (1983) for a collection of essays by women of color that explore how the first- and second-wave (white) feminist movements both co-opted and marginalized the concerns of feminists of color.

15. See, for example, Veysey's section on the pursuit of the "well rounded man" (1965, pp. 197–202) and the discussion of football in establishing "the academic man" (Rudolph, 1990, pp. 373–416).

16. Although there are obvious differences in status and condition of residential education for African American and Native American students during the nineteenth and twentieth centuries, see Lomawaima (1995) for an excellent discussion of how the control of minds rested on the control of bodies in federal Indian schools.

17. Peggy Pascoe (2001) makes a similar argument in "Democracy, Citizenship, and Race: The West in the Twentieth Century."

References

Apple, Michael (1987). "Gendered Teaching, Gendered Labor." In T. Popkewitz (Ed.), *Critical Studies in Teacher Education: Its Folklore, Theory and Practice* (pp. 55–83). London: Falmer.

Apple, Michael (1994). "Is Change Always Good for Teachers? Gender, Class and Teaching in History." In K. M. Bornman and N. Greenman (Eds.), *Changing American Education: Recapturing the Past or Inventing the Future?* Albany: State University of New York Press.

Bledstein, Burton J. (1978). *The Culture of Professionalism: The Middle Class and the Development of Higher Education in America.* New York: Norton.

Blount, Jackie (1999). "Manliness and the Gendered Construction of School Administration in the USA." *International Journal of Leadership in Education, 2, 2, 55–68.*

Butler, Judith (1990). *Gender Trouble: Feminism and the Subversion of Identity.* New York: Routledge.

Cherniavsky, Eva (1995). *That Pale Mother Rising: Sentimental Discourse and the Imitation of Motherhood in 19th-century America.* Bloomington, IN: Indiana University Press.

Cooper, Anna Julia (1988). *A Voice from the South.* New York: Oxford University Press.

Cubberly, Edward (1974). "An Educator on the New Immigrants." In S. Cohen (Ed.), *Education in the United States: A Documentary History* (p. 2162). New York: Random House. (Original work published 1909)

Dean, Mitchell (1994). *Critical and Effective Histories: Foucault's Methods and Historical Sociology.* London: Routledge.

Etzioni, Amitai. (Ed.). (1969*). The Semi-Professions and Their Organization: Teachers, Nurses and Social Workers.* New York: Free Press.

Faragher, John Mack, and Florence Howe (1988). *Women and Higher Education in American History.* New York: Norton.

Foucault, Michel (1972*). The Archaeology of Knowledge, and the Discourse on Language* (A.M. Sheridan Smith, Trans.). New York: Pantheon.

Foucault, Michel (1984a). "Nietzsche, Genealogy, History." In P. Rabinow (Ed.), *The Foucault Reader* (pp. 75–100*).* New York: Pantheon. (Original work published 1971)

Foucault, Michel (1984b). "Truth and Power." In P. Rabinow (Ed.), *The Foucault Reader* (pp. 51–75). New York: Pantheon. (Original work published 1972)

Foucault, Michel (1990). *The History of Sexuality: An Introduction. Volume 1.* (R. Hurley, Trans.). New York: Vintage. (Original work published 1978)

Foucault, Michel (1991). "Politics and the Study of Discourse." In G. Burchell, C. Gordon and P. Miller (Eds.), *The Foucault Effect: Studies in Governmentality* (pp. 53–72). Chicago: University of Chicago Press.

Foucault, Michel (1994). *The Order of Things: An Archaeology of the Human Sciences.* New York: Vintage. (Original work published 1970)

Foucault, Michel (1995). *Discipline and Punish* (A. Sheridan, Trans.). New York: Vintage. (Original work published 1975)

Gitlin, Andrew (1996). "Gender and Professionalization: An Institutional Analysis of Teacher Education and Unionism at the Turn of the Twentieth Century." *Teachers College Record, 97*(4), 588–615.

Glazer, Penina Migdal, and Miriam Slater (1987). *Unequal Colleagues: The Entrance of Women into the Professions, 1890–1940.* New Brunswick, NJ: Rutgers University Press.

Graves, Karen (1998). *Girls' Schooling During the Progressive Era: From Female Scholar to Domesticated Citizen.* New York: Garland.

Hall, G. Stanley (1903). "Coeducation in the High School." *National Education Association Journal of Proceedings and Addresses* 42.

Heyning, Katharina (2001). 'The Early Childhood Teacher as Professional: An Archaeology of University Reform." In J. A. Jipson and R. T. Johnson (Eds.), *Resistance and Representation: Rethinking Childhood Education* (pp. 77–105). New York: Peter Lang.

Hoffman, Nancy (1981). *Woman's "True" Profession: Voices from the History of Teaching.* Old Westbury, NY: The Feminist Press.

Horowitz, Helen Lefkowitz (1984). *Alma Mater: Design and Experience in the Women's Colleges from Their Nineteenth-Century Beginnings to the 1930's.* Boston: Beacon.

Kliebard, Herbert (1995). *The Struggle for the American Curriculum 1893–1958.* New York: Routledge.

Labaree, David F. (1992). "Power, Knowledge, and the Rationalization of Teaching: A Genealogy of the Movement to Professionalize Teaching." *Harvard Educational Review, 62*(2), 123–154.

Labaree, David F. (1995). "A Disabling Vision: Rhetoric and Reality in Tomorrow's Schools of Education" *Teachers College Record, 97*(2), 166–205.

Labaree, David F. (1996). "The Trouble with Ed. Schools." *Educational Foundations*, Summer, 27–45.

Labaree, David F. (1997). *How to Succeed in School Without Really Learning: The Credentials Race in American Education.* New Haven, CT: Yale University Press.

Lather, Patti (1987). "The Absent Presence: Patriarchy, Capitalism and the Nature of Teacher Work." *Teacher Education Quarterly, 14*(2), 25–38.

Leach, Mary (1988). "Teacher Education and Reform: What's Sex Got to Do with It?" *Philosophy of Education 1988*. Proceedings of the Fifty-Fourth Annual Meeting of the Philosophy of Education Society. Normal: Illinois State University.

Lomawaima, Tsianina (1995). "Domesticity in the Federal Indian Schools: The Power of Authority over Mind and Body." In J. Terry and J. Urla (Eds.), *Deviant Bodies: Critical Perspectives on Difference and Science and Popular Culture* (pp. 197–219). Bloomington: Indiana University Press.

Moraga, Cherie, and Gloria Anzaldua (1983). *This Bridge Called My Back: Writings by Radical Women of Color*. New York: Kitchen Table, Women of Color.

Odem, Mary E. (1995). *Delinquent Daughters: Protecting and Policing Adolescent Female Sexuality in the United States, 1885–1920*. Chapel Hill: University of North Carolina Press.

Pascoe, Peggy (2001). "Democracy, Citizenship, and Race: The West in the Twentieth Century." In H. Sitkoff (Ed.), *Perspectives on Modern America: Making Sense of the Twentieth Century* (pp. 227–246). New York: Oxford.

Patton, Cindy, and Benigno Sanchez-Eppler (Eds.) (2000). *Queer Diasporas*. Durham, NC: Duke University Press.

Pellegrini, Ann (1997). *Performance Anxieties: Staging Psychoanalysis, Staging Race*. New York: Routledge.

Popkewitz, Thomas (1993). "U.S. Teacher Education Reforms: Regulatory Practices of the State, University and Research." In *Changing Patterns of Power: Social Regulation and Teacher Education Reform* (pp. 263–302). Albany, NY: State University of New York Press.

Popkewitz, Thomas (1994). "Certification to Credentialing: Reconstituting Control Mechanisms in Teacher Education." In K. Borman and N. Greenman (Eds.), *Changing American Education: Recapturing the Past or Inventing the Future?* (pp. 33–70). Albany, NY: State University of New York Press.

Popkewitz, Thomas (2000). "Curriculum as a Problem of Knowledge, Governing and the Social Administration of the Soul." In B. Franklin (Ed.), *Curriculum and Consequence: Herbert Kliebard and the Promise of Schooling* (pp.75–102). New York: Teachers College Press.

Readings, Bill (1996). *The University in Ruins*. Cambridge, MA: Harvard University Press.

Rousmaniere, Kate (in press). "Historical Research." In K. Bennett de Marrais and S. D. Lapan (Eds.), *Perspectives and Approaches for Research in Education and the Social Sciences*. Lawrence Earlbaum.

Rubin, Gayle (1993). "Thinking Sex: Notes for a Radical Theory for the Politics of Sexuality." In H. Abelove, M. Barale and D. Halperin (Eds.), *The Lesbian and Gay Studies Reader* (pp. 3–44). New York: Routledge.

Rudolph, William (1990). *The American College and University: A History.* Athens, GA: University of Georgia. (Original work published 1962)

Sanger, Margaret (1970). *The Birth Control Review Vol. I, Vols. 1–3, 1917–1919.* New York: Da Capo. (Original work published 1919 as "Birth Control and Racial Betterment." *The Birth Control Review,* 3(2), 11–12.

Schneider, Dorothy, and Carl Schneider (1993). *American Women in the Progressive Era, 1900–1920.* New York: Facts on File.

Sklar, Kathryn Kish (1976). *Catherine Beecher: A Study in American Domesticity.* New York: W. W. Norton.

Solomon, Barbara Miller (1985). *In the Company of Educated Women.* New Haven, CT: Yale University Press.

Sommerville, Siobhan (2000). *Queering the Color Line: Race and the Invention of Homosexuality in American Culture.* Durham, NC: Duke University Press.

Spillers, Hortense (1987). "Mama's Baby, Papa's Maybe: An American Grammar Book." *Diacritics, 17*(2), 65–81.

Stoler, Ann Laura (1995). *Race and the Education of Desire: Foucault's History of Sexuality and the Colonial Order of Things.* Durham, NC: Duke University Press.

Terry, Jennifer (1991). "Theorizing Deviant Historiography." *d i f f e r e n c e s : A Journal of Feminist Cultural Studies, 3*(2), 55–74.

Tyack, David, and Elisabeth Hansot (1982). *Managers of Virtue: Public School Leadership in America, 1820–1980.* New York: Basic Books.

Veysey, Laurence (1965). *The Emergence of the American University.* Chicago: University of Chicago Press.

Weems, Lisa (1999). "Pestalozzi, Perversity and the Pedagogy of Love" In W. Letts and J. Sears (Eds.), *Queering Elementary Education* (pp. 27–37). Boulder, CO: Rowman Littlefield.

Weiler, Kathleen (1988). *Women Teaching for Change: Gender, Class and Power.* South Hadley, MA: Bergin and Garvey.

Weis, Lois (1995). "Gender and the Reports: The Case of the Missing Piece." In R. Ginsburg and D. Plank (Eds.), *Commissions: Reports, Reforms and Educational Policy* (173–192). Westport, CT: Praeger.

Young-Bruehl, Elisabeth (1996). *The Anatomy of Prejudices.* Cambridge, MA: Harvard University Press.

SECTION TWO: DANGERS

PART ONE:
In Tutelage

Michel Foucault:
Marxism, Liberation, and Freedom

James D. Marshall

There are many forms of oppression, of which economic oppression is but one and, according to Michel Foucault, not the form of oppression to which all other forms of oppression are to be reduced.[1] No doubt he was influenced here by his early mentor and teacher, Louis Althusser. But if Althusser was a heretic from strict Marxism, there were other examples in French Marxist thinking such as Henrei Lefebrve who, as early as 1935, had argued from the basis of the family towards a form of liberation and joy. For his "efforts" he was later to be expelled from the French Communist Party and to become an important member and contributor to the movement and journal *Arguments*. But Althusser and Lefebrve were still Marxists. Foucault was not and indeed was quite critical of Marxism. What was wrong with Marxist views of liberation from oppression according to Foucault? We will look here at classical Marxism and the neo-Marxist writings of Paulo Freire.

Foucault often said such things as, "to be happy it is [not] enough to cross the threshold of discourse and to remove a few prohibitions" [author's brackets] (Foucault, 1977a, p. 114). In relation to the notion of the subject, he said (Foucault, 1982, p. 216): "Maybe the target nowadays is not to discover what we are, but to refuse what we are." An interpretation of these aphorisms in some education literature that appeals to Foucault seems to involve the unearthing of power relations in education, especially those that impinge on the subjectivity of the young. These power relations can be found at a number of levels, at that of institutional structures including curricula, at the level of the discourses/practices of teaching and learning, and of course, at all levels in between. However, it did not require Foucault to unmask the power relations omnipresent at the institutional and curriculum level for inspired-inspired sociology of education had already trodden that path (e.g., Apple, 1979; Young, 1971) even though Foucault brought new understanding to that arena with his concept of governmentality (Foucault, 1979a), and the new ways in which we can govern the self.

Foucault asks new questions about power. Within the typical liberal approach to power, questions are asked such as: Is power being exercised?

And, if so, by whom, on whom, and by what means? He rejects traditional notions of the subject and, in particular, that of a continuous and ultimate identity through neo-Kantian appeals to autonomy, especially where autonomy is interpreted as a form of moral autonomy, and rationality is conceived and exercised in terms of Weberian bureaucratic rationality. Instead, his strategy is to "promote new forms of subjectivity through the refusal of this kind of individuality (that linked to the 'state's' institutions) which has been imposed upon us for several centuries" (Foucault, 1982, p. 216). Foucault does not see the state as Marxists do, yet it might be argued that the institutions that he wishes to talk about—the asylum, the hospital, the prison, and so on, are usually provided by the state. (I have placed scare quotes around the state when I use the word in Foucault's sense.) Indeed his notion of governmentality is not concerned with Governments but with *how* people come to be governed and how they come to govern or discipline themselves. Thus he does not posit a theory of the state and the functions of the state because, for him, that would still not answer the question, "How does the state ensure governmentality?"

There is little doubt here that Foucault was influenced by Henri Bergson and the teaching of Bergson in lycées and tertiary institutions, especially when he was at the École Normale Supérieure and attended assiduously the lectures of Maurice Merleau-Ponty on Bergson (Eribon, 1991, p. 32). Also, he was examined on Bergson for his aggregation (licence to teach philosophy). Within French philosophy in the late nineteenth and early twentieth centuries, Bergson's work represents a movement away from the early scientific positivism of Comte and Durkheim. Respect for the achievements of the mathematical sciences is replaced by a humanist suspicion of the sciences in relation to human beings (Matthews, 1996, p. 4). Whereas we could have a scientific (or in Bergson's term, "analytic") knowledge of the self, even of our mental lives, this was not for Bergson proper *self-knowledge.* Such analytic knowledge, even of our inner thoughts, say, was knowledge of the self that was subsumed under thoughts of a *general* kind, and thus thoughts that any human being could have. Thus, these thoughts in question might be subsumed under certain psychological generalisations, say, of the human mind. Conceived in this analytic way they were universal and essentially timeless and detached from the very individuality which they sought according to Bergson.

The self-knowledge that Bergson wishes to emphasise, whilst in time, is in time in a much more present sense than in analytic, absolute, or mathematical time. He calls this "durée" or duration. "Earlier than" or "in the future" are always relevant to the *present* and not in spatial or absolute time and because they are always in the present, where I am now; they are always different because I am always changing or *becoming*. My history related always to the present becomes a *unique* history. In a space-time-analytic history it is possible that anyone might have had that history— thereby, it is no longer unique and *mine* (e.g., Bergson, 1913). Whilst Foucault scarcely acknowledges Bergson, he is a forerunner in French philosophy in attacking the social sciences, and Foucault was well acquainted with his work.

However, Foucault does not always totally reject the knowledge available through the human sciences as Bergson did. But whilst he does critique the knowledge of the human sciences, he sees that knowledge as being sometimes important and useful—why else would he have encouraged a young student to study Freud, as he did in California (Miller, 1993, p. 282)? Rather than totally rejecting that knowledge he sees it instead as potentially dangerous, as possibly imposing a view of the self upon individuals that may leave them in tutelage, that is, under the guardianship or "protection" of others, whether directly or indirectly. This is the basis then of his attack upon autonomy and thus upon liberal education.

In liberal approaches to education, at the microlevel of the interaction between teacher and learner, the production of docile bodies and the constitution of normalised forms of subjectivity, Foucault's work on power was clearly innovative in its challenge to the authority of the teacher. He challenges it in two ways at least. First, philosophically, his work challenges liberal education philosophy (and liberal education) and its use of authority as the fundamental concept for describing and understanding the "processes" of the transmission of knowledge, or as R. S. Peters puts it, the processes of initiation. (Here I use "liberal" in Foucault's wide sense to include Marxism and neo-Marxism.) In R. S. Peters's seminal text, *Ethics and Education* (Peters, 1966), "power" has but four mentions, two of those in footnotes. It is authority in the de jure sense, and the authority of the teacher, that carries the liberal educator through processes that are potentially instructional and noneducational but potentially manipulative and indoctrinating. Even if such issues are addressed by liberal education, the appeal is to the liberal authority of rationality and proper liberal (i.e., rational) processes. Power is not on centre stage but off in the wings, as a last resort to come to civil aid (to build upon his military metaphors—Peters, 1966, p. 238). Second, Foucault challenges the relationship between teacher and learner and the sorts of human relationship that underlie that relationship. Phillipe Ariès (1962) noted that in the mediaeval school the teacher was not responsible for discipline over students; this changed for a number of reasons related to parents' concerns and demands, the demands of society, the requirements of mass education, and changing knowledge about childhood. Discipline is now an accepted aspect of modern schooling. However, Foucault's account of discipline in *Discipline and Punish* is different from that of Peters and liberalism. It is concerned with how individuals are constituted in certain ways so that they fall initially under the tutelage of parents and teachers and eventually of other adults and the "state" and its institutions. In this source it brings together two uses of "discipline" that, for whatever reason, liberal education had separated— discipline in a legal and military sense as a form of order, and discipline as in "the study of the disciplines." Foucault talks of this as disciplinary power (Foucault, 1979b. See further, Marshall, 1996.). Later he is to use discipline in a number of other senses and particularly when talking of the self in the sense of *self-discipline.*

In much early writing on Foucault in education, discovering disciplinary power in educational practices therefore might be seen, and often is, as a form of *liberation*. It is almost as if unearthing a power relationship *explains* what these discourse and practices are doing to the young. As power is usually seen in education as oppressive (the remnants of the liberal tradition), the unearthing of these relationships becomes a fundamental prolegomenon to liberating individuals from tutelage. Changing discourses and practices will bring about liberation, it is thought or assumed. Not necessarily so, Foucault argues, because if it is power that does the explaining, power *itself* is in need of explanation.

The solution to tutelage, Foucault argues, is to care for the self, to *work* on the self, "by which one attempts to develop and transform oneself, and to attain to a certain mode of being" (Foucault, 1984, p. 282). This is not a selfish or narcissistic enterprise but involves a highly personalised approach to philosophy—that philosophy is concerned with the self and with how the self is to be conceived and perceived, and with how, for Foucault, it is to exercise its freedom. But Foucault is chary of talking of this as *liberation* of the self (Foucault, 1984, p. 282). Indeed he had always been concerned and suspicious of such talk (Foucault, 1991: in Trombadori, 1991, et passim).

For Foucault the self was not an individuated substance that had a continuous identity through time.

It is not a substance. It is a form, and this form is not primarily or always identical to itself. You do not have the same type of relationship to your self when you constitute yourself as a political subject who goes to vote or speaks at a meeting and when you are are seeking to fulfill your desires in a sexual relationship. Undoubtedly there are relationships and interferences between these different forms of the subject: but we are not dealing with the same type of subject. (Foucault, 1984, p. 290)

By saying that the subject is a form I understand that he is saying that it is a placeholder—like a logical x—and that placeholder can be filled with different particulars—a and b, say. Clearly, for Foucault, in the example that he provides, a and b are not identical. But this move permits the constitution of new and different particulars to fill the placeholder, and thereby one is not tied to an ongoing identity of self. This later notion of the self—the self that can be cared for (Foucault, 1984)—is different from his earlier accounts of the self. It is not the dispersed and decentered self that he seemed to hold in an almost structuralist manner but is more like the embodied self of Bergson. Foucault was often called a structuralist, but on several occasions he emphatically denied that that was the case—e.g., in the foreword to the English editions of *The Order of Things.*

But if the self is to exercise freedom it must not be in tutelage. First we need to look at Foucault's concerns with the notion of liberation, which arise, I will argue, from a set of dissatisfactions with Marxist and neo-Marxist ideology. Foucault said that it was difficult to talk about power relations without Marxist concepts (Foucault, 1977b, p. 110). Duccio Trombadori noted in 1978 when he interviewed Foucault (Trombadori, 1991) that:

After a decade of almost uninterrupted enthusiasm for Marxist "language," many people were circulating his [Foucault's] vocabulary, and the "micro-physics of power" became symptomatic of a radical, libertarian aspiration. Beyond the questions of fashion, this peculiar ideological transition deserved, and still deserves, some consideration. (author's brackets) (p. 15f)

However, according to Trombadori (1991), Foucault saw Marxism as entering into the European resistance movements:

as no more than a fragile ideological covering. Or rather, the troublesome scaffolding of "indomitable discursivities"...which somehow got in the way (so Foucault thinks) of a more substantial, deeper expression of libertarian needs that we are ready to strike at power in its intimate rationality and in its capacity to "govern" individuals.

Nevertheless Foucault (1991) acknowledged the importance of the events of May–June 1968 but argued that certain Marxist hyper-theorizations of those events were inadequate because they did not capture what it was that the students were questioning and revolting against. Nevertheless

> May of '68 was an experience of exceptional importance, without a doubt...without May of '68, I would never have done the things I'm doing today: such investigations as those on the prison, sexuality etc., would be unthinkable. The climate of 1968 was decisive for me in these matters. (Foucault, 1991, p. 144)

How was it, he asked, that there were serious expressions of dissatisfaction being expressed by students in societies as diverse as Sweden, Poland, Germany and Tunisia—all of which he had experienced? The revolt of the Tunisian students in 1968, just before the events in France, was an "outburst of radical revolt" marked not only by violence and intense involvement but also by the consequences and sacrifices. In Tunisia, unlike "daddy's darlings" in Paris, students faced the risk of fifteen years in prison. What he saw in Tunisia was a set of intolerable conditions produced by capitalism, colonialism, and neocolonialism, and to which "the theoretical Marxist preparation offered to students was not very in-depth" (Foucault, 1991, p. 137). The real debates amongst these students were concerned with strategies and tactics on what to do, and whilst Foucault believed that a political perception was necessary for initiating a revolt, questions of theory, its scientific status, etc. were of only secondary concern for these students. In fact they functioned more in the debates "as a means of deception than as a truthful, correct and proper criterion of conduct" (ibid.).

Foucault is objecting also to the turn that Marxism had taken in the academy. This involved the Marxist claim to adjudicate theoretically on the "scientificity" of science. Not only was it a central concern of institutions but it also came to dominate the daily lives of students (Foucault, 1991, p. 59) and, as "hypo-Marxism," interfered in the course of the events of May–June 1968.

Foucault continues

> I think my answer is that the dissatisfaction came from the way in which a kind of permanent oppression in daily life was being put into effect by the state or by other institutions and oppressive groups. That which was ill-tolerated and continuously questioned, which produced that sort of discomfort, was "power." And not only state power, but also that which was exercised within the social body through extremely different channels, forms and institutions. It was no

longer acceptable to be governed in certain ways. I mean "government" in an extended sense; I'm not referring just to the government of the state and the men who represent it, but also to those men who organise our daily lives by means of rules, by way of direct or indirect influences, as for instance the mass media. (1991, p. 144)

If power is the answer given to the question of the cause of this dissatisfaction, "power is that which must be explained" (Foucault, 1991, p. 148). It needs to be explained, he believed in 1978, because whilst to date he had written histories of power, power itself must be explained, but not because that would explain questions that had been raised concerning power in those histories. Hence he is to turn to a series of works on governmentality based upon his College de France Lectures of 1978—as in "Governmentality" which was first published in *Aut Aut* (September–December), 1978.

But he was always somewhat suspicious of Marxism and its claims of liberation for such persons as the alienated worker and alienated peasant. This suspicion stemmed from at least two sources: the underlying humanist (and Marxist) notion of a "real" self and that liberation per se was only a *prolegomenon* for an ethics. If, as suggested in a 1984 interview, his later ethical work on the self was to be interpreted as a process of liberation, then Foucault reasserted such suspicions:

I have always been somewhat suspicious of the notion of liberation, because if it is not treated with precautions and within certain limits, one runs the risk of falling back on the idea that there exists a human nature or base that, as a consequence of certain historical, economic, and social processes, has been concealed, alienated, or imprisoned in and by mechanisms of repression. According to this hypothesis, all that is required is to break these repressive deadlocks and man will be reconciled with himself, rediscover his nature or regain contact with his origin, and re-establish a full and positive relationship with himself. I think this idea should not be accepted without scrutiny. (1984, p. 282)

Of course liberation is important for Foucault. It not only exists or existed, as many colonials or former colonials are well aware, but it is a *precondition* of ethics, both logically and temporarily. Without liberation, talk of ethics is pointless, even perhaps nonsensical. Sartre was wrong, from his position, in asserting that the slave in chains, whilst clearly not liberated, was free to choose (as Simone de Beauvoir had also argued against him at least as early as 1939). Of course not being in "chains" is necessary for making choices and thereby exercising those choices, but liberation, which is then a precondition for freedom, does not, on its own, indicate what choices and practices should be chosen. For Foucault then, such talk of liberation not only presupposes forms of humanism in Marxism and existentialism but does not tell us how, as individuals, to exercise our freedom post-liberation. Marxism can, of course, but at the cost of acting in the interests of the revolution and not necessarily in the interests of the individual (one of Camus's critiques), and Sartrean existentialism can also, but at the cost of existentialist angst. Also talk of liberation seems often to presuppose that once freed from one set of chains, that is the end of the matter. But other chains may appear in such simplistic reversals of oppression (a point noted by Foucault in fleeing from France to Sweden in his twenties). This is to treat liberation and oppression as binary opposites, whereas it is much more complex. We must go "beyond" such binary oppositions if we are to liberate.

For Foucault then we need an ethics of freedom to define practices of freedom, if society and individuals "are to be able to define admissible and acceptable forms of existence or political society" (Foucault, 1984, p. 283). That is why he is suspicious of liberation, not because of the need to strategise practices and tactics of liberation, but because this may be seen as sufficient, not just as work well done, but as work successfully accomplished if not completed! That would be to prioritise practices of liberation over practices of freedom, and whilst there must clearly be temporal priorities here, these are not the logical priorities for an *ethics* of freedom.

But this distinction between liberation and freedom may become blurred, Foucault notes, in any analysis of power. Power relations cover an extreme range from individual human relationships, to family relationships, to pedagogical relationships, and to political life. For Foucault, power relations are always mobile and reversible. But in political life, in its widest sense, power relationships can become blocked or frozen so that it becomes impossible to adopt strategies and tactics that can modify them, and states of freedom no longer exist in fact. The power relation becomes immobile, "preventing any reversibility by economic, political or military means." This he refers to as a state of *domination* (Foucault, 1984, p. 283) and as a state from which we must be liberated. In particular liberation and a struggle for liberation may exist side by side. Here we can consider the example of sexuality and the practice of homosexuality, where the liberation of the practice may not liberate homosexuals whose freedom to practice homosexuality is repressed by other practices, for example, in employment and in the law (partnership, property, etc.). Thus whilst there is liberation of the practice, the struggle for liberation goes on, against practices that constrain freedom to act upon choices. Mere liberation of the practice in law may miss the ethical aspects of freedom that must accompany liberation. Liberation is not achieved because the modes in which freedom is to be practised, or the *how* of freedom, has not been considered. Of course, subsequent to the liberation legislation on homosexuality permitting the practices further legislation has been passed, for example, of a nondiscriminatory character, which provides political and ethical guidelines for homosexuals to practice their freedom.

Foucault sees, if not defines, ethics as the practice of freedom (1984, p. 284): "for what is ethics, if not the practice of freedom, the conscious (*réfléchie*) practice of freedom....Freedom (i.e., liberty) is the ontological condition of ethics. But ethics is the considered form that freedom takes when it is informed by reflection." For the Greeks who *problematised* their freedom, ethos was concerned with how the individual problematised his (or her) freedom and this was "evident in his clothing, appearance, gait, in the calm with which he responded to every event, and so on" (ibid., p. 286). If freedom is already problematised in this way, he adds, "extensive work by the self on the self is required for this practice of freedom to take shape in an *ethos* that is good, beautiful, honourable, estimable, memorable, and exemplary." There are major educational issues raised here—issues that, as usual, Foucault addresses quite cursorily (Marshall, 1996, chapter five). True, education and/or schools were not a focus for Foucault, but there are a number of issues here.

We can consider these at least from the earlier Foucault:

1. Foucault directs our attention to a number of shaping-up processes—learning to speak, read, and write—which the liberal education framework would not normally see as being contrary to the interests of the child and therefore not involving power. But for Foucault power is productive. Do we use the concept of power in relation to these practices then?

2. Submitting oneself to the discipline of the disciplines may lead us to become dominated and thus, if not repressed, to remain in the tutelage of others.

3. Modern power—surveillance, examination, and discipline—was developed in institutions such as the school. The knowledge associated with modern power is heavily associated with the human sciences that purport to give us knowledge about our selves. Both Bergson and Foucault dispute this thesis.

4. Autonomy is a central aim of liberal education, yet Foucault seems to hold that it is a sham and that far from being able to exercise our freedom, we may remain in a position of tutelage.

Apart from the issues above, in the later Foucault there are at least these:

What is the pedagogical relationship between the learner and the mentor?

How would it be possible for his approach to ethics to be part of the ethos of the school?

While this takes us in the later Foucault to questions of *how* to care for the self, it is not possible to pursue those matters here (but see Marshall, 1999; 2001), for our concern is with liberation, the precondition of such pursuits. The neo-Marxist Paulo Freire is, perhaps, the best-known educator to have recently emphasised the liberatory features and functions of an appropriate form of literacy. According to Freire, a proper form of literacy permits human beings to pursue their historical and ontological vocation of *becoming more fully human* (Freire, 1993, chapter one). By becoming more fully human Freire means:

> more critically aware of one's world and in creative control of it. The more one engages in conscious action to understand and transform the world—one's reality—in a praxis of reflection and action, the more fully human one becomes. (Lankshear, 1987, p. 68)

As human beings we are to become involved then in creating and naming our world, and in so doing we create our own being instead of being passively created by a world "made" by other people. Freire is claiming, similarly to Foucault, that we need not stay in tutelage to other people.

But they arrive at this position from very different standpoints. Freire believes in something that is akin to there being a "real" human nature. Not only does some such view of human nature underlie his thoughts on education and naming of the world, but he is arguing that we must pursue this ontological insight. We must become more human, that is, critically reflective, to develop this human nature "in a praxis of reflection and action." Foucault would see this as a version of humanism. He had critiqued this humanist assumption in Marxism on several occasions.

Also, Freire seems to be running together the notion of liberation and an ethics or the practices of freedom. As we have seen, in Foucault liberation is a precondition of an ethics. For Freire one is also acting in an ethical way in the very practices of naming the world, and to become more fully human in so doing is itself an ethical prescription. The ethics here are prescribed by Freire. If so, then is one still not in some form of tutelage?

But does Foucault have an ethics? In saying that ethics is the practice of freedom he does not, however, say how we should practice our freedom so as to be ethical. In other words, he does not provide a "full-bodied" account of ethics. Hacking (1986, p. 239) sees Foucault as being quite Kantian on ethics and, indeed, part of Foucault's doctorate was to translate a work of Kant's.

For Kant the moral law in a particular situation has to be *made* by us and is universally binding. For Hacking the innovation here by Kant was not the application of reason but the notion of *construction*. Though Foucault's approach leads one away "from the letter and the law of Kant," yet it shares with Kant the "notion of constructing morality." Thus, though he does not provide a full-bodied ethics he is being Kantian in the sense that we have to construct our ethics. It is we who have to decide how to practice our freedom. Hacking (1986, p. 239) concludes his paper, entitled "Self-Improvement," thus:

> Those who criticise Foucault for not giving us a place to stand might start their critique with Kant.

Endnote

1.   This is an amended version of an invited paper originally presented at the inaugural Foucault and Education Conference preceding the AERA Conference in New Orleans, 2000. Another amended version was published in *Educational Philosophy and Theory,* 34(4): 413–418 (2002). This chapter looks at Bergson's notion of the self and self-knowledge and extends the critique of Marxist notions of liberation by looking at the work of Paulo Freire.

References

Apple, Michael (1979). *Ideology and Curriculum.* London: Routledge and Kegan Paul.

Ariès, Phillipe (1962). *Centuries of Childhood: A Social History of Family Life.* New York: Vintage.

Bergson, H. (1913). *An Introduction to Metaphysics.* (T. E. Hulme, Trans.). London: Macmillan.

Eribon, Didier (1991). *Michel Foucault.* (Betsy Wing, Trans.). Cambridge, MA: Harvard University Press.

Foucault, Michel (1977a). "Power and Sex." Republished in Lawrence D. Kritzman, Ed. (1988), *Michel Foucault: Philosophy, Politics, Culture* (pp. 110–124). New York: Routledge.

Foucault, Michel (1977b). "Truth and Power." Republished in C. Gordon (1980), *Power Knowledge: Selected Interviews and Other Writings 1972–1977* (pp. 109–133). New York: Pantheon.

Foucault, Michel (1979a). "On Governmentality," *Ideology and Consciousness,* 6: 5–26.

Foucault, Michel (1979b). *Discipline and Punish: The Birth of the Prison.* New York: Vintage.

Foucault, Michel (1982). "Afterword." In H. Dreyfus and P. Rabinow (Eds.), *Michel Foucault: Beyond Structuralism and Hermeneutics.* Brighton: Harvester.

Foucault, Michel (1984). "The Ethics of the Concern of the Self as a Practice of Freedom." In Paul Rabinow, Ed. (1997), *Michel Foucault: Ethics, Subjectivity, Truth* (pp. 281–301). New York: The New Press.

Foucault, Michel (1991). *Michel Foucault: Remarks on Marx* (Duccio Trombadori, Ed.; R. James Goldstein and James Cascaito, Trans.). New York: Semiotext(e).

Freire, Paulo (1993). *Pedagogy of the Oppressed* (Myra Bergman Ramos, Trans.). New York: Continuum.

Hacking, Ian (1986). "Self-Improvement." In David Couzens Hoy (1986) *Foucault: A Critical Reader* (pp. 235–240). Oxford: Blackwell.

Lankshear, C. J. (1987). *Literacy, Schooling, Revolution.* London: Falmer.

Marshall, James D. (1996). *Michel Foucault: Personal Autonomy and Education.* Dordrecht, The Netherlands: Kluwer.

Marshall, James D. (1999). "Performativity: Lyotard and Foucault through Searle and Austin," *Studies in Philosophy and Education,* 18(5): 309–317.

Marshall, James D. (2001). "Caring for the Adult Self." In D. Aspin, J. Chapman, M. Hatton, & Y. Sawano (Eds.), *International Handbook on Lifelong Learning.* Dordrecht, The Netherlands: Kluwer.

Matthews, Eric (1996). *Twentieth-Century French Philosophy.* Oxford: Oxford University Press.

Miller, James (1993). *The Passion of Michel Foucault.* New York: Simon and Schuster.

Peters, R. S. (1966). *Ethics and Education.* London: George Allen and Unwin.

Trombadori, Duccio (1991). "Introduction: Beyond the Revolution." In Duccio Trombadori (Ed.), *Michel Foucault: Remarks on Marx* (R. James Goldstein and James Cascaito, Trans.). New York: Semiotext(e).

Young, M. F. D. (1971). *Knowledge and Control: New Directions for the Sociology of Education.* London: Collier-Macmillan.

Foucauldian "Indiscipline" as a Sort of Application: Qu(e)er(y)ing Research/Policy/Practice

Patti Lather

To change one's understanding of the reasons for one's practice, or the meanings of one's practice—is it, or is it not, under this understanding of theory, to change one's practice?

—Sedgwick, 1997: 22–23

The work of Foucault has changed the terms of debate across a wide range of "fields of knowledge." While it would be most un-Foucauldian to identify him as the originator of this or that, his work crystallizes ways of thinking about the space of knowledge that characterize what he terms our "contemporaneity" (1991b: 40). From emphasizing the insurrection of subjugated knowledges, through contesting taken-for-granted categories and concepts, to articulating post-humanist subjectivity, his focus on denaturalizing the regularities that govern our thought has proven richly usable across the human sciences. Central here are literature and history as well as the "inexact" or "social" sciences, certainly including educational research.[1]

There are critics. In terms of this paper, among the most interesting is art historian Jeremy Gilbert-Rolfe, who argues that the U.S. reception of Foucault in comparison to, especially, Derrida and Deleuze is suspicious in serving as a "transitional model" for those wanting a return to a kind of social realism. This is due to Foucault's focus on institutional power and "the realism of the sign rather than the thing" that makes him readily subsumed into a "Frankfurt School Hegelianism." What results is a culturally redemptive practice "deprived of its Nietzschean volition" (Gilbert-Rolfe 1999: 73, 80).

Taking such criticism into account in arguing his "generative" methodological usefulness, my engagement with Foucault in this paper is threefold. First, I want to put his concept of positivities to work in my continuing interest in a more expansive idea of science, a science appropriate to an era of blurred disciplinary boundaries, the global uprising of the marginalized, and what George Marcus (1997) terms the need to put high theory to work.[2] Second, I explore what a more expansive science might look like in relation to both what Jim McGuigan refers to as "the policy turn in cultural studies" (2001) and Nietzsche's idea of a Gay Science. Finally, I explore what this might mean in terms of the long-running aporia of the relationship of research to policy and practice, including the degree to which the research/policy/practice nexus is about separate albeit relational entities or, in a more Foucauldian vein, about seeing it all as discursive practice.[3] To do this, I look at two examples of policy-inflected research. In the first example, I use queer theory to think about my own efforts in *Troubling the Angels: Women Living with HIV/AIDS* (Lather & Smithies, 1997). In the second, I address what a Foucauldian approach to policy analysis might open up via the work of Bent Flyvbjerg (2001) in the context of Danish urban development and planning.

Discursive Formations and Positivities

> There exists a problem that is not without importance for political practice: that of the status...of scientific discourses. That is what I have undertaken to analyze historically—choosing the discourses which possess not the strongest epistemological structure (mathematics or physics), but the densest and most complex field of positivity (medicine, economics, the human sciences). (Foucault, 1991a: 65)

In his effort to analyze "the pure experience of order and of its modes of being" (1970: xxi), Foucault uses the concept of positivities repeatedly in ways that I have been tracking for several years. There is something he refers to as the "positive" basis of knowledge, that which makes knowledge and theory possible, the space in which the order of knowledge is constituted. This is the "positivity" in which ideas appear, sciences are established, experience is reflected in philosophies, rationalities are formed, all perhaps to be dissolved sooner rather than later.

The positivity of discourses, "their conditions of existence, the systems which regulate their emergence, functioning and trans-formation," become the "objects of a political practice" in a way that is quite other to the "consciousness" and "triumphant reason" assumed to underwrite politics (1991a: 69). This "mode of being of things" (1970: xxii) is presented to understanding out of both established and emerging configurations, simultaneities, and mutations that constitute the general space of knowledge. Empirical entities inhabit positivities that are thoroughly imbued with finitude out of the endless erosion of time and perspective. Such positivities include "the codes of language, perception, and practice" that rise up for awhile and make possible a particular understanding of "the order of things" (1970: xxi). Within such an archaeological framework, for Foucault, the analysis of "actual experience," whether from the perspective of phenomenology, positivism, or eschatology (e.g., liberalism, Marxism) is a humanism that denies the "Promise-Threat" of Nietzsche's notion "that man would soon be no more" (1970: 322). In contrast, Foucault's methodological interest is in studying the modifications of the configurations that produce both "the order of positivity" and "the order of foundations" (1970: 340).

Foundations has to do with "the old theory of representation" (1970: 339) with its successor regimes of truth, ontology of continuity, and permanent tables of stable differences. In contrast, the order of positivities is an "analytic of finitude" that historicizes discourse formations within "an ontology without metaphysics" (340). In the interplay of what belongs to the order of foundations and what belongs to the order of positivities, we find the heart of modern thought. In his focus on the specificity of actual practices as opposed to heavily overcoded unities such as class, race, gender, and/or sexuality, what Foucault teaches us is that, post-foundationally, we have to historicize the very terms our analysis is organized around. Situating our object of study as a Foucauldian positivity, then, allows us to analyze "the ordering codes and reflections upon order itself" (Foucault, 1970: xxi).

Working within and against a return to "a kind of social realism by way of Foucault" (Gilbert-Rolfe, 1999: 81), in this move from foundations to positivities, Foucault, along with the interruptions of Derrida and Deleuze, helps me to think against myself in contexts across research/policy/practice.[4] Ontologically, this entails moving from foundations to positivities. In post-foundational thought, one epistemologically situates oneself as curious and unknowing versus the more typical sort of mastery project. This is a methodology of "getting lost" where we think against our own continued attachments to the philosophy of presence and consciousness that undergirds humanist theories of agency. Methodologically assuming no privileged signifier, no exclusivity, no priority or predominance, here is where the journey of thinking differently begins. In contrast to a new "successor regime" (Harding, 1991), the very terms that a Foucauldian analysis is organized around are positioned as moments in the politics of truth. This is a refusal of a "universal Foucaultianism" (Gilbert-Rolfe, 1999: 83) and an insistence on a more Nietzschean Foucault that opens educational research up to questions it can hardly permit itself to think. What happens if this sort of "indisciplined" thinking is "applied" to the issue of policy-relevant methodologies?[5]

From Foundations to Positivities:
The (Im)Possibilities of the Human Sciences

> I absolutely will not play the part of one who prescribes solutions....My role is to address problems effectively, really: to pose them with the greatest possible rigor, with the maximum complexity and difficulty so that a solution does not arise all at once because of the thought of some reformer or even the brain of a political party....It takes years, decades of work carried out at the grassroots level with the people directly involved....Then perhaps a state of things may be renewed. (Foucault, in *Remarks on Marx*, 1991b: 157–159)

In Foucauldian terms, policy is one of the three technologies of governmentality, the others being diplomatic/military and economic.[6] Policy is to regulate behavior and render populations productive via a "biopolitics" that entails state intervention in and regulation of the everyday lives of citizens in a "liberal" enough manner to minimize resistance and maximize wealth stimulation. The shaping of subjectivity via the disciplining of bodies requires the tools of social policy, particularly its production of discursive norms that work to "police" populations to do the "right" thing. Naming, classifying, and analyzing: all work toward disciplining through normalizing. Such governmentality is "as much about what we do to ourselves as what is done to us" (Danaher, Schirato, & Webb, 2000: 83). It is, contrary to those who see Foucault as a pessimist and determinist, much about how understanding such processes might raise possibilities for doing otherwise.

One example of an effort to discipline and normalize the research/policy/practice relationship is the recent National Research Council report, *Scientific Research in Education* (2002), which attempts to negotiate between the federal government and the educational research community what it means to do scientific educational research.[7] Based on efforts since the Reagan administration to codify proper scientific method in assessing the outcomes of educational programs, the report attempts to soften congressional disdain for educational research, disdain quite evident in a 1998 report, *Education at a Crossroads: What Works and What's Wasted in Education Today*. Rather than a focus on randomized experimental trials as the gold standard, the NRC report attempts inclusivity regarding a range of approaches to educational research, both "quantitative" and "qualitative." In spite of such rhetorical moves toward a "big tent" of legitimate methods in educational research, its major effect is to reinscribe what I am calling "This IS Your Father's Paradigm" in its delineation of science. What is happening when at the very time there is a philosophical trend against certainty in the social sciences, "this continual and noisy legislative activity" (Elden, 2002: 146), with all of its normalizing authority, is working at the federal level to discipline educational research to a narrowly defined sense of science-based evidence?

John Willinsky's (2001) call to broaden and deepen major federal policy statements regarding the translation of educational research into practice provided a wake-up call for me regarding these movements at the federal level. Rather ingeniously, Willinsky attaches a critical agenda to one that is decidedly instrumentalist and even shocking in its lack of attention to the last twenty years of "utilization" research on why "'top-down linear' R&D models of the 1950's and 1960's" didn't work (7). Arguing for democratic forms of collaboration and exchange rather than "heavy-handed intentions of driving educational practice" (7), Willinsky foregrounds the "productive tensions and radical challenges that mark this play of interpretations within social science research" (7). Worried about "research-wielding technocrats" (9), I was scared to death by his article. The fifteen-year timeline of the Strategic Education Research Program of the National Research Council might very well change the face of educational research in a way that seems much about going backward.

How, then, is one to make sense of "the re-assertion of Science with a capital S in policy studies again" (Muller, 1997: 201)? In contrast, across the more high-status areas of science, there is increasing recognition of the value of an expansive definition of science (e.g., Goenka, 2002). What does it mean that educational research is being told what science is by Congress when the autonomy of science has been long established as central to scientific quality (Feuer, Towne, & Shavelson, 2002)?

Foucault's is a very different take on the demarcation issue in science. In chapter ten of *The Order of Things*, Foucault turns to the matter of the status of the human sciences. Here he argues that to look at the social sciences as "pre-paradigmatic" is to buy into some "maturation" narrative that belies his insight that the human sciences are about "constantly demystifying themselves" rather than making themselves more precise (1970: 356, 364). Distinguishing between "the sciences proper" and "the sciences of man," Foucault's questioning at the archaeological level locates the human sciences in the interstices of the mathematizable and the philosophical. "This cloudy distribution" (1970: 347) is both their privilege and their precariousness. "Dangerous intermediaries in the space of knowledge" (348), essentially unstable, uncertain as sciences, "the complexity of the epistemological configuration in which they find themselves" (348) is their particular positivity. As what Nietzsche terms the "unnatural sciences" (1974: 301), they are opposed to the "great certainty" of the natural sciences by their address "to man in so far as he speaks, lives and produces" (Foucault, 1970: 351). While some of language, life, and labor is mathematizable, this is "the simplest way of providing positive knowledge about man with a scientific style, form, and justification" (351). Language, meaning, the limits of consciousness, the role of representations, this is the stuff of human seeking to know. Rather than lacking in exactitude and rigor, the human sciences are more a "'meta-epistemological' position" in being about "finitude, relativity, and perspective" (355). Here their very "haziness, inexactitude and imprecision" (355) is the surface effect of the forms of positivity proper to the human sciences: "blurred, intermediary and composite disciplines multiply[ing] endlessly" (358). Across the biological (Comte) and economic (Marx) models of earlier centuries, we arrive via the linguistic/interpretive turn (Freud) to a focus on the need for a "reflexive form of knowledge" where there is "always something still to be thought" (372). The "primacy of representation" is "the very field upon which the human sciences occur" (362–363). "Unveil[ing] to consciousness the conditions of its forms and contents" (364) is its task.

Whether this is "truly scientific" or not is a "wearisome" discussion (1970: 365). The human sciences do not answer to criteria of objectivity and systematicity, the formal criteria of a scientific form of knowledge, but they are within the positive domain of knowledge as much as any other part of the modern episteme. There is no internal deficiency here; they are not "stranded across the threshold of scientific forms" (366). They are not "false" sciences; "they are not sciences at all" (366). They assume the title in order to "receive the transference of models borrowed from the sciences" (366). Enacting "a perpetual principle of dissatisfaction, of calling into question, of criticism and contestation" (373), such knowledges are tied to a praxis of the representations we give to ourselves of ourselves, a "counter-science" (379) that "unmakes" us as it "traverse[s], animate[s], and disturb[s] the whole constituted field of the human sciences...threatening the very thing that made it possible for man to be known" (381). Here is where we learn to think again, "in the process of disappearing" (385), opening ourselves to a future thought of the knowledge of things and their order.

Toward a Counter-Science:
The (Im)Possibilities of a Gay Policy Analysis

> It's true that certain people...are not likely to find advice or instructions in my books to tell them "what is to be done." But my project is precisely to bring it about that they "no longer know what to do," so that the acts, gestures, discourses that up until then had seemed to go without saying become problematic, difficult, dangerous. (Foucault, quoted in Miller, 1993: 235)

In order to flesh out the concept of a policy-relevant counter-science, in this final section, I turn to two examples of Foucauldian-inflected research that serve as contrast to the NRC report with its disciplining and normalizing effort to standardize educational research in the name of quality and effectiveness. In *The Order of Things*, by "counter-science," Foucault is referring to those knowledges that "'unmake' that very man who is creating and re-creating his positivity in the human sciences" (1970: 379). Elsewhere, Foucault situates science as a discursive event where the "inexact knowledges" become "a *field of strategic possibilities*" (1998: 320, original emphasis). Noting how his own work is tied to "that strange and quite problematic configuration of human sciences" (311), Foucault's interest is in "undoing and recomposing" the very ground he stands on. Here demarcation issues are refused; distinctions are seen as uncertain and "the play of immediacies" becomes the point of analysis (306).

The "privilege accorded to...'the sciences of man'" is based on the "'political arithmetic'" (1998: 323) that makes particular kinds of discourse both possible and necessary. This is not so much about concepts on their way to formation or even the price paid for scientific pretensions but rather of understanding claims to scientificity as discursive events. Such an understanding of the human sciences is more about "the play of its differences, its interstices, its distances—in some sense its blanks rather than its full surfaces" (321) than it is about foundational epistemological claims. It is out of this positivity that I delineate a counter-science invested in "unfold[ing] as broadly as possible" the historical space in which it has come to rest (327).

A couple of years ago, I was asked to speak as a feminist poststructuralist to the question of the relationship of educational research to policy and practice.[8] I presume this invitation was, in part, due to *Troubling the Angels: Women Living with HIV/AIDS* (Lather & Smithies, 1997) and the possibilities it raises for research that might be of use in struggles for social justice. Such a positioning might be termed "the interventionist, critical edge of deconstruction" (Niranjana, 1992: 161). In the spirit of a Foucauldian "indiscipline" as a way to come to such a question freshly, I first sketch my understanding of what queer is via Eve Sedgwick's edited collection, *Novel Gazing*, intended to articulate "queer specificity" in terms of interpretive practices (1997: 2) and then turn to the relation of my work to policy and practice.[9]

Queer is a "technology of the self" (Foucault, 1994d) that hinges on undertaking particular, performative acts of experimental filiation that are preoccupied with social codification and regulatory labeling. This peculiar self-performativity is "strangely relational" (Barber, 1997: 403) to others: Misfits are idealized in a "queer relationality" (404), where each refuses mastery in moving toward the greatest possible proximity while guarding against the traps of projection and identification so that each can remain strange to the other. This entails the risk of being despised and using this toward a mode of joyful experimentation with being in order to ignite novel ethical possibilities.

To queer one's practice, then, is to explore a manner of living on that is advanced as counter to and discontinuous with the violating yet perversely enabling epistemic configuration within which one finds oneself. These ruptures are, although never finally achieved, ever enacted as an investment in perversion, as a force of intervention in the normalizing procedures of subjectification. In excess, untimely, such interventions advance by transvaluing impropriety in ways that break with conventions in order to open up another time-space. This is a persistent effortfulness that makes a present by generating fresh, "deroutinizing methodologies" (Sedgwick, 1997: 3) that work at the most stretched and ragged edges of one's competence. The move is toward recognitions, pleasures, and discoveries that are more reparative than suspicious, a working of positive affect toward experiencing surprise via making mistakes. The goal is practices that take the terror out of error, that aim at making mistakes sexy, creative, even cognitively powerful. Instead of the banality of the merely deidealized/disenchanted, the goal is to assemble and confer plenitude on an object that will then have resources to offer. This is an erotic generosity that is about "helping one save oneself" (Litvak, 1997: 85). It is not cure so much as undertaking a different range of affects, ambitions, and risks in terms of extracting sustenance from the objects of a culture, even if that culture is committed to not sustaining the very queerness that might generate some way out of the present exhaustions. The exhaustions Sedgwick addresses are those of the hermeneutics of suspicion that have guided critical literary criticism. In my case, I am looking for some way out of the exhaustions of the usual ways of making sense of the relationship of research to policy and practice.

Having written a book that was recently referred to as having "at least an implicit...applied and policy edge" (Rapp, 1999: 17), my interest is in how queer practices can be used to see what might open up in terms of (re)thinking the research/policy/practice relationship. *Troubling the Angels* uses what Barber refers to as "the violating yet perversely enabling epistemic configuration" (1997: 403) that is the ground of queer theory toward different practices of knowing and doing. Organized as a hypertextual, multilayered weaving of data, method, and the politics of interpretation, the book looks at how twenty-five Ohio women in HIV/AIDS support groups make sense of the disease in their lives. Combining sociological, political, historical, therapeutic, and policy analysis along with the privileging of ethnographic voice, the book moves toward destabilizing practices of telling stories that belong to others. Interspersed among the interviews, there are [angel] intertexts, which serve as "breathers" between the themes and emotions of the women's stories; a running subtext where the authors spin out their tales of doing the research; factoid boxes on various aspects of the disease; and a scattering of the women's writing in the form of poetry, letters, speeches, and e-mails.

The book is written within what might best be characterized as "an era resolutely inimical to master narratives" and an "increasing popular suspicion of 'expertise'" (Muller, 2000: 268). This era is also marked, paradoxically, by quantitative indicators of school quality becoming the gold standard in spite of the global trend against certainty in the social sciences. In such a place, the usual way of making sense of the relationship of research to policy and practice is to divide academics into two groups: critics invested in entertaining doubts about the constitutive grounds of knowledge who worry that "to pursue positive knowledge of any kind...is to become sucked into the power machine" (Muller, 2000: 280) and those invested in considerations of administrative usefulness. As McGuigan notes (2001), this has been a tension in cultural analysis at least since Adorno and might be best situated as a tension to be exacerbated rather than resolved in addressing critical engagement with the policy process.

What queer thinking offers by way of shaking up is a persistent effortfulness that becomes constitutive of a kind of critical practice that is generous and pleasurable in the risks it takes toward what Sedgwick terms a reparative rather than a suspicious/paranoid counterpractice (1997). This is quite other to the too great investment in disciplinary power with its "expectations of imminent governmental enlightenment and reason" (2001: 199) that worries McGuigan. Less a knowledge than a pragmatics of interruption, queer research is, according to William Haver (1997), an unworking, "thinking as departure," nomadic: "a hiatus in the very possibility for cultural (re)production—rather than something that 'is' Queer" (284).

From this perspective, *Troubling the Angels* might be seen as a practice of rupture, full of stuck places and difficult issues of truth, interpretation, and responsibility that attests to the possibilities of its time yet, in the very telling, registers the limits of itself as a vehicle for claiming truth. Staging a set of anxieties that haunts feminist ethnography, conscious of itself as a system of conventions, its aspiration is to consolidate a critical public, both on the political level of HIV/AIDS support and activism and in the reception of feminist ethnography as a critical tool. Unpacking *Troubling the Angels* in terms of its queer performativity, I submit the following as practices toward a counter-science.

- Complicating, accessing competing layers of the real; using the ruins of correspondence theories of the real[10] as a fruitful site for practices of doing and reporting research in a way that attempts to be readable to a broad audience while including a focus on major tensions in doing social inquiry, including a critique of one's own interests and investments in emancipatory work (Jones & Brown, 2001: 71). One example of this is the refusal to deliver the women in our study to the reader in a tidy tale. Such a move breaks the realist frame, with researchers both getting in and out of the way (Piontek, 2000).

- Refusing mastery by writing in a tentative authorial voice, constructing a strange relationality of knowing by not-knowing in a way that does not reinscribe itself as a new one-best-way to knowing.

- Using the loss of certainty and ethnographic authority to explore new textual practices that enact such tensions in a way that stages the problems of representation. One example of this is enacting the tensions around honoring "voices" and the demand for interpretive work on the part of the researcher. This is a tension that the book addresses via its use of a split text, where the interview data are presented at the top and the "confessional" and interpretive tales of the researchers are on the bottom.

- Queering angels in order to work against crowd-pleasing sentiment and narrative simplicity. Attempting to write in such a way that the addressee becomes aware of the stakes of language, the book grafts codes in order to articulate across different registers the historical moment of women living with HIV/AIDS. Angels, for example, are presented as a tangled web of meanings and surveyed across theology, popular culture, poetry, fiction, art, and philosophy. Familiar images of angels are mobilized and then undercut, troubled, as part of a flood of too much too fast in order to break down the usual codes we bring to reading about the lives of others.

Troubling confessional writing and the romance of voice, the book moves away from a more innocent moment of "giving voice," what feminist anthropologist Kamala Visweswaran has termed "the university rescue mission in search of the voiceless" (1994: 69). Instead, "voice" is situated as partial, perspectival and situated: in time, bodies, and political and philosophical regimes.

As much limit case as model, part of a "lateral extension" (Foucault, 1998/1968: 327), what I offer with my own work is not so much privileged example as a "doxology" (329): the description of the uses that might made of a conceptual ensemble as a particular play of form on the ordering of the empirical. My search in the book was for the sort of doubled practices that "let the story continue," as Britzman (2000) refers to the work of representation in a post-foundational era. Caught within the incomplete rupture with philosophies of the subject and consciousness,[11] I have appropriated contradictory available scripts to create alternative practices of feminist research as a site of being and becoming in excess of intention. From the consolations of empowerment to a sort of self-abjection at the limit, the book was generated out of the very impossibilities of representation as it faces the problems of doing feminist research in this historical time.

As a second example toward a policy-relevant counter-science, I turn to *Making Social Science Matter* (2001) where Bent Flyvbjerg applies Foucauldian "indiscipline" to the areas of Danish urban development and planning. Arguing for a move from a narrowly defined epistemic science to one that comes at techne[12] from the side of a value rationality that takes power into account, Flyvbjerg envisions a social science that can hold its own in the Science Wars by contributing to society's practical rationality in clarifying where we are and where we want to be. The "physics envy" that presently characterizes dominant social science discourses is self-defeating.[13] The objectivist strands of the social sciences, the parade of behaviorism, cognitivism, structuralism, and neopositivism: All have failed to successfully study human activity in a way modeled after the assumedly cumulative, predictive, and stable natural sciences.[14]

While perhaps laboring too much to bring the Plato/Hobbes/Kant/ Habermas strain together with Machiavelli/Nietzsche/Foucault, Flyvbjerg's argument for a practical philosophy of ethics that takes power into account "as a point of departure for praxis" (2001: 70) is very helpful in delineating a Foucauldian policy analysis. Noteworthy in Flyvbjerg's articulation is the focus on the context of practice as a disciplining of interpretation. Mandating on-the-ground empirical work, theories are constantly confronted with praxis toward public deliberation so that social science becomes a sort of public philosophy. Case studies assume prime importance in such a Foucauldian policy analysis. As Flyvbjerg notes, even Donald Campbell came to this conclusion.[15] Critical cases, strategically chosen, provide "far better access for policy intervention than the present social science of variables" (2001: 86). Flyvbjerg's value-oriented social science proceeds via (1) getting close to the people being studied, (2) focusing on particular practices, (3) using case studies, (4) using historical and narrative analysis, (5) proceeding dialogically, and (6) securing feedback from those under study (2001: 63–72). His own case study demonstrates how power works and how research can exacerbate inequalities and breaks with the sort of scientism that believes that science holds a reliable method of reaching the truth about the nature of things. In the context of a study of an urban renewal project that was at first disastrous in reproducing social inequalities, Flyvbjerg articulates a social science that approaches what Bourdieu terms "fieldwork in philosophy" (quoted in Flyvbjerg: 167). In such a laboratory, against a narrow scientism in policy analysis and program evaluation, the urgent questions become: Where are we going with democracy in this project? Who gains and who loses and by which mechanisms of power? Given this analysis, what should be done?

"Simultaneously sociological, political and philosophical" (Flyvbjerg: 64), this is a Gay Science that does not divest experience of its rich ambiguity because it stays close to the complexities and contradictions of existence. Focusing on practices as event, detecting forces that make life work, sociality and history are seen as the only foundations we have. Instead of emulating the natural or, in Foucauldian terms, "exact" sciences, the goal is getting people to no longer know what to do so that things might be done differently, so that we might "produce something that doesn't yet exist" (Foucault, 1991b: 121). Critical here is Foucault's analytics of power, especially "power with." Real change comes, according to Foucault, from changing our selves, our bodies, our souls, our ways of knowing (1991b). To make difficult what we take for granted as the good, is to see, in fact, what Nietzsche saw: that "perhaps there has never been a more dangerous ideology...than this will to good" (Flyvbjerg, 2001: 95). This is the first step in becoming moral, this realization that, in Foucauldian terms, "everything is dangerous, which is not exactly the same as bad. If everything is dangerous, then we always have something to do" (1983: 343).

Rather than some vanguard, to see practices of a counter-science relevant to policy analysis as both dangerous and something we have to do is to see it as likely as not to cause another generation of problems, reaction formations, and unexpected and by no means necessarily positive outcomes (Becker, 2000; Muller, 1997: 205). The sort of "indisciplined" policy analysis offered here might help us situate ourselves in the perpetual state of always beginning again that Foucault sees as the condition of the social sciences. To make difficult what we take for granted as the good is to move into a social science that takes values and power seriously in efforts toward a progressive praxis, a social science that matters in struggles for social justice.[16] This is the yes of the setting-to-work mode of post-foundational theory that faces unanswerable questions, the necessary experience of the impossible, in an effort to foster understanding, reflection, and action instead of a narrow translation of research into practice.

Conclusion: Indisciplined Knowing

> The more that policy work drives toward planning and implementation, the less
> can it entertain doubts about its constitutive grounds. (Muller, 2000: 278)

To think about the relation of policy and research in such a place of
Foucaultian "indiscipline," what I have offered might be viewed, in a
Lacanian register, as "the hysteric's discourse" (Fink, 1995). Here "a
truly scientific spirit" is commanded by "that which does not work, by
that which does not fit. It does not set out to carefully cover over
paradoxes and contradictions" like that of the master's discourse with its
imperative to be obeyed within its guise of reason. The hysteric sees the
heart of science as "taking such paradoxes and contradictions as far as
they can go" (Fink, 1995: 135) rather than endorsing a monolithic
science "based on a set of axiomatic mathematizable propositions,
measurable empirical entities, and pure concepts" (138). In short, the
Science Wars continue; the line between a narrowly defined scientism
and a more capacious scientificy of disciplined inquiry remains very
much at issue. In terms of the desirability of degrees of formalization,
mathematized and not, generic procedures, and rigorous differentiations,
there is virtually no agreement among scientists, philosophers, and
historians as to what constitutes science except, increasingly, the view
that science is but one discourse among others, a cultural practice and
practice of culture. To operate from a premise of the impossibility of
satisfactory solutions means to not assume to resolve but, instead, to be
prepared to meet the obdurancy of the problems and obstacles as the very
way toward producing different knowledge and producing knowledge
differently. Foucault terms this "the absolute optimism" of "a thousand
things to do" (1991b: 174), where our constant task is to struggle against
the very rules of reason and practice inscribed in the effects of power of
the social sciences. What follows is the syllabus for a course taught in
2001 on Foucault and policy analysis in education.

Appendix

Foucault, Educational Research and Policy Analysis
Ed P&L 925L49, O6958-7
Winter Quarter, Tuesday, 4:30–6:48, Room: Ram 336
Patti Lather, Instructor

This course will look at the relationship between the thought of Michel Foucault and educational research in the context of policy analysis. Whether Foucault is read as historian or philosopher, stucturalist or poststructuralist, critical or postcritical, his analysis of how power works through practices of surveillance, classification, exclusion, regulation, and normalization has great implications for educational inquiry. How is the modern subject of knowledge produced by our very efforts to know it? How does a focus on the microphysics of power change our understanding of social practices? Of what use is Foucault's theory of governmentality in educational policy analysis? These and other questions will be addressed through the following readings in a seminar format where students will be expected to both co-lead class discussions and explore the implications of such questions in their emerging sense of research project.

Reading
Required of everyone

Michel Foucault, *The Order of Things: An Archaeology of the Human Sciences*. New York: Random House, 1970 (original work published 1966).
Thomas Popkewitz and Marie Brennan, eds., *Foucault's Challenge: Discourse, Knowledge and Power in Education*. New York: Teachers College Press, 1998.
Cop-Ez reader. "Booklet of readings" (listed at end of syllabus)

Choose one of the following
Michel Foucault, *The Archaeology of Knowledge and the Discourse on Language*, trans. A. M. Sheridan Smith. New York: Pantheon, 1972 (original work published 1971).
Michel Foucault, *Discipline and Punish: The Birth of the Prison*, trans. Alan Sheridan. New York: Random House, 1978 (original work published 1975).

Michel Foucault, *The History of Sexuality, Vol. I: An Introduction*, trans. Robert Hurley. New York: Random House, 1978 (original work published 1976).

Michel Foucault, *Power/Knowledge: Selected Interviews and Other Writings, 1972–1977*, Colin Gordon, ed. and trans. New York: Pantheon, 1980.

Choose one of the following secondary sources

Gilles Deleuze, *Foucault*, trans. Sean Hand. Minneapolis: Univ. of Minnesota Press, 1988 (1986).

David Halperin, *Saint Foucault: Towards a Gay Hagiography*. New York: Oxford University Press, 1995.

Geoff Danaher, Tony Schirato, and Jen Webb, *Understanding Foucault*. London: Sage, 2000.

Lois McNay, *Foucault: A Critical Introduction*. NY: Continuum.

Recommended

Catherine Marshall, ed. *Feminist Critical Policy Analysis: A Perspective from Primary and Secondary Schooling*. London: Falmer, 1997.

Student Assignments

1. Working alone or in pairs, pick a week to lead class discussion OR give 15-minute midterm oral report on secondary source book. 30%

2. 2–3 pp. review of secondary source on Foucault. Due at midterm, along with oral report on emerging focus of final paper. 30%

3. Write 10–12 pp. paper on implications of Foucault for your emerging sense of project. Use course reading and discussion to inform your paper, with particular focus on second Foucault book that you choose. 40%

Policies and Procedures

Absences: Contact instructor, preferably ahead of time, to arrange for make-up work.

Incompletes: Written request no later than last class meeting. Include timeline for getting work done next quarter. Incompletes are evaluated with higher expectations, given additional time to do work, and I give minimal feedback.

Late work: Not accepted without prior arrangement.

Course Schedule

Jan. 2: Introduction to course and one another. Background on Foucault and educational policy analysis.

Jan. 9: *The Order of Things*, Part I plus Reading 1.

Jan. 16: *The Order of Things*, Part II plus Reading 2.

Jan. 23: Readings 3–5.

Jan. 30: Midterm work due, including oral reports on emerging projects (everyone) and secondary sources.

Feb. 6: Popkewitz and Brennan, Introduction and ch. 1. Plus 2–3 other chapters.

Feb. 13: Readings 6–8

Feb. 20: Readings 9–12

Feb. 27: *The Order of Things*, second time around: What we know now that we didn't know before. Readings 13–14.

March 6: Final oral reports on uses of Foucault to your project.

Monday March 12, final work due, 4 PM, box in Ramseyer 121.

Reading Booklet

1. Diane Levy, But What's the R2? Considering the Increased Use of Qualitative Methodologies in Public Policy Research. Paper presented to American Anthropology Association annual meeting, San Francisco, November 2000.

2. Bradley A. Levinson and Margaret Sutton (2001), "Introduction: Policy as/in Practice—A Sociocultural Approach to the Study of Educational Policy." In Margaret Sutton and B. Levinson, eds., *Policy as Practice: Toward a Comparative Sociocultural Analysis of Educational Policy*. Westport, CT: Ablex, 1–22.

3. James Scheurich, "Policy Archaeology: A New Policy Studies Methodology." *Journal of Educational Policy*, 9(4), 1994, 297–316.

4. Brian Hoepper, "Messy Realities": Theorizing Policy-Making Processes. Chapter 4 from unpublished dissertation, Educating Globally: A Critical Portrayal. University of Queensland, 1998.

5. Nancy Campbell, "Governing Mentalities: Reading Popular Culture." Chapter 2 of *Using Women: Gender, Drug Policy, and Social Justice*. New York: Routledge, 2000, 33–54.

6. James Marshall, "Foucault and Educational Research." In Stephen Ball, ed., *Foucault and Education: Discipline and Knowledge*. London: Routledge, 1990, 11–28.

7. Michael Peters, "Foucault, Discourse and Education: Neoliberal Governmentality." Chapter 4 of *Poststructuralism, Politics and Education*. Westport, CT: Bergin and Garvey, 1996, 79–91.

8. Dephne Meadmore, Caroline Hatcher, and Erica McWilliam, "Getting Tense about Genealogy." *Qualitative Studies in Education*, 13(5), 2000, 463–476.

9. Johan Muller, "Critics and Reconstructors: On the Emergence of Progressive Educational Expertise in South Africa." In Thomas Popkewitz, ed., *Educational Knowledge: Changing Relationships Between the State, Civil Society, and the Educational Community*. Albany: SUNY Press, 2000, 265–283.

10. Wanda Pillow, "Decentering Silences/Troubling Irony: Teen Pregnancy's Challenge to Policy Analysis." In Catherine Marshall, ed., *Feminist Critical Policy Analysis I: A Perspective from Primary and Secondary Schooling*. London: Falmer, 1997, 134–152.

11. Julie Laible, "Feminist Analysis of Sexual Harassment Policy: A Critique of the Ideal of Community." In Catherine Marshall, ed., *Feminist Critical Policy Analysis I: A Perspective from Primary and Secondary Schooling*. London: Falmer, 1997, 201–215.

12. Peter Moss, Jean Dillon, and June Statham, "The 'child in need' and 'the rich child': Discourses, constructions and practice." *Critical Social Policy*, 20(2), 2000, 233–254.

13. Ian Hunter, "Assembling the School." In Andrew Barry, Thomas Osborne, and Nikolas Rose, eds., *Foucault and Political Reason: Liberalism, Neo-liberalism and Rationalities of Government*. Chicago: University of Chicago Press, 1996, 143–166.

14. Thomas Popkewitz, "The Culture of Redemption and the Administration of Freedom as Research." *Review of Educational Research*, 1998, 68(1), 1–34.

Endnotes

1. See appendix for my course syllabus, Foucault, Educational Research and Policy Analysis, that includes a sampling of the writing on Foucault and educational research that is pertinent to policy analysis.

2. "High theory" refers to the Euro-male pantheon of philosophical writing of those such as Kant and Hegel, their critics Nietzsche and Heidegger, and the Marxist variant kept alive in the Frankfurt School. Based in the German academic tradition, its French inflection includes Lacan, Althusser, Foucault, Derrida, and Deleuze. See Spivak, 1999, for an excellent discussion of the setting-to-work mode of deconstruction.

3. Foucault's teacher, Althusser, argued that philosophy is class struggle at the level of theory, thereby blurring the distinctions. See, for example, the essays in *Philosophy and the Spontaneous Philosophy of the Scientists* (1990) where Althusser posits theory as practice and articulates theoretical research. For the argument that policy is practice, see Levinson and Sutton (2001). One could go on here, but given my interest in the uses of Foucault for policy-relevant methodologies (e.g., Scheurich, 1994), I move between keeping research/policy/ practice conceptually separate and situating them as a sort of Deleuzean assemblage, a multiplicity that is not so much about what it is as "what it functions with" (1987: 4). This is in keeping with Foucault's definition of policy as a technology that is "the set of means necessary to make the forces of the state increase from within" (1994c: 69).

4. Note 3 illustrates one way I use Deleuze to keep concepts moving in the context of policy analysis. For Derrida, see my 2003 paper, "Applied Derrida: (Mis)Reading the Work of Mourning in Educational Research." *Educational Philosophy and Theory*, 35(3), 257–270.

5. Foucault uses "indiscipline" to describe a mechanism by which a marginalized population/practice is created to exert pressure that cannot be tolerated by the very process of exclusions and sanctions designed to guard against irregularities and infractions (1994a: 36). In articulating a counter-science, I use the term as a within/against move that is an homage to Nietzsche's idea of "the gay science" as an "unnatural science" (1974: 301) that leads to greater health by fostering ways of knowing that escape from normativity.

6. See Burchell, Gordon, and Miller, 1991, for an elaboration of the concept of governmentality.

7. National Research Council, 2002. As what Foucault terms "a kind of tribunal of reason" in delineating the scientificity of science (1991b: 60), the NRC, serving as scientific advisor to the government since 1863, is trying to speak against the ESEA Act (signed into legislation this past January) which "virtually mandates" (Cochran-Smith, 2002: 188) that, to be funded, educational research must be evaluated "using experimental or quasi-experimental designs…with a preference for random-assignment experiments" (Section 9101).

8. American Educational Research Association annual conference, Seattle, April 2001. Symposium: How does research speak to policy and practice, how does it not?

9. In the sections that follow, I draw on Sedgwick's notion of what queer is in order to enact a Gay Policy Analysis. A Gay Policy Analysis can be understood as a specific or localized instance of Foucault's notion of counter-science and Nietzsche's notion of a Gay Science. Sedgwick's work is helpful in articulating a queer specificity in interpretive strategies in educational policy/research/practice. It provides a means of bearing out what Foucault sees as counter-science and what I mean by a Gay Policy Analysis. That is, by drawing on queer performativity in a Gay Policy Analysis, the following sections demonstrate/speak to specific instances or particularities of enacted counter-sciences.

10. Correspondence theories assume a one-to-one relationship between the word and the thing.

11. For a discussion of paths beyond "the philosophy of the subject" and "the philosophy of consciousness," see Foucault, 1994b: 176.

12. Flyvbjerg (2001) sets his book up around Aristotle's distinctions of episteme, techne, and phronesis. His major argument is that we must move from narrowly epistemological, universalistic ideas of science to a science that integrates the context-dependency of the art and craft of techne with the practical deliberation about values toward a praxis of phronesis. Here Foucault is used to reconstruct the concept of phronesis by bringing "explicit considerations of power" to bear in delineating a practical knowledge/ethics/wisdom adequate for our time (55).

13. This phrase, credited to Freud, was used in the *New York Review of Books* (Flyvbjerg, 2001: 26–27).

14. There are of course multiple critiques of the natural sciences as cumulative, predictive, and stable. See, for example, Latour, 1993.

15. Flyvbjerg quotes Campbell: "qualitative common-sense knowing is not replaced by quantitative knowing....This is not to say that such common-sense naturalistic observation is objective, dependable, or unbiased. But it is all that we have. It is the only route to knowledge—noisy, fallible, and biased though it may be" (2001: 73).

16. See Foucault, 1991a, p. 70, for a delineation of the distinctions between progressive and reactionary politics.

References

Althusser, Louis (1990). *Philosophy and the spontaneous philosophy of the scientists and other essays*. London: Verso.

Barber, Stephen (1997). Lip-reading: Woolf's secret encounters. In *Novel gazing*, Eve Sedgwick, ed. (pp. 401–443). Durham, NC: Duke Univ. Press.

Becker, Howard (2000). Afterword: Racism and the research process. In *Racing research/Researching race: Methodological dilemmas in critical race studies*, France Winddance Twine and Jonathan Warren, eds. (pp. 247–253). New York: New York University Press.

Britzman, Deborah (2000). If the story cannot end. In *Between hope and despair: Pedagogy and the remembrance of historical trauma*, Roger Simon, Sharon Rosenberg and Claudia Eppert, eds. (pp. 27–57). Lanham, MD: Rowman and Littlefield.

Burchell, Graham, C. Gordon, and P. Miller, eds. (1991). *The Foucault effect: Studies in governmentality*. Chicago: University of Chicago Press.

Cochran-Smith, Marilyn (2002). What a difference a definition makes: Highly qualified teachers, scientific researchers, and teacher education. *Journal of Teacher Education*, 53(3), 187–189.

Danaher, Geoff, Tony Schirato, and Jen Webb (2000). *Understanding Foucault*. London: Sage.

Deleuze, Giles, and Felix Guattari (1987). *A thousand plateaus: Capitalism and schizophrenia* (Brian Massumi, Trans.). Minneapolis: University of Minnesota Press.

Education at a crossroads: What works and what's wasted in education today (1998). Subcommittee on Oversight and Investigations of the Committee on Education and the Workforce. 105th Congress, July 17, 1998.

Elden, Stuart (2002). The war of races and the constitution of the state: Foucault's *Il faut defendre la societé* and the politics of calculation. *boundary 2*, 29(1), 125–151.

Feuer, M. J., L. Towne, and R. J. Shavelson (2002). Scientific culture and education research. *Educational Researcher*, 31(8), 4–14.

Fink, Bruce (1995). *The Lacanian subject: Between language and jouissance*. Princeton, NJ: Princeton University Press.

Flyvbjerg, Bent (2001). *Making social science matter: Why social inquiry fails and how it can succeed again*. Cambridge: Cambridge University Press.

Foucault, Michel (1970). *The order of things: An archaeology of the human sciences*. New York: Vintage.

Foucault, Michel (1980). *Power/knowledge: Selected interviews and other writings 1972–1977*. New York: Pantheon.

Foucault, Michel (1983). On the genealogy of ethics: An overview of work in progress. In *The Foucault reader*, Paul Rabinow, ed. (pp. 340–372). New York: Pantheon.

Foucault, Michel (1991a). Politics and the study of discourse. In *The Foucault effect: Studies in governmentality*, Graham Burchell, C. Gordon, and P. Miller, eds. (pp. 53–72). Chicago: University of Chicago Press.

Foucault, Michel (1991b). *Remarks on Marx: Conversations with Duccio Trombadori*. New York: Semiotext(e). (Original work published 1981)

Foucault, Michel (1994a). The punitive society. In *Michel Foucault: Ethics, subjectivity and truth*. V. 1, Paul Rabinow, ed. (pp. 23–38). New York: The New Press.

Foucault, Michel (1994b). Sexuality and solitude. In *Michel Foucault: Ethics, subjectivity and truth*. V. 1, Paul Rabinow, ed. (pp. 175–184). New York: The New Press.

Foucault, Michel (1994c). Security, territory and population. In *Michel Foucault: Ethics, subjectivity and truth*. V. 1, Paul Rabinow, ed. (pp. 67–72). New York: The New Press.

Foucault, Michel (1994d). Technologies of the self. In *Michel Foucault: Ethics, subjectivity and truth*. V. 1, Paul Rabinow, ed. (pp. 223–252). New York: The New Press.

Foucault, Michel (1998). On the archaeology of the sciences: Response to the epistemology circle. In *Michel Foucault: Aesthetics, method, and epistemology*. V. 2, James D. Faubion, ed. (pp. 297–334). New York: The New Press. (Original work published 1968)

Gilbert-Rolfe, Jeremy (1999). Nietzchean critique and the Hegelian commodity, or the French have landed. *Critical Inquiry* 26(Autumn), 70–84.

Goenka, Shifalika (2002). A day in the field that changed my methodology. *British Medical Journal*, 324 (Feb. 23), p. 493.

Harding, Sandra (1991). *Whose science? Whose knowledge? Thinking through women's lives*. Ithaca, NY: Cornell University Press.

Haver, William (1997). Queer research: Or, how to practice invention to the brink of intelligibility. In *The eight technologies of otherness*, Sue Golding, ed. (pp. 277–292). London: Routledge.

Jones, Liz and Tony Brown (2001). "Reading" the nursery classroom: A Foucauldian perspective. *Qualitative Studies in Education*, 14(6), 713–725.

Lather, Patti (2003). Applied Derrida: (Mis)Reading the work of mourning in educational research. *Educational Philosophy and Theory*, 35(3), 257–270.

Lather, Patti and Chris Smithies (1997). *Troubling the angels: Women living with HIV/AIDS*. Boulder, CO: Westview Press.

Latour, Bruno (1993). *We have never been modern* (Catherine Porter, trans.). Cambridge, MA: Harvard University Press.

Levinson, Bradley A., and Margaret Sutton (2001). Introduction: Policy as/in practice—A sociocultural approach to the study of educational policy. In *Policy as Practice: Toward a Comparative Sociocultural Analysis of Educational Policy*, Margaret Sutton and B. Levinson, eds. (pp. 1–22). Westport, CT: Ablex.

Litvak, Joseph (1997). Strange gourmet: Taste, waste, Proust. In *Novel Gazing*, Eve Sedgwick, ed. (pp. 74–93). Durham, NC: Duke University Press.

Marcus, George (1997). Critical cultural studies as one power/knowledge like, among, and in engagement with others. In *From sociology to cultural studies: New perspectives*, Elizabeth Long, ed. (pp. 399–425). Oxford: Blackwell.

McGuigan, Jim (2001). Problems of cultural analysis and policy in the information age. *Cultural Studies/Critical Methodologies*, 1(2), 190–219.

Miller, James (1993). *The passion of Michel Foucault*. New York: Simon and Schuster.

Muller, Johan (1997). Social justice and its renewals: A sociological comment. *International Studies in Sociology of Education*, 7(2), 195–211.

Muller, Johan. (2000). Critics and reconstructors: On the emergence of progressive educational expertise in South Africa. In *Educational knowledge: Changing relationships between the state, civil society, and the educational community*, Thomas S. Popkewitz, ed. (pp. 265–284). Albany: SUNY Press.

National Research Council (2002). *Scientific research in education*. Committee on Scientific Principles for Education Research, Richard J. Shavelson and Lisa Towne, eds. Washington, DC: National Academy Press.

Nietzsche, Friedrich (1974). *The gay science*, trans. Walter Kaufmann. New York: Vintage Books.

Niranjana, Tejaswini (1992). *Siting translation: History, post-structuralism and the colonial context*. Berkeley: University of California Press.

Piontek, Thomas (2000). Language and power in postmodern ethnography: Representing women with HIV/AIDS. In *Hybrid spaces: Theory, culture, economy*, Johannes Angermuller, Katherina Bunzmann, and Christina Rauch, eds. (pp. 97–112). Hamburg, Germany: LIT. (Distributed in North America by Transaction Publishers/Rutgers University)

Rapp, Rayna (1999). *Testing women, testing the fetus: The social impact of amniocentesis in America*. New York: Routledge.

Scheurich, James Joseph (1994). Policy archaeology: A new policy studies methodology. *Journal of Educational Policy*, 9(4), 297–316.

Sedgwick, Eve (1997). Paranoid reading and reparative reading: Or, you're so paranoid, you probably think this introduction is about you. In *Novel*

Gazing: Queer readings in fiction, Eve Sedgwick, ed. (pp. 1–40). Durham, NC: Duke Univ. Press.

Spivak, Gayatri (1999). The setting to work of deconstruction. *A critique of postcolonial reason* (pp. 423–431). Cambridge, MA: Harvard University Press.

Visweswaran, Kamala (1994). *Fictions of feminist ethnography*. Minneapolis: University of Minnesota Press.

Willinsky, John (2001). The strategic education research program and the public value of research. *Educational Researcher* 30(1), 5–14.

Studying Schools
with an "Ethics of Discomfort"

Valerie Harwood and Mary Louise Rasmussen

Introduction

> Few people criticize hospitals...for segregating the sick in order to best treat
> them. Similarly, some students who are living in gay or lesbian environments
> and struggling with their sexual identity need special attention in order to best
> function in the larger, mainstream society. We're kind of like an educational
> hospice along the way to college and life.
>
> —Linebarger in Martin, 2001

In the excerpt above, Wally Linebarger, a teacher at the Walt Whitman Community School (WWCS) in Dallas, USA,[1] blurs the lines between discourses of illness and sexuality. Linebarger does this via the construction of an "educational hospice" for students purportedly struggling with their sexual or gender identifications. This *blurring of lines* is significant because it places Linebarger's "gay" or "lesbian" students in a relationship with woundedness. When such connections are formed, young people who are identified as "gay" or "lesbian" may become pathologized by virtue of their sexual identification, a connection that may take hold and come to be considered axiomatic among people who study schools. This is one of many examples of a familiar discourse that may arise when studying schools.[2] In the instance of discourses of sexuality, one might ask, "How do schools form relations to discourses of sexuality that enable sexual and gender identifications to be essentialized and LGBTI[3] identified young people to be invested with wounded identities?" It is when discourses habitually become so familiar that there is no longer any pause for reflection and they are able to appear truthful and comfortable. It therefore seems imperative to challenge this comfort that enables teachers such as Linebarger to publicly construct a metaphorical educational hospice where LGBTI adolescence is conflated with woundedness.

One means to challenge such comfort is to engage in what Foucault (1997a) calls "an ethics of discomfort." In this task we take as our springboard a piece by Foucault titled "For an Ethics of Discomfort." This short piece is a book review of Jean Daniel's *L'Ere des Ruptures* and was first published in *Le Nouvel Observateur* in April 1979. Drawing on what Merleau-Ponty considers to be one of the essential political tasks, Foucault writes, "Never consent to being completely comfortable with your own certainties" (1997a: 144). Foucault also provides some directions on how to turn down comfort. He cautions that "everything perceived is only evident when surrounded by a familiar and poorly known horizon" (1997a: 144). We suggest that this sense that something can be familiar, yet poorly known, is worthy of reconsideration.

This chapter sets out a way of interrogating the familiar in schooling through the application of an ethics of discomfort. To do this we draw on research related to a study of people in Australia and the United States who work to support LGBTI identified students in high school settings (Rasmussen, 2003). An ethics of discomfort is used to consider one of the findings of this research, that is, the tendency to conflate LGBTI adolescence with woundedness in educational discourses. First, we elaborate on how we conceive of Foucault's ethics of discomfort and consider how this ethics can be informed by his suggestion that "everything is dangerous" (Foucault, 1997c: 256). Here we suggest that these two Foucaultian notions can be employed to inform the study of schoolings' poorly known horizons. To illustrate this point we analyze "horror stories" produced in relation to LGBTI adolesence. We then discuss how an ethics of discomfort can be applied to an interrogation of these "horror stories" by scrutinizing repetition and thaumaturgy as processes that make the poorly known comfortable.

Drawing on Foucault's "Ethics of Discomfort"

As outlined above, an ethics of discomfort engages the notion of a "familiar and poorly known horizon." This notion provides a tactical space, a space where an ethics of discomfort can be brought into play. In relation to this, in "The Masked Philosopher," Foucault (1997b) refers to "manifest truth" and the replacement of one "manifest truth" with a new one. What we see in this "replacement" is, according to Foucault, not the commencement of a new entity with no antecedent or relation to the previous, but on the contrary,

...the new manifest truth is always a bit of an idea from the back of your mind. It allows you to see again something you had never completely lost sight of; it gives the strange impression that you had always sort of thought what you had never completely said, and already said in a thousand ways what you had never before thought out. (Foucault, 2002: 447–448)

Thus, in studying schools with an ethics of discomfort, one can become vigilant for those shadows that cast an illusion of new ideas upon the ground of the familiar. Related to the above point, it is important to note that studying schools with an ethics of discomfort does not mean enlisting in a search to make our horizons known. Toward this we invoke a point made by Foucault at the end of the first volume of *The History of Sexuality*. On the last page the remark is made, "Let us consider the stratagems by which we are induced to apply all our skills to discovering its secrets, by which we are attached to the obligation to draw out its truth, and made guilty for having failed to recognize it for so long" (Foucault, 1976: 159). Further, a relevant consideration can be drawn from the point that, in the search for the truth of sex "we became dedicated to the endless task of forcing its secret, of exacting the truest of confessions from a shadow" (Foucault, 1976: 159). This vital point can be underscored by considering Foucault's comments in "What Is Enlightenment?" about a "critical ontology of ourselves":

The critical ontology of ourselves must be considered not, certainly, as a theory, a doctrine, nor even as a permanent body of knowledge that is accumulating; it must be conceived as an attitude, an ethos, a philosophical life in which the critique of what we are is one and the same time the historical analysis of the limits imposed on us and an experiment with the possibility of going beyond them. (Foucault, 1997d: 319)

An ethics of discomfort does not imply the construction of a theory or doctrine, but rather, it enlists an approach that takes as its ethos the practice of unsettling certainty and its limits. On this basis, an ethics of discomfort does not seek to find "facts" to solve the poorly known through the injunction of locating a known. On the contrary, an ethics of discomfort seeks to consider how it is that the *poorly known is poorly known*. Thus, in considering the "poorly known horizon" we are not seeking to replace one truth with another, nor are we advocating the search for a truth to make our horizons known. As Foucault states,

...an obvious fact gets lost, not when it is replaced by another which is fresher or cleaner, but when one begins to detect the very conditions which made it obvious: the familiarities which served as its support, the obscurities upon which its clarity was based, and all these things that, coming from far away, carried it secretly and made it such that "it was obvious." (1997a: 143)

The purpose of analyzing these certainties is not to become more certain, nor to bring about a reversal, but to corrupt the pleasantry of certitude. In this way the idea of a poorly known horizon paradoxically provides an opportunity to fashion an ethics of discomfort: a means to craft a practice that assumes that "everything is dangerous." To clarify, Foucault argues that,

...what I want to do is not the history of solutions—and that's the reason why I don't accept the word *alternative*. I would like to do the genealogy of *problématiques*. My point is not that everything is bad, but that everything is dangerous, which is not exactly the same as bad. If everything is dangerous, then we always have something to do. So my position leads not to apathy but to a hyper- and pessimistic activism. [Emphasis in original] (1997c: 256)

Here we interpret Foucault's strategy to perceive everything is dangerous as making an important distinction from a strategy that perceives that everything is bad. Saying everything is dangerous eschews the binary of the good and the bad. This tactic gives us something to do and enables us to move away from a search for solutions. In this regard an ethics of discomfort provides a means to move away from apathy and hone a "hyper- and pessimistic activism" (Foucault, 1997c: 256) that unsettles the comfort of certitude. This Foucaultian ethics distinguishes itself from an ethics that courts a knowledgeable certainty of morality. It is an ethics that is not tied to the formulation of codes and principles of moral behavior or to notions of certainty.

The combination of an ethics of discomfort and everything is dangerous can be used to provide a way to reconsider what Foucault described as our relationship to truth. This possibility can be illustrated by again drawing on a statement from "The Masked Philosopher," where Foucault suggests, "What is philosophy if not a way of reflecting, not so much on what is true and what is false, as on our relationship to truth?" (327). Further to this, Foucault comments, "It should be added that it is a way of interrogating ourselves: If this is the relationship we have with truth, how must we behave?" (Foucault, 1997b: 327). Taking this from Foucault, if we have a relationship to truth, the question that needs to be asked is what is this relationship to truth—or perhaps more accurately, how are our relationships to truth manifested and more pressingly, how can we notice/catch/see/raise our awareness of these relationships? What is crucial here is that considering the poorly known horizon does not lead to a perusal of *what is truth*, but rather, a deliberate questioning that asks, *how is this relation to truth formed?*

In the following section we recount "horror stories" of LGBTI adolescence. Our aim is not to determine their veracity or to formulate an appropriate "moral" response. Rather, we go on to consider how an ethics of discomfort might be applied to the production of these persuasive stories entwining woundedness and LGBTI adolescence.

"Horror Stories" of LGBTI Adolescence

W/e speak out knowing we continue to come to terms with our dislocatedness in a society where our queer youth "belong to two groups at high risk of suicide: youth and homosexuals." (Gibson, 1994, in Grace & Benson, 2000: 107)

The quotation above presents with familiarity in research related to LGBTI identified young people (Macgillivray & Kozik-Rosabal, 2000; Rogers, 1998; Unks, 1995: 1–5). This sense of risk was repeated in interviews Mary Louise Rasmussen conducted with people working in programs designed to support LGBTI identified teachers and students in high school settings in Australia and the United States. Christopher Rodriguez of the Hetrick Martin Institute[4] (HMI) in New York describes himself as "an advocate for young people, for high risk youth" (Rodriguez in Rasmussen, 2003: 173). For Rodriguez it appears that "young people" and "high risk youth" are synonymous. Rodriguez goes on to state, "It's common knowledge that GLBT youth are more at risk of depression and suicide. More so than just about any other population of young people" (Rodriguez in Rasmussen, 2003: 173).[5] This common knowledge about LGBTI young people as a population "at risk" is echoed below by one of the founders of the HMI, Joyce Hunter:

58% of the kids coming to the agency [HMI] at that time were victims of violence in their schools....Young person after young person told stories about how they had been discriminated against by students and staff in the public schools in the communities in which they lived. (Hunter in Rasmussen, 2003: 173)

In a similar vein to Rodriguez and Hunter, Gail Rolf, coordinator of Project 10 in the Los Angeles Unified School District, conveys this sense of risk in the quote below. Rolf states,

We know just looking at the statistics that kids are killing themselves in drugs, numbing themselves out as a way of avoiding the pain they are feeling. They are getting themselves pregnant as a way of hiding. They are subject now to HIV infection and other STDs, they are having high risk sex and are engaging in tremendously risky behaviors and I am very concerned about that. (Rolf in Rasmussen, 2003)

Margaret Edwards,[6] one of the Australian participants in Rasmussen's (2003) research, argues that being young and "dealing with sexuality and identity problems" doubles people's troubles:

That's one of the things we focus on a lot in our workshops...kids who are dealing with sexuality and identity problems have got a double whammy, because not only are they dealing with adolescence and what that means and puberty and growth changes and emotional ups and downs, but they are also dealing with "Heh, I am different to other people." They are scared. They are frightened. They are dealing with two parallel things happening and it's very confusing. (Edwards in Rasmussen, 2003: 174)

In the excerpts above, people who work to support LGBTI identified adolescents emphatically express their concerns regarding the hapless plight of these young people. Through the expression of these concerns there appears to be some consensus that LGBTI adolescence is a difficult and risky period where young people are liable to engage in "tremendously risky behaviours" (Rolf in Rasmussen, 2003: 174).

There can be no denying that communities of young people experience violence and self-harm, regardless of their sexual or gender identifications. Our objective here is not to discount the existence of violence and self-harm but to interrogate the conflation of woundedness and sexuality. While avoiding debates relating to the veracity of the "horror stories" recounted above, we are perturbed by the tendency to *naturally* conflate woundedness and LGBTI adolescence. When LGBTI identified young people are perceived as an acutely endangered minority, other discourses may be formed whereby these same young people are perceived to be at risk and in *need* of a range of protections and services within and outside schools. The production of such a relationship may thus underpin schools' role in the pathologization of *all* young people who are LGBTI identified. Such a relationship to truth also sustains other divisions that accompany the maintenance of the heterosexual/homosexual binary in educational contexts.[7] Our reservations regarding the conflation of woundedness and LGBTI adolescence prompt us to consider how schools form relations to discourses of sexuality that enable young people's sexual and gender identifications to be essential-ized and subsequently intertwined with woundedness.

Applying an Ethics of Discomfort

In this last section we suggest how an ethics of discomfort can be specifically applied to the intertwining of sexual and gender identifications with woundedness. As outlined earlier, an ethics of discomfort takes the perspective that "everything is dangerous," an approach, as Foucault suggests, that means that "we always have something to do" (Foucault, 1997c: 256). This notion of "something to do," and what Foucault further clarifies as a "hyper- and pessimistic activism" (1997c: 256) seems to imply an ongoing form of practice, yet it would seem that more is required to move from an understanding of everything as dangerous to being able to locate the familiar and the certain. Toward this we draw on Foucault's suggestion that "it seems to me that the critical question today must be turned back into a positive one: In what is given to us as universal, necessary, obligatory, what place is occupied by whatever is singular, contingent, and the product of arbitrary constraints?" (1997d: 315). Related to this, Foucault makes the point that "criticism is no longer going to be practiced in the search for formal structures with universal value, but rather, as a historical investigation into the events that have led us to constitute ourselves and to recognize ourselves as subjects of what we are doing, thinking, saying" (1997d: 315). Reading these statements alongside one another it could be said that what is given to us as universal, necessary, obligatory are the very practices that inscribe and reinscribe these same formal structures. In this way it can be argued that the naturalness of the "horror story" forms a poorly known horizon that conceals the singular, the contingent, and the products of arbitrary constraints. This act of conceal-ment can be used strategically in the application of an ethics of dis-comfort, which is to suggest that the singular, the contingent, and the product of arbitrary constraints can become targets of an ethics of dis-comfort. These are fragments that can be used tactically to make known the processes that create certainty's poorly known horizon.

We have identified two interrelated processes that facilitate the application of an ethics of discomfort in this study of the conflation of woundedness and LGBTI adolescence: "repetition" and "thaumaturgy." An effect of these processes is that they obscure the knowledge of the young person. Indeed, it could be argued that this obscuration forms part of what is *poorly known* in the poorly known horizon. For example, Gordon notes what appears to be the tendency of adults who themselves identify as LGBTI to construct LGBTI adolescence "almost pietistically, as the territory of an inevitable martyrdom" (Gordon, 1999: 19). In this construction, LGBTI identified young people may be unquestioningly contrasted to two groups in order to become situated as martyrs, namely their heterosexual-identified peers and LGBTI identified adults. Here we suggest that it is through processes of repetition and thaumaturgy that this contrast becomes poorly known, and as such can remain un-problematized and unmarked in discourse. While a consideration of these two processes is efficacious for our purposes here, they are by no means intended to be prescriptive. Other studies of schooling that seek to question the familiar may analyze alternative processes to facilitate the application of an ethics of discomfort.

Repetition

One means by which to engage in the practice of problematization using an ethics of discomfort is through an analysis of processes of repetition in educational discourses. These processes of repetition are instrumental in forming particular relationships to truth for those involved in their reiteration. We study two aspects of such processes of repetition: the potential effects of such processes remaining unchallenged, and the potential effects of such processes of repetition that are challenged but sustained for strategic reasons. The process of repetition we have chosen to consider in this instance is the recounting of "horror stories" (Macgillivray, 2000: 321) in discourses relating to LGBTI adolescence. In repeating these "horror stories," researchers and young people gradually form particular relationships to truth that become difficult to question.

Relations to truth that are unchallenged and taken as axiomatic are exemplified by Andre Grace and Fiona Benson, who, as mentioned previously, are comfortable in repeating Gibson's research finding that "queer youth 'belong to two groups at high risk of suicide: youth and homosexuals'" (Gibson, 1994 in Grace & Benson, 2000: 107). In a similar vein, Ian MacGillivray argues,

> We as a society are in a crisis situation. Ending the antigay violence that leads youth to kill themselves or others should be our first priority. I know of no better way to do this than making all people, but especially educators, aware of the horror stories that many GLBTQ[8] students live through. (Macgillivray, 2000: 321)

Macgillivray notes that repeating such "horror stories" may have deleterious effects:

> Focusing narrowly on the horror stories does have its consequences. The director of a local support group for GLBTQ youth explains that *some of her group members, who are otherwise healthy and well-adjusted, seem to get caught up in the drama and pathology created around being GLBTQ and develop self-destructive behaviors because it is expected of them.* They report feeling like there's something wrong with them if they do not also have *horror stories* about being GLBTQ to share. [Emphasis ours] (Macgillivray, 2000: 320–321)

In this process of repetition, the disturbing experiences of some LGBTI identified young people are transferred onto *all* young people who adopt LGBTI identifications. Young people may even "develop self-destructive behaviors" (Macgillivray, 2000: 320–321) in order to authenticate their sexual or gender identification. Similarly, researchers such as Grace and Benson may not hesitate to confirm these same young people in their state of abjection.

Unchallenged processes of repetition can therefore be viewed as implicated in the solidification of "horror stories." Once solidified, these "horror stories" may be understood as obligatory experiences or "rites of passage" for all LGBTI identified young people. These stories and experiences are not evidence of authenticity; rather, they are part of the processes through which people learn "to recognize themselves as subjects of 'sexuality'" (Foucault, 1982: 208). Being vigilant to and challenging such processes of repetition may be considered part of the application of an ethics of discomfort. The aim is to locate these stories and experiences that have become so familiar to unsettle the certainty of their authority and evidence.

Another aspect of repetition that might be considered in the framework of an ethics of discomfort are such processes that are acknowledged as perilous but are sustained for strategic reasons. In other words, we apply an ethics of discomfort to a consideration of arguments that advocate the repetition of "horror stories." For example, the repetition of "horror stories" is acknowledged as problematic by Macgillivray because he is cognizant of the potential adverse effects of "sending the message that if one is GLBTQ, then these horror stories should be his or her own experience" (Macgillivray, 2000: 321). Still, he goes on to argue that "we as a society are in a crisis situation so repeating these stories may be worth the risk at this time" (321). Moreover, it is apparent from Macgillivray's (2000) own research that such an emphasis on "horror stories" can have a negative effect on young people. Yet it seems such effects are not sufficiently deleterious to dispel his belief that the repetition of such stories is of strategic value. The strategic value of "horror stories" of LGBTI adolescence is also noted by Kevin Jennings, the executive director of GLSEN (Gay, Lesbian, and Straight Education Network) in the United States. He remarks,

> And here's another thing that's very disturbing to me. We have been cornered for a long time into portraying gay students as victims, really. That *we had to hammer home the suicide statistics, the violence statistics, the drop-outs, the drug addiction, as a way of generating sympathy for gay youth.* And I think that's a very problematic strategy, that it pathologizes gay youth, it victimizes them and portrays them as deserving of pity, and I personally try as hard as I can not to do that anymore. But then you get that other kind of problem which is that when I start to talk about the many wonderful gay youth...people start saying "Oh, we are all better now, we don't need to do anything!" [Emphasis ours] (Jennings in Rasmussen, 2003: 175, 176)

The certitude provided by conflating LGBTI adolescence with woundedness is strategically important. For Jennings, this conflation has become integral to providing benefactors with a worthy motivation for supporting LGBTI community organizations. Nevertheless, he questions the inclination of people working to support LGBTI identified young people, himself included, to deploy discourses that construct these young people as victims.

While repetition of these "horror stories" may have deleterious effects, according to Macgillivray and Jennings, disturbing this conflation may also be a dangerous strategy. This tension is suggestive of how an ethics of discomfort can be deployed to perform a "hyper- and pessimistic activism" that can interrogate the complexities—and politics—of repetition and its certainty. It may also prompt further consideration of the interrelationship of these two processes.

Thaumaturgy

Another process we consider in the application of an ethics of discomfort revolves around the notion of thaumaturgy. We contend that thaumaturgical processes complement processes of repetition so integral to the production of the familiar but poorly known horizon. Our use of the term "thaumaturgy" is drawn from Foucault's (1989) analysis of the psychiatric doctor in *Madness and Civilization: A History of Insanity in the Age of Reason*. In this work Foucault describes the psychiatric doctor as "thaumaturge" and, by extension, the psychiatric institution as thaumaturgical. Foucault points to the esotericism of the doctor's knowledge as part of the doctor's "power to unravel insanity" (275). Positioned as thaumaturgical, the psychiatric institution can be understood in terms of "miracles," it becomes *natural* that the psychiatric facility is *for people with problems*. Whilst the doctor as thaumaturgical might be considered "the classical case" of thaumaturgy, we argue that this can be extended to other medicalizing discourses. It is in this sense that thaumaturgy can be used in this study of the conflation of LGBTI adolescence and woundedness, a conflation that is partially made possible through recourse to such medicalizing notions. Below, we point to some thaumaturgical processes that naturalize "horror stories" of LGBTI adolescence and consider how the application of an ethics of discomfort might disturb such processes.

In the quotation that opens this chapter, the designation of the Walt Whitman Community School as an educational hospice echoes the thaumaturgical role of the psychiatric facility. Professionals in both institutions *naturally* offer treatments to *people with problems*, in order that they may "best function in the larger, mainstream society" (Linebarger in Martin, 2001). In a similar way, Christopher Rodriguez, a professional working in an organization dedicated to supporting LGBTI identified young people, invokes a "common knowledge" (Rodriguez in Rasmussen, 2003: 173) of the woundedness of LGBTI young people. It is in the invocation of this common knowledge that these performances of sexual and gender identifications are magically transformed into evidence of their discrete and wounded sexual and gender identifications. Thus, it becomes *natural* that Rodriguez should conceive of himself as "an advocate for young people, for high risk youth" (Rodriguez in Rasmussen, 2003: 173). This is one element in the alchemy that conflates LGBTI adolescence and woundedness in educational discourses.

The process described above seems natural and familiar, yet upon inquiry it may appear mysterious and inscrutable. An ethics of discomfort can employ the notion of thaumaturgy to be alert to the context and participants involved in sustaining these mysterious and inscrutable practices. This provokes the question, "How can teachers and researchers studying schools apply an ethics of discomfort that is alert to these thaumaturgical processes?" A means to respond can be demonstrated by an analysis of the following quote, which affirms the connection between youth suicide and LGBTI identified young people:

> It seems likely that young Australian gays and lesbians will be at greater risk of suicide as compared with heterosexual youth....If Australian research ignores the connection between homosexuality and youth suicide, young gays and lesbians will remain hidden as a possible high-risk group, and attempts to formulate effective suicide prevention strategies may be seriously undermined. (Macdonald & Cooper, 1998: 24)

Ron Macdonald and Trudi Cooper draw heavily on medicalizing research to hammer home their belief in the woundedness of LGBTI identified young people. They attach this belief to the construction of effective suicide prevention strategies for young people who, to their eyes, remain hidden from the gaze of such strategies. This line of thought not only reinscribes the conflation of LGBTI adolescence with woundedness, but it goes on to argue the necessity of such a conflation and to berate those who do not realize this connection. Thus Macdonald and Cooper become part of the process of making the poorly known horizon of LGBTI woundedness, *poorly known*.

Using thaumaturgy in this way, we can get at how those who study and work in schools may make the poorly known poorly known. This enables us to interrogate the "magical ways" whereby Macdonald and Cooper can argue that the prevalence of LGBTI youth suicide is obscured and Rolf can "*know*...that (LGBTI) kids are killing themselves in drugs, numbing themselves out as a way of avoiding the pain they are feeling" (Rolf in Rasmussen, 2003: 174). In this way a study of thaumaturgical processes can be used to study schooling's discourses and apply an ethics of discomfort to excavate below the surface of the familiar in discourse.

Conclusion

In this chapter we have advocated that those who study schools need to consider the familiar yet miraculous shifts through which it is possible to see how relationships to "truth" are formed and sometimes become difficult to shake. An ethics of discomfort can make these miraculous shifts fathomable by locating processes of repetition and thaumaturgy. Being alert to repetition and thaumaturgy also helps to emphasize the singular, the contingent, and the products of arbitrary constraints so often obscured in the production of "horror stories" of LGBTI adolescence.

Yet while advocating the application of an ethics of discomfort, we recognize that this ethics needs to be strategically applied. As a result, although discourses of risk tend to pathologize all LGBTI identified young people, these discourses may remain familiar and poorly known for tactical reasons. An ethics of discomfort that adopts the maxim that everything is dangerous may therefore be perceived to have strategic limitations, especially in an economy where notions of risk produce financial premiums. As such, we are aware that an ethics of discomfort may be effective in engraving a question mark upon the surface of certitude, while simultaneously this questioning may not be acted upon because of strategic considerations. The example of Jennings, cited above, is a salient reminder; while we advocate the necessity of arguing that everything is dangerous, we recognize that an ethics of discomfort must always be applied within the constraints imposed by contemporary educational contexts. It is our contention that the interstices between the awareness of, and the application of, an ethics of discomfort accentuate the necessity of a process of continuous questioning of the certitudes that underpin the production of wounded knowledges.

Endnotes

1. The WWCS caters primarily to young people who identify as lesbian, gay, bisexual, and transgender.

2. There are other familiar features pertaining to the production of discourses related to sexualities and schooling worthy of further consideration but beyond the scope of this chapter. One is the tendency to exclude from public rhetoric any discussion of the economic and racial dividing practices imbricated in LGBTI identified young people's associations with woundedness. Thus "race" and "class" may, in certain instances, become the unmarked background in discourses of sexuality and schooling. For further discussion see Rasmussen, M. L. (2002), Safety and Subversion and the Role of Agency in the Production of Sexualities in School Spaces. American Educational Research Association, Annual Conference, New Orleans, April.

3. Lesbian, gay, bisexual, transgender, and intersex.

4. "HMI was founded in 1979 in response to an incident in a NYC group home. A 15-year-old boy was beaten and sexually assaulted by other residents. Group home staff addressed the incident by discharging the young man, explaining to him that the attack would not have happened if he were not gay. When Doctors Emery S. Hetrick and A. Damien Martin learned of the case, they marshalled the support of concerned adults and founded the Institute for the Protection of Lesbian and Gay Youth (IPLGY). The Institute was renamed in their honor after their deaths." This information is drawn verbatim from the Institute web site, see http://www.hmi.org/ about.htm (accessed 22/08/02).

5. The quotes presented here represent only a small sample of the many discourses that "support" the widely produced knowledge that sexual minority young people are "at risk." A comprehensive list of the oft-quoted risk factors associated with sexual identity, drawn from research compiled by the Hetrick Martin Institute, Joyce Hunter, and the National Gay and Lesbian Task Force et al., can be found at http://www.drizzle.com/ ~kathleen /wla/lgbyout.htm (accessed 28/08/010).

6. Edwards is a schoolteacher in Wagga Wagga, a rural town in the state of New South Wales.

7. For further discussion relating to the production of the heterosexual/ homosexual binary in school settings, see Leck, G. M. (2000), Heterosexual or Homosexual? Reconsidering Binary Narratives on Sexual Identities in Urban Schools. Education and Urban Society, 32(3), pp. 324–348.

8. Gay, lesbian, bisexual, transgender, queer.

References

Foucault, M. (1976). *The history of sexuality, Volume I: An introduction* (Harmondsworth, England: Peregrine, Penguin).

Foucault, M. (1982). The subject and power. In H. L. Dreyfus & P. Rabinow (Eds.), *Michel Foucault: Beyond structuralism and hermeneutics* (New York: Harvester Wheatsheaf).

Foucault, M. (1989). *Madness and civilization: A history of insanity in the age of reason* (London: Routledge).

Foucault, M. (1997a). For an ethics of discomfort. In S. Lotringer & L. Hochroth (Eds.), *The politics of truth: Michel Foucault* (New York: Semiotext(e)).

Foucault, M. (1997b). The masked philosopher. In P. Rabinow (Ed.), Michel Foucault: *Ethics, subjectivity and truth, the essential works of Michel Foucault, Vol. 1* (New York: The New Press).

Foucault, M. (1997c). On the genealogy of ethics: An overview of work in progress. In P. Rabinow (Ed.), *Michel Foucault: Ethics, subjectivity and truth, the essential works of Michel Foucault, Vol. 1* (New York: The New Press).

Foucault, M. (1997d). What is enlightenment? In P. Rabinow (Ed.), *Michel Foucault: Ethics, subjectivity and truth, the essential works of Michel Foucault, Vol. 1* (New York: The New Press).

Foucault, M. (2002). For an ethic of discomfort. In J. D. Faubion (Ed.), *Michel Foucault: Power, the essential works of Michel Foucault, Vol. 3* (London: Penguin).

Gordon, A. (1999). Turning back: Adolescence, narrative, and queer theory. *GLQ: A Journal of Lesbian and Gay Studies,* 5(1), pp. 1–24.

Grace, A. P. & Benson, F. J. (2000). Using autobiographical queer life narratives of teachers to connect personal, political and pedagogical spaces. *International Journal of Inclusive Education,* 4(2), pp. 89–109.

Leck, G. M. (2000). Heterosexual or homosexual? Reconsidering binary narratives on sexual identities in urban schools. *Education and Urban Society,* 32(3), pp. 324–348.

Macdonald, R. & Cooper, T. (1998). Young gay men and suicide: A report of a study exploring the reasons which young men give for suicide ideation. *Youth Studies Australia,* 17(4), pp. 23–27.

Macgillivray, I. K. (2000). Educational equity for gay, lesbian, bisexual, transgendered, and queer/questioning students. *Education and Urban Society,* 32(3), pp. 303–323.

Macgillivray, I. K. & Kozik-Rosabal, G. (2000). Introduction. *Education and Urban Society,* 32(3), pp. 287–302.

Martin, T. (2001). To be gay, and happy, at school, *Student.com,* http://www.student.com/article/gayschool/2001; accessed 22/02/01.

Rasmussen, M. L. (2002). Safety and subversion and the role of agency in the production of sexualities in school spaces. *American Educational Research Association,* Annual Conference, New Orleans, April.

Rasmussen, M. L. (2003). *Becoming subjects: A study of the production of sexualities in high school settings in Australia and the United States of America.* Unpublished doctoral dissertation, University of South Australia, Adelaide.

Rogers, M. (1998). *Breaking the silence: A study of lesbian youth in the current, social and South Australian educational context.* Masters dissertation, Faculty of Education, University of South Australia.

Unks, G. (Ed.) (1995). *The gay teen: Educational practice and theory for lesbian, gay, and bisexual adolescents* (New York: Routledge).

PART TWO:
Inter-views

Care of the Self:
The Subject and Freedom

Elizabeth Adams St.Pierre

Readers of these chapters that demonstrate how scholars in education have put the theories and methods of Michel Foucault to work in their various projects will no doubt find that Foucault is very different from himself. That is, they will see that contributors, notwithstanding their careful reading of his work, interpret and construct Foucault differently based on their individual experiences and desires. For instance, my interests have led me to focus in this chapter on a particular theory of the subject, *care of the self*, that Foucault (e.g., 1982/1988, 1983/1984, 1984/1985a, 1984/1985b, 1984/1988, 1985/1986, 1997) wrote about late in his life. This is not the same Foucault who, earlier in his career, proposed other theories of the subject because, in the course of his life's work, Foucault changed his mind. He writes that he is inclined "to begin and begin again, to attempt and be mistaken, to go back and rework everything from top to bottom" (Foucault, 1984/1985b, p. 7). Those who use him may also be so inclined. If readers, therefore, are looking for the "real" Foucault in these pages, they will be disappointed. In like fashion, if they expect contributors to be "true" to Foucault, they will be disappointed, for Foucault is not himself. Further, one seldom reads Foucault in a vacuum but with, against, and through other scholars. For instance, I think simultaneously with Foucault and, among others, Jacques Derrida, Gilles Deleuze, Friedrich Nietzsche, Judith Butler, and Gayatri Spivak and find fruitful convergences between Derrida's deconstruction (1967/1974) and Foucault's (1971/1984) splitting analytics that "disturbs what was previously considered immobile; fragments what was thought unified; shows the heterogeneity of what was imagined consistent with itself" (p. 82). Together, these theories take on a provocative and irresistible energy.

But since both Foucault and his readers are multiple and changing, mastering Foucault is impossible. I can perhaps explain the futility of trying to understand Foucault once and for all in terms of subjectivity and freedom, my lifelong passion, by invoking Judith Butler's (1995) comment on the agency of the subject, "That the subject is that which must be constituted again and again implies that it is open to formations that are not fully constrained in advance" (p. 135). The freedom[1] of Foucault lies in the fact that each of us must constitute him again and again for our projects and our lives as we reconstitute ourselves. And as we work hard to think differently than we have before, we go back to Foucault differently and find him again, and he is different, so we can move with him again into another thinking space. This is indeed the freedom of a subject constituted, not in advance of the world, but in material and discursive relations[2] that always offer the possibility of transformation. This is what Foucault teaches us about the subject and about freedom.

Foucault (1967/1998) understood quite well the provisional nature of interpretation, which I have been describing, as is illustrated in the following comment, "If interpretation can never be completed, this is quite simply because there is nothing to interpret. There is nothing absolutely primary to interpret, for after all everything is already interpretation" (p. 275). Simply put, there is no "original" Foucault to find. In fact, Foucault (1971/1984) writes that the search for an origin is fruitless since it is "an attempt to capture the exact essence of things, their purest possibilities, and their carefully protected identities; because this search assumes the existence of immobile forms that precede the external world of accident and succession" (p. 78). Well, Foucault is certainly not immobile, and, rather than think of his work as a stable, unified, and coherent foundation that we are obliged to master and be true to, it is perhaps more useful to think of it, in the words of Gilles Deleuze, whom Foucault admired, as a "line of flight" that takes us "across our thresholds, toward a destination which is unknown, not foreseeable, not preexistent" (Deleuze & Parnet, 1977/1987, p. 125).

Given his comment about Nietzsche that follows, we might assume that Foucault wouldn't mind being a line of flight, "The only valid tribute to thought such as Nietzsche's is precisely to use it, to deform it, to make it groan and protest. And if commentators then say that I am being faithful or unfaithful to Nietzsche, that is of absolutely no interest" (Foucault, 1972, pp. 53–54). I would imagine that all of us who use Foucault make him groan and protest in some way, so rather than be obsessed with essentializing questions about the truth of Foucault, we might ask ethical questions like Linda Alcoff's (1991), which focus on where our work with Foucault goes and what it does there. Indeed, where do we land once Foucault has flung us out of the constraints of what we have been told are the "universal necessities of human existence" (Foucault, 1988, p. 11)? What is our responsibility for the new truths we produce as we think with a man who writes, "I believe too much in truth not to suppose that there are different truths and different ways of speaking the truth" (Foucault, 1984/1988, p. 51)? What adventures will we encounter and how do we comport ourselves as we move with Foucault in the spaces of the unthought?

There is a pleasure in this work of thinking with Foucault that is sometimes so seductive it is difficult not to become enamoured of him. And that is why we are obliged to remember Nietzsche's (quoted in Spivak, 1974) warning that "One seeks a picture of the world in *that* philosophy in which we feel freest; i.e., in which our most powerful drive feels free to function" (p. xxvii). Judith Butler (1995) elaborates, "For the question of whether or not a position is right, coherent, or interesting is, in this case, less informative than why it is we come to occupy and defend the territory that we do, what it promises us, from what it promises to protect us?" (pp. 127–128). What does Foucault promise us? *And what does he protect us from thinking?* The latter is the most difficult question for those who love Foucault, but it is the ethical question we must inevitably ask of our fondest attachments. In short, how do we accomplish deconstruction's double bind of working under erasure, of simultaneously using and troubling a body of work that is both "inaccurate yet necessary" (Spivak, 1974, p. xiv)?

I have struggled to keep these questions in mind as I have used Foucault's work to think differently about the subject, to, as Gayatri Spivak (1974) explains, "make room for the 'irruptive emergence of a new concept,' a concept which no longer allows itself to be understood in terms of the previous regime" (p. lxxvii). Foucault, and others, have given us analyses with which to examine existing conceptions of the subject and to open up that category to reinscriptions. Foucault (1982) writes that the goal of his work "has been to create a history of the different modes by which, in our culture, human beings are made subjects" (p. 208). Further, he suggests that our project in regard to subjectivity might be to "refuse what we are" (Foucault, 1982, p. 216) and "to get free of oneself" (Foucault, 1984/1985, p. 8). I suspect that I can best honor Foucault by being wary of my attachment to him, by working to get free of the subject he has allowed me to think and be so that I might think and be a different subject. For me, this work is always about employing deconstruction's ethical imperative of practicing a "persistent critique" of "what one cannot not want" (Spivak, 1993, p. 46). Clearly, there is much to think about here for those of us who are fond of Foucault.

But back to interpretation. That there is no original truth of Foucault to uncover does not mean that we can get away with a facile reading of his work. Foucault (1983/1984b) writes that "everything is dangerous" (p. 343), and it is certainly dangerous to read him carelessly. Foucault (quoted in Dreyfus & Rabinow, 1982) acknowledges that "we are condemned to meaning" (p. 88), but Spivak (1992) cautions that our search for original meaning "belongs to that group of grounding mistakes that enables us to make sense of our lives" (p. 781). Similarly, she points out that "any act must assume unified terms to get started" (Spivak, 1993, p. 130). So we cannot escape the fact that we are always organizing and centering Foucault, making him *mean* something, as we work with him. Therefore, we should read him long and hard because we will no doubt be asked to account for the Foucault each of us constructs. At some point, the Foucault police *will* come after us. When they do, we should be able to explain the enabling conditions of *our* Foucault, our desires in putting him to work, and the effects of our projects on real people.

I think that's what this book is about—how each of us has constructed a Foucault to suit our experiences, desires, and projects. And I have written several introductory pages about interpretation to warn you that my Foucault will be different from everyone else's. I do hope you haven't latched on to a particular Foucault so tightly that you cannot hear all the others. If so, you will miss the marvelous multiplicity of Foucault effects that are gathered here to encourage you to follow your own line of flight with him into some space you have not yet thought.

Getting Free of Oneself

I have been obsessed with subjectivity and freedom all my life, long before I had the comforting language of Judith Butler, Jane Flax, Gayatri Spivak, Joan Scott, Michel Foucault, Jacques Derrida, and Gilles Deleuze, among others, to theorize why certain experiences[3] and not others were available in my life. I have always understood that I was subjected by discourse and cultural practice. Trinh's (1989) description of how we are inscribed by language and culture reflects my own experiences, "You try and keep on trying to unsay it, for if you don't, they will not fail to fill in the blanks on your behalf, and you will be said" (p. 80). Like many of us who are in love with language, I always knew it was not neutral, transparent, steady, and stable, but precarious, productive, and governed by a "grammar of disequilibrium" (Deleuze,

1994, p. 27). I understood as a child that discourse can create violent structures and unequal power relations within which people falter, languish, and fade.

But I also understood the possibilities of freedom that exist side by side with subjection[4] "when the language system overstrains itself [and] begins to stutter, to murmur or to mumble [so that] the entire language reaches the limit that sketches the outside and confronts silence" (Deleuze, 1994, p. 28). When language misfires, structures crack and lives can open up. John Rajchman (1985), who writes beautifully about Foucault, describes Foucault's vision of freedom, of getting free of oneself, as "a constant 'civil disobedience' within our constituted experience" (p. 6) as we "rebel against those ways in which we are already defined, categorized, and classified" (p. 62). Within discourse and cultural practice, I have used what Judith Butler variously calls "subversive repetition" (1990, p. 147) and "subversive citation" (1995, p. 135) in limit-work, described by Foucault (1997) as work that transforms "the critique conducted in the form of a necessary limitation into a practical critique that takes the form of a possible crossing-over of an obstacle" (p. xxxiii). Butler (1995) explains that "to be constituted by language is to be produced within a given network of power/discourse which is open to resignification, redeployment, subversive citation from within, and interruption and inadvertent convergences with other such networks. 'Agency' is to be found precisely at such junctures where discourse is renewed" (p. 135). The freedom of the subject, then, lies in these propitious junctures of language and practice that enable new mappings for crossing over limits we once thought foundational and necessary. In my day-to-day experiences, I have been intrigued by those who have learned to work those junctures, to open up spaces within which they thrive, experts at resignification.

When I am feeling particularly subjected by the discourses and practices that shut me down and close me off into the concept *woman,* I remember Foucault's (1982/1988) comment that people "are freer than they feel, that people accept as truth, as evidence, some themes that have been built up at a certain moment during history, and that this so-called evidence can be criticized and destroyed" (p. 10). His statement that focuses on the *contingency* of debilitating regimes of truth has encouraged me to interrogate the concept *older woman,* a perilous category that I and all women[5] who live long enough will inhabit. I believe that, in every sense and in every site, this critique is my life's work, and I have found poststructural theories of language, lived experience, and the subject useful in opening up that category and keeping it in play. My desire is that the deconstructive work I and other women accomplish in this regard will spread like a virus in a ravenous epidemic that will overturn and displace the conceptual order that articulates and perpetuates this stricken concept within which women of a certain age gasp after centuries of strangulation.

What might such a post-revolutionary, deconstructive politics look like, a politics that has no intention of imposing a successor regime? Brian Massumi (1992), writing about Deleuze and Guattari's work, says that this kind of freedom does

> not presume a revolution that can right all wrongs but one that attempts to pry open the vacant spaces that would enable you to build your life and those of the people around you into a plateau of intensity that would leave afterimages of its dynamism that could be reinjected into still other lives, creating a fabric of heightened states between which any number, the greatest number, of connecting routes would exist. Some might call that promiscuous. Deleuze and Guattari call it revolution. The question is not, Is it true: But, Does it work? What new thoughts does it make possible to think? What new emotions does it make possible to feel? What new sensations and perceptions does it open in the body? (p. 8)

This is not the same, for example, as the Marxist revolution that will put an end to all domination.

Butler, Spivak, Foucault, Deleuze and Guattari—they all envision a freedom very different from that we are used to thinking about. I have long since lost faith in and given up believing in a mighty revolution that will save us, but I know that the more subtle revolutions these scholars describe are possible because I see such freedom practiced every day in women's lives as they find those junctures, those rhizomatic routes, that open up vacant spaces, heightened states of possibility. At a certain point in my life, I knew I needed to study this freedom more carefully, and, longing for a "philosophy of praxis" (Gramsci, 1971, p. 388), I designed a research project that took me home to talk with the older women of my hometown who first taught me deconstruction—women beautifully promiscuous and exquisitely practiced in the double move of both being and subverting *woman*.

Postmodern Homework

Ethnographers are warned against transforming their "homeland to the site of the hunt" (Clough, 1992, p. 58), but Kamala Visweswaran (1994) writes that "many feminist theorists identify home as the site of theory" (p. 111). Like other feminist ethnographers, I went home to do fieldwork and theory work, worrying a great deal initially about nostalgia, a cultural practice of redemption and a reaction formation to poststructuralism[6] and its shattering of foundations and origins. "In a world of loss and unreality, nostalgia rises to importance as the phantasmal, parodic rehabilitation of all lost frames of reference" (Foster, quoted in Stewart, 1988, p. 228). In fact, Baudrillard (1983/1993) explains, "when the real is no longer what it used to be, nostalgia assumes its full meaning" (p. 347). However, the longing for places, perhaps for those "growing-up places" (Pratt, 1984, p. 17) that we all carry around with us, should not necessarily be seen as reactionary (Massey, 1994, p. 151), nor should homelessness be valorized over home (Game, 1991, p. 148). Further, it seems irresponsible to insert those in cultures we inscribe as ruins in the double bind of being both "romanticized as those who can (still) speak and on the other hand coldly judged and dismissed because they speak 'incorrectly' and 'inefficiently'" (Stewart, 1988, p. 228). I find a troubling sense of teleology in the opposition to nostalgia, as if being attached to what we imagine the past to be and what we value in it is automatically suspect, whereas being attached to where we are going and what we might become is valorized. Nostalgia is surely another of those modernist constructs that postmodernist ethnographers who go home to do "fieldwork, textwork, and headwork" (Van Maanen, 1995, p. 4) must rethink as they trouble classical theories that represent time as a continuous line and history as continuous progress, an "afterwards explainable in terms of what had gone before" (Augé, 1995, p. 24).

With appropriate postmodern angst, I went home to study my early subjection by talking with some of the older white women of Milton (a pseudonym) who had taught me how to be a woman. But it was not just the past I studied. I went home to interrogate disturbing "memor[ies] of the future" (Deleuze, 1986/1988, p. 107) I might have had had I not left Milton. I was dismayed at how easily I dropped back into place among womanly discourses I thought I had overcome (subversive repetition takes one only so far). Such an easy recovery of a subject I thought I had outlived and one I believed I would never live taught me something about time as well as the subject. During fieldwork in Milton, I lived time differently, and I wrote, "this story has no beginning and no end but has always been, and I slip into it over and over again in different places, and it is as if I too have always been there" (St.Pierre, 1997b, p. 379). Indeed, had I ever left Milton? Could I ever leave?

Time became big trouble in my study. When time ceases to measure, it can no longer produce the "before" or "after" Aristotle proposed in his *Physics*. How does one think a subject not ordered by classical linear time—by past, present, and future—but produced within a folded, "crumpled" (Serres, 1990/1995, p. 60) time so that time distant touches time near, so that an "hour" is the same as a "year" and both can be lived simultaneously? This is the subject I became during fieldwork when time was at once "a thousand different paces, swift and slow" (Braudel, quoted in Popkewitz, 1997, p. 23) *and* a simultaneity. Such a subject was almost too hard to think, and it's still too hard to think except when I am that subject. Such a subject breaks down every conceptual order I know, and I could think only so far into that breakdown while I was in Milton.

Of course, the failure of the classical conception of time in my project and the emergence of a different subject forced the collapse of the entire structure of qualitative inquiry that I had studied in courses and in textbooks. Like many qualitative research studies, mine was out of control almost immediately. I tend to believe that if qualitative research projects are not in a state of emergency most of the time, researchers have probably stopped reading, thinking, and listening to their data (whatever that is!). I recommend leaping into the abyss of discomfort and uncertainty that surely accompanies every study but is seldom described in the literature and *working* that confusion as rigorously as our imaginations allow. Spivak reminds us that we are always limited by our imaginations. She writes, "what I cannot imagine stands guard over everything that I must/can do, think, live" (Spivak, 1993, p. 22). But poststructural researchers have a special advantage in this regard in that deconstruction demands that we put foundational concepts of qualitative inquiry like *data* (St.Pierre, 1997a), the *field* (St.Pierre, 1997b), *interviewing* (Scheurich, 1995) and *validity* (Lather, 1993) as well as others like *time* and the *subject* under erasure, so it's not uncommon to find oneself stranded in the debris of conventional qualitative inquiry, which has not yet made the "postmodern turn" (Hassan, 1987).

The difficulty for the poststructural researcher lies in trying to function in the ruins of a particular kind of qualitative inquiry after the theoretical move that authorizes its foundations has been interrogated and its limits breached so profoundly that its center can no longer hold. But as Derrida (1966/1978) explains, "There is no sense in doing without the concepts of metaphysics in order to attack metaphysics. We have no language—no syntax and no lexicon—which is alien to this history; we cannot utter a single destructive proposition which has not already slipped into the form, the logic, and the implicit postulations of precisely what it seeks to contest" (p. 250). So we make do with these concepts that are both inaccurate yet necessary even as we subvert them, and, in doing so, qualitative inquiry comes loose from its moorings and becomes increasingly different from itself. Of course, one might say that the entire enterprise has always already been unstuck. So perhaps our question should be how else might we structure qualitative inquiry and to what ends? I believe poststructural researchers are producing a different qualitative inquiry and that it behooves us to pay attention to its effects. Everything is dangerous.

The study that produced these postmodern complications is a combination of an interview study with 36 older, white southern women who live in my hometown and an ethnography of the small, rural community in which they live. I used Foucault's (e.g., 1982/1988, 1983/1984, 1984/1985a, 1984/1985b, 1984/1988, 1985/1986, 1997) ethical analysis, *care of the self*, which I will discuss shortly, to investigate the "arts of existence" or "practices of the self" the women have used during their long lives in the construction of their subjectivities. Notwithstanding my romance with the new subject I was beginning to think and be, I had to shift my attention to another subject that seemed more fitting for Milton and its older women, who live within classically ordered and stable time and space and talked with me mostly of their everyday practices, of the things they do that make them who they are. Of course, that other subject I was beginning to love intruded on my study in rude and raucous ways, but I focused instead on a theory of the subject that best suited the women's description of themselves, a subject constituted within practice.

This is not the study I set out to accomplish, and, like many interviewers, I was fortunate that the women I talked with answered questions I should have asked. Despite my poststructural inclinations, I began the study looking for *meaning*, and I positioned the women as repositories of knowledge and wisdom I might uncover if I asked the right questions. But I was not skilled enough to get them to tell me the secret of life, which is, of course, what I wanted to know. They responded to my questions about knowledge with answers about how, in day-to-day life, one creates a particular aesthetics of existence in ethical relations with oneself and others. They talked about "learning to take care of yourself"; about "listening to older people, especially your mother"; about "remaining cheerful as you do your duty"; about "living your life so you have a clear conscience"; about "practicing self-discipline." They were *enacting* care of the self, but I couldn't hear them. I did not read the last two volumes of Foucault's *History of Sexuality* (1984/1985b, 1985/1986), in which he describes this theory in detail, until after I had collected much of my data, so his theory of a subject constituted in practice was not available to me as I listened to the women. It was only later, when there was such a lack of fit between my epistemological approach and my data about praxis—what Lather (1991) describes as the "self-creative activity through which we make the world"—that I found his ethical analysis, which he describes as a "historical ontology in relation to ethics through which we constitute ourselves as moral agents" (Foucault, 1983/1984, p. 351). Foucault's ontological theory of the subject worked for this particular study, but I have not forgotten that other subject, the one lost in time, who continues to deterritorialize the "weariest kind of thought" (Deleuze & Guattari, 1980/1987a, p. 5) that overcodes my life.[7]

Care of the Self—The Theory

In the course of his work, Foucault moved through various conceptions of the subject: a subject dispersed in discourse (e.g. Foucault, 1979), a subject constituted in discourse (e.g., Foucault, 1961/1965, 1975/1979), and a subject constituted in practice. As I have explained, it is the latter conception that I used in my study with some of the older white women of Milton and that is discussed in the last two volumes of his three-volume series, the *History of Sexuality* (1976/1978, 1984/1985b, 1985/1986), and in other writings (e.g., 1982/1988, 1983/1984, 1984/1985a, 1984/1987, 1984/1988, 1984/1997, 1988, 1997).

Foucault originally announced that his history of sexuality would be a six-volume study concentrating "on the eighteenth and nineteenth centuries, and including volumes on women, children, and perverts" (Davidson, 1986, p. 230). Its purpose was "to define the regime of power-knowledge-pleasure that sustains the discourse on human sexuality in our part of the world" (Foucault, 1976/1978, p. 11). According to Davidson (1994), the back cover of the first volume, *History of Sexuality: An Introduction*, which is the only volume of that series that Foucault published, identified five forthcoming volumes as follows: Volume 2, *The Flesh and the Body*; Volume 3, *The Children's Crusade*; Volume 4, *Woman, Mother, Hysteric*; Volume 5, *Perverts*; and

Volume 6, *Population and Races* (p. 65). However, Foucault's interests changed after he completed the first volume, and he began to write a new series of books that focused on a different kind of subject, one that had appeared about 2000 years earlier in "Greco-Roman culture, starting from about the third century B.C. and continuing until the second or third century after Christ" (Foucault, 1983/1984, p. 359), thus serving the Greeks for about 600 years.

Three volumes of the history of sexuality were eventually published. Volume One, *History of Sexuality: An Introduction*, the first book in the six-volume study he abandoned, is similar to his other genealogies and examines sexuality in the eighteenth and nineteenth centuries. The second volume, *The Use of Pleasure* (1984/1985b), and the third volume, *The Care of the Self* (1985/1986), are the first two volumes of the new series, and they examine care of the self for the ancient Greeks. In his biography of Foucault, Macey (1993) explains that the fourth volume, *The Confessions of the Flesh,* which would have been the third volume of the new series, was actually the first book Foucault wrote in the new series, though he never finished it. Foucault was very ill at that time, and there was an urgency to publish what he had already written in the new series on sexuality. Evidently, he was uncertain about the order of publication of the texts and even considered publishing the new series as a single book of about 750 pages. Eventually, he put the almost finished *Confessions of the Flesh* aside, "accepted the advice of Nora [Pierre Nora, his editor at Gallimard] and others and settled for the simultaneous publication of the two volumes in the chronological order of their content" (Macey, 1993, p. 466). Foucault died in July 1984 before completing *Confessions of the Flesh,* which has never been published and, according to both Macey (1993, p. 466) and Rabinow (1997, p. 183), probably never will be.

Readers who had expected Foucault to publish the books announced eight years earlier on the back cover of *History of Sexuality: An Introduction* were surprised to read in the introduction to *The Use of Pleasure* that he had abandoned that project. In an interview with Alessandro Fontana, Foucault (1984/1988) remarks that one of the reasons he had begun the new project was that "I very nearly died of boredom writing those books; they were too much like the earlier ones" (p. 47). Those familiar with his work often cite his more formal and inspiring words from the introduction to *The Use of Pleasure*, in which he explains the eight-year gap between the publication of the first and second volumes as a "long detour" (Foucault, 1984/1985b, p. 7) during which he moved in a new direction in his work, expanding the domains of his genealogical analyses of truth and power to include the subject. Deleuze (1990/1995) writes that "it takes him years of silence to get, in his last books, to this third dimension…about establishing different ways of existing" (p. 92). Foucault (1984/1985b) explains that this detour was one of those "times in life when the question of knowing if one can think differently than one thinks, and perceive differently than one sees, is absolutely necessary if one is to go on looking and reflecting at all" (p. 8). He says that philosophy is that "critical work that thought brings to bear on itself," and he wonders "to what extent it might be possible to think differently, instead of legitimating what is already known" (Foucault, 1984/1985b, p. 9). During the eight years of detour, Foucault (1984/1985b) studied ancient Greek

> texts written for the purpose of offering rules, opinions, and advice on how to behave as one should: "practical" texts, which are themselves objects of a "practice" in that they were designed to be read, learned, reflected upon, and tested out, and they were intended to constitute the eventual framework of everyday conduct. These texts thus served as functional devices that would enable individuals to question their own conduct, to watch over it and give shape to it, and to shape themselves as ethical subjects: in short, their function was "etho-poetic." (pp. 12–13)

These texts describe a *"style of liberty"* [italics added] (Foucault, 1984/1988, p. 49) made possible through the application of "intentional and voluntary actions by which men not only set themselves rules of conduct but also seek to transform themselves, to change themselves in their singular being, to make their life into an *oeuvre* that carries certain aesthetic values and meets certain stylistic criteria" (Foucault, 1984/ 1985b, pp. 10–11).

The Greeks called this ethical work *epimeleia heautou,* or care of the self, and it appeared very early in Greek culture as a widespread imperative, which, "consecrated by Socrates, philosophy took up again and ultimately placed at the center of that 'art of existence' which philosophy claimed to be" (Foucault, 1985/1986, pp. 43–44). The theme of the art of existence broke loose of philosophy to some extent and "gradually acquired the dimensions and forms of a veritable 'cultivation of the self'" (Foucault, 1985/1986, p. 44), with attendant attitudes, modes of behavior, activities, a way of living, and an entire social practice.

His new project had larger implications for his thinking about *relations,* and he found that the relation to oneself cannot be accounted for in the power relations or relations between forms of knowledge he had described in his earlier work. Thus, he reorganized his whole system to account for it. Accordingly, he revised his domains or axes of genealogy to include the following: (1) "a historical ontology of ourselves in relation to truth through which we constitute ourselves as subjects of knowledge"; (2) a "historical ontology of ourselves in relation to a field of power through which we constitute ourselves as subjects acting on others"; and (3) "a historical ontology in relation to ethics through which we constitute ourselves as moral agents" (Foucault, 1983/1984, p. 351). The latter domain, care of the self, studies the self's relation to itself, *rapport à soi,* by exploring the ancient Greek concept that, since the self is not given, it must be created as a work of art.

His new project also had implications for his thinking about *technologies.* Foucault's earlier archaeological and genealogical analyses had examined the problems of truth and power, what he called *technologies of sign systems,* "which permit us to use signs, meanings, symbols, or signification" as well as *technologies of power,* "which determine the conduct of individuals and submit them to certain ends or domination, an objectivizing of the subject" (Foucault, 1982/1988, p. 18). He had also identified *technologies of production,* "which permit us to produce, transform, or manipulate things" (Foucault, 1982/1988, p. 18). In his new project, he foregrounds a third domain of existence, the problem of individual conduct, or *technologies of the self,* "which permit individuals to effect by their own means or with the help of others a certain number of operations on their own bodies and souls, thoughts, conduct, and way of being, so as to transform themselves in order to attain a certain state of happiness, purity, wisdom, perfection, or immortality" (Foucault, 1982/1988, p. 18).

In conjunction with his new focus, his interest in *governmentality,* which previously had focused on how individuals are governed, regulated, and normalized by institutions, shifted to how individuals govern themselves. Foucault (quoted in Rabinow, 1997) writes that "the concept of governmentality makes it possible to bring out the freedom of the subject and its relationship to others—which constitutes the very stuff of ethics" (p. xvii).

Care of the self is often called Foucault's ethical analysis, the third axis of his analyses after archaeology and genealogy, which examine the domains of systems of knowledge and the modalities of power. Davidson (1986) cautions that "ethics neither displaces genealogy and archaeology or makes them irrelevant, but it does alter the final methodological implications of both....An attempt to study modern sexuality would have to combine all three axes of analysis, the self, power, and knowledge" (p. 230).

Foucault (1984/1985b) explains the purpose of the second and third volumes of the new series as follows: in *The Use of Pleasure*, he explores the moral/ethical dimension of the ancient Greeks and three major techniques of the self that they practiced: dietetics, economics, and erotics; in *The Care of the Self*, he describes the cultivation and elaboration of the self made possible by the Greek techniques of the self just mentioned as well as the manner in which sexual activity was problematized "in the Greek and Latin texts of the first two centuries of our era" (p. 12).

Interestingly, Foucault learned that, for the Greeks, ethics was not related to the moral precepts of religious institutions or to the rewards or punishments of an afterlife but focused instead on how one might live an ethical life in relation to others in order to make "one's life into an object for a sort of knowledge, for a *techne*—for an art" (Foucault, 1983/1984, p. 362). The ancient texts he studied indicated that the Greeks were interested in ethics as a means to give "the maximum possible brilliance to their lives" (Foucault, 1983/1984, p. 362). This idea that the self is the chief *work of art* to which one should attend on a day-to-day basis—for self-improvement, not self-absorption—is very different from the idea of the self in Christianity, which brought about a "profound transformation in the moral principles of Western society" (Foucault, 1988, p. 22) in that it made the renunciation of the self a condition of salvation. Foucault (1988) points out that today, "we find it difficult to base rigorous morality and austere principles on the precept that we should give ourselves more care than anything else in the world" (p. 22). Christian morality is a "morality of asceticism [that] insists that the self is that which one can reject" (Foucault, 1988, p. 22). As a result, "there has been an inversion between the hierarchy of the two principles of antiquity, 'Take care of yourself' and 'Know thyself.' In Greco-Roman culture knowledge of oneself appeared as the consequence of taking care of yourself. In the modern world, knowledge of oneself constitutes the fundamental principle" (p. 22).

In his ethical analysis, Foucault situates ethics as one element within the larger theme of morality, which he defines generally as "a set of values and rules of action that are recommended to individuals through the intermediary of various educational institutions, churches, and so forth" (Foucault, 1984/1985b, p. 25). He proposes that morality is composed of three elements: (1) a culture's moral code, (2) the "real behavior of individuals" (Foucault, 1984/1985b, p. 25), and (3) "the manner in which one ought to conduct oneself...as an ethical subject of this action" (Foucault, 1984/1985b, p. 26). He does not write a great deal about moral codes, since he found them to be similar across cultures, nor does he discuss people's actual behavior. Rather, he focuses on the third element of morality, care of the self, how one should conduct oneself in relation to codes of action and to others.

Care of the self has four major aspects: (1) the ethical substance—the part of oneself that will be worked on by ethics: "for Christians it was desire, for Kant it was intentions, and for us now it's feelings" (Foucault, 1983/1984, p. 252); (2) the mode of subjection—the way in which one is invited to become ethical, e.g., divine law, the Greeks' desire to "give your existence the most beautiful form possible"; (Foucault, 1983/1984, p. 353); (3) the self-forming activity or elaboration—all the activities that elaborate the self, that one performs on oneself in order "to transform oneself into the ethical subject of one's behavior" (Foucault, 1984/1985b, p. 27); and (4) the telos—the goal of this exercise, to "become pure, immortal, or free, or masters of ourselves" (Foucault, 1983/1984, p. 355).

It is important to remember that the subject of care of the self is constructed through *practice*. Foucault (1983/1984) writes, "so it is not enough to say that the subject is constituted in a symbolic system. It is not just in the play of symbols that the subject is constituted. It is constituted in real practices—historically analyzable practices. There is a technology of the constitution of the self which cuts across symbolic systems while using them" (p. 369). Foucault stresses that the Greek word *heautou* implies significant labor. Thus, *epimeleia heautou,* care of the self, involves more than self-absorption or self-attachment or preoccupation with the self, but implies "a sort of work, an activity; it implies attention, knowledge, technique" (Foucault, 1983/1984, p. 360) in everyday activities. One treats one's life as an object for a certain kind of knowledge, "for a *techne*—for an art" (p. 362), and Greek ethics is centered on the "aesthetics of existence" (Foucault, 1983/1984, p. 348). For the ancient Greeks, the kind of relationship one ought to have with oneself, *rapport à soi,* was not just self-awareness but deliberate self-formation in which "the individual delimits that part of himself that will form the object of his moral practice, defines his position relative to the precept he will follow, and decides on a certain mode of being that will serve as his moral goal. And this requires him to act on himself, to monitor, test, improve, and transform himself" (Foucault, 1984/1985b, p. 28). Since it is ontological and not psychological, ethics involves activities and social practices more than contemplation. Indeed, care of the self is "not a rest cure" (Foucault, 1985/1986, p. 51)—there are things to be done if one wishes to be ethical.

To facilitate self-formation grounded in practice, "a demanding, prudent, 'experimental attitude is necessary; at every moment, step by step, one must confront what one is thinking and saying with what one is doing, *with what one is.*' For Foucault in 1983, the key to appraising the values held dear by *any* philosopher was therefore 'not to be sought in his ideas, as if it could be deduced from them, but rather in his philosophy-as-life, in his philosophical life, his ethos'" (Foucault, quoted in Miller, 1993, p. 339). In fact, each culture produces patterns, practices, conventions, and events that may be used in the constitution of the self; the individual doesn't necessarily invent them. The ancient Greeks elaborated and used certain practices in the cultivation of the self that are still used today, including studying with a teacher or philosopher, keeping a journal, taking care of one's body, practicing abstinence, and conducting periodic administrative reviews of progress toward one's goal of becoming an ethical subject of one's actions.

Care of the self was not, however, an aesthetics of existence for everyone in ancient Greece. At first, it was available only to an elite group of free men. However, it was not required, was a matter of free choice, was not juridical or prescribed by any institution or disciplining authority, and was not used to normalize society. The principle of this ethics is a radical freedom that operates not only as *choice* but also as *resistance* to self-forming practices. Care of the self describes a permanent political relationship between self and self in which one's goal is to both produce oneself as the ethical subject of one's actions as well as to create one's life as a work of art. Further, the final relation to oneself achieved as a result of the practices of the self is an "ethics of control" (Foucault, 1985/1986, p. 65) that hinges on self-mastery and temperance in all matters. Care of the self was not aimed solely at individual perfection but also at preparing one to participate in society. If one has mastered oneself, one should not fear dominating others. Foucault (1984/1987) explains how one's relationship with oneself affects one's relationship with others as follows:

But if you care for yourself correctly, i.e., if you know ontologically what you
are, if you also know of what you are capable, if you know what it means for
you to be a citizen in a city, to be the head of a household in an *oikos*, if you
know what things you must fear and those that you should not fear, if you know
what is suitable to hope for and what are the things on the contrary which
should be completely indifferent for you, if you know, finally that you should
not fear death, well, then, you cannot abuse your power over others. (p. 8)

One's relationship with others, of course, moves one into the social and
political realm.

Though intrigued with care of the self, Foucault did not find the
ancient Greeks either admirable or exemplary. Nor, since he urges us to
accept our historicity, did he think care of the self could simply be
overlaid on contemporary society. He did, however, think that care of the
self has something to offer us today, especially given that contemporary
politics does not appear much concerned with an ethical subject. Perhaps
for this reason, when asked in an interview if we "should actualize this
notion of the care of the self, in the classical sense, against this modern
thought" (Foucault, 1984/1987, p. 14), he replies, "Absolutely, but I am
not doing that in order to say, 'Unfortunately we have forgotten the care
for self. Here is the care for self. It is the key to everything.' Nothing is
more foreign to me than the idea that philosophy strayed at a certain
moment of time, and that it has forgotten something and that somewhere
in her history there exists a principle, a basis that must be rediscovered"
(Foucault, 1984/1987, p. 14). Deleuze (1986/1988) elaborates here and
explains that the Greek view of the body and its pleasures that Foucault
describes in his genealogy "was related to the agonistic relations between
free men, and hence to a 'virile society' that was unisexual and excluded
women; while we are obviously looking here for a different type of
relations that is unique to our own social field" (p. 148). Foucault's and
Deleuze's point is that the concept of ethical self-formation through
technologies of the self can indeed be reconfigured based on the moral
codes, self-forming activities, and relationships available in postmodern
culture.

Care of the Self in Milton

I have described care of the self in Milton in great detail elsewhere
(St.Pierre, 1995) and, for ethical and political reasons, I am leery of
writing anything much about Milton women here in the reductive limits
of a few hundred words.[8] Thus, I will only touch on some of the major
aspects of my study to illustrate how the analysis worked in producing

one interpretation of Milton women's lives. As is usual, there was not a complete fit between the theory and my data. For instance, the arena of Foucault's ethical study is sexual relations, though one might also examine other arenas of relations and attendant codes such as those of the workplace, the schoolroom, the family, and friendship in considering ethical self-formation. In my study, I identified the arena of friendship relations as the site of self-constitution and theorized that these older women's subjectivities have been and are aesthetically stylized to a great extent within those friendship relations. The women I interviewed have spent most of their lives in the small town of Milton, where everyone knows everyone else, many are longtime friends, and friendship is highly valued.

Most of the women's arts of existence are practiced at home or with their friends; there was little mention of men in my study. I believe their relations with their women friends serve as sites of resistance and freedom. Foucault (1984/1985b) explains that moral codes are "transmitted in a diffuse manner, so that, far from constituting a systematic ensemble, they form a complex interplay of elements that counterbalance and correct one another, and cancel each other out at certain points, thus providing for compromises or loopholes" (p. 25). I believe friendship relations in Milton are private spaces, loopholes, with attendant practices the women both find in their culture and invent that encourage subversive citation and the disruption of the fierce public codes that aim to keep women in their place.

The moral codes I identified in Milton are Christianity, patriarchy, racism, and what I call the "white southern woman's code," which is a local, particular interpretation of the other three. These women, who ranged in age from 60 to 95 at the time of the interviews, seldom mentioned race unless I asked specific questions about it. Neither did the women discuss gender or sexuality or class. None of the women identified themselves as feminists, and almost all said they were Christian. In general, difference was unmarked, unaccounted for, and silenced. I did not believe my role in the study was to liberate these women from what might be perceived as false consciousness; rather, I studied their practices of the self that produced subjects for whom difference was unintelligible or silenced.

I theorized the four aspects of care of the self for these older women according to Milton's codes. The ethical substance—the part of the self to be worked on by ethics—is the sinful part of a humanist self, that part of a unified, stable self that is flawed and unable to sustain the love and duty expected by one's personal God. These women are good Christian women who find solace in their faith and their churchwork. Going to church to find peace and strength when they don't know how to keep on living is a well-practiced art of existence.

I believe their mode of subjection—the way in which one is invited to become ethical—is, officially, through divine law and, unofficially, through the women's desire, much like that of the ancient Greeks, to have a beautiful existence as defined by their culture. There is much aesthetic stylization in Milton—a great emphasis on the details of "making your life beautiful," as one woman said. I am reminded of a luncheon given in my honor in which the hostess floated a single impatien blossom in a small crystal salt dish by each guest's plate. This kind of whimsical loveliness and attention to detail is commonplace and demonstrates women's love for each other. Gestures like these are only small examples of the *care for others*, which has its own complicated structure and well-defined practices in Milton.

Their arts of existences, practices of the self, or self-forming activities—all the practices one performs to transform oneself into the ethical subject of one's behavior—are many, are related to resistance, ambivalence, or accommodation to the codes, and include the following: gender, religion, education, kinship, widowhood, and old age, and a practice I call "cheerfulness, significance, and pride." Education, one of those arts of existence, was terribly significant in Milton women's lives, perhaps because it was so hard to come by during the Depression years. I heard over and over again from women who had lost their parents, their husbands, their brothers and sisters, their best friends, their children, their financial security, their social status, their health, "Tell the girls you teach to get an education because nobody can take it away from you." In order to continue their education past formal schooling, these women and their mothers have organized and maintained at least nine book and study clubs: The Shakespeare Club (1898–present), the Women's Literary Club (1901–about 1975), the Tuesday Study Club (1919–present), the Current Book Club (1930–present), the Saturday Book Club (1930–present), the Cosmopolitan Club (1935–present), the Tuesday/Thursday Topics Club (1951–1975), the Wednesday Literary Club (1948–present), and the Pickwick Papers Literary Club (1967–present). They do research, write and present papers at club meetings, read controversial books on occasion, invite guest speakers from neighboring universities to lecture, and privilege scholarship in their clubs. Membership in the clubs is highly desirable in the community.

The practices of widowhood were the hardest to hear. None of the widows I interviewed had remarried, and, therefore, they have had to construct a complex network of care for each other to make sure that a friend who can't drive has a ride to the doctor or a friend in the hospital has someone with her around the clock. Being a widow is not necessarily bad, and some women have found freedom in being alone and designing their lives to suit themselves. Several have inherited large tobacco plantations, are very wealthy in their old age, have taken on political tasks in the county, and are enjoying power and influence they did not have as wives.

The telos of Milton women—the goal of their work—is to be immortal and live forever with God. However, the path to immortality is marked by other goals that contribute to an "ethics of pleasure" and an "ethics of control" (Foucault, 1985/1986, p. 65).

For the ancient Greeks, care of the self was a truly social practice. There was "a ready support in the whole bundle of customary relations of kinship, friendship, and obligation," and "the care of the self appears as intrinsically linked to a 'soul service,' which includes the possibility of a round of exchanges with the other and a system of reciprocal obligations" (Foucault, 1985/1986, p. 54). Foucault's words could just as easily have been written to describe care of the self among Milton women. Within friendship relations, they practice self-formation in elaborate, aesthetic rituals that privilege what they value—learning something new every day, self-discipline, an attention to detail that expresses beauty and love, doing their duty to themselves and others, and remaining cheerful in the face of adversity. Their practices of the self in friendship relations—practices that both accommodate and resist the codes that control them—move into their more public practices in their churches, their jobs, and their community and mark their patriarchal culture in very distinct ways.

Conclusion

Foucault (quoted in Rajchman, 1985) writes that "each time I have attempted to do theoretical work, it has been on the basis of elements from my experience—always in relation to processes that I saw taking place around me. It is in fact because I thought I recognized something cracked, dully jarring, or disfunctioning in things I saw, in the institutions with which I dealt, in my relations with others, that I undertook a particular piece of work, several fragments of an autobiography" (pp. 35–36). No doubt, most research projects begin because something is cracked in our lives. I watched my mother and her friends (and me not far enough behind) moving into that vicious category *older woman*, and I determined to understand the conditions of its existence, how it is maintained, and how it is disrupted, not for everyone certainly, but for a group of women I had known all my life.

My research project necessarily set me on the trail of theories of subjectivity, and I read widely in that area, particularly in feminist and poststructural theory. Many theories of subjectivity were at work in my study, not just Foucault's care of the self, even though it became the most significant. Reading theory is, of course, marvelous and often a luxury, but the thrill of qualitative research is taking theory to the field and putting it to work as we talk with and observe people as they go about their daily lives. This is the work of *interpretation*,[9] of using theory to make sense of living, to make a *contingent* sense of living, since different theories allow us to interpret differently. I continue to be enthralled by Foucault's (1971/1972) question, "How is it that one particular statement appeared rather than another?" (p. 27). How is it that one particular subject appeared rather than another? What other theories are available, or what other theories might we invent, that can open up the subject for different configurations and make possible different lives?

Foucault found the ancient Greeks' theory of an ethical subject, care of the self, a promising possibility and thought some variation of it might be useful in today's world. Of course, I found so many convergences between the theory and my participants' lives that I believe a variation of care of the self, indeed, *is* working in Milton. And I use that theory now in my own life and pay a great deal more attention these days to (1) my *practices*, to the things I do, and need to do, every day that make me, I hope, an ethical subject and (2) to the *relations*, including my relation with myself, within which I am constituted and constitute myself differently.

So I took theories of subjectivity with me to the field. I also took theories of time and space that I had read much about in the poststructural literature. Those bodies of theory helped me capture and close off into thought a subject I was (became?) that would have been unintelligible without them. Not surprisingly, the subject lost in time I have begun to think and be is also, like Foucault's subject, a subject constituted in practice, for I cannot separate thinking this subject from being/doing this subject. Indeed, I could never have thought this subject unless I had accomplished all those practices that qualitative researchers call fieldwork, unless I had thrown myself into the thick of things with the older women of Milton, and unless I had let myself go native as ethnographers are wont to do as we lose ourselves in "being there." Foucault described particular subjects during his life that he needed to think and live, and he has inspired me to describe mine.

This work of opening up the subject, of keeping it in play, does indeed require, as Foucault (1984/1985b) says, that we "work in the midst of uncertainty and apprehension" as we "begin and begin again" (p. 7). He also says that what motivates us to do this work of reinvention is not only that we find something jarring in our lives but also *curiosity,* a curiosity that "enables one to get free of oneself" (p. 8). I believe this is one of the most seductive but difficult ideas in the postmodern turn—that the subject itself is a *construction,* a product of curiosity, imagination, and desire. But therein lies our freedom, the freedom to problematize who we are and then think of who we might become. My desire is that we problematize the subject so that it proliferates, runs amuck, and overturns the conceptual orders that control our imaginations and shut down lives. No doubt this problematization, this art of existence, will occupy me for the rest of my life.

Endnotes

1. See my discussion of *freedom* in relation to *power* and *resistance* in the essay, "Poststructural Feminism in Education: An Overview" (St.Pierre, 2000). John Rajchman (1985) explains that, for Foucault, "freedom is not liberation, a process with an end. It is not liberty, a possession of each individual person. It is the motor and principle of his skepticism; the endless questioning of constituted experience" (p. 7). Foucault certainly does not reject the concept *freedom*, and it becomes particularly important in his ethical analysis, *care of the self.* He writes that "there is no sovereign, founding subject, a universal form of subject to be found everywhere....I believe, on the contrary, that the subject is constituted through practices of subjection, or, in a more autonomous way, through practices of liberation, of liberty, as in Antiquity, on the basis, of course, of a number of rules, styles, inventions to be found in the cultural environment" (Foucault, 1984/1988, pp. 50–51). He explains further that "Freedom is the ontological condition of ethics. But ethics is the considered form that freedom takes when it is informed by reflection" (Foucault, 1997, p. 284). Nor does Foucault, who is suspicious of revolution, reject liberation struggles, "You have situations where liberation and the struggle for liberation are indispensable for the practice of freedom" (1984/1997, p. 283). In this essay, I mostly use freedom in the way it is used in care of the self; that is, that since the subject is not given in advance, she can indeed create herself as a work of art.

2. See my discussion of discourse in the essay, "Poststructural Feminism in Education: An Overview" (St.Pierre, 2000) and also Paul Bové's (1990) lovely essay, "Discourse." Of course, discourses can be material, but when I speak of *relations*, I often make a distinction between discursive and material relations, as I do between discourse and cultural practice. For me, this is a feminist strategy that insists we not forget the materiality of lived experiences and practices, what Hal Foster (1996), after much useful poststructural critique of the *real* and *reality*, writes about in his book *The Return of the Real.* Foucault (1997) acknowledges that not all practices are discursive: "The study of forms of experience can thus proceed from an analysis of 'practices'—discursive or not—as long as one qualifies that word to mean the different systems of actions insofar as they are inhabited by thought as I have characterized it here" (p. 201). My purpose is not to maintain a binary logic but to acknowledge differences in relations and practices.

3. In her essay "Experience," Joan Scott (1992) explains that experience is not a foundational concept or the "origin of knowledge" (p. 25) but that which has to be explained. Subjects are constituted, subjected, through the experiences they are able to have given the discourses and practices available in their culture, and Scott urges us to denaturalize lived experience and not assume it is "uncontestable evidence as an originary point of explanation" (p. 24). This is not to say, however, that we are not concerned with the experiences people have, since they are, as Althusser (1971) explains, indicators of ideologies at work, ideologies that might be repressive. Scott encourages us to acknowledge the *reality* (a concept I use only under erasure) that people describe as their experiences and, at the same time, to examine the conditions that make those experiences possible and intelligible.

4. Subjection is not necessarily in opposition to some free state, since, in one sense, subjection simply implies the making of a subject. Butler (1997) explains this interpretation as follows, "No individual becomes a subject without first becoming subjected or undergoing "subjectivation" (p. 11). However, subjection is not neutral but involves all sorts of power relations. Different modes of subjection allow different practices of freedom. Disciplinary power, for example, "maintains the disciplined individual in his subjection" (Foucault, 1975/1979, p. 187), a subjection that may not be particularly desirable. Subjection carries at least a double meaning, as Butler (1997) writes, in that "the subject is itself a site of this ambivalence in which the subject emerges both as the *effect* of a priori power and as the *condition of possibility* for a radically conditioned form of agency. A theory of the subject should take into account the full ambivalence of the conditions of its operation" (pp. 14–15). Of course, Foucault recommends that we refuse subjection—the way we have been made into a subject—and he finds this refusal a practice of freedom.

5. I continue to use the categories *older woman* and *woman* even as I interrogate them. In Milton, these categories were defined traditionally, and women were/are carefully subjected as *southern women* and, more specifically, *southern ladies*. Overlapping cultural, linguistic, and material practices, many invented by the women themselves, discipline, regulate, and subvert these categories.

6. The terms *poststructuralism* and *postmodernism* are often used interchangeably; however, there are acknowledged differences in their meaning. Lather (1993) differentiates these two terms as follows: postmodernism "raises issues of chronology, economics (e.g., post-

Fordism) and aesthetics whereas poststructural[ism] is used more often in relation to academic theorizing 'after structuralism'" (p. 688). See Ursula Kelly's (1997) chart (pp. 25–26) for a helpful visual representation of modernism, postmodernism, structuralism, and poststructuralism. See Michael Peters's (1999) careful essay in which he distinguishes between these terms.

Postmodernism is an American term which refers to "the new stage of multinational, multiconglomerate consumer capitalism, and to all the technologies it has spawned" (Kaplan, 1988, p. 4) as well as to the avant garde in the arts, "the erosion of the older distinction between high culture and so-called mass or popular culture" (Jameson, 1988, p. 14). Jameson (1984) sees postmodernism as a "cultural dominant" (p. 56) that began to emerge after World War II with late consumer capitalism. The term postmodernism first appeared in architecture, indicating a different way of organizing space and, by extension, a different relationship between space and time. Jane Flax (1990) writes that "postmodern discourses are all deconstructive in that they seek to distance us from and make us skeptical about beliefs concerning truth, knowledge, power, the self, and language that are often taken for granted within and serve as legitimation for contemporary Western culture" (p. 41). See John Rajchman's (1987) essay for a genealogy of postmodernism.

Poststructuralism is a French term that represents the European avant garde in critical theory (Huyssen, 1990). Michael Peters (1999) writes that poststructuralism is a "specifically philosophical response to the alleged scientific status of structuralism." David Harvey (1989) writes that "In philosophy, the intermingling of a revived American pragmatism with the post-Marxist and poststructuralist wave that struck Paris after 1968 produced what Bernstein calls 'a rage against humanism and the Enlightenment legacy.' This spilled over into a vigorous denunciation of abstract reason and a deep aversion to any project that sought universal human emancipation through mobilization of the powers of technology, science, and reason" (p. 41).

In an interview with Gerard Raulet published in 1983, Foucault troubles the use of the terms postmodern and poststructural. He asks, "What are we calling postmodernity? I'm not up to date" (Foucault, 1983, p. 204). After a question by Raulet about modernity, Foucault responds, "I've never clearly understood what was meant in France by the word 'modernity'.... I feel troubled here because I do not grasp clearly what that [modernity] might mean, though the word itself is unimportant; we can always use any arbitrary label. But neither do I grasp the kind of problems intended by this term—or how they would be common to people thought of as being 'post-modern.' While I see clearly that behind what was known as structuralism, there was a certain problem—broadly speaking, that of the subject and the recasting of the subject—I do not understand what kind of problem is common to the people we call post-modern or post-structuralist" (p. 205).

Judith Butler (1992) too worries that very different theories are grouped under the term postmodern, that such carelessness results in "an excuse not to read and not to read closely," and that, as a result, a critic can more easily "dispense with them all at once" (p. 5). She writes, therefore, "I don't know what postmodernism is, but I do have some sense of what it might mean to subject notions of the body and materiality to a deconstructive critique" (p. 17).

[As is evident in the series of quotations in this note, deconstruction is often used in conjunction with both postmodernism and poststructuralism.]

I believe Butler is right in that these terms are used to describe the work of scholars whose work is quite dissimilar and who might refuse the labels. But this sort of collapsing of difference happens over time with any large theoretical framework (e.g., humanism) as those who have *not* read the theories at all or not read them carefully use the terms in an acknowledgment that something different and, perhaps, significant has occurred even if they aren't familiar with it. We are always creating categories—assimilating difference into the same—for convenience's sake, if nothing else, and that is why I find deconstruction useful in that it requires that we persistently critique those categories and keep them in play. Briefly, in my own work, I seem to use *poststructural* in relation to theory and *postmodern* in relation to practices, to space/time, and to aesthetics. I find I am less interested in some "true" meaning of these terms than in how they are taken up and used by different scholars and in the effects of that use.

7.   Deleuze and Guattari's (1980/1987) figurations—the nomad, haecceity, rhizome, schizoanalysis, the middle, deterritorialization, and so forth— many of which can be found in their book, *A Thousand Plateaus: Capitalism and Schizophrenia*, have helped me begin to describe a subject I am and have always been that was simply unintelligible and indescribable before I read their work. The experience of this new subject, quite an overturning in my life, has once again brought home to me the importance of language in the construction of subjectivity since I needed the new language/thought of the figurations for a new subject. Of course, other modes of expression, for example, painting, dance, and drama, enable lines of flight for those less in love with language. Though the new theory of the

subject I was beginning to describe in this study helped me think differently about myself, about time/space, about qualitative inquiry, and so forth, it did not work well with the women of Milton. Foucault's theory of the subject in care of the self was a closer fit with the data, so close, in fact, that I had to consider once again the powerful sedimentary effects of the ancient Greeks' culture on modern Western culture. I also had to consider a dilemma that confronts researchers living and working in one theoretical framework who study people who live and work in another. What are the ethical and political implications of using, say, poststructural theories to inscribe the lives of those who would, if they had the language, describe themselves as humanists? Because of complications such as these, I decided to save the new subject I was beginning to think for myself and not impose it on the women of Milton. I continue to think this elusive subject and to read and write around it, but thinking, reading, and writing will never be enough because it was the juxtaposition of the *figurations* of Deleuze and Guattari and the material conditions of *this particular study* that produced this subject who mostly rests now. To find language to describe this subject, I will have to *really be* her again, intensely and perilously, perhaps in the deterritorialized field(s) of another worrisome ethnography. No doubt the conjunction of other reading and other studies can produce different subjects for any of us who can hear them.

8. In fact, to date, I have resisted turning my dissertation into a book because I am lost in the "crisis of representation" (Marcus & Fischer, 1986). I have written elsewhere (St.Pierre, 1997c) about my practice of writing around that book rather than writing it. I *do* write at it, worried all the while about the violence of inscribing lives. No doubt something will come to me in the writing—it usually does. Perhaps it is the new subject who will write the book, or write something.

9. Interpretation is not innocent, and we bear the burden of responsibility for the interpretation we produce. Foucault (1971/1984) writes the following about interpretation, "If interpretation were the slow exposure of the meaning hidden in an origin, then only metaphysics could interpret the development of humanity. But if interpretation is the violent or surreptitious appropriation of a system of rules, which in itself has no essential meaning, in order to impose a direction, to bend it to a new will, to force its participation in a different game, and to subject it to secondary rules, then the development of humanity is a series of interpretations" (p. 86). Derrida (1966/1978), too, writes of the danger of interpretation, "There are thus two interpretations of interpretation, of structure, of sign, of play. The one seeks to decipher, dreams of deciphering a truth or an

origin which escapes play and the order of the sign, and which lives the necessity of interpretation as an exile. The other, which is no longer turned toward the origin, affirms play and tries to pass beyond man and humanism, the name of man being the name of that being who, throughout the history of metaphysics or of ontotheology—in other words, throughout his entire history—has dreamed of full presence, the reassuring foundation, the origin and the end of play" (p. 292).

References

Alcoff, L. M. (1991). The problem of speaking for others. *Cultural Critique,* *20(*Winter), 5–32.

Althusser, L. (1971). Ideology and ideological state apparatuses (Notes towards an investigation). In *Lenin and philosophy and other essays* (pp. 127–186). New York: Monthly Review Press.

Augé, M. (1995). *Non-place: Introduction to an anthropology of supermodernity* (J. Howe, Trans.). New York: Verso. (Original work published 1992)

Baudrillard, J. (1993). The precession of simulacra (P. Foss, P. Patton, & P. Beitchman, Trans.). In J. Natoli & L. Hutcheon (Eds.), *A postmodern reader* (pp. 342–375). Albany: State University of New York Press. (Original work published 1983)

Bové, P. A. (1990). Discourse. In F. Lentricchia & T. McLaughlin (Eds.), *Critical terms for literary study* (pp. 50–65). Chicago: University of Chicago Press.

Butler, J. (1990). *Gender trouble: Feminism and the subversion of identity.* New York: Routledge.

Butler, J. (1992). Contingent foundations: Feminism and the question of "postmodernism." In J. Butler & J. W. Scott (Eds.), *Feminists theorize the political* (pp. 3–21). New York: Routledge.

Butler, J. (1995). For a careful reading. In S. Benhabib, J. Butler, D. Cornell, & N. Fraser (Eds.), *Feminist contentions: A philosophical exchange* (pp. 127–143). New York: Routledge.

Butler, J. (1997). *The psychic life of power: Theories in subjection.* Stanford, CA: Stanford University Press.

Clough, P. T. (1992). *The end(s) of ethnography: From realism to social criticism.* Newbury Park, CA: Sage.

Davidson, A. I. (1986). Archaeology, genealogy, ethics. In D. C. Hoy (Ed.), *Foucault: A critical reader* (pp. 221–233). Cambridge, MA: Basil Blackwell.

Davidson, A. I. (1994). Ethics as ascetics: Foucault, the history of ethics, and ancient thought. In J. Goldstein (Ed.), *Foucault and the writing of history* (pp. 63–80). Cambridge, MA: Blackwell.

Deleuze, G. (1988). *Foucault* (S. Hand, Trans.). Minneapolis: University of Minnesota Press. (Original work published 1986)

Deleuze, G. (1994). He stutters. In C. V. Boundas & D. Olkowski (Eds.), *Gilles Deleuze and the theater of philosophy* (pp. 23–29). New York: Routledge. (Original work published 1993)

Deleuze, G. (1995). *Negotiations: 1972–1990.* (M. Joughin, Trans.). New York: Columbia University Press. (Original work published 1990)

Deleuze, G., & Guattari, F. (1987). *A thousand plateaus: Capitalism and schizophrenia.* (B. Massumi, Trans.). Minneapolis: University of Minnesota Press. (Original work published 1980)

Deleuze, G., & Parnet, C. (1987). Many politics. In *Dialogues* (H. Tomlinson & B. Habberjam, Trans.). New York: Columbia University Press. (Original work published 1977)

Derrida, J. (1974). *Of grammatology* (G. C. Spivak, Trans.). Baltimore: The Johns Hopkins University Press. (Original work published 1967)

Derrida, J. (1978). Structure, sign and play in the discourse of the human sciences. In J. Derrida, *Writing and difference* (A. Bass, Trans.) (pp. 278–293). Chicago: University of Chicago Press. (Lecture delivered 1966)

Dreyfus, H. L., & Rabinow, P. (1982). *Michel Foucault: Beyond structuralism and hermeneutics* (2d ed.). Chicago: University of Chicago Press.

Flax, J. (1990). Postmodernism and gender relations in feminist theory. In L. J. Nicholson (Ed.), *Feminism/Postmodernism* (pp. 39–62). New York: Routledge.

Foster, H. (1996). *The return of the real: The avant-garde at the end of the century.* Cambridge, MA: MIT Press.

Foucault, M. (1965). *Madness and civilization: A history of sanity in the age of reason* (R. Howard, Trans.). New York: Vintage Books. (Original work published 1961)

Foucault, M. (1972). *The archaeology of knowledge and the discourse on language* (A. M. Sheridan Smith, Trans.). New York: Pantheon Books. (Original work published 1971)

Foucault, M. (1972). *Power/Knowledge: Selected interviews and other writings, 1972–1977* (C. Gordon, Ed.; C. Gordon, L. Marshall, J. Mepham, K. Soper, Trans.). New York: Pantheon Books.

Foucault, M. (1978). *The history of sexuality. Volume I: An introduction* (R. Hurley, Trans.). New York: Vintage Books. (Original work published 1976)

Foucault, M. (1979). What is an author? In J. V. Harari (Ed.), *Textual strategies: Perspectives in post-structuralist criticism* (pp. 141–160). Ithaca: Cornell University Press. [no translator given]

Foucault, M. (1979). *Discipline and punish: The birth of the prison* (A. Sheridan, Trans.). New York: Vintage Books. (Original work published 1975)

Foucault, M. (1982). The subject and power. In H. L. Dreyfus & P. Rabinow (Eds.), *Michel Foucault: Beyond structuralism and hermeneutics* (2d ed.) (pp. 208–226). Chicago: University of Chicago Press.

Foucault, M. (1983). Structuralism and post-structuralism: An interview with Michel Foucault (G. Raulet, Interviewer; J. Harding, Trans.). *Telos, 55,* 195–211.

Foucault, M. (1984). Nietzsche, genealogy, history. In P. Rabinow (Ed.), *The Foucault reader* (pp. 76–100). New York: Pantheon Books. (Reprinted from *Hommage à Jean Hyppolite*, pp. 145–172, 1971, Paris: Presses Universitaires de France)

Foucault, M. (1984). On the genealogy of ethics: An overview of work in progress. In P. Rabinow (Ed.), *The Foucault reader* (pp. 340–372). New York: Pantheon Books. (Interview conducted 1983)

Foucault, M. (1985a). Final interview: An interview with Michel Foucault (G. Barbadette & A. Scala, Interviewers). *Raritan: A Quarterly Review, 5*(1), 1–13. (Interview conducted 1984)

Foucault, M. (1985b). *The history of sexuality. Volume 2: The use of pleasure* (R. Hurley, Trans.). New York: Vintage Books. (Original work published 1984)

Foucault, M. (1986). *History of sexuality. Volume 3: The care of the self* (R. Hurley, Trans.). New York: Vintage Books. (Original work published 1985)

Foucault, M. (1987). The ethic of care for the self as a practice of freedom. In J. Bernauer & D. Rasmussen (Eds.), *The final Foucault* (R. Fornet-Betancourt, H. Becker, A. Gomez-Müller, Interviewers; J. D. Gauthier, Trans.) (pp. 1–20). Cambridge, MA: The MIT Press. (Interview conducted 1984)

Foucault, M. (1988). Technologies of the self. In L. H. Martin, H. Gutman, & P. H. Hutton (Eds.), *Technologies of the self: A seminar with Michel Foucault* (pp. 16–49). Amherst: University of Massachusetts Press.

Foucault, M. (1988). Truth, power, self: An interview with Michel Foucault (R. Martin, Interviewer). In L. H. Martin, H. Gutman, & P. H. Hutton (Eds.), *Technologies of the self: A seminar with Michel Foucault* (pp. 9–15). Amherst: University of Massachusetts Press. (Interview conducted 1982) [no translator given]

Foucault, M. (1988). An aesthetics of existence (A. Fontana, Interviewer; A. Sheridan, Trans.). In L. D. Kritzman (Ed.), *Politics, philosophy, culture: Interviews and other writings, 1977–1984* (pp. 47–53). New York: Routledge. (Reprinted from *Panorama*, April 25, 1984)

Foucault, M. (1997). *Ethics: Subjectivity and truth.* (P. Rabinow, Ed.; R. Hurley et al., Trans.). New York: The New Press.

Foucault, M. (1997). The ethics of the concern of the self as a practice of freedom (H. Becker, R. Fornet-Betancourt & A. Gomez-Müller, Interviewers; P. Aranov & D. McGrawth, Trans.). In P. Rabinow (Ed.), *Ethics: Subjectivity and truth* (pp. 281–301). New York: The New Press. (Original work published 1984)

Foucault, M. (1998). Nietzsche, Freud, Marx. In *Aesthetics, method, and epistemology* (J. D. Fabion, Ed.; R. Hurley et al., Trans). (pp. 269–278). New York: The New Press. (Original work published 1967)

Game, A. (1991). *Undoing the social: Towards a deconstructive sociology.* Toronto: University of Toronto Press.

Gramsci, A. (1971). *Selections from the prison notebooks* (Q. Hoare & G. Nowell Smith, Eds. & Trans.). New York: International Publishers.

Harvey, D. (1989). *The condition of postmodernity: An inquiry into the origins of cultural change.* Cambridge, MA: Blackwell.

Hassan, I. (1987). *The postmodern turn: Essays in postmodern theory and culture.* Columbus: Ohio State University Press.

Huyssen, A. (1990). Mapping the postmodern. In L. J. Nicholson (Ed.), *Feminism/Postmodernism* (pp. 234–277). New York: Routledge.

Jameson, F. (1984). Foreword. In J. F. Lyotard, *The postmodern condition: A report on knowledge* (pp. vii–xxi). Minneapolis: University of Minnesota Press.

Jameson, F. (1988). Postmodernism and consumer society. In E. A. Kaplan (Ed.), *Postmodernism and its discontents: Theories, practices* (pp. 13–29). New York: Verso.

Kaplan, E. A. (1988). Introduction. In E. A. Kaplan (Ed.), *Postmodernism and its discontents: Theories, practices* (pp. 1–9). New York: Verso.

Kelly, U. A. (1997). *Schooling desire: Literacy, cultural politics, and pedagogy.* New York: Routledge.

Lather, P. (1991). *Getting smart: Feminist research and pedagogy with/in the postmodern.* New York: Routledge.

Lather, P. (1993). Fertile obsession: Validity after poststructuralism. *Sociological Quarterly, 34*(4), 673–693.

Macey, D. (1993). *The lives of Michel Foucault: A biography.* New York: Random House.

Marcus, G. E. & Fischer, M. M. J. (1986). A crisis of representation in the social sciences. In *Anthropology as cultural critique: An experimental moment in the human sciences* (pp. 7–16). Chicago: University of Chicago Press.

Massey, D. (1994). *Space, place, and gender.* Minneapolis: University of Minnesota Press.

Massumi, B. (1992). *A user's guide to capitalism and schizophrenia: Deviations from Deleuze and Guattari.* Cambridge, MA: MIT Press.

Miller, J. (1993). *The passion of Michel Foucault.* New York: Doubleday.

Peters, M. (1999). (Posts-) modernism and structuralism: Affinities and theoretical innovations. *Sociological Research Online, 4*(3). www.socresonline.org.uk.

Popkewitz, T. S. (1997). A changing terrain of knowledge and power: A social epistemology of educational research. *Educational Researcher, 26*(9), 18–29.

Pratt, M. B. (1984). Identity: Skin, blood heart. In E. Bulkin, M. B. Pratt, & B. Smith (Eds.), *Yours in struggle: Three feminist perspectives on anti-semitism and racism* (pp. 11–63). Ithaca, NY: Firebrand Books.

Rabinow, P. (1997). Introduction: The history of systems of thought. In P. Rabinow (Ed.), *Ethics: Subjectivity and truth* (pp. xi-xlii). New York: New Press.

Rajchman, J. (1985). *Michel Foucault: The freedom of philosophy.* New York: Columbia University Press.

Rajchman, J. (1987). Postmodernism in a nominalist frame: The emergence and diffusion of a cultural category. *Flash Art, 137* (Nov-Dec), 49–51.

Scheurich, J. J. (1995). A postmodernist critique of research interviewing. *International Journal of Qualitative Studies in Education, 8*(3), 239–252.

Scott, J. W. (1992). Experience. In J. Butler & J. W. Scott (Eds.), *Feminists theorize the political* (pp. 22–40). New York: Routledge.

Serres, M. (1995). *Conversations on science, culture, and time* (with B. Latour; R. Lapidus, Trans.). Ann Arbor: University of Michigan Press. (Original work published 1990)

Spivak, G. C. (1974). Translator's preface. In J. Derrida, *Of Grammatology* (G. C. Spivak, Trans.) (pp. ix-xc). Baltimore: Johns Hopkins University Press.

Spivak, G. C. (1992). Acting bits/Identity talk. *Critical Inquiry, 18*(4), 770–803.

Spivak, G. C. (1993). *Outside in the teaching machine.* New York: Routledge.

Stewart, K. (1988). Nostalgia—a polemic. *Cultural Anthropology: Journal of the Society for Cultural Anthropology, 3*(3), 227–241.

St.Pierre, E. A. (1995). *Arts of existence: The construction of subjectivity in older, white southern women.* Unpublished doctoral dissertation, The Ohio State University, Columbus.

St.Pierre, E. A. (1997a). Methodology in the fold and the irruption of transgressive data. *International Journal of Qualitative Studies in Education, 10*(2), 175–189.

St.Pierre, E. A. (1997b). Nomadic inquiry in the smooth spaces of the field: A preface. *International Journal of Qualitative Studies in Education, 10*(3), 363–383.

St.Pierre, E. A. (1997c). Circling the text: Nomadic writing practices. *Qualitative Inquiry, 3*(4), 403–417.

St.Pierre, E. A. (2000). Poststructural feminism in education: An overview. *International Journal of Qualitative Studies in Education, 13*(5), 477–515.

Trinh, M. H. T. (1989). *Woman, native, other: Writing postcoloniality and feminism.* Bloomington: Indiana University Press.

Van Maanen, J. (1995). An end to innocence: The ethnography of ethnography. In J. Van Maanen (Ed.), *Representation in ethnography* (pp. 1–35). Thousand Oaks, CA: Sage.

Visweswaran, K. (1994). *Fictions of feminist ethnography*. Minneapolis: University of Minnesota Press.

Technologies of the Self in Classrooms Designed as "Learning Environments": (Im)possible Ways of Being in Early Literacy Instruction

Dawnene D. Hammerberg

Introduction

Literacy education at the elementary school level is often built on the assumption that everybody in the classroom is an individual with varying needs, attitudes, abilities, and social backgrounds. The work of contemporary elementary school teachers typically involves daily focused efforts to meet individual needs one-on-one or in small groups (e.g., Clay, 1991a, 1991b; Fountas & Pinnell, 1996; Holdaway, 1979; Routman, 1994; Taberski, 2000). In materials written for teachers about individualized instruction, a primary concern surfaces: What is the rest of the class doing while the teacher is working with just a few? (see, e.g., Cambourne, 2001; Fountas & Pinnell, 1996).

In response to this concern, elementary classrooms are often designed as "learning environments," which are defined as classrooms that are organized and managed for independence by containing centers and various literacy activities to engage the rest of the class (e.g., Fountas & Pinnell, 1996, p. 43). Classrooms designed as learning environments (as opposed to rooms that hold whole classes in rows) operate on a conception of literacy instruction that makes individuals responsible for managing their own behaviors. To engage in the learning environment, then, requires more than a knowledge of literacy skills; it also requires self-regulation through a set of techniques that one uses to be, act, and think appropriately in the learning environment.

Michel Foucault (1988b) refers to such techniques as "technologies of the self." Technologies of the self are those "which permit individuals to effect by their own means or with the help of others a certain number of operations on their own bodies and souls, thoughts, conduct, and way of being, so as to transform themselves in order to attain a certain state of happiness, purity, wisdom, perfection, or immortality" (p. 18). In this chapter, I use Foucault's (1988b, 1990a, 1990b) concept of technologies of the self to analyze what it means to be a literacy learner within the contexts of early literacy pedagogy and elementary school classrooms that are designed as learning environments.

The purpose of my analysis is to disentangle the technologies of the self that are implicit in elementary school learning environments and to show that literacy learning is not only a problem of teaching reading or writing but more significantly, a problem of managing and training technologies of the self. While technologies of the self are techniques of *self*-constitution, they are at one and the same time techniques of administration and regulation (Foucault, 1977; Rose, 1990, 1996). This insight counters much of what is written about "independence" and "thinking for oneself" in the pedagogical literature about early elementary school learning environments.

My methodological approach involves examining four specific techniques that make classrooms function as learning environments and that make selves appear as "independent": (1) the spatial design of the classroom; (2) training for independence in order to use that design; (3) the curriculum content available in the learning environment; and (4) the transference and internalization of classroom design, training, and curriculum into the idea of a "private" or "individualized" self of the child. In the end, I consider these techniques of being and becoming "literacy learners" in the learning environment a function of pedagogical practices and discursive constructions.[1] Or, as Nikolas Rose (1990) puts it: "Thoughts, feelings and actions may appear as the very fabric and constitution of the intimate self, but they are socially organized and managed in minute particulars" (p. 1).

Foucault, Techniques, Technologies, and Studying Learning Environments

In my analysis, "technologies" are understood in Foucault's (1988b) terms: as matrices of practical reason through which human beings organize and develop knowledge about themselves (p. 18). In *Technologies of the Self*, he writes that "[t]he main point is not to accept this knowledge at face value but to analyze these so-called sciences as very specific 'truth games' related to specific techniques that human beings use to understand themselves" (p. 18). As a context, he then names four major types of techniques that human beings use to understand themselves, and he calls them "technologies": technologies of sign systems, technologies of power, technologies of production, and technologies of the self. While Foucault switches between using the term "techniques" and "technologies" in this chapter as well as in other places (e.g., 1988a, p. 146; 1990b, p. 11), I wish to keep the term "technologies" in order to explicate how ways of being individuals and understanding oneself in the classroom extend beyond a handful of "techniques" one can use. "Technologies," as a term, suggests a manner of training and a sense of power. Foucault (1988b) echoes this sentiment by writing that the four major types of technologies are each "associated with a certain type of domination. Each implies certain modes of training and modification of individuals, not only in the obvious sense of acquiring certain skills but also in the sense of acquiring certain attitudes" (p. 18).

While it is clear that Foucault's term "technologies of the self" never appears in educational descriptions of learning environments, the framework of providing individualized instruction (and the corresponding need to keep the rest of the class occupied) makes it necessary for young students to effect by their own means (or with the help of others) a certain number of operations on their own bodies, thoughts, conduct, and ways of being while the teacher is otherwise occupied. And while Foucault (1988b, 1990a, 1990b) didn't have literacy instruction in mind when he used "technologies of the self" to explain the construction of sexuality and the obligation to tell the truth about oneself, the same concept is applicable in the study of early literacy education as a way to understand the construction of an "appropriate learner" in the classroom and the obligation to be self-regulated and independently "on task" within early elementary school literacy pedagogy.

A technology of the self therefore involves a different sense of technology from the Frankfurt school notion of instrumental reason and also a different sense of technology from commonplace notions of inventions, accessories, or appendages. Technologies of the self in the classroom are not consciously created as tools to promote an individual's self-regulation or self-constitution, but instead, technologies of the self as used and understood here are functions of *being* in the learning environment and living in the pedagogy: ways of operating on one's own body and soul, thoughts and conduct, so as to transform oneself into an "appropriate" early literacy learner today within the discourses of early literacy pedagogy.

Invite Them; They Are There:
Classroom Design and Pedagogical Reason

The spatial design of a classroom *as* a learning environment must be understood, first and foremost, as an effect of trends in early literacy pedagogy that call for individualized instruction. Individualized instruction is the cornerstone of contemporary literacy pedagogy and drives instructional techniques such as guided reading (e.g., Clay, 1991a, 1991b; Fountas & Pinnell, 1996; Holdaway, 1979; Routman, 1994), where the teacher works with small groups of two to four students who are reading at similar levels or are practicing similar reading strategies.

Guided reading, as one individualized approach, is intended to be used in early elementary classrooms, such as kindergarten or first grade, and in these situations the demand for the teacher's attention is often quite high. Things come up: how to spell a word, how to tie a shoe, how to keep a noisy pencil quiet. Quite often, it is not an easy challenge, when working with individuals in small guided reading groups, to ensure that the remainder of the class is self-occupied. Fountas and Pinnell (1996) state:

> When initiating guided reading, the first challenge for the teacher is to manage the classroom to be able to work in a focused, uninterrupted way with small clusters of students. A critical question is, While I am working with a group in guided reading, what are the rest of the children doing? (p. 53)

Managing the classroom to provide individualized instruction means establishing a larger classroom framework so that things don't come up while the teacher is working in focused and uninterrupted ways with a few students: no noisy pencils, no untied shoes, no questions about spelling or recess or math. Indeed, the expectation that students will be self-regulated and independent while the teacher is otherwise occupied defines the "nature of effective literacy instruction" in first-grade classrooms (e.g., The National Research Center on English Learning and Achievement,[2] 1998, p. 12; Morrow, Tracey, Woo, & Pressley, 1999).

Fountas and Pinnell (1996) describe a *learning environment that is designed for independence and self-regulation* in this way:

> A classroom organized for literacy learning invites children to use print in purposeful ways: Wherever possible, written language—materials for reading and writing—are incorporated naturally and authentically. Individuals and groups of children are able to interact with the materials independently, regularly freeing the teacher to work with individuals or small groups. The setting is safe and supportive and enables all learners to develop confidence, take risks, learn to work independently, and develop social skills. In short, an

organized and well-designed classroom enables the teacher to observe, support, and meet the learning needs of each child. (p. 43)

Social constructivist psychologies of learning underpin the spatial design of the classroom as an "invitation." Under social constructivist pedagogy, students are seen as independent and active participants in their own learning, and education is largely seen as a social engagement. Students are invited to this social engagement called "literacy education" to construct particular understandings of reading and writing by interacting with others who are at the party.[3]

Classrooms organized as invitations are described as "print rich" and are specifically designed to incorporate materials for reading and writing in ways that are described as "natural."[4] But make no mistake about it: The natural look is planned and timed. There are big books and leveled books,[5] literature and references, posters with directions, and chart pads with poems and songs. There are name charts and word charts, alphabet charts and pocket charts, clipboards, whiteboards, easels, word walls, and organizational bins. Everything has a place and everything is labeled: chart paper, lined paper, post-its, markers, pencils, clock. There are message boards and sign-in sheets for areas of the room relegated to specific activities (or centers): places to buddy read; nooks for writers to get feedback; plastic letters on overhead projectors to make shadows of words on the wall; tables with writing materials, staplers, hole punchers, glitter, whiteout tape, scissors, glue. There are student collections of stories read, class editions of stories written, and the products of shared experiences (like interactive writing) are proudly displayed at eye level for everyone to revisit. Long benches or tables serve as dividers, and other moveable objects make the organization flow. Talking (or whispering) is encouraged if it's about reading or writing or if it's to help each other know what to do.

A classroom such as this, then, "invites" particular ways of being (e.g., regulated, constructive, independent). Since the spatial design of the learning environment is meant to support the type of "happy" education that is seen as social, constructive, and inviting, the technologies implicit within this type of environment enable individuals to effect by their own means (or with the help of others) ways of being "happy," in a "socially constructive" sense. The enactment of this type of "happiness" is encouraged through and takes place in the spatial arrangements of the classroom: the provision of centers, their distribution in space, and the obligations that such a design suggests. As students work and engage with the materials and each other, they are operating on their thoughts and actions to fit themselves into the learning environment as it is arranged in space and in the timing of routines.

Contextualized within the spatial and temporal design of the learning environment, then, are particular expectations of how the environment itself *should* lead to particular effects of learning (e.g., leveled book boxes *should* lead to students finding developmentally appropriate materials, or plastic letters on an overhead projector *should* lead to students making word shadows on the wall).[6] The spatio-temporal design of the learning environment is believed to render certain emotional and cognitive states (e.g., constructive, independent, happy), as the learning environment itself becomes a directive for how to act, think, feel, and be. At the level of spatial design, the possible ways of being an appropriate learner in the classroom are defined paradoxically by a pedagogical package of social constructivism and individualization.

Appropriate Conduct Required: Training for Independence

The appearance of appropriate and independent learning in this environment is practiced in relation to the management strategies of teachers, who themselves are managed by a sense of developmentally appropriate materials and self-monitored proof of learning, the reason of contemporary "best practices." Apparent independence requires students to adopt a series of self-monitoring techniques via teacher-management strategies. Knowing how to keep track of the books you've read independently, how to pick the best leveled book bin independently, and how to get right to listening at the listening center are learned behaviors. They are therefore teacher-monitored and pedagogically organized ways of acting on the self. The student, in other words, only appears as "independent" in light of contemporary pedagogical reason that states, "Don't bother the teacher at this time."[7]

Knowing appropriate ways of not bothering the teacher is such a large part of the *successful* learning environment that explicit training toward self-conduct and body-management is the basic task for the first six weeks of the school year. As a fundamental principle of learning in a learning environment, "powerful demonstrations" are seen as necessary (Fountas & Pinnell, 1996, pp. 43–44). The National Research Center on English Learning and Achievement (1998) overtly states that "[w]hether elementary-level students are self-regulated may depend on what the teacher expects of the students, with self-regulation most likely if those expectations are accompanied by teaching students how to do appropriately matched literacy tasks for themselves and by arranging the room to facilitate such self-regulation (e.g., having bins of leveled books, with the students taught how to decide which bin to choose from)" (p. 2). While techniques of self-regulation are reinforced year-round, and specifically any time new tasks are introduced, the beginning of the school year is the time to slowly (and "powerfully") demonstrate how to use the materials and work areas of the classroom.

The art of living and being in the learning environment is exercised daily and is a work of the self on the self, but it is also the internalized transformation of teaching into self-action.[8] For example, the work board that records where children are expected to be each day in the learning environment is set up early and introduced slowly in terms of the work areas of the room. Routines for knowing when to leave one learning center and move to another are modeled and practiced for weeks at a time. Centers are introduced one by one, routines and expectations are established, and every aspect of conduct is described and played out in minute detail.

A specific instance of the latter occurs around dramatic play centers. If there is a drama center, designed like a dentist's office, the teacher might act out loud (in front of the whole class) how to be a patient in the waiting room by choosing to read a magazine that is there. Later, the teacher might ask the students to think of other kinds of reading or writing that people might do in dentists' offices: taking phone messages at the receptionist's desk, filling out prescriptions, reading a story to comfort a baby doll, looking up numbers in phone books, or sending out appointment notices. In these think-out-loud demonstrations, the teacher is showing how to be and think like a literacy learner in the learning environment. These demonstrations are to be transformed into individual action and independent behavior at a later time, when the teacher is otherwise busy.

As another instance of training for appropriate use of classroom design, Fountas and Pinnell (1996) discuss getting a book from the classroom library:

> [I]n the classroom library, show children how to take out books and how to use them on the rug or at a table. For some groups, you may even want to show them how to turn the pages carefully so that books are not damaged and others can use them. You may want to show them how to share books with a partner so that both can see the pictures. Then, show them how to put away each book in its place. Be sure to notice and praise children's efforts. (p. 62)

The above describes how to teach the routine of getting and using any book in general; imagine the training required to explain the use of leveled book bins. While to an outside observer it may seem that children are "free" to work on a variety of literacy tasks, each engaging in different activities, the technologies available to be happy and free are quite formalized and specific in an attempt to monitor and regulate thinking, acting, and learning when the teacher is not there to direct. Thus, pedagogies rooted in "independent learning" construct a subject whose every tiny action is anticipated, regulated, and made normal before children can be "left on their own" in the learning environment.

These examples indicate that by the time students are ready to engage meaningfully in the classroom as a learning environment, they have heard it all, practiced it all, and enjoyed the printed materials that are up and around the room many times over. Yet, in time, this rigorous training is made invisible, because the system only works if students have made the training "their own" and can maintain themselves "independently." The routines learned through training become technologies of the self that allow individuals to act on themselves (no longer with the help of others) in ways that appear "independent" or "productive."

Self-regulation Toward What?
Curriculum Content and Pedagogies of "Meaningful" Learning

It is important to note that, in research on effective early literacy instruction, as well as in teacher's manuals and teacher resources, any discussion about training for independence in the learning environment is closely associated with a prerequisite that the independent activities are "meaningful" or "authentic" (e.g., Cambourne, 2001; Fountas & Pinnell, 1996, chapter 5; McCarrier, Pinnell, & Fountas, 2000; National Research Center on English Learning and Achievement, 1998). While the purpose of designing a classroom as a learning environment may be based in the pedagogical reason of individualized instruction, the management of the self by the self in the learning environment is meant to be about high academic engagement in "meaningful" activities while the teacher is otherwise occupied. This section therefore considers what the meaning of "meaningful" is in the context of a learning environment rooted in the pedagogical reason of individualized instruction and the cognitive psychologies of developmental learning.

Seeing children as individuals who need instruction focused on internal capacities and differences stems from child-study movements of the late 1800s and consequent psychological theories of learning (see Coles, 1998, pp. 107–110; Kliebard, 1987, pp. 42–51; Popkewitz, 1991, chapters 5–6). In terms of literacy learning, psychological notions hold that reading and writing processes occur "in the head" through the use of a core group of cognitive skills and abilities (e.g., decoding skills, reading strategies, knowledge of story structure, learning behaviors). Instructional approaches that focus on this core group of skills imagine that there is a fixed and decipherable message within the phonological-graphemic code of an alphabetic sign system, promoting the idea that meaning is static and lies primarily at the word level. In cognitive-psychological terms, reading comprehension occurs after readers decode each word and "listen" to the words and messages in their heads (e.g., Adams, 1996; Gough, 1984; McGuiness, 1997). This core group of skills for deciphering a text's meaning is broken down into developmental levels that are used to analyze a student's reading behavior, which is retrospectively taken as evidence of cognition. The assertion of core skills thus becomes a universal standard against which individual capacities and differences may be located, compared, and "fixed."

Recall that "[a] classroom organized for literacy learning invites children to use print in purposeful ways" (Fountas & Pinnell, 1996, p. 43). Here, the meaning of "purposeful" involves the extent to which students feel "invited" to practice the core group of cognitive skills and abilities as they are integrated throughout the centers and activities of the learning environment. The types of learning activities that are available in the learning environment maintain a sense of developmental appropriateness (e.g., leveled book bins) and a psychological notion of reading (e.g., combining letters to form words on the overhead projector). In order for print to be used in purposeful ways, a certain way of valuing, liking, and using print is believed to be located in the head, residing in "memory," and "seen" as evidence of purposeful cognition. Psychologized curricular goals, then, appear in the handling and judgment of bodies, souls, thoughts, conduct, and ways of being.

This psychological and developmental notion of reading as an in-the-head process (as opposed to a social process, for example) plays out in the purportedly social and constructive atmosphere of the learning environment. As a case in point, Cambourne's (2001) article entitled "What Do I Do with the Rest of the Class?" sets forth three criteria for determining whether a teaching-learning activity in the learning environment has been successful: (1) engagement in activity; (2) internalization and transfer (e.g., of a skill or concept); and (3) promotion of collaborative, independent, and interdependent learning (pp. 124–126). In other words, the success of a teaching-learning activity is attached to how well the students can independently (yet collaboratively) become engaged enough to internalize an early literacy skill or concept. Here, it becomes less about the social "nature" of the environment, and more about what cognitive skills social constructivism can yield.

The rules and order of the "natural" learning environment thus take up the rules and order of alphabetic print (e.g., static notions of text and purposes for reading), which construct the appropriate desires, attitudes, and social engagements of individuals themselves. To govern one's self within this framework calls for thoughts, conducts, and ways of being that make the child appear "as literate," or, at least, as "becoming literate," in a strictly individualized, psychological, phonics-driven sense. This effectively links ways of being a "good literacy learner" to knowledge about letters, words, directionality, and other concepts about print. Thus, while students are trained to act on their own in their own literacy development, the modification and training of individuals are afforded through the regulatory effects of psychologized curricular content in basic literacy instruction.[9]

Further, while the learning environment is meant to invite collaborative and social constructions of "meaningful" literacy engagements, the notion of "meaningful" is delimited to psychologized notions of curriculum content as *staggered* or *tiered*. In other words, social constructivist pedagogy falls short of socially constructing just anything at any time. To be truly "meaningful" in the context of early literacy pedagogy, a child's thoughts and actions must be engaged at an appropriate level, and working with a vision of literacy as a psychological, in-the-head, staggered, decoding, and print-bound process.

As we have seen, for the classroom to even *be* a learning environment, as opposed to a room that holds a class, students need to be clued in to how to use the areas of the room through training. It is important to emphasize therefore, that the meaningfulness of the task is not necessarily determined by the student but instead, by the pedagogical reason that exists in the design of literacy activities. Through the reason of pedagogy, a literacy activity or task is believed to be "meaningful" when students are engaged in learning opportunities described as "authentic." Tasks are believed to be "authentic" if they closely match a "real" reading or writing experience. Playing in the pretend dentist's office is "authentic" to the extent that the literacy activities one engages in while there are close to real reading or writing activities that might actually occur in a real dentist's office. And pushing plastic letters around on overhead projectors is "meaningful" to the extent that it mimics "real" decoding. It turns out to be all good and authentic when "meaningfulness" meshes with psychological theories of learning: After all, tasks that are found nowhere else but in the learning environment can look "authentically meaningful" in a classroom filled with students in perceived need of individualized, cognitively based, leveled instruction.

However, activities such as appropriately reading in a dentist's office, or choosing the right book bin, or planning what you should do next based on the organizational chart on the wall would be artificial (i.e., not "authentic") on the playground or in the after-school lives of many children. A kind of academic language, artificial anywhere else, is a part of the fabric of the learning environment, no matter how "meaningfully authentic" the tasks aim to be. For example, if a teacher asks what is going on in the "dentist's office," any metacognitive confessions express self-knowledge about the academic "authenticity" at hand. Thus, the supposedly "authentic" social construction of knowledge in the learning environment can be somewhat distinct from the cultural practices (texts, figures of speech, movements, syntax, knowledge) of the very individuals for whom we want to design "authenticity." While the pedagogical drive is toward authentic and meaningful experiences, the tasks are only "authentic" in the social and cultural contexts of the learning environment.

In sum, in determining what is "meaningful" and "authentic" in the learning environment, we can see how the thoughts, feelings, and actions attributed to individuals are socially prepared toward particular curriculum content.[10] This involves an a priori understanding that personal mental attributes "reside" in each individual's mind, which separates the self from the sociocultural contexts of learning, at the same moment when the learning environment is described as socially constructive.

Attitudinal Adjustments: The Transference and Internalization of Classroom Design, Training, and Curriculum

On one level, the classroom setting and routines are meant to encourage children to learn a specific academic content by engaging meaningfully with each other and with the environment. An underlying (though not necessarily secondary) purpose is to enable individuals and groups of students to work together without conflict. Here, the techniques individuals use to work together without conflict appear as characteristics of the individual, instead of contingent upon a framework of pedagogical reason, the minute particulars of training, and the contexts of being in the learning environment. In this section, I turn to the ways in which mechanisms of self-control, an effect of classroom management strategies and curriculum content, are spoken and internalized in terms of the individual, not in terms of the entire learning environment and early literacy pedagogy. How is it possible, I ask, that techniques of pedagogical reason and carefully orchestrated operations of entire learning environments get transformed into personal descriptors of the individual's ability and attitude?

The above analysis has indicated how, beyond merely "inviting" children to engage in "meaningful" literacy activities, the organization of the classroom with all of its print-rich materials is meant to modify students' attitudes so that they may work in self-motivated, independent, peaceful, happy ways. Indeed, disciplinary issues can be a detriment if teachers are trying to work in focused and uninterrupted ways with a small portion of the class, and, as current literature suggests, fewer disciplinary problems are attributed to good classroom management strategies. For example, the study put out by the National Research Center on English Learning and Achievement (1998) informs us that "the teachers with the most engaged and best performing students were superb classroom managers, with the result that there were few disciplinary encounters because the students were so engaged with academics" (p. 2). The goal for the "superb classroom manager," then, is to establish a classroom environment where the child has little room to be a discipline problem because he or she is so engaged with academics at all times.

Before teachers, as superb classroom managers, can proactively curb possible discipline problems, individuals with personalities and attitudes have to be identified and defined, and this act constitutes a fundamental principle of learning environments. In terms of early literacy pedagogy, the "discovery" of what kind of self each person *is* necessarily precedes knowing how to care for each individual. Against an invisible backdrop of training, classroom management techniques, and curricular content, culturally constituted selves are thought to stand out as "individuals."

The expectation that attitudes and personalities come into the classroom almost already formed drives contemporary notions of how to care for the child in the learning environment. Contemporary psychological notions of individuality make attitude, self-motivation, self-discipline, and positive self-images a part of an individual's personality. This type of belief emphasizes individual freedom and stems from Enlightenment philosophies where individuals are viewed as self-sufficient beings (see Hacking, 1999, pp. 14–16). It is as if first there are individual "selves," and then they are assembled and managed in learning environments.

Popkewitz (1998) notes that there are two senses of management: "teaching-as-management, which focuses on the organization of lessons and classroom behavior, and teaching as managing the personality, attitudes, and beliefs of individuals, which forms part of the grid of 'reason' of the teacher" (p. 66). This distinction is important because the procedural concerns about classroom management are more than a concern over providing time for guided reading groups or providing an invitation to engage in "meaningful" academic reading and writing tasks. Classroom management today also has to do with the acknowledgment that students come to school with various personalities and attitudes, some of which might need to be curbed.

There may be and often are children who resist the learning environment as it stands: those who do not think the learning environment is too terribly inviting. There may be and often are children who don't accept plastic letters on overhead projectors as invitations to make word shadows on the wall but instead feel invited to throw them (problem of discipline) or aimlessly push them around (problem of meaningfulness). But the proactive teacher, through training, demonstrates all the intricacies of being a self-regulated *learner* with this tool. The teacher asks students to think of words they know to make with the letters, points out where in the room one could look to find words to make, shows what fun it is to see shadows of words on the wall, demonstrates how to record a list of all words made, and has students come up to practice and think out loud. At various times the teacher might even model being a disruptive student, as a demonstration of how *not* to be at the overhead—a training in self-discipline for the times when the teacher is not there to control.

The thinking out loud and practicing and training of how to be at the overhead all take place, at first, in the context of a large group experience, and it may be practiced for weeks as a part of a morning routine. As a matter of self-constitution, however, the rigorous training disappears at the moment when a student is (or is not) independently learning with this tool. At this moment, the action (no matter the training) is believed to be transferred to the mind and personality of the student as a seemingly free agent holding plastic letters.

The transformation of a teacher's demonstrations into an individual's actions in the learning environment is not too far from Stoic technologies of the self (Foucault, 1988b), whereby individuals transformed the truths of teaching into action. Today, however, students demonstrate whether they have internalized the truths of teaching by explaining themselves (not Stoic), as well as through their actions. For example, at the end of the day, the teacher might ask the students to tell what they did during "center time" or write what they did in their journals. Access to the "reality" of what students know is characterized by the accessible information gleaned by teachers (e.g., how students are behaving in the learning environment, whether they are self-selecting appropriately leveled books), and this is evidenced through what children do in action and what they confess. This access into the "reality" of what a self knows is revealed day after day in ways that "show" that the individual has internalized the demonstrations of how to be in the learning environment, an enactment of specific technologies of the self.

If the learning environment and the training have been done "correctly," then the goal of providing an academically engaging environment becomes transferred to the self-management of individuals. Superb classroom management, then, is not only about the organization of the room and the establishment of routines but also about the management of perceived motivations, attitudes, and behaviors. The two senses of management—the establishment of routines in a structured environment and the management of personalities within that environment—collapse into one under current belief systems where individuality is considered a matter of personal motivation and attitude toward the structured routines.

Under psychological notions of learning, the individual is made and defined in the context of the environment: responsible, motivated, reliable or efficient instead of lazy, goofy, troubled, or distracted. Any of these traits, among many others, become combined into personal descriptors that reach into hearts and souls, impressing upon the future well-beings of individual selves, transforming lives, feelings, hopes, and desires. A particularized sense of self is thus made manifest through a narrow range of descriptors built around management routines, curriculum content, and idealized notions of attitudinal adjustments.

The point is that since the learning environment "invites" a particular set of technologies of the self, and since these technologies are then considered to be transferred into the "heads" of individuals through the pedagogy and the training, it becomes a problem of the student, not the training nor the demands of a socially constructivist learning environment, if the student does not operate the appropriate mechanisms for self-conduct. Whatever an individual's heart might desire is therefore contextualized by the conventions and curriculum of the classroom, as selves are formed and individuals are defined as having specific potentials and/or needs. Individuals who learn to align themselves with the conventions of the classroom attain a certain state of happiness, purity, or wisdom (in terms of Foucault's [1988b] definition of technologies of the self, p. 18). They do not get in trouble; they learn what they're supposed to learn; they're likely to get nice feedback, and most importantly, they show themselves in positive lights that shine into their futures. But individuals who resist the conventions of the classroom appear as having further "needs" to be met. In this way, if the individual is *not* using the well-appointed, print-rich classroom in the intended ways, it is not a problem of the classroom, not a problem of the pedagogy, not a problem of the curriculum content, not a problem of the training, not a problem of the meaninglessness of the task, but a problem of the individual (Popkewitz, 1998, p. 65).

The effect of attaching "needs" and "potential" to the individual is that technologies of the self in early elementary school learning environments appear as though they are disconnected from the sociohistorical contexts in which they are formed and practiced. Yet if there are social, cultural, or political effects of understanding technologies of the self as contextualized in the learning environment and contingent upon the reason of pedagogy, it is to acknowledge that an individual's attitude, needs, potentials, and sense of self are the transference and internali-zation of classroom design, training, and curriculum.

Conclusion: (Im)possible Ways of Being
in the Classroom as a Learning Environment

For Foucault, technologies of the self was a useful theoretical concept to explain the construction of sexuality and the obligation to tell the truth about oneself (Foucault, 1988b, pp. 16–17; see also Foucault, 1990a, 1990b). In "Technologies of the Self" (1988b), he sketched out shifts in the development of the hermeneutics of the self in Greco-Roman philosophy and in the Christian spirituality of the first centuries. In his work, he found the intelligibility of a decentered self located in the structure and systems of discourses/practices.

In this chapter, we too have found intelligibility of what it means to be a young child in the learning environment by decentering the child and locating the self instead within the structure and systems of early literacy pedagogy and corresponding practices of learning environments. In this concluding section, I will first highlight what it means to be a young child within the structure and systems of early literacy discourses/practices, and then I will move our discussion to possible implications and further questions in terms of the immediacy of our teaching practices.[11]

I'd like to make perfectly clear that my purpose throughout this analysis has not been to annihilate learning environments or to call pedagogies that require a sense of self-regulated independence necessarily "bad." Instead, my intent has been to denaturalize how students appear as selves in the learning environment and to identify how the reason of pedagogy implicit in the learning environment *makes* individuals into particular kinds of selves. It is nothing new that institutionalized notions of "good literacy learning" determine the practices of children in schools.[12] However, it is something new to denaturalize our reasoning in order to become aware of the constraints of our pedagogy so that we may consider effects and alternatives from within those constraints.

In order to denaturalize our reasoning and articulate constraints, to be a young child within the structures and systems of the learning environment means the following in terms of self-constitution:

1. A classroom "designed for independence" is a function of trends in early literacy pedagogy that call for individualized instruction. Therefore, the constitution of oneself as "independent" must be understood in relation to contemporary pedagogical reason that requires a teacher to work with small groups.

2. Knowing how to be independent or self-regulated does not come from "within"; it is carefully trained and managed. Therefore, the constitution of oneself as a "literacy learner" must be understood as the transference and internalization of training.

3. The training of independence is closely related to leveled curricular outcomes and a sense of what is "meaningful" in terms of cognitive, psychological goals. The types of tasks (print-based) that are embedded in a "print-rich" learning environment continually define, construct, and recirculate notions of "potential" and "success" as attached to the individual's "mind" and "abilities," viewed as separate from the social contexts of the learning environment. Therefore, the constitution of oneself as a "good literacy learner" becomes delimited by psychological, in-the-head literacy processes, even as the learning environment portrays a sense of socially constructive learning.

4. The techniques used to govern oneself in the learning environment are internalized in such a way that they are described as a part of a private self, as opposed to a part of the system. However, the constitution of one's seemingly personal thoughts, feelings, attitudes, and actions must be understood as socially prepared and organized. Therefore, we should be cautious of assigning personal descriptors of appropriate attitude and abilities to a child's self, when they are more accurately descriptors of what it means to be an "appropriate learner" in a fabricated learning environment and early literacy pedagogy.

5. While examples of the normalization that Foucault (1977) offers in *Discipline and Punish* are not difficult to find in education, the kinds of normalization that occur in the learning environment disappear into the very centers and activities and become ways of appearing "independent" and "productive" as a matter of self-constitution. When the making of the self as a literacy learner is organized and managed in minute particulars, and when, simultaneously, that organization disappears, as an individual's thoughts, feelings, and actions are stripped of the sociohistorical context and attached solely to the individual's head and attitude, then the construction of inner control (e.g., Clay, 1991a) becomes dangerously invisible. Judgments about a child's private self become closely tied to the normalizing forces of early literacy pedagogy and curricular content based in cognitive psychology that is rarely questioned for its sociohistorical specificities.

In terms of the immediacy of teaching practice, some very real questions entangled in sociohistorical specificities might occur. For example: What are the unintended effects (today) of designing classrooms as learning environments? How does the pedagogical reason implicit in learning environments operate on selves in ways that run counter to the theoretical underpinnings of contemporary early literacy pedagogy? And, what does it mean in terms of self-constitution when dispersed features of the learning environment are attributed to the self?

We can see, as we think about questions like these (and you might have others), that the process of self-constitution in elementary learning environments is wrapped in pedagogies that make an individual into an object of case study in terms of psychological norms.[13] This is an unintended effect for a social constructivist pedagogy that subscribes to self-reflection and shared connections in the social construction of knowledge. And we can see that techniques for operating on the self in ways that appear independent, authentic, or meaningful are, instead, rigorously trained and curricular. This runs counter to the theoretical underpinnings of early literacy pedagogy, which demands authenticity and meaningfulness in task as well as an appeal toward "independence" and "thinking for oneself." And in terms of self-constitution, we can see that, despite appearances to the contrary, personal characteristics of individuals are not "of" the individual but are instead defined and formed in terms of an entire pedagogical package. This means that the hearts, souls, and futures of individuals rest within the contexts and permissions of learning environments as opposed to resting "within" the individual.

Knowing all of this, even from within the constraints of current pedagogical reason, we might consider the possibility that there are other ways of being, doing, and living in classrooms designed as learning environments. If we know that technologies of the self are what we do to be and live in the learning environment, we might historicize ourselves within the same model, and take responsibility for the learning contexts that make certain ways of being possible and impossible. We might become more cautious about attributing the dispersed features of the pedagogy, as articulated throughout the learning environment, onto an individual's sense of self. Or we might subscribe to a different ethics of self-constitution that would make leveled book bins and plastic letters on overhead projectors seem strange. An important thing to note, as we consider the immediacy of teaching practice, is that particular brands of technologies of the self do not exist a priori to the contexts and permissions of a particular historical-social environment.

Dangerous coagulations, you might say. So true. But if the uses of Foucault in the study of education can assist us in understanding the (self-)constitution of individuals in the classroom, perhaps we can begin by acknowledging that literacy learning is not only a problem of teaching reading but also a problem of technologies of the self. This means realizing that *how* we regulate and *how* we discipline permit individuals to effect by their own means (or with the help of others) certain techniques of being, certain technologies of the self. Possible and impossible ways of being in a learning environment, then, become a matter of using this knowledge tactically to (re)define options, pedagogically and socially.

Endnotes

1. The discourses and contexts of early literacy pedagogy, including the idea of a "learning environment," produce the very idea of "literacy learner" (as opposed to student or pupil), thus constituting its objects as subjects in the making. Accordingly, far from existential or phenomenological notions of "Being," I view the discourse and contexts of early literacy pedagogy as constitutive of the possible and impossible "ways of being" in the learning environment.

2. The authors of this CELA report include Michael Pressley, Richard Allington, Lesley Morrow, Kim Baker, Eileen Nelson, Ruth Wharton-McDonald, Cathy Collins Block, Diane Tracey, Gregory Brooks, John Cronin, and Deborah Woo [Online]. Available: http://cela.albany.edu/1stgradelit/literacy.html#publish [February 26, 1999].

3. See the underlying theories of classroom learning environments as described by Fountas & Pinnell, 1996, pp. 43–44.

4. For non-exhaustive options of activities and materials that might be found in a "print-rich" learning environment, see e.g., Calkins (1983, 1994), Cox (1999), Fountas & Pinnell (1996, pp. 45–46), Morrow (1988), Routman (1994, chapter 15).

5. Leveled books are instructional texts that are organized by "developmental" reading levels, so that teachers may select "just right" books for the reading abilities of their students (see, e.g., Pinnell & Fountas, 1999).

6. We should note that any literacy pedagogy produces a sense of what should happen when confronted with a particular task. For example, for students living at the end of the 1800s in the United States, standing with your toes on a line instigated a form of recitation literacy in which students practiced loosening and wagging their tongues in unison (Myers, 1996, pp. 64–65; Rice, 1893, pp. 176–177). The difference, however, is that in contemporary situations, the context of the learning environment dictates what should happen even if the teacher is occupied elsewhere, as opposed to a teacher standing in front and overtly monitoring every move (or tongue-wagging, as the case may be).

7. Indeed, "independence" within a different pedagogical reason is not always a valued trait and therefore not trained (e.g., within the pedagogical reason

of cultural unity and the erasure of dialects in the 1800s in the United States, whole-group recitation of the Bible and oral language exercises were the modus operandi of literacy instruction, and "independence" in these activities was not appreciated).

8. Foucault (1997) writes that "[n]o technique, no professional skill can be acquired without exercise; nor can one learn the art of living, the techne tou biou, without an askesis that must be understood as a training of the self by the self" (p. 235). Askesis, as the rigorous training of the self by the self (through exercise and the transformation of teaching), functions similarly in the rigorous training of how to be a learner in the learning environment.

9. For examples of basic literacy instruction, see the Committee on the Prevention of Reading Difficulties in Young Children (1998).

10. We should fully appreciate, however, that psychological notions of literacy, including an understanding of the self as a collection of cognitive skills, are quite different from other notions (past and present) of appropriate literacy instruction. A different curricular content or pedagogy would produce a different sense of self. For example, sociocultural approaches to language and literacy (e.g., Erickson, 1984; Ferdman, 1991; Gee, 1992; Pérez, 1998) more closely connect literacy acts to cultural contexts, social practices, and issues of power (e.g., Gee, 1996, chapter 3). From a sociocultural perspective, "literacy" is more than a collection of cognitive skills, because there is believed to be a social dimension to meaning making (Green & Dixon, 1996, p. 292), which involves multiple literacies (Scribner & Cole, 1981; Street, 1984) that change based on specific situations, purposes, audiences, and texts (Cazden, 1988; Cook-Gumperz, 1986; Gee, 1992; Heath, 1983; Pérez, 1998; Street, 1984). The thoughts, feelings, and actions of individuals socially prepared for "multiple literacies" might entail a different sense of self from psychological notions of literacy (e.g., an obligatory acknowledgment of the identity resources, knowledge resources, cultural practices, and contextualized purposes required when constructing meaning).

11. While there is sometimes a tendency in this line of research to ban thinking about the immediacy of practice and while some readings of Foucault make resistance look futile (Mayo, 2000; Muckelbauer, 2000), it is, for me, an unacceptable conclusion to end this analysis without going at least some length to consider implications. What does it mean, in terms of teaching practice, to acknowledge that an individual's needs and potentials are the

transference of classroom design, training, and curriculum? What does it mean to understand that technologies of the self are what we do to be and live in the learning environment?

12. For a portrait of the ways in which contingent and historical notions of literacy have determined what children do in schools, see Myers (1996).

13. From this we can see that current processes and models available for self-constitution in the learning environment are quite different from a search for an ethics of self-constitution or the project of "ethical work (travail éthique)," which is to historicize one's connected position to the work "that one performs on oneself, not only in order to bring one's conduct into compliance with a given rule but to attempt to transform oneself into the ethical subject of one's behavior" (Foucault, 1990b, p. 27; see also Foucault, 1984; Dreyfus & Rabinow, 1986; Poster, 1989, chapter 3). For individuals to make such a shift within the context of learning environments would take structures and systems of discourses/practices that would allow for a particular kind of work by the self on the self in ways that would encourage an ethics of self-constitution and historicize one's connected position vis-à-vis those very technologies of the self.

References

Adams, M. J. (1996). *Beginning to read: Thinking and learning about print.* Cambridge, MA: MIT Press.

Calkins, L. M. (1983). *Lessons from a child: On the teaching and learning of writing.* Exeter, NH: Heinemann Educational Books.

Calkins, L. M. (1994). *The art of teaching writing* (New ed.). Portsmouth, NH: Heinemann.

Cambourne, B. (2001). What do I do with the rest of the class?: The nature of teaching-learning activities. *Language Arts, 79,* (2), 124–135.

Cazden, C. B. (1988). *Classroom discourse: The language of teaching and learning.* Portsmouth, NH: Heinemann.

Clay, M. (1991a). *Becoming literate: The construction of inner control.* Portsmouth, NH: Heinemann.

Clay, M. (1991b). Introducing a new storybook to young readers. *Reading Teacher, 45,* 263–273.

Coles, G. (1998). *Reading lessons: The debate over literacy.* New York: Hill and Wang.

Committee on the Prevention of Reading Difficulties in Young Children. (1998). *Preventing reading difficulties in young children.* Washington, DC: National Academy Press, U.S. Dept. of Education, Office of Educational Research and Improvement, Educational Resources Information Center.

Cook-Gumperz, J. (Ed.). (1986). *The social construction of literacy.* Cambridge, England: Cambridge University Press.

Cox, C. (1999). *Teaching language arts: A student- and response-centered classroom* (3rd ed.). Boston: Allyn and Bacon.

Dreyfus, H., & Rabinow, P. (1986). What is maturity? In D. Hoy (Ed.), *Foucault: A critical reader.* New York: Blackwell.

Erickson, F. (1984). School literacy, reasoning, and civility: An anthropologist's perspective. *Review of Educational Research, 54,* 525–545.

Ferdman, B. M. (1991). Literacy and cultural identity. In M. Minami & B. P. Kennedy (Eds.), *Language issues in literacy and bilingual/multicultural classrooms* (pp. 347–390). Cambridge, MA: Harvard University Press.

Foucault, M. (1977). *Discipline and punish: The birth of the prison.* New York: Pantheon.

Foucault, M. (1984). What is enlightenment? In P. Rabinow (Ed.), *The Foucault reader.* New York: Pantheon.

Foucault, M. (1988a). The political technologies of individuals. In L. H. Martin, H. Gutman, & P. H. Hutton (Eds.), *Technologies of the self: A seminar with Michel Foucault* (pp. 145–162). Amherst: University of Massachusetts Press.

Foucault, M. (1988b). Technologies of the self. In L. H. Martin, H. Gutman, & P. H. Hutton (Eds.), *Technologies of the self: A seminar with Michel Foucault* (pp. 16–49). Amherst: University of Massachusetts Press.

Foucault, M. (1990a). *The history of sexuality, volume 1: An introduction.* New York: Vintage.

Foucault, M. (1990b). *The history of sexuality, volume 2: The use of pleasure.* New York: Vintage.

Foucault, M. (1997). Writing the self. In A. I. Davidson (Ed.), *Foucault and his interlocutors* (pp. 234–247). Chicago: University of Chicago Press.

Fountas, I., & Pinnell, G. S. (1996). *Guided reading: Good first teaching for all children.* Portsmouth, NH: Heinemann.

Gee, J. P. (1992). Socio-cultural approaches to literacy (literacies). *Annual Review of Applied Linguistics, 12,* 31–48.

Gee, J. P. (1996*). Social linguistics and literacies: Ideology in discourses.* Bristol, PA: Taylor & Francis.

Gough, P. B. (1984). Word recognition. In P. D. Pearson (Ed.), *Handbook of reading research* (pp. 225–254). New York: Longman.

Green, J., & Dixon, C. (1996). Language of literacy dialogues: Facing the future or reproducing the past. *Journal of Literacy Research, 28,* 290–301.

Hacking, I. (1999). *The social construction of what?* Cambridge: Harvard University Press.

Heath, S. (1983). *Ways with words.* New York: Cambridge University Press.

Holdaway, D. (1979). *The foundations of literacy.* Sydney, Australia: Ashton Scholastic.

Kliebard, H. M. (1987). *The struggle for the American curriculum: 1893–1958.* New York: Routledge.

Mayo, C. (2000). The uses of Foucault. *Educational Theory, 50,* (1), 103–116.

McCarrier, A., Pinnell, G. S., & Fountas, I. C. (2000). *Interactive writing: How language and literacy come together, K-2.* Portsmouth, NH: Heinemann.

McGuiness, D. (1997). *Why our children can't read and what we can do about it: A scientific revolution in reading.* New York: Simon & Schuster.

Morrow, L. M. (1988). Young children's responses to one-to-one story readings in school settings. *Reading Research Quarterly, 23,* 89–107.

Morrow, L. M., Tracey, D., Woo, D., & Pressley, M. (1999). Characteristics of exemplary first-grade literacy instruction. *Reading Teacher, 52,* (5), 462–477.

Muckelbauer, J. (2000). On reading differently: Through Foucault's resistance. *College English, 63,* (1), 71–94.

Myers, M. (1996). *Changing our minds: Negotiating English and literacy.* Urbana, IL: National Council of Teachers of English.

National Research Center on English Learning and Achievement (CELA). (1998). The nature of effective first-grade literacy instruction, *Report Series 1107.* Albany, NY: CELA.

Pérez, B. (1998). *Sociocultural contexts of language and literacy.* Mahwah, NJ: Lawrence Erlbaum.

Pinnell, G. S., & Fountas, I. C. (1999). *Matching books to readers: Using leveled books in guided reading, K-3.* Portsmouth, NH: Heinemann.

Popkewitz, T. S. (1991). *A political sociology of educational reform: Power/knowledge in teaching, teacher education, and research.* New York: Teachers College Press.

Popkewitz, T. S. (1998). *Struggling for the soul: The politics of schooling and the construction of the teacher.* New York: Teachers College Press.

Poster, M. (1989). *Critical theory and poststructuralism: In search of a context.* Ithaca, NY: Cornell University Press.

Rice, J. M. (1893). *The public-school system of the United States.* New York: Century.

Rose, N. (1990). *Governing the soul: The shaping of the private self.* New York: Routledge.

Rose, N. (1996). *Inventing our selves: Psychology, power, and personhood.* New York: Cambridge University Press.

Routman, R. (1994). *Invitations: Changing as teachers and learners K-12.* Portsmouth, NH: Heinemann.

Scribner, S., & Cole, M. (1981). *The psychology of literacy.* Cambridge, MA: Harvard University Press.

Street, B. V. (1984). *Literacy in theory and practice.* New York: Cambridge University Press.

Taberski, S. (2000). *On solid ground: Strategies for teaching reading K-3.* Portsmouth, NH: Heinemann.

Everything Is Dangerous: Pastoral Power and University Researchers Conducting Interviews

Cathy A. Toll and Thomas P. Crumpler

As university researchers, we have noble intentions. We interview teachers, both preservice and inservice, in order to help them and to help the profession. We see the research interview as a journey (Kvale, 1996) on which we and the research participants together explore the territory of their work lives. We refer to those being interviewed as "participants," not subjects, because we don't want to act *on* these individuals; rather we want to act *with* them. We create friendly atmospheres in the interviews, because we are concerned that the participants are comfortable and find the experience positive. We smile a lot and murmur encouraging words. Our goal is to make room for participants' voices, to provide insight into the previously unexplored aspects of their lives, in order to improve the lot of educators everywhere. We wish to uncover subjugated knowledges, knowledges of those who have not been seriously listened to in the past, those "located low down on the hierarchy, beneath the required level of cognition or scientificity" (Foucault, 1980c, p. 82).

However, research interviews are dangerous acts. Following Foucault (1983a), we don't intend "dangerous" to necessarily mean "bad"; rather we intend "dangerous" to indicate that interviews have the *potential* to be harmful. For instance, research interviews reflect an attempt for us to "know" another person, to produce truths about them; while it is not inherently dangerous to want to learn more about someone else, there is potential danger in such an endeavor because one risks constructing the other as an object of one's own perceptions. Or, for example, we risk reducing participants to data, and we risk speaking for the participants as we analyze and report on these data. Such research sometimes implies that participants are static and that we can understand them by understanding what they say in one or two interviews. Moreover, despite our best attempts not to generalize, all too often we hint that our conclusions about interview participants apply to other preservice or inservice teachers like them.

It troubles us to consider our research interviews as dangerous, given our good intentions. Therefore, we seek further insight regarding the apparent contradiction between wanting to do good and engaging in an activity that might move from the dangerous to the bad or harmful. Foucault's (1983b) notion of pastoral power assists us in this work because it describes just such acts, done in order to help but nonetheless involving engagement with discourses that are always dangerous and that potentially may also be bad.

Foucault described pastoral power as historically exemplified in the activities of Christian clerics, where the exercise of power takes place through caring for others. It is now exemplified in the activities of welfare states, such as in the work of social security agencies, the medical establishment, and police forces. Pastoral power can be identified when the following ensemble of characteristic practices are present:

1. Salvation: When there is a focus on saving the individual. (Historically, this focus was on the individual's soul; in the present, it is on the individual's physical and emotional well-being.)

2. Self-sacrifice: Where "expert" subjects are willing to sacrifice themselves for those being cared for.

3. Attention to the Individual: Where individuals as well as populations are deemed as in need of looking after.

4. Knowing Minds and Souls: Where experts seek to understand others' minds and souls and have access to their innermost thoughts and secrets. (Foucault, 1983b)

We will examine two research projects that featured interviews in order to illustrate moments when our efforts to be good and kind interviewers, for the good of the teachers we interview, have perhaps had unintended consequences. Our specific examples demonstrate how the interview process is indicative of the operation and complexities of pastoral power. In the concluding section, we consider the implications of these insights, whether the "dangerous" has become the "bad" in regard to the interview process, and suggest some approaches for rethinking the place, role, and effects of the research interview.

Two Research Studies

One of the studies we examined was conducted by Tom in order to investigate teachers' use of technologically enhanced classrooms. Tom interviewed three preservice teachers, all female, who were undergraduate interns in a yearlong Professional Development School placement. The school was in a small city in Illinois. Tom's goal was to learn these teachers' views of educational technology, specifically computers. He wished to understand their classroom experiences in using such technology and how they might transfer knowledge about technology to instructional practice.

The other study was conducted by Cathy, in order to investigate the development of critical educators' stances.[1] She interviewed fourteen teachers, five male, nine female, with a wide variety of experiences in schools. All participants taught in an urban area, and all were connected to some extent to *Rethinking Schools*, a newspaper that advocates social justice and equity through the alteration of teaching practices, curricula, school structures, and education policy. Cathy's goal was to learn how these critical educators came to their practices and what sustained them in a time when standards and testing were forcing many educators to reprioritize their goals.

Pastoral Power in Action

The operation of pastoral power as characterized by Foucault and delineated above is evident throughout these interviews. Discourses of salvation, self-sacrifice, attention to the individual, and knowing minds and souls can be identified, converging to indicate how the practices characteristic of pastoral power shape subject positions as well as the kinds of relations and interactions they can have with each other. For instance, when Tom began one interview, he was careful to explain the process carefully and to ask the participant if it was okay with her:

> Dr. C: I'm sitting here with Cindy, and we're going to finish our interview for the [school district] research project. And Cindy, I'm going to ask you some questions and tape record to make a copy of these responses. I'll transcribe them so that your identity is not known, is this okay?

> Cindy: Yes.

Dr. C: And once I begin to write about you, I'll give you your choice: If
           you want me to use your name, I will. If you want to make up
           another name for yourself, we can do that, too. It depends on
           how you feel, some people feel—I mean, anonymity is important
           and I want to let you decide.

We find several interesting aspects to this segment, which
demonstrates how a discourse of care is imbricated in the construction of
subject positions. The speakers' labels are notable because Tom was
given a title, "Dr. C," whereas Cindy was just that, a first name. In
addition, Tom told Cindy that he would give her a choice regarding
whether he would use her real name in writing about the project, but then
he told her anonymity is important. Tom appeared to be giving a choice
while also indicating the "best" choice for Cindy to make—because he
cares about her, of course, and wants to protect her. In this way, Tom and
Cindy's subject positions are established in a pattern of tutelage and
redemption: he as the caring "pastor," Cindy as the recipient of his
concern.

Salvation. In Cathy's project, the operation of pastoral power is also
evidenced in ministering to the well-being of interview participants. In
this case, it was an interview with a teacher early in her career. That
teacher talked of the struggle in preparing to move to a new school but
also her hope that she will find like-minded colleagues from whom she'll
learn. Cathy strived to build the self-esteem of this teacher—in other
words, to provide a bit of salvation—by assuring her that others would
learn from her, the newer teacher, as well.

T: But it's been hard. It's been hard to even try to think about, I still
           have to pack up my room (laughs). But also to take, I have kind
           of taken some solace in saying, well, I know that there are other
           teachers in this [new] building who feel the way I feel, so I don't
           have to feel like this is all on my own shoulders. You know, like
           I do now. There are other teachers who want this. And, and
           that's exciting, you know, that I'll be in a building with teachers
           who think that way.

C: Yeah, I interviewed two of them today, right before you. And
           they'll learn from you as well.

Although Foucault's description of pastoral power (1983b) can at
times convey the sense that it is the member of the flock (in this case, the
interviewee) whose salvation is being attempted, one could argue that
pastoral power operates in a way that enables both shepherd and
shepherded to appear saved. In the example above, Cathy experiences the

"salvation" of being a reassuring mentor to the relatively new teacher. She has learned to govern herself and secure her own salvation as "the good researcher" through picking up on the desires of those deemed needy or in need of reassurance.

Self-sacrifice. Just as the cleric is willing to sacrifice herself/himself for the salvation of the flock, we recognize moments in our research interviews when we will give up our own position in order to honor ideas presented by participants. For instance, one interview participant went on at length about matters not pertinent to Cathy's interests, and the interview extended beyond the time Cathy had scheduled for it. But rather than interrupt the speaker or explicitly redirect her, Cathy continued to appear interested and supportive, smiling and responding pleasantly, while attempting redirection in a subtle, inoffensive manner, in order to not to hurt the participant's feelings. This care for the participant led to a much lengthier interview than Cathy imagined and to a much later three-hour drive home.

In a second instance, a participant, in describing his own path to teaching, spoke ill of teacher education programs, which Cathy experienced as a veiled criticism of the kind of work she does as a university professor. However, she bore this hinted-at insult with kindness and patience, as any good pastor would.

> T: And at that time people, teachers I worked with, encouraged me to go back and get a degree and become a teacher. And luckily there happened to be a very innovative program at UW-M that allowed me to do that in short order and without having to take a lot of courses, but having to student teach for a year as opposed to a semester. And that allowed, I thought that was a very positive program, very student-centered, sort of a remnant of the '60s....I don't think actually I would've gone into teaching had it not been that flexibility of the program, because I have a very low tolerance for bullshit, and one finds a lot of that in schools of education. I've since gone back and gotten my master's, I'm actually in a doctoral program at a different school. Um, I still have low tolerance for bullshit.

This excerpt exemplifies the operation of pastoral power both to free participants to say what is on their minds—even if what is said offends the interviewer—and also to require researchers to self-sacrifice rather than respond to participants' offenses and risk shutting down the conversation. Both researchers and participants are caught in a matrix of power-knowledge—the researcher needing participants' continued cooperation to get "the data" and participants needing researchers to hear what they think. Pastoral power sets such dynamics in play that, far from liberating or giving voice, may actually or potentially close down a more productive conversation.

Attention to the individual. Foucault suggested that pastoral power is evident in the focus on the individual as much as the population as a whole (1983b). Although Foucault does not say so explicitly, one might wonder if such individualization is essential to the effectiveness of pastoral power: The recipient feels the care of the pastor, feels special. Of course, a focus on the individual is what the research interview is all about. The interview allows the researcher to attend to one individual for an extended period of time; in return, that individual may feel cared for by the researcher.

Knowing minds and souls. The research interview privileges us to hear many things about participants. Although participants are not *forced* to reveal anything they don't want to, the nature of pastoral power is such that we reveal ourselves as kind and caring for the well-being of the participant, and participants respond by answering virtually all of our questions. For instance, a preservice teacher that Tom interviewed revealed her level of comfort with educational technology, and in the process she appeared to challenge her self-knowledge by admitting that, although she did know some things about technology, she really did have things to learn as well.

> Dr. C: Okay, the first thing I want to ask you, this is your, uh, question about your level of proficiency before you came into the PDS program. Please describe your level of proficiency with technology prior to joining the PDS and specifically maybe you could say some things about what applications you feel comfortable using.
>
> A: Now or then?
>
> Dr. C: This was before, what strategies for use in your classrooms were you already familiar with, and maybe on a scale of 10, what was your overall comfort level when using technology?
>
> A: Okay, well, as I was applying for the PDS and found out that it was technology-based, I thought, yes, I know about technology, but then unfortunately, when I got there, I realized that I really didn't know as much as I thought I knew. So, uh...I was comfortable using Microsoft Works and Word, like word processing, and a little bit with spreadsheet, but just very little. And then, like a lot of other girls came in with PowerPoint knowledge and I had never had the program to work with. So those were things that...I was not competent in yet. Um, strategies for using computers in the classroom...uh, I really

wasn't, I had not seen computers used too much in the classroom, that was a learning experience that I needed to encounter and...what was my overall comfort level? I thought I was probably about an 8, but really I...came to learn a few things.

In another case, a participant in Cathy's study shared information about his adolescent sexual experiences. There was nothing in the interview that specifically asked for such information; again, this kind of sharing may be a reflection of the kind of subject position taken by interview participants in the context of how pastoral power operates.

T: And I got into that through, um, you know, I wanted to know about my own, um, sexuality as an adolescent, so I started reading books so I could, um, take care of myself in that domain. And that was an important thing for a young guy to be, ah, knowledgeable about. Um, that's what I want to accomplish with the kids. I want them to become independent readers like I became, and I want them to understand that one of the reasons they are turned off to books is, is that someone else is telling them what to read.

C: Well, it seems to me that a lot of adolescents, ah, who are, ah, struggling either to understand sexuality or to fit into a larger world, don't think of turning to books.

T: Right.

C: How come you connected with books at that point?

T: Well, my parents didn't teach me, and the school system didn't teach me about sexuality and what my friends were telling me—I grew up in sort of—it became ghetto-ized, you know, with the de-industrialization of society, and, um, I didn't trust what they were saying. I knew some of the things they were saying were just, um, they were just being like players, as we say, just playing on me, and it was older boys. And so I had to have a little bit of a cool pose, and when they would tell me junk, I'd be like, yeah, yeah, and go along with what they were saying. But in my mind I knew that they might be playing me, I didn't trust 'em. So, I don't know really—that's pretty much it. You know, I had a girlfriend, and we wanted to, ah, experiment—and she didn't know, and that was, ah, somehow we went to those books. And at first it was a lot of pictures, you know, and then after a while we came to understand all the language—to use the dictionary.

This participant's discussion of sex supports Foucault's argument that "it is in the confession that truth and sex are joined, through the obligatory and exhaustive expression of an individual secret" (1978, p. 61). The discourse of the research interview positions the participant as confessant who, if she/he is to be truthful, must reveal confidentialities, with sex being the ultimate truth to be revealed.

It is also interesting to note Foucault's argument that the confessional contributed to making sex something to be interpreted: The "truth" resulted not from the confession alone but from the cleric's interpretation of what was confessed. Thus, "by making sexuality something to be interpreted, the nineteenth century gave itself the possibility of causing the procedures of confession to operate within the regular formation of a scientific discourse" (1978, p. 67). Isn't this exactly what is taking place in this analysis? As researchers, we, Cathy and Tom, are interpreting the research participant's decision to discuss his adolescent sexuality during an interview.

Pastoral Power and Doing Interviews: Is the Dangerous Also the Bad?

Our well-intentioned teacher interviews led to the creation of regimes of truth and to the construction of some participants as acquiescent and others as resistant. These effects are not unique to such interviews. In fact, ethnographic/qualitative researchers have given great attention to such effects and to the danger in failing to recognize that such truths and constructions derive from the research act rather than from any objective "reality" (Guba & Lincoln, 1994; Lather, 1991). However, we would like to give some examples of where and how the circulation of pastoral power seems dangerous:

1. In the construction of regimes of truth
2. In limiting subject positions of participants
3. In encouraging the telling of secrets
4. In constructing participants as resistant

We will also highlight aspects of pastoral power in particular that function discursively to create some of the dangerous effects as bad ones.

Regimes of truth. Foucault's notion of regimes of truth conveys the sense that what is true in any situation depends on parameters constructed by the discourse of that situation. In other words, there is skepticism toward absolute truth in favor of thinking about how what is taken as true depends upon the rules by which knowledge and power are enacted. Foucault describes the workings of regimes of truth in this way:

Each society has its regime of truth, its "general politics" of truth; that is, the types of discourse which it accepts and makes function as true; the mechanisms and instances which enable one to distinguish true and false statements, the means by which each is sanctioned; the techniques and procedures accorded value in the acquisition of truth; the status of those who are charged with saying what counts as true. (Foucault, 1980b, p. 131)

We suggest that regimes of truth are discursively delineated not just in societies but also in subsets of societies, for instance, in research interviews. Our own interviews reinforce regimes of truth that indicate what is acceptable and what is "correct" during the interview, both in terms of content and process. For instance, Cathy was interviewing a teacher who interrupted the interview to say hello to a colleague, then apologized for the interruption. Cathy reassured her it was okay:

T: And I pick and choose those things that I know I can incorporate
        into my classroom. Hi, Sue (laughs). Sorry.

C: That's okay.

The regimes of truth for research interviews such as this include the rule that the person being interviewed will speak only in response to the researcher's questions and will not initiate her/his own topic. Therefore, when this participant chose to greet her colleague, she felt a need to apologize. Cathy, then, as the good interviewer, reassured the participant that this interruption was acceptable. This indicates how in "forgiving" the participant's "transgression," the operation of pastoral power is in danger of fixing such subject positions as shepherd and flock, savior and the saved, without being interrogated. On occasion, the participant may introduce a topic not expected by the interviewer, as when one of the participants in Cathy's project discussed his adolescent sexuality. However, we see this instance as an illustration of the fact that the power is not exercised by the researcher alone; the regime of truth is created by the discourse of the interview, not by the researcher, and the participant is responding to what seems to be asked of him within that.

Creating binary subject positions. The regimes of truth created by a research interview shape what is acceptable knowledge as well as what is acceptable procedure during the interview. An even-greater danger, however, is that these regimes of truth construct the participants in the interview, often in binary form. We see evidence of this particularly when participants are judged as being either acquiescent or resistant during interviews. Our goal in providing the following examples is not to contend that acquiescence and resistance are "wrong" but rather to show ways that the interview process constructs them as possibilities, thereby constructing the participants as being one kind or the other.

The acquiescence attributed to the research participant below illustrates how the interview shaped her. The participant appeared to be describing a situation that troubled her, in which her students could not all use the computers at the same time, because there weren't enough. By the end of the segment she put an optimistic spin on it, noting that she and her cooperating teacher were fortunate for what they had. In this way, she becomes a "good" research participant, not a complaining one, even though she was asked to describe a challenge. Note, too, the way Tom urged the participant to take her time, which was intended to reassure her but also interrupted her, establishing Tom's privilege in the interview.

Dr. C: Great, okay, good. Um, I'd like to ask you a little about sort of a challenge you might have faced. What would you consider, do you consider, the greatest challenge for you, as a teacher, in designing and implementing a technology-based instruction? And maybe you could say, were you able to overcome this challenge, and why or why not?

B: Mm…I have to think about that one for a m…

Dr. C: Take your time, take your time.

B: Um, just finding something that…is going to be relevant to everyone and that all the students are going to be able to do because I think that, just logistics-wise, making sure that you have, all the students are going to be able to be involved and do it because you can't, obviously, always have them all there on the computers at the same time. I mean it depends how you're using it, but a lot of the times you have the students go to the computer. So it was just, you always had to find some sort of activity, also, that was something that was relevant and not just busy work for the students who were not using the computers before they rotated. So Linda helped me a lot with that t—you know, in things that relate so when they're at the computer, they're not doing something completely different, you know, at their tables, things that were…along the same lines. So, I think I've gotten better at that…finding relevant activities where everyone can be involved and everyone's getting their turn.

Dr. C: Yeah, so it sounds like are you saying there was a sense of rotating the kids in and out.

B: Mm hmm, because not everyone could always, you know, be
there at the same time. So, in a perfect world maybe, but...I
mean, we were lucky to have what we had.

Telling secrets. In addition to the manner in which the interview
process establishes acquiescence as a desirable subject position and
shapes judgments of the interview participant, such acquiescence often
manifests as the telling of secrets. Some participants reveal aspects of
their personal or professional life in an apparent attempt to be the "good"
interviewee, to give the interviewer what is wanted. For instance, one
participant reveals practices she used as a school administrator to "work
the system" to hire the teachers she preferred.

T: I knew how the seniority terms worked and I knew that if I was
going to post a position, and I wanted [specific teacher's name],
I'd put down that I needed somebody with Cognitively Guided
Instruction training and that they had to have experience in an
inclusion classroom, and it was going to be a three/four split.
And I ruled. (laugh)

Some researchers might take a psychological perspective and argue
that the telling of secrets is dangerous only if the interview participant
feels forced to do so. However, from the perspective that a research
interview exists within a power-knowledge matrix, the act of telling
secrets is dangerous when one considers the discursively created sense
that telling secrets is essential to telling the truth (Foucault, 1978). From
this perspective, the discourse of the interview creates the sense that a
good interview is one in which something previously hidden is revealed.
Thus, telling secrets is not really an option, it is required of the interview.
When researchers and participants fail to understand this, when they
operate as though the interview is a safe space for the participant to
choose to tell secrets (or not to), then the effect of the interview may
become a bad one.

Resistance. Taking up the other part of the binary, the subject
position of resister, can lead to further dangers. Cathy noticed this in an
interview when the participant, who teaches at a university, wanted to
stress the dangers of a professor speaking for others, leading to a warning
against the same thing occurring in Cathy's work.

T: I think that there are real dangers in taking any sort of the stance
that I took around social justice writ large and then proceeding to
differentiate *my* world from what goes on in anti-social justice-
(laughs) oriented institutions. The dangers are *profound*
presumptuousness, so I want to at least acknowledge that and,
well, if it ever shows up in your work, I'll, I may or may not find

> out. But, I think one of the dangers around people who, you
> know, who pursue this issue, particularly white people who
> pursue it, is a kind of posturing, a kind of self-aggrandizing, a
> kind of sense of superiority, and I try hard, I hope, to struggle
> against that.

There is perhaps a more significant example of resistance related to Cathy's interview project. The pool of potential interview participants consisted of teachers with some relationship to the newspaper *Rethinking Schools*. This newspaper is a visible and respected forum for the voices of critical educators, and therefore those connected with it have a venue to make their own voices heard. They don't need Cathy or any other researcher, and they challenge some aspects of the circulation of pastoral power from within. This may explain the examples of resistance found in her interviews, but it may be even more useful in explaining the lack of response Cathy received when she asked for participants to review transcripts and to meet in a "member checking" focus group. Perhaps these teachers were extending as much pastoral care to Cathy as she was to them. They wanted to be kind to this rather unknown researcher and help her out, but there was a limit to what they had time for. Among the dangers of these acts of resistance and care are that the participants from *Rethinking Schools* can easily be construed as difficult or uncooperative. The limited range of subject positions allowed to interview participants provides a likelihood that participants' responses may be outside those that are "allowed" and approved of.

The Dangerous into the Bad. Pastoral power is in some sense homologous with Foucault's concept of disciplinary power, in which power is exercised "*within* the social body rather than *from* above it" (1980a, p. 39, emphasis in original). Pastoral power appears benign, exerted not out of any desire for power but out of caring and a wish to help those being cared for. In this way, the subjects produced through such circulation of power willingly participate in the attendant discourse, because clearly it is for their own good.

There is a discursive logic that sheds light on the manner in which pastoral power produces the dangerous effects described above. As in any situation in which power is exercised, these interviews create a power-knowledge matrix in which regimes of truth are constructed. The strategies we use as well-intended researchers have normalizing effects (Foucault, 1977) in establishing the acceptable behavior of the participants, and it is here, in such normalizing effects, that we see the transition from the dangerous into the bad. Gracious compliance with the wishes of the pastor is the presumed response of the "flock," and thus a great deal of acquiescence is manifested. We create a "quiet, ordered, and private scenario in which peoples' abilities and knowledges about themselves are gently and quietly shaped in a gentle, 'caring' institution" (Marshall, 1990, p. 15).

On the other hand, those who choose not to participate in this shepherd-flock game are left with resistance as their descriptor and course of action. Even those who resisted to some degree, however, also participated "appropriately" (i.e., according to our wishes) during much of the interview. Clearly, the regime of truth discursively created during research interviews had a strong influence on the behaviors of the interviewees. This brings into question the extent to which participants' statements can be seen or treated as pure data and pure voice. Let us emphasize, however, that this discussion is not about a one-way exercise of power in which we dominate the interview participants. Rather, we suggest that power is a matrix where "the 'wielders' of power [are] just as inextricably caught in its webs as the supposedly powerless" (McHoul & Grace, 1993, p. 7). The self-sacrifice we experienced and the participants' resistance are two examples of the manner in which such discursively created power has effects on all participants in this web.

Revisioning the Research Interview

The ideas discussed so far make us reconsider the research interview. Our good intentions seem suspect when we recognize how they in themselves are part of the discourse of the interview and serve in part to construct the participants in that interview. Moreover, we recognize that the research interview *is* surveillance, and thus we struggle to continue believing in the benign nature of what we do. We seek subjugated knowledges (Foucault, 1980c), but the discourse of the research interview may forbid them from being revealed, because pastoral power constrains as much as it frees (Foucault, 1980b).

Thus, instead of freeing the research participants to reveal themselves in a safe space that makes their voices known, as we intend to do, we may be confining participants to playing a role in which they are constructed as the cared-for and ministered-to. We demand their confession as a requirement of their participation. In this way, our goal of caring for and ministering to participants becomes another way we gain and maintain authority while seeking to open space for interviewees to tell their stories. Our position as researchers is thus secure and our surveillance seemingly benign.

We also question the concept of the research interview itself. If we view it as a journey, then there must be a destination, a place where we end up. Given the pastoral intent of such interviews, this journey appears directed toward intimate knowledge of participants, which results not from just "allowing" participants to speak but from "knowing" them, with all of the interpretive intent inherent in coming-to-know. If we were interested only in making voices heard, then we would distribute transcripts of the interviews and consider our work complete. But of course that isn't what we do; we "make sense" of the interviews, deciding which of the participants' knowledges are of most value and how best to reveal them. We also recognize that what we are documenting is not so much about these teachers' professional lives as it is about the way these teachers have been constructed by the interviews.

We are left with the question, then, of how we wish to conceptualize research interviews in the future. Our research gains integrity when we recognize and make visible in each study the manner in which the discourse of the interview constructs subjectivities and knowledges. Moreover, insights based on Foucault's notion of pastoral power enable us to recognize its circulation within interviews; although we cannot eliminate its operation, we can indeed make it visible to those with whom we share our research and acknowledge that it influences the construction of the interviews and their participants, ourselves included.

On the other hand, such an effort to "come clean," to thoroughly examine our practices and intents (to "examine our conscience") could in itself be seen as an effect of pastoral power. Foucault claimed that pastoral power required the self-sacrifice of those who exercise it; in a sense, such self-sacrifice takes place when we put our work up for critical examination. Furthermore, a pastoral intent is evident when such an examination of our research is conducted in order to lead us to being "better" researchers who are fairer to interviewees. The very objective of this project appears to reflect a discourse in which pastoral power creates knowledge of the "good" researcher who tends to the flock of the researched *and* his or her own ethical behavior.

One approach to these troubling issues is to consider the subject of our research to be *our* participation in the research interview. We might examine our desires in developing and conducting our interviews, the manner in which our desires are shaped and changed by the interview, the subjectivities we help create, normalize, or reinforce through the interview, and how we are constructed by the discourses of the interviews. By considering these topics, we would be altering the purpose of the interview and perhaps making the effects of pastoral power visible and therefore less dangerous. It would be interesting to approach a potential interview participant and explain that we wish to talk to them about their practice, so that we can learn more about ourselves as we participate in the interview! Surely many potential participants would be confused and perhaps disconcerted. On the other hand, we might open up new avenues for discussion with teachers, as we explain our desire *not* to take care of the teachers or behave like their saviors. It would also be interesting to consider the circular complexities of this as discussed above. What new regimes of truth, subjectivities, and knowledges constructed in this altered research environment might emerge?

Another approach to research interviews might be to understand them genealogically rather than empirically. Foucault (1984) describes a genealogy as different from a history, because it follows the "complex course of descent" of a phenomenon, by identifying "the accidents, the minute deviations—or conversely, the complete reversals—the errors, the false appraisals, and the faulty calculations that gave birth to those things that continue to exist and have value for us" (p. 81). A genealogy requires that one "record the singularity of events" by seeking them "in sentiments, love, conscience, instincts" (p. 76). In addition, Foucault speaks of "the genealogical fragments in the form of so many traps, demands, challenges, what you will" (1980c, p. 87).

Flynn (1994) reminds us that genealogies consider the effects of power, a project we have already begun in this chapter. However, Flynn also notes the emphasis Foucault places on bodies, including factors that affect the conditions of bodies and the way power disciplines and controls bodies. In addition, Rabinow refers to Foucault's genealogical approach as presenting "a series of discrete elements that, while following their own periodicity and their own dynamics, assemble at the same conjuncture" (1994, p. 203).

A genealogy of research interviews would examine not just interviews themselves but the position of interviews within educational research, that is, the development of interviewing as a valued practice among educational researchers. This work would build on existing work by Foucault in which he analyzes confessional practices in Christianity (1978) and the emergence of the medical interview (1973). In addition, such a genealogy would consider the manner in which interviews position researchers and teachers within their professions and in society at large as well as how interviews position participants within the interviews and within the research process. Such a genealogy would provide an extensive analysis of the manner in which research interviews make possible the discursive construction of power and the effects of that power in shaping participants, the profession, and the field.

A genealogy of the interview would also examine the current value of caring in the education profession (Noddings, 1994) and expose caring's effects on the desires of educational researchers as it leads to the exercise of pastoral power in research interviews. When the pastoral intent of researchers is understood as discursively created rather than a personal characteristic that ennobles the researcher, the dangers of interviews will be increasingly evident. The goal is not necessarily to eradicate such intent—again, as a discursively constructed practice, it cannot be easily done away with—but rather to make it visible and to interrogate it for all its effects, rather than trusting in its "goodness." Foucault (1983a) described three "domains" in his genealogy of ethics:

> First, an historical ontology of ourselves in relation to truth through which we constitute ourselves as subjects of knowledge; second, an historical ontology of ourselves in relation to a field of power through which we constitute ourselves as subjects acting on others; third, an historical ontology in relation to ethics through which we constitute ourselves as moral agents. (p. 237)

This current examination of our research interviews approaches the second and third domains. It considers the manner in which the discourse of the research interview constructs us as subjects acting in relation to others as well as moral agents. There is much more to probe in these two domains, however, and there is also a need to probe the first domain, how we constitute ourselves as subjects of knowledge. It may be that the very structure of interviews, including the "inter-spaces" or gaps that exist between the interviewer and the interviewee, provides a way to more thoroughly examine these domains.

Conclusion

Foucault claimed that "everything is dangerous, which is not exactly the same as bad. If everything is dangerous, then we always have something to do" (1983a, pp. 231–232). Foucault saw danger as essential to truth-speaking, in the sense that a truth-speaker (*parrhesiast*) is always speaking within a discourse where power operates. If there is no risk of danger, then the speaker is not relaying a truth; rather, s/he is saying the obvious or speaking to please others (Rabinow, 1994). Of course, for Foucault, truth was what a discourse said was true; he wasn't referring to an absolute "Truth" that existed beyond discourse (1980b).

This idea assists us in understanding that our research interviews cannot be *without* danger. Our participants must speak within the confines of the threat that they might, for instance, misspeak, or their ideas might be criticized, or they may say something embarrassing. In other words, if a research participant's speech is not mere compliance with the interviewer, then danger will be present, because the participant will not know how her/his words will be received nor what effect they will have. We cannot make interviews entirely safe.

On the other hand, interviews are not safe for us as researchers, either. We may desire to help teachers, we may perceive ourselves as caring individuals, and yet our participation in research interviews leads us to engage in a discourse that has all the dangers—and potential—of any discourse: "Discourse can be both an instrument and an effect of power, but also a hindrance, a stumbling-block, a point of resistance and a starting point for an opposing strategy" (Foucault, 1978, p. 101).

When we recognize the limitations of the interview and our limitations as interviewers, we are left with choices. We can construct *ourselves* differently, relinquishing our pastoral postures, and continue our interviews despite the risks to participants; we can construct *interviews* differently, in order to make the dangers more visible to ourselves and the participants; or we can construct our *research* differently, perhaps taking a genealogical approach that focuses on the effects of power's circulation and the construction of subjectivities in our interactions with preservice and inservice teachers. These issues provide ethical as well as methodological dilemmas, which may be best understood by continuing to trouble the research interview.

Endnote

1. The term "critical educator" is used here to refer to individuals implementing a critical pedagogy in which "first, students learn to perceive social, economic and political contradictions in what they know and what they are told. Second, they learn to take action against the oppressive and dominant elements within these contradictory situations" (Morgan, 1997, p. 6).

References

Flynn, T. (1994). Foucault's mapping of history. In G. Gutting (Ed.), *The Cambridge companion to Foucault* (pp. 28–46). New York: Cambridge University Press.

Foucault, M. (1973). *The birth of the clinic: An archaeology of medical perception* (A. M. Sheridan Smith, Trans.). New York: Vintage.

Foucault, M. (1977). *Discipline and punish: The birth of the prison* (A. Sheridan, Trans.). New York: Vintage.

Foucault, M. (1978). *The history of sexuality: An introduction, Volume 1.* (R. Hurley, Trans.). New York: Vintage.

Foucault, M. (1980a). Prison talk. In C. Gordon (Ed.), *Power/knowledge: Selected interviews and other writings, 1972–1977* (pp. 37–54). New York: Pantheon.

Foucault, M. (1980b). Truth and power. In C. Gordon (Ed.), *Power/knowledge: Selected interviews and other writings, 1972–1977* (pp. 109–133). New York: Pantheon.

Foucault, M. (1980c). Two lectures. In C. Gordon (Ed.), *Power/knowledge: Selected interviews and other writings, 1972–1977* (pp. 78–108). New York: Pantheon.

Foucault, M. (1983a). On the genealogy of ethics: An overview of work in progress. In H. L. Dreyfus & P. Rabinow (Eds.), *Michel Foucault: Beyond structuralism and hermeneutics* (2d ed., pp. 229–52). Chicago: University of Chicago Press.

Foucault, M. (1983b). The subject and power. In H. L. Dreyfus & P. Rabinow (Eds.), *Michel Foucault: Beyond structuralism and hermeneutics* (2d ed., pp. 208–26). Chicago: University of Chicago Press.

Foucault, M. (1984). Nietzsche, genealogy, history. In P. Rabinow (Ed.), *The Foucault reader* (pp. 76–100). New York: Pantheon.

Guba, E. G., & Lincoln, Y. S. (1994). Competing paradigms in qualitative research. In N. Denzin & Y. S. Lincoln (Eds.), *Handbook of qualitative research* (pp. 105–117). Thousand Oaks, CA: Sage.

Kvale, S. (1996). *InterViews: An introduction to qualitative research interviewing.* Thousand Oaks, CA: Sage.

Lather, P. (1991). *Getting smart: Feminist research and pedagogy with/in the postmodern.* New York: Routledge.

Marshall, J. D. (1990). Educational research. In S. J. Ball (Ed.), *Foucault and education: Disciplines and knowledge* (pp. 11–28). New York: Routledge.

McHoul, A., & Grace, W. (1993). *A Foucault primer.* New York: New York University Press.

Morgan, W. (1997). *Critical literacy in the classroom: The art of the possible.* London: Routledge.

Noddings, N. (1994). An ethic of caring and its implications for instructional arrangements. In L. Stone (Ed.), *The education feminism reader* (pp. 171–183). New York: Routledge.

Rabinow, P. (1994). Modern and countermodern: Ethos and epoch in Heidegger and Foucault. In G. Gutting (Ed.), *The Cambridge companion to Foucault* (pp. 197–214). New York: Cambridge University Press.

Appendix

Below is a list of Internet sites focused on Michel Foucault. The search that procured these was restrictive; all sites had to have the complete name "Michel Foucault." Even so, over 100,000 Internet locations were returned. From this massive list we reviewed approximately the top 100 and pared these down. Our purpose in assembly was to demonstrate the range of ways in which Foucault has appeared—in academic disciplines and otherwise—as a topic in cyberspace. Listed below, therefore, are sample sites that focus on Foucault as a central topic and approach his name from multiple directions.

The list was compiled in late 2002. Given the ever-changing nature of the World Wide Web, we make no claim for link viability at press time. It should be noted that we have no professional connection to any of these sites, nor do we vouch in any way for the "authenticity" of sites or their particularized use of Foucault's work.

Institut Mémoires de L'édition Contemporaine
http://www.imec-archives.com

The eJournal website:
Critical Thinkers Resources, Michel Foucault Resources
Contains links to other sites, recommended reading, and a bibliography. Hosted by Patrick Jennings.
http://www.synaptic.bc.ca/ejournal/foucault.htm

Welcome to the World of Michel Foucault
The Foucault Pages at CSUN, dedicated to exploring the work of French philosopher and social critic Michel Foucault. Maintained by Bernardo Attias at California State University Northridge.
http://www.csun.edu/~hfspc002/foucault.home.html

Michel Foucault: Resources
Contains a Foucault quote of the month, bibliography, and links to other sites. Hosted by Clare O'Farrell at Queensland University of Technology.
http://www.foucault.qut.edu.au/

Foucault, info.
Search for news about Michel Foucault, scan Foucault texts by theme or keyword. Nonprofit information site, "a repository for all things Michel Foucault."
http://foucault.info/

PopCultures.com: Theorists and Critics: Michel Foucault
Includes general links, primary and secondary literature by and about Foucault, newsgroups, and discussion links. Hosted by PopCultures.com, "The comprehensive guide to cultural studies and popular culture on the Internet." Maintained by Sarah Zupko.
http://www.popcultures.com/theorists/foucault.html

Michel Foucault trading card
Card [3] Michel Foucault. "Creative knowledge you can put in your pocket." Hosted by Theory.org.uk—social theory for fans of popular culture.
http://www.theorycards.org.uk/card03.htm

I Was Michel Foucault's Love Slave
Prose by Carol Lloyd and illustrated by Jordin Isip. Hosted by Salon.com, San Francisco, California
http://www.salon.com/feb97/loveslave970210.html

Online Audio Recordings from UC Berkeley Lectures and Events
Contains audio recording of Foucault's lecture "The Culture of the Self" on April 12 & 19, 1983, at the University of California, Berkeley.
http://www.lib.berkeley.edu/MRC/audiofiles.html

Who Is Michel Foucault? A primer for Pre-Post-Structuralists
Focus on art history and art criticism. Hosted by John Haber, New York, New York.
http://www.haberarts.com/foucault.htm

Dictionary for the Study of the Works of Michel Foucault
Courtesy of Lois Shawver. Hosted by Postmodern Therapies NEWS, a newsletter for those interested in postmodernism.
http://www.california.com/~rathbone/foucau10.htm

Michel Foucault Quotations
Hosted by MemorableQuotations.com, a collection of quotations gleaned from the writings and speeches of "the world's most memorable individuals."
http://www.memorablequotations.com/foucault.htm

Foucault funk: The Michel Foucault Postmodern Blues
Downloadable MP3 song. Lyrics by Michel Foucault, Gary Radford, and Marie Radford. Music by Stephen Cooper and Gary Radford. Created by the Professors, a band composed of "a group of academics dedicated to the enjoyment of classic blues and rock."
http://www.scils.rutgers.edu/~band/profs/foucault.html

The Rhetoric of Foucault
Focusing primarily on power, feminism, sexuality, identity, and knowledge within the writings of French philosopher Michel Foucault. Designed and produced by undergraduate students and Minnesota State University, Moorhead, Minnesota.
http://www.mnstate.edu/borchers/Teaching/Rhetoric/RhetoricWeb/Foucault/foucault.html

Queer History and Foucault
Discusses "privately homosexual Foucault." Hosted by PlanetOut.com.
http://www.planetout.com/pno/news/history/archive/foucault.html

Michel Foucault – NEXUS (1926-1984)
Part of the Fathers and Mothers of Management and Organizational Behavior Project by David Boje at New Mexico State University.
http://cbae.nmsu.edu/~dboje/foucault.html

Sociology at Hewett...Michel Foucault
Explains Foucault as a good example of relativistic thinking. Hosted by the Hewett School, a secondary school in Norwich, Norfolk, UK.
http://www.hewett.norfolk.sch.uk/curric/soc/POSTMODE/post5.htm

"Technologies of the Self": Foucault and Internet Discourse
Paper by Alan Aycock, Department of Anthropology, University of Wisconsin–Milwaukee
http://www.ascusc.org/jcmc/vol1/issue2/aycock.html

The World of Michel Foucault
Book review of James D. Faubion's *The Essential Works of Michel Foucault* by M.S. Nagarajan appearing in *The Hindu*: Online Edition of India's National Newspaper on Sunday, September 16, 2001.
http://www.hinduonnet.com/thehindu/2001/09/16/stories/1316017t.htm

Michel Foucault and Pornography
Article by Wendy McElroy hosted by WendyMcElroy.com, a site for "Individualist Feminism and Individualist Anarchism."
http://www.zetetics.com/mac/eris.htm

World History Timeline: Timeline of Human Evolution, Culture and Knowledge
As part of the timeline, Foucault shows up situated between the fossil coelacanth and Sigmund Freud. The timeline offers "an outline of 15 billion years of chemical and biological evolution of the universe, in which the cultural history on Earth has been elaborated extensively." Hosted by Tom Schoepen, Ghent, Belgium.
http://users.pandora.be/worldhistory/milestones_frame.html?pages/foucault.htm

Contributors

Bernadette Baker is an Associate Professor in the Department of Curriculum and Instruction at the University of Wisconsin-Madison. Her research interests are in historiography and history of curriculum, philosophy of education, international curriculum studies, 'post'-literatures, and disability studies. She co-founded both the Foucault and Education Special Interest Group and the Postcolonial Studies and Education Special Interest Group of AERA. She has published widely in educational journals and is the author of the Peter Lang (2001) monograph *In Perpetual Motion: Theories of Power, Educational History, and the Child.*

Thomas Crumpler is a faculty member in the Center for Reading and Literacy at Illinois State University. His areas of interest include learner-directed assessment, drama and critical literacy, and arts-based approaches to educational research.

Inés Dussel is the Director of the Education unit of FLACSO/Argentina. She teaches in the Masters and Doctoral programs at FLACSO and the University of San Andres, Argentina. Her academic interests focus on the history of education and pedagogy, postmodern theories of education, and issues of identity and difference in schooling. She is preparing a book on the historical construction of the schooled body through studies of the wearing of school uniforms in Argentina, France, and the United States.

Dawnene Hammerberg is an Assistant Professor in the Department of Curriculum and Instruction at the University of Wisconsin-Madison. She teaches courses on literacy and language development and manages the licensure program for reading teachers and reading specialists. Her research examines early literacy curriculum and instruction to determine how it constitutes and governs individuals and how it maintains a particular social conception of what it means to read and write well.

Valerie Harwood is a lecturer in Foundations of Education, Faculty of Education, at the University of Wollongong, Australia. Her research interests are in the areas of youth studies and the construction of child and youth psychopathology.

Katharina E. Heyning is an Associate Professor at the University of Wisconsin-Whitewater. In 1996 she co-founded the Foucault and Education Special Interest Group of AERA and currently manages the group's website. Her research interests include the history of reform and change of teacher education, certification and licensure, and the teaching of social studies in elementary school.

Kenneth Hultqvist was a Professor of Education at the Stockholm Institute of Education, Sweden. His interests have been in the governing systems of reasoning in education and other related areas of knowledge and practice. Sadly, Kenneth passed away during the printing of this book. He will be dearly missed by his colleagues in education and the Foucault arenas.

David Kirk is a Professor in the School of Sport and Exercise Sciences at Loughborough University. His interest in Foucault stems from an ongoing research program focused on the social construction of the body in and through school physical education and sport and the relationship of this process to wider social processes of corporeal regulation.

Patti Lather is a Professor in the Cultural Studies in Education Program at Ohio State University where she teaches qualitative research in education and gender and education. Her primary scholarly interest is in putting the post to work in feminist research methodology and critical theory. She is presently working on a manuscript, *Getting Lost: Feminist Efforts toward a Double(d) Science*.

James Marshall is Professor Emeritus (former Dean of Education) at the University of Auckland, New Zealand. His interests are in educational philosophy and French poststructuralism, especially Michel Foucault. He is the author/editor of a number of books and monographs, including recently *Michel Foucault: Personal Autonomy and Education* (1996), *Wittgenstein: philosophy, postmodernism, pedagogy* (1999), and *Education Policy* (1999). (The last two with Michael Peters). A co-edited book with Michael Peters and Paul Smeyers entitled *Nietzsche's Legacy* was published in 2001. In addition he has contributed to a number of edited collections and has published widely in international journals in educational philosophy, education, social theory and policy. A second book on Foucault and an edited collection entitled *Poststructuralism, Philosophy, Pedagogy* are in press.

Erica McWilliam is a Professor of Education and an Assistant Dean of Research in the Faculty of Education at the Queensland University of Technology. The first two decades of her career in education were spent in secondary schools in both the State and private sectors. Her educational publications cover a wide spectrum, as is evidenced in her publications on teaching and learning, research methodology and training, leadership and management, and postmodernity. She is currently series editor of 'Eruptions', with Peter Lang Publishing, New York.

Thomas S. Popkewitz is a Professor in the Department of Curriculum and Instruction at the University of Wisconsin-Madison. His research focus is about "thought" as a cultural/historical practice. He is writing a book about cosmopolitanism, a European Enlightenment notion about universal reason which is assembled and reassembled in schooling to order who the child is, should be, and who is not that "reasonable" child. He is also co-editing books on educational partnerships, comparative studies on welfare systems of the child and family, and Dewey's pragmatism as it travels internationally and connects with different modernities.

Mary Lou Rasmussen is a lecturer at Deakin University, Victoria, Australia. Currently she is researching the nexus between consumption, globalization and *Queer as Folk*. She is also studying Butlerian notions of melancholia in relation to the production of sexualities and genders in educational contexts. In addition, Mary Lou is involved in developing an international collaborative research project utilizing ethnographic work to consider how gender and sexual identities are created in diverse school and community contexts.

Elizabeth Adams St.Pierre is an Associate Professor in the Language Education Department at the University of Georgia. She is an Affiliated Faculty member of both the Women's Studies Department and the university's Qualitative Research Program. Her research agenda is grounded in poststructural theories of language and focuses on three related and overlapping areas: language and literacy studies, poststructural feminism, and qualitative research methodology. Specific projects are the construction of subjectivity in older women, the reading practices of adult expert readers, literacy practices in adult women's book clubs, and the critique of conventional qualitative research methodology.

Cathy Toll is a faculty member in the Center for Reading and Literacy at Illinois State University. Her areas of interest include the politics of literacy and of schools, school/curriculum change, and teacher professional development. She uses poststructuralist, feminist, and critical lenses in her work.

Lisa Weems is an assistant professor in the department of educational leadership and the director of the Center for Education and Cultural Studies at Miami University in Oxford, Ohio. Her current research includes an ethnographic study of high school girls, science and technology; queer theorizing on race and sexualities; and construction of reciprocity within discourses of qualitative research.